a D. Van Nostrand Publication

EN FRANÇAIS

PRACTICAL CONVERSATIONAL FRENCH

Second Edition

Dana Carton

Anthony Caprio

THE AMERICAN UNIVERSITY

 Heinle & Heinle Publishers, Inc.
Boston, Massachusetts 02210 U.S.A.

Cassette Tapes

NUMBER OF CASSETTES: 10

RUNNING TIME: 10 hours (approximate)

CASSETTE CONTENTS

CHAPTER DIALOG: First at normal speed and again with pauses for student response and repetition.

STRUCTURAL PRACTICE: The starred chapter **exercices d'application** and **exercices de synthèse** in four-phased sequences: cue—pause for student response—correct response by native speaker—pause for student repetition

PRONUNCIATION: Practice with pauses for student repetition in each chapter.

DICTATION: Listening comprehension/writing practice for each chapter.

CHANSON: Musical renditions of all songs in the book.

ENTRACTES: Selected practice from **Entractes 1, 2, 3** on Cassette 10.

Cassette tapes are available from the publisher. For information and orders, please write to Heinle & Heinle Publishers, Inc., 51 Sleeper St., Boston, Massachusetts 02210.

10 9 8 7 6 5 4 3 2

Preface

EN FRANÇAIS: *Practical Conversational French, Second Edition* presents the essential elements of French for beginning courses through everyday situations of immediate practical interest to students. The book's format enables students to learn to speak the language quickly. Having mastered the vocabulary and structures of this text, anyone can use French confidently in travel to a French-speaking country or in daily life.

EN FRANÇAIS fits well into one semester or two-quarter courses, yet includes sufficient materials to satisfy the needs of a full-year program. For extension courses or adult education programs, EN FRANÇAIS offers compact units of instruction allowing for instant communication in French. The instructor may choose those parts of each chapter that best suit the needs of a class. The **dialogues, entractes,** and folksongs are especially successful in such courses.

In preparing the Second Edition, we have made every effort to retain those features of the first edition that have proved effective in encouraging a rapid and thorough acquisition of practical conversational French.

The Second Edition has several significant revisions:

1. The book has been reorganized and streamlined into 19 chapters to fit the needs of beginning courses more effectively.
2. Two new chapters of high student interest (**Échange de cadeaux** and **Une Soirée**) have been included.
3. Several new **entractes** featuring practical expressions and vocabulary have been incorporated for expanded situational practice, and others have been placed earlier in the book to increase their accessibility.
4. The book has been enriched throughout with many student-directed exercises.
5. Each chapter has a new section on Pronunciation covering all basic French sounds, reinforced by examples from the chapter.
6. All chapters and **entractes** now include suggestions for **projets** and **activités**—innovative learning devices to build student confidence by encouraging immediate application of skills in a creative and stimulating fashion.
7. A new Instructor's Manual, available from the publisher, includes suggestions for using the text materials in a variety of course situations, additional exercises, guidelines for testing, and an answer key.
8. The new tape cassette program, described on the copyright page, has been substantially expanded.

EN FRANÇAIS, Second Edition, includes 19 chapters and 21 **entractes.** Each unit is a separate entity, thereby facilitating independent study and permitting the student to assimilate the materials fully. Each chapter centers on a different situation and contains the following closely interrelated materials:

Proverbe: A French proverb, related (often humorously) to the content of the chapter.

Chapter Outline: A complete listing of the chapter contents.

Photo: The chapter photo is related thematically to the content of the chapter and shows some aspect of life in a francophonic country.

Dialogue: A unique dialog format consisting of a main speaker, **"Vous,"** and a French-speaking person in a typical real-life encounter. The dialog is made up of practical, down-to-earth sentences that are the most basic and necessary in the given situations. Each dialog contains word blocks (alphabetized), allowing for easy substitution of related expressions. This dialog format allows every student to express a wide variety of ideas by using only one grammatical structure. Individualized responses are consequently encouraged in a realistic fashion. Each dialog is accompanied by an on-page English equivalent, allowing students to know exactly what they are saying. The use of **"Vous"** as main speaker throughout the text enables students to picture themselves in the everyday experience presented.

Exercices d'application: Following each dialog and preceding the grammatical explanations, the exercises require using the vocabulary and basic structures presented in the dialog.

Verbe(s) irrégulier(s): The chosen verb or verbs are always closely related to the content of the chapter.

Structures: Based on the content and structures of each dialog, these sections provide a thorough grounding in the fundamentals of French grammar. Illustrations of each grammatical point are drawn from the preceding sections of the chapter and are identified by quotation marks, thereby underlining the structural unity of the chapter as a whole. Explanations are intentionally succinct, straightforward, and in English, in order to facilitate self-study and individualized instruction.

Exercices de synthése: These exercises, by using the grammar and vocabulary introduced in the preceding five sections, encourage students to strengthen the conversational skills developed in the earlier portions of the chapter. Emphasis is consistently placed on personalization, variety, and high student interest.

Expansion: This section thematically complements the situational context of the chapter and includes exercises for practice.

Prononciation: NEW to the Second Edition, these sections highlight the basics of contemporary French pronunciation. In keeping with the modular orientation of EN FRANÇAIS, the practice phrases provided are entirely drawn from the chapter.

Improvisation: This exercise in improvisation allows students to use all the elements they have learned in the preceding lesson. Besides developing skill in writing, students will gain further fluency in spoken French in a creative, constructive fashion.

Projet(s): NEW to the Second Edition, these projects encourage creative student application of the vocabulary and structures of the chapter. Students respond with enthusiasm to these personalized exercises, which may be used either as in-class activities or assigned for out-of-class preparation.

Activité(s): NEW to the Second Edition, these lively in-class activities are excellent confidence builders, as students effectively learn to rely on their own abilities to communicate in French. In keeping with the modular orientation of the book, these exercises require only the vocabulary and structures of the chapter at hand. Many of the activities create a "learning-by-doing" experience by encouraging students to employ highly practical vocabulary in facsimiles of real-life situations.

Chanson: A means of vocabulary expansion, the French folksongs are related whenever possible to the content or structures of the chapter. All songs have been transposed into the key of G and have appropriate chord indications in order to facilitate accompaniment by amateur musicians.

ENTRACTES: Each chapter is followed by an **entracte.** These exercises consist of grammatically simple questions that evoke brief responses, in which a wide variety of substitutions are possible. Each question relates directly to the student and to his or her daily life. Each allows for a large range of different reactions and for substantial vocabulary accumulation. The **entractes** are independent units and serve as a distinct enhancement of the points covered in the lessons themselves. Each **entracte** contains a section entitled **Springboards for Conversation.** The questions involve each student directly, thereby stimulating class participation. Through the use of guided, structured conversation, the springboard questions provide a lively repetition of vocabulary and grammatical structures, enhancing rapid acquisition of the basic language skills. Many **entractes** also contain **projets or activités.**

Dana Carton
Anthony Caprio

ACKNOWLEDGMENTS

Grateful acknowledgment is extended to the many users of the first edition for their comments and suggestions based on classroom experience. Special thanks are due the respondents to our survey questionnaire: Léon Applebaum, North Seattle Community College; Jeanne E. Calo, Trenton State College; Reginald Hyatt, Ripon College; Joan Quilter, De Anza College; Sam Sykes, Christopher Newport College; and Glenn J. Van Treese, Sweet Briar College. The following reviewers critiqued the manuscript for the Second Edition: Eileen Coates, Valparaiso University; Russell B. Everett, East Stroudsburg State College; and Lois Sutton, Baylor University.

Table des matières

Exercices de synthèse / Expansion: **En autobus, En métro, En taxi** / Expansion: **À la gare,**
En train / Expansion: **À l'aéroport, En avion**
Prononciation: [ʒ], [g] / Improvisations / Projet / Activité
Chanson: **Il était un petit navire**

16 En Vacances   305

Dialogue / Exercices d'application / Verbe irrégulier: **courir**
Structures: 1. Third-Person Pronouns, Indefinite Pronouns and Expressions,
      2. Complementary Infinitives
Exercices de synthèse / Expansion: **Qu'emportez-vous lorsque vous partez en vacances**
Prononciations: [ɲ] / Improvisation / Projet / Activité
Chanson: **À la claire fontaine**

17 À la banque   325

Dialogue / Exercices d'application / Verbe irrégulier: **lire**
Structures: 1. Subjunctive Mood: Formation   2. Subjunctive Mood: Uses
Exercices de synthèse / Expansion: **À la banque**
Prononciation: [z], [s] / Improvisation / Projet / Activités
Chanson: **La Marseillaise**

18 Échange de cadeaux   345

Dialogue / Exercices d'application / Verbes irréguliers: **devoir, falloir, offrir**
Structures: Past-Participle Agreement

Chapitre

1

Bonjour	Getting Acquainted

Proverbe: C'est simple comme bonjour.	Proverb: It's as easy as A B C. (*Literally:* It's as easy as hello.)

«Permettez-moi de vous présenter mon ami.»

DIALOGUE

VOUS: Bonjour, Monsieur / Madame / Mademoiselle.[1]

UN MONSIEUR / UNE DAME: Bonjour, Monsieur / Madame / Mademoiselle.

VOUS: Je m'appelle_____. Et vous?
　　　　　　　　　　(votre nom)

LE MONSIEUR / LA DAME: Je m'appelle _____.

VOUS: Pardon?

LE MONSIEUR / LA DAME: Je m'appelle _____.

VOUS: Enchanté(e), Monsieur / Madame / Mademoiselle.

LE MONSIEUR / LA DAME: Moi de même.

VOUS: Permettez-moi de vous présenter **mon ami.**

```
mon amie
mes enfants
ma femme
mon frère
mon mari
ma mère
mes parents
mon père
mon professeur
ma sœur
Monsieur _____.
Madame _____.
Mademoiselle _____.
```

LE MONSIEUR / LA DAME: Enchanté(e).

VOUS: Comment allez-vous, Monsieur / Madame / Mademoiselle?

LE MONSIEUR / LA DAME: Très bien, merci. Et vous?

VOUS: **Très bien,** merci.

YOU: Hello, (Sir / Madam / Miss).

A GENTLEMAN / A LADY: Hello.

YOU: My name is _____. And yours? (Literally: And you?)

THE GENTLEMAN / THE LADY: My name is _____.

YOU: Pardon?

THE GENTLEMAN / THE LADY: My name is _____.

YOU: Delighted (to know you).

THE GENTLEMAN / THE LADY: Likewise (I am too).

YOU: Allow me to present my *friend*.

```
friend (feminine)
children
wife
brother
husband
mother
parents
father
professor / teacher
sister
Mr. _____
Mrs. _____
Miss _____
```

THE GENTLEMAN / THE LADY: Delighted (to know you).

YOU: How are you?

THE GENTLEMAN / THE LADY: Very well, thanks. And you?

YOU: *Very well*, thanks.

---

1. The standard abbreviations for these terms are **M., Mme, Mlle.** The plurals—**Messieurs, Mesdames, Mesdemoiselles**—are abbreviated **MM., Mmes, Mlles.**

Bien
Assez bien
Comme ci, comme ça
Pas mal
Pas très bien

Well
Rather well
So–so
Not bad
Not very well

LE MONSIEUR /LA DAME: Au revoir, Monsieur / Madame / Mademoiselle.

VOUS: **Au revoir,** Monsieur / Madame / Mademoiselle.

THE GENTLEMAN / THE LADY: Good-by.

YOU: *Good-by.*

À bientôt
Bonne nuit
Bonsoir
À demain
À tout à l'heure
À plus tard
À lundi
À mardi
À mercredi
À jeudi
À vendredi
À samedi
À dimanche

See you soon.
Good night.
Good evening.
See you tomorrow.
See you later.
See you later.
See you Monday.
See you Tuesday.
See you Wednesday.
See you Thursday.
See you Friday.
See you Saturday.
See you Sunday.

EXERCICE D'APPLICATION

What do you say:

1. to greet someone?
2. to introduce yourself?
3. to someone after he or she has been introduced to you?
4. to introduce your friend to someone? to introduce your spouse? your parents? your brother or sister? your children? your teacher?
5. to ask about someone's health?
6. to tell someone that you are feeling very well? rather well? not very well?
7. when you are leaving?
8. to let someone know that you will be seeing him or her again soon?
9. to let someone know that you will see him or her on Monday? on Tuesday? on Wednesday? on Thursday? on Friday? on Saturday? on Sunday?

VERBES IRRÉGULIERS: aller, être, s'appeler

aller	to go		
je vais	*I go, I am going, I do go*	**nous allons**	*we go*
tu vas	*you go*	**vous allez**	*you go*
il va	*he goes*	**ils vont**	*they (masculine) go*
elle va	*she goes*	**elles vont**	*they (feminine) go*
on va	*one goes*		

aller is used with expressions of health:

«**Comment allez-vous?**»
—**Je vais bien, merci.** *I am fine, thanks.*

Comment ça va? *How are you? How are things?*
—**Ça va bien, merci.** *Fine, thanks.*

Ça va? *Everything going O.K.?*
—**Oui, ça va.** *—Yes, everything's fine.*
          (Informal. Used between friends.)

être	to be		
je suis	*I am*	**nous sommes**	*we are*
tu es	*you are*	**vous êtes**	*you are*
il est	*he is*	**ils sont**	*they (masculine) are*
elle est	*she is*	**elles sont**	*they (feminine) are*
on est	*one is*	**ce sont**	*they are, these are, those are*
c'est	*it is, this is, that is*		

«**C'est** simple comme bonjour.»

s'appeler	to be named		
je m'appelle	*my name is*	**nous nous appelons**	*our name is, our names are*
tu t'appelles	*your name is*	**vous vous appelez**	*your name is, your names are*
il s'appelle	*his name is*	**ils s'appellent**	*their (masculine) names are*
elle s'appelle	*her name is*	**elles s'appellent**	*their (feminine) names are*

«**Je m'appelle** _____. Et vous?»

Comment **vous appelez-vous?** _What's your name?_

Comment **s'appelle**-t-il? _What's his name?_
—Il **s'appelle** Pierre. _His name is Pierre._

Comment **s'appelle**-t-elle? _What's her name?_
—Elle **s'appelle** Henriette. _Her name is Henriette._

STRUCTURES

1.   **Subject Pronouns**

je	_I_		**nous**	_we_
tu	_you_		**vous**	_you_
il	_he_		**ils**	_they (masculine)_
elle	_she_		**elles**	_they (feminine)_
on	_one, people_			

tu is used informally between close friends, relatives, children, and to pets:

Bonjour, Paul. Comment vas-**tu?** _Hello, Paul. How are you?_

on is used in a general sense:

On parle français ici. _French is spoken here._ (Literally: _One speaks French here._)

vous is both singular and plural. It may be used when speaking politely or formally to one person, or when addressing a group of people:

Bonjour, Monsieur. Comment allez-**vous?**
Bonjour, Monsieur. Bonjour, Madame. Comment allez-**vous?**

2.   **Possessive Adjectives**

All nouns in French are either masculine or feminine. Possessive adjectives agree in gender (masculine / feminine) and in number (singular / plural) with the noun they modify:

	Masculine Singular	Feminine Singular	Masculine Plural Feminine Plural
my	**mon** frère	**ma** sœur	**mes** frères / **mes** sœurs
your	**ton** frère	**ta** sœur	**tes** frères / **tes** sœurs
his / her	**son** frère	**sa** sœur	**ses** frères / **ses** sœurs
our	**notre** frère	**notre** sœur	**nos** frères / **nos** sœurs
your	**votre** frère	**votre** sœur	**vos** frères / **vos** sœurs
their	**leur** frère	**leur** sœur	**leurs** frères / **leurs** sœurs

ses = sã

«Permettez-moi de vous présenter **mon ami / mes enfants / ma femme / mon frère / mon mari / ma mère / mes parents / mon père / mon professeur / ma sœur.**»

Exception: Before a feminine noun beginning with a vowel, **mon / ton / son** are used instead of **ma / ta / sa**:

«Permettez-moi de vous présenter **mon amie.**»
Son amie s'appelle Henriette. *His / her friend's name is Henriette.*

EXERCICES DE SYNTHÈSE

A.* *Employez la forme correcte du verbe* **aller:**

1. Je _vai_ bien.
2. Comment _vas_-tu?
3. Elle _va_ bien.
4. _allez_-vous à Paris?
5. Nous _allon_ à Rome.
6. Ils _vont_ bien.
7. Elles _vont_ bien.

B.* *Employez la forme correcte du verbe* **être:**

1. Je _suis_ sa sœur.
2. Elle _sont_ en France.
3. Nous _somme_ vos parents.
4. C' _est_ simple comme bonjour.
5. Tu _es_ mon frère.
6. Ils _sont_ en France.
7. Vous _êtes_ mon ami.

êtes = ĕt

C.* *Do you say* **Comment vas-tu?** *or* **Comment allez-vous?** *to:*

↑ only one person   *↑ more than*

1. votre ami?
2. votre sœur?
3. Monsieur La France?
4. votre frère?
5. Madame La France?
6. votre professeur de français?
7. votre femme?
8. votre mari?
9. votre amie?
10. vos parents?   *Comment allez-vous*

D.* *When addressing someone in French, do not use the family name after* **Monsieur,**
Madame, *or* **Mademoiselle:**

EXEMPLE: Dites *(say)* «bonjour» à Madame La France.
                    «Bonjour, Madame.»

Dites «bonjour» à:

1. Mademoiselle Vincent
2. Madame La France et Madame Martin = mesdame = plural madame
3. Monsieur La France et Monsieur Martin
4. votre professeur

E.* *Transformez. Employez la forme convenable de l'adjectif possessif:*

EXEMPLE: Permettez-moi de vous présenter ma mère. (père)
                    Permettez-moi de vous présenter mon père.

1. sœur ma	4. ami mon	7. parents mes = mã
2. femme ma	5. amie mon	8. enfants mes
3. mari mon → mõ	6. professeur mon	

EXEMPLE: Comment s'appelle ta mère? (père)
                    Comment s'appelle ton père?

1. sœur?	4. amie?	6. père?
2. frère?	5. mère?	7. professeur?
3. ami?		

EXEMPLE: Comment s'appelle la mère de Marc?   what's marc's mothers name?
                    Comment s'appelle sa mère?   what's his mothers name?

1. le père de Marc? son	4. l'ami de Marc? son	6. la femme de Marc? sa
2. la sœur de Marc? sa	5. l'amie de Marc? son	7. le professeur de Marc? son
3. le frère de Marc? son		

\\ before a vowel

F.* *Employez la forme convenable de l'adjectif possessif:*

1. Mon père va bien.
2. Ta mère va bien.
3. Mes enfants vont à Paris. = mãs
4. Son frère s'appelle Jean.
5. Notre professeur est français.
6. Votre père et votre mère sont vos parents.
7. Permettez-moi de vous présenter mon mari et mes enfants.

8. Notre sœur s'appelle Francette.
9. Leur amie s'appelle Henriette.
10. Leur père s'appelle Georges.
    père

G. *Répondez à ces questions:*

1. Comment vous appelez-vous?
2. Comment allez-vous?
3. Comment ça va?
4. Comment va votre mère? votre père? etc.
5. Comment s'appelle votre mère? votre père? votre ami? etc.
6. Comment s'appelle votre professeur de français?

EXPANSION: Formules de politesse

1. **Permettez-moi de me présenter.** *Allow me to introduce myself.*
   Je suis _____. *I am _____.*
2. **Oui, s'il vous plaît.** *Yes, please.*
3. **Avec plaisir.** *With pleasure.*
4. **Merci, non.** *No thanks.*
5. **Merci beaucoup.** *Thank you very much.*
6. **Salut!** *Hi! 'Bye!*
7. **De rien. / Pas de quoi. / Je vous en prie.** *You're welcome. / Don't mention it.*
8. **Excusez-moi. / Pardon.** *Excuse me. / Sorry.*
9. **Il n'y a pas de mal.** *That's all right.*
10. **C'est la vie!** *That's life!*
11. **C'est dommage. / Quel dommage.** *Too bad. / What a pity.*
12. **Je suis très fatigué(e) aujourd'hui.** *I'm very tired today.*
13. **Bien sûr!** *Of course!*
14. **C'est très gentil de votre part.** *That's very kind of you.*

What do you say:

1. to refuse when someone offers you a cigarette? *merci, non*
2. to accept when someone asks if you would like a drink?
3. to greet a close friend?
4. to apologize when you step on someone's toes?
5. to thank someone for giving you a gift?
6. when someone thanks you for something you've done for him or her?
7. when someone offers you seconds at dinner and you're very hungry?

8. when you're exhausted and someone asks you how you are?
9. when you find out that your friend is ill?
10. when someone offers to accompany you to your destination?
11. when someone steps on your foot and says to you: "Oh, pardon!"?
12. when something is obviously true?
13. to introduce yourself to someone?

PRONONCIATION

1.   Sound (Phonetic Symbol): [ɔ̃]

SPELLING:	on om *not doubled, not*
ENGLISH SOUND RESEMBLED:	Vowel sound in words *bone* and *home*
PRONUNCIATION:	Round and protrude lips tensely. Constrict throat slightly. Do not pronounce the final /n/ or /m/ as in English. Mouth remains open throughout entire sound.

EXAMPLES FROM THIS CHAPTER:

b**on**jour   **on** va
m**on** frère   nous all**on**s
t**on** mari   ils v**on**t
s**on** père   elles s**on**t
n**on**   pard**on**
                     b**on**soir

NOTES:

1. The spellings **on** and **om** lose their nasal quality when followed by a vowel or by another **n** or **m**. Examples from this chapter: **comme   comment   nous sommes**
Quel dommage!   bonne nuit

2. The possessive adjectives **mon, ton, son** and the personal pronoun **on** retain the nasal sound when they are followed by a vowel, with the second syllable picking up the sound [n]. Examples from this chapter: **mon ami (e)**   [mɔ̃-na-mi]
on est   [ɔ̃-ne]

3. The sound [ɔ̃] is dropped completely from **monsieur: Bonjour, Monsieur.**

2.   Sound (Phonetic Symbol): [R]

SPELLING: **r, rr, rh**

PRONUNCIATION: [R] has various pronunciations depending upon the French-speaking region where it is used. The Parisian [R] may be obtained by letting the vocal cords vibrate while slightly constricting the back of the throat, as if gargling. In some French-speaking areas the [R] sound is produced by trilling the tongue against the front teeth. Notice that when the /r/ sound appears in the middle or at the end of a word, it is pronounced very softly.

EXAMPLES FROM THIS CHAPTER: **mère**   **frère**

                               père   **mari**

                               merci   **sœur**

                               pardon   **très**   (tR̄ɛ̄)

3.   Silent Letters

Final consonants are generally not pronounced in French, except for the letters **c, f, l,** and **r.**

EXAMPLES FROM THIS CHAPTER:

SILENT FINAL CONSONANT	PRONOUNCED FINAL: **c f l r**
nous	**bonjour**
vous	**sœur**
parents	**professeur**
très	**avec plaisir**
nuit	**adjectif**
à plus tard	**il**
assez bien	**mal**
tu vas	
allons	
enfants	
pas	
beaucoup	

NOTES:

a. The final consonant **r** is <u>not</u> pronounced in the infinitive verb ending **-er** or in the word **monsieur: aller, s'appeler, monsieur.**

b. The final third-person plural verb ending **-ent** is not pronounced: **ils s'appellent**

c. The final vowel **e** is not pronounced in French, but it does cause the preceding consonant to be pronounced. Examples from this chapter:

madame	**je m'appelle**
bonne	**tu t'appelles**
frère	**il s'appelle**
	elle s'appelle

IMPROVISATION

Complétez ce dialogue. Employez le vocabulaire et les structures de la leçon:

UN AMI: Salut!
VOUS: Salut!
VOTRE AMI: Comment vas-tu aujourd'hui?
VOUS: _____
VOTRE AMI: _____
VOUS: _____
VOTRE AMI: _____
VOUS: _____
VOTRE AMI: _____
VOUS: _____
VOTRE AMI: _____
VOUS: C'est la vie.

PROJET

Using the family members given in the dialogue (**ma mère, mon père, etc.**), along with **mon ami, mon amie,** and **mon professeur de français,** draw up a listing of names. You may wish to attach photos where appropriate.

EXAMPLE: Mon père s'appelle Peter.
　　　　　　Mon frère s'appelle John, etc.

ACTIVITÉS

1. Say hello to the person sitting on your right. Introduce yourself. Find out that person's name. Ask how he or she is feeling today. Introduce the person sitting on your right to the person sitting on your left.
2. Ask the person sitting on your right if he or she can remember the name of the person sitting on your left: «**Comment s'appelle-t-il? / Comment s'appelle-t-elle?**» If he or she cannot remember, [**J'ai oublié.** *(I've forgotten.)*], you may be able to supply the information: «**Il / Elle s'appelle** _____.» If neither of you can remember, apologize to your classmate (**«Pardon!»**) and inquire again: «**Comment vous appelez-vous?**»

FRÈRE JACQUES

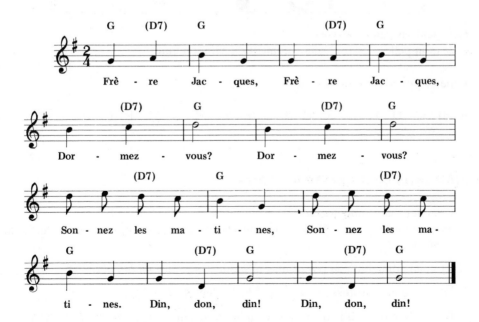

Entracte

1

THE ALPHABET

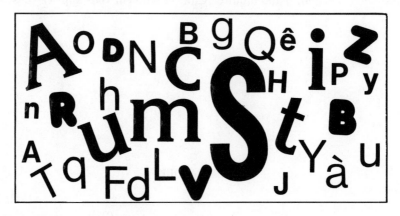

Comment vous appelez-vous?
—Je m'appelle _____. Voilà comment s'écrit mon nom _____.

Répétez après votre professeur:

A B C D E F G H I J K L M N O P Q R S T U V W X Y Z

SPRINGBOARDS FOR CONVERSATION

1. Comment vous appelez-vous?
   Je m'appelle _____. Voilà comment s'écrit mon nom [nom = nom de famille *(last name)*]: _____.

   Et voilà comment s'écrivent mes prénoms *(first and middle names):* _____.

2. Épelez le mot professeur: *P, R, O, F, E*, deux *S, E, U, R*.

   Épelez le mot l'étudiant: *L*, apostrophe, *E* accent aigu, *T, U, D, I, A, N, T*.

14

Épelez le mot très: *T, R, E,* accent grave, *S.*

Épelez le mot hôtel: *H, O* accent circonflexe, *T, E, L.*

Épelez le mot français: *F, R, A, N, C* cédille, *A, I, S.*

Épelez le prénom Jean-Marc: *J* majuscule, *E, A, N,* trait d'union, *M* majuscule, *A, R, C.*

Épelez Noël: *N, O, E* tréma, *L.*

NOTES:

a. An accent mark over the letters **e** and **o** often indicates that the letter **s** used to follow the vowel in the spelling of that particular word. The **s** often remains in the English spelling. For example:

épelez	(English: *spell*)
étudiant	(English: *student*)
hôtel	(English: *hostel*)
forêt	(English: *forest*)
château	(English: *castle*)

b. **ç** (accent cédille) appears only before the letters **a, o, u,** and is pronounced [s]. Without the addition of the cedilla, the letter **c** followed by **a, o, u,** would be pronounced [k]. The cedilla, by maintaining the [s] sound, often reveals a relationship in meaning between two words of the same family.

EXAMPLES:

français *(French)*	**France** *(France)*
ça *(that,* colloquial)	**cela** *(that)*
commençons *(let's begin)*	**commencer** *(to begin)*

3. Êtes-vous marié(e)? Quel est votre nom de jeune fille *(maiden name)?* Épelez-le. Quel est le nom de jeune fille de votre mère? de votre grand-mère?

4. Avez-vous un sobriquet, un surnom ou un diminutif *(nickname)?* Épelez-le.

5. Épelez le prénom de votre mère, de votre père, de votre sœur, de votre frère, de votre meilleur(e) ami(e), de votre chien, etc.

6. Comment s'appelle votre professeur de français? Comment s'écrit son nom?

7. Regardez votre voisin(e) de gauche. Comment s'appelle-t-il/elle? Comment s'écrit son nom?

Regardez votre voisin(e) de droite. Comment s'appelle-t-il / elle? Comment s'écrit son nom?

Il / Elle s'appelle _____.
Voilà comment s'écrit son nom: _____.

PROJET

Livre d'alphabet. Make a children's alphabet book using line drawings, pictures from magazines, etc. to illustrate each word. EXAMPLE: *A* . . . **Animal,** *B* . . . **Ballon,** etc. You may wish to consult the **Vocabulaire** at the end of this book for vocabulary ideas.

ACTIVITÉ

Have a **tombola** *(raffle)* in class. (Prizes are optional and may consist of anything.) Everyone has a partner who will dictate, letter by letter, his or her full name. As names are spelled out by one student, they are written down on a small piece of paper by another. These pieces of paper are then folded and placed in **la tombola.** Winning names are drawn from **la tombola** and again spelled out loud for all to hear.

Chapitre

2

| Comment demander son chemin | Asking Directions |

Proverbe: Qui cherche, trouve. Proverb: He who seeks, finds.

«Vous voyez. La Tour Eiffel est très loins d'ici.»

DIALOGUE

VOUS: Pardon, Monsieur. Pouvez-vous m'aider? Je me suis perdu(e). Je cherche **la Tour Eiffel.**

YOU: Excuse me, sir. Can you help me? I'm lost. I'm looking for the *Eiffel Tower.*

la banque	bank
la bibliothèque	library
la cathédrale	cathedral
le château	chateau, castle, manor
le cinéma	movies
la gare	train station
les jardins publics	public gardens
le musée	museum
le parc	park
la poste	post office
la préfecture de police	police station
la sortie	exit
la station de taxis	taxi stand
le syndicat d'initiative	tourist office
les toilettes	restroom(s)

dc

UN MONSIEUR: C'est très loin d'ici, vous savez.
VOUS: Comment puis-je y aller? = allā
LE MONSIEUR: **Continuez tout droit.** Puis. . . .

A MAN: It's very far from here, you know.
YOU: How can I get there?
THE MAN: Continue (going) straight ahead. Then. . . .

Tournez à gauche (rue Manin)	Turn left (at / onto Manin Street)
Tournez à droite (aux feux)	Turn right (at the traffic light)
Allez au premier (deuxième / troisième) carrefour	Go to the first (second / third) intersection
Allez par là	Go that way
Prenez la première rue à droite	Take the first road on the right
Prenez la direction «Paris»	Go towards Paris
Suivez / Prenez le boulevard Hamilton	Follow / Take Hamilton Boulevard
Continuez / Restez sur la route 6 (jusqu'à . . .)	Continue / stay on Route 6 (as far as / until you get to . . .)
Continuez jusqu'à la route 6	Continue to Route 6
Continuez vers le nord / le sud / l'est / l'ouest	Continue (going) north / south / east / west
Allez jusqu'à la deuxième rue à droite / gauche	Go two blocks / Go until you get to the second street on your right (left).

Vous: Je suis désolé(e), mais je ne vous comprends pas très bien. Parlez un peu plus lentement, s'il vous plaît.

Le Monsieur: Voici le plan de la ville. Vous voyez. La Tour Eiffel est très loin d'ici.

Vous: Ah oui. Vous avez raison.

Le Monsieur: Alors. Prenez **le métro.**

> l'autobus / le bus
> un taxi

Vous: Où est la station de métro la plus proche?

Le Monsieur: Là-bas. Juste devant **l'église** (*f.*).

> l'aéroport (*m.*)
> l'Ambassade (*f.*) des États-Unis
> l'Arc de Triomphe (*m.*)
> l'arrêt d'autobus (*m.*)
> l'ascenseur (*m.*)
> l'école (*f.*)
> l'entrée (*f.*)
> l'escalier (*m.*)
> l'hôpital (*m.*)
> l'hôtel (*m.*)
> l'Opéra (*m.*)
> l'université (*f.*)

Vous: Merci bien. Au revoir, Monsieur.

Le Monsieur: Au revoir, Monsieur / Madame. Et bonne chance!

You: I'm sorry, but I don't understand you very well. Speak a little more slowly please.

The Man: Here's a map of the city. You see. The Eiffel Tower is very far from here.

You: Ah yes. You're right.

The Man: So. Take *the subway*

> the bus
> a taxi

You: Where is the nearest subway station?

The Man: Over there. Just in front of the *church.*

> airport
> U.S. Embassy
> Arch of Triumph
> bus stop
> elevator
> school
> entrance
> stairs
> hospital
> hotel
> Opera House
> university

You: Thank you. Good-by.

The Man: Good-by. And good luck!

EXERCICES D'APPLICATION

1. Turn to the student next to you and ask directions to the restrooms, the exit, the stairway, or to a nearby building. Begin with: «**Pardon, Monsieur / Madame / Mademoiselle. Pouvez-vous m'aider? Je cherche . . . .**»
2. Ask where the nearest _____ is. Use **le plus proche** with masculine nouns and **la plus proche** with feminine nouns.

EXEMPLE: **l'hôpital**
Où est **l'hôpital** le plus proche?

la bibliothèque, la banque, la poste, la gare, le parc, le syndicat d'initiative, la station de métro, l'arrêt d'autobus, la station de taxis, l'hôtel, l'université, la sortie

VERBES IRRÉGULIERS: pouvoir, prendre, savoir, connaître

pouvoir	*to be able*		
je peux	*I can, I am able*	**nous pouvons**	*we can*
tu peux	*you can*	**vous pouvez**	*you can*
il / elle peut	*he / she can*	**ils / elles peuvent**	*they can*

«**Pouvez-vous** m'aider?»

Exception: **Puis-je?** = *Can I?*
«Comment **puis-je** y aller?»

prendre	*to take*		
je prends	*I take, I am taking*	**nous prenons**	*we take*
tu prends	*you take*	**vous prenez**	*you take*
il / elle prend	*he / she takes*	**ils / elles prennent**	*they take*

«**Prenez** la première rue à droite.»
«**Prenez** le métro / l'autobus / le taxi:»

Like **prendre: apprendre**   *to learn*
                comprendre   *to understand*

«**Je** ne vous **comprends** pas très bien.»

savoir	*to know*		
je sais	*I know*	**nous savons**	*we know*
tu sais	*you know*	**vous savez**	*you know*
il / elle sait	*he / she knows*	**il / elles savent**	*they know*

«C'est très loin d'ici, **vous savez.**»

savoir means *to know* in the sense of "to have knowledge":

> **Savez-vous** où est la Tour Eiffel?
> *Do you know where the Eiffel Tower is?*

savoir + infinitive means *to know how:*

> **Savez-vous** parler français?
> *Do you know how to speak French?*

connaître *to know*			
je connais	*I know*	**nous connaissons**	*we know*
tu connais	*you know*	**vous connaissez**	*you know*
il / elle connaît	*he / she knows*	**ils / elles connaissent**	*they know*

Connaître means *to know* in the sense of "being acquainted with" a person or a thing (a city, a restaurant, a book, a road, etc.) through contact or experience.

Connaître is never followed by **comment** *(how),* **où** *(where),* **quand** *(when),* **que** *(that),* or **si** *(if):*

> **Je connais** Paris. *I know Paris.*
> **Connaissez-vous** Danièle? *Do you know Danièle?*

STRUCTURES

1.   Definite Articles: le, la, l', les *(the)*

All French nouns are either masculine or feminine. Most nouns are made plural by adding the letter **s** to the singular.

	Singular	Plural
Masculine	**le taxi**	**les taxis**
	le musée	**les musées**
Feminine	**la cathédrale**	**les cathédrales**
	la bibliothèque	**les bibliothèques**

le and la become l' before nouns that begin with a vowel or with a mute h:

l'église   l'hôtel   l'ascenseur   l'université
l'hôpital   l'entrée   l'escalier   l'école

2.   **Indefinite Articles: un, une** *(a, an);* **des** *(some)*

	Singular	Plural
Masculine	**un taxi** **un ascenseur**	**des taxis** **des ascenseurs**
Feminine	**une église** **une rue**	**des églises** **des rues**

3.   **-er Verbs: Present Tense**

The infinitives of many French verbs end in **-er.** The infinitive is the form you will find when you look up a verb in the dictionary. The English equivalent is *to _____.* For example, **parler** means *to speak.* The present tense of **-er** verbs is formed by adding the appropriate endings to the base or stem of the verb. The base is found by dropping the **-er** ending from the infinitive. For example, the base of **parler** is **parl-:**

je parl**e**	nous parl**ons**
tu parl**es**	vous parl**ez**
il parl**e**	ils parl**ent**
elle parl**e**	elles parl**ent**
on parl**e**	

There are often three possible English meanings for each form:

je parle = *I speak, I am speaking, I do speak*

Some common **-er** verbs used in everyday conversation:

acheter[1]	*to buy*	**continuer**	*to continue*
adorer	*to adore*	**cuisiner**	*to cook*
aider	*to help*	**danser**	*to dance*
aimer	*to like, to love*	**détester**	*to detest*
chanter	*to sing*	**donner**	*to give*
chercher	*to look for*	**écouter**	*to listen (to)*
commencer[1]	*to begin*	**étudier**	*to study*

1. See **Appendice,** page 390.

expliquer	*to explain*	**oublier**	*to forget*
fermer	*to close*	**parler**	*to speak*
fumer	*to smoke*	**regarder**	*to look (at)*
habiter	*to live (in)*	**téléphoner (à)**	*to telephone*
inviter	*to invite*	**tourner**	*to turn*
jouer	*to play*	**travailler**	*to work*
manger[1]	*to eat*	**trouver**	*to find*
marcher	*to walk*	**visiter**	*to visit (a place)*
montrer	*to show*	**voyager**[1]	*to travel*
nager[1]	*to swim*		

Note that **je** becomes **j'** before verbs beginning with a vowel. **Elle** remains **elle:**

> **J'**aime voyager.
> **Elle** aime voyager.

4.   Imperatives

A command or order (the imperative) in French is formed by using the present tense of the verb without the subject pronoun. You can give an order to an individual (**tu, vous**), or to a group of people (**nous, vous**):

> «**Continuez** tout droit.»
> «**Tournez** à gauche.»
> «**Tournez** à droite.»
> «**Allez** au premier carrefour.»
> «**Prenez** le métro.»

> **Prends** le métro. *Take the subway.* (**tu** form)

> **Allons!** *Let's go!* (**nous** form)

Exception: **-er** verbs and the verb **aller** drop the letter **s** in the second person singular (**tu**) command form:

> **Parle** plus lentement, Francette.
> *Speak more slowly, Francette.*

Negative imperative:

> **Ne prenez pas** le métro.
> *Don't take the subway.*

---

1. See **Appendice,** page 390.

5.   Contractions with the Definite Article

a. The preposition **à** *(to) contracts with* **le** and **les:**

> à + le → au
> à + les → aux
> à + la *remains* à la
> à + l' *remains* à l'

> «Allez **au** premier carrefour.»
> «Tournez à droite **aux** feux.»

b. The preposition **de** *(of, from, about)* contracts with **le** and **les:**

> de + le → du
> de + les → des
> de + la *remains* de la
> de + l' *remains* de l'

> Nous sommes loin **du** parc. *We are far from the park.*

> loin **de** = *far from*

> loin **de** + **le** parc → loin **du** parc

des *(some)* is also the plural of **un / une** *(a, an).*

de is also used to express possession or relationship:

> Voici l'adresse **de** Pierre. *Here's Pierre's address.*
> Où est la mère **de** Marc? *Where is Marc's mother?*
> Quelle est l'adresse **du** professeur? *What is the professor's address?*

6.   Negation

a. To make a sentence negative, place **ne** before the conjugated verb and **pas** after it. **Ne** becomes **n'** when the following verb begins with a vowel or a mute **h:**

> «Je suis désolé(e), mais je **ne** vous comprends **pas** très bien.»
> Nous **n'**allons **pas** à Paris. *We aren't going to Paris.*

b. Pas is used alone when there is no verb:

> **Pas** aujourd'hui! *Not today!*
> **Pas** moi! *Not I!*
> **Pas** vrai! *Not true!*

EXERCICES DE SYNTHÈSE

A.* *Employez la forme correcte du verbe* **pouvoir:**

1. Vous _____ prendre le métro.
2. _____ -je y aller?
3. Je _____ vous aider.
4. Nous _____ parler plus lentement.
5. Elle _____ prendre l'autobus.
6. Elles _____ continuer tout droit.
7. _____ -tu m'aider?

B.* *Employez la forme correcte du verbe* **prendre:**

1. Je _____ le métro.
2. Tu _____ un taxi.
3. Nous _____ l'autobus.
4. Ils _____ la première rue à gauche.
5. Vous _____ la première rue à droite.
6. Il _____ l'autobus.

C. *Ask the person on your left if he or she knows the person on your right:* «**Connaissez-vous Monsieur / Madame / Mademoiselle?**» *If the answer is* «**Non**», *introduce them:* «**Permettez-moi de vous présenter _____.**» *Don't hesitate to ask:* «**Pardon, comment vous appelez-vous?**»

D. *Employez l'article défini* (**le, la, l', les**):

1. _____ métro, _____ métros
2. _____ hôtel, _____ hôtels
3. _____ entrée, _____ entrées
4. _____ taxi, _____ taxis
5. _____ bibliothèque, _____ bibliothèques
6. _____ université, _____ universités
7. _____ sortie, _____ sorties

E. *Employez l'article indéfini* (**un, une, des**):

1. _____ taxi, _____ taxis
2. _____ rue, _____ rues
3. _____ sortie, _____ sorties
4. _____ ascenseur, _____ ascenseurs
5. _____ bibliothèque, _____ bibliothèques
6. _____ syndicat d'initiative, _____ syndicats d'initiative
7. _____ station de métro, _____ stations de métro
8. _____ cathédrale, _____ cathédrales

F. *Répondez par «oui» ou par «non» selon le cas:*

EXEMPLE: Aimez-vous nager?
Oui, j'aime nager. *Ou,*
Non, je n'aime pas nager.

Aimez-vous . . . . . .

1. parler?
2. danser?
3. cuisiner?
4. fumer?
5. marcher?
6. prendre le métro?
7. voyager?
8. jouer?
9. travailler?
10. étudier?
11. téléphoner?
12. chanter?

G. *Répondez par «oui» ou par «non» selon le cas:*

EXEMPLE: Savez-vous nager?
Oui, je sais nager. *Ou,*
Non, je ne sais pas nager.

Savez-vous . . . . . .

1. danser?
2. cuisiner?
3. nager?
4. parler français?
5. étudier?
6. jouer?
7. fumer?

H.* *Transformez. Remplacez les mots en italique:*

1. EXEMPLE: Je *téléphone à* mon ami. (aimer)
J'aime mon ami.

inviter, chercher, aider, parler de, parler à, écouter, adorer, téléphoner à, aimer

2. EXEMPLE: Il *étudie* beaucoup. (fumer)
Il fume beaucoup.

parler, cuisiner, expliquer, fumer, marcher, nager, oublier, téléphoner, travailler, voyager, manger

3. EXEMPLE: Ils *étudient* beaucoup. (fumer)
                      Ils fument beaucoup.

parler, cuisiner, expliquer, fumer, marcher, nager, oublier, téléphoner, travailler, voyager, manger

4. EXEMPLE: Vous *jouez* bien. (danser)
                      Vous dansez bien.

commencer, cuisiner, danser, expliquer, jouer, nager, parler, travailler, chanter

5. EXEMPLE: Nous *aimons* la ville. (adorer)
                      Nous adorons la ville.

détester, adorer, visiter, regarder, parler de, chercher

I.*   *Employez:* **à la, à l'** *ou* **au:**

EXEMPLE: Je vais **au** cinéma.

Je vais _____.

1. l'hôtel
2. la cathédrale
3. l'église
4. le château

5. la poste
6. la banque
7. l'aéroport
8. la bibliothèque

9. l'université
10. le parc
11. l'hôpital

J.*   *Employez* **de la, de l'** *ou* **du:**

EXEMPLE: L'hôtel est loin **de la** gare.

L'hôtel est loin _____.

1. l'église
2. l'hôpital
3. la station de métro
4. l'arrêt d'autobus

5. la bibliothèque
6. le syndicat d'initiative
7. l'aéroport
8. l'université

9. le musée
10. le parc
11. la cathédrale

K.   *Employez* **du, de l'** *ou* **de la** *dans les phrases suivantes. Puis traduisez:*

1. C'est le livre _____ professeur.
2. Henriette est une amie _____ frère de Jean.

3. C'est la maison _____ amis de Pierre.
4. C'est le livre _____ sœur d'Antoine.
5. Voilà l'adresse _____ hôtel.
6. Quelle est l'adresse _____ professeur?
7. Voilà l'adresse _____ école.
8. C'est la mère _____ ami de Marc.
9. Voilà l'entrée _____ bibliothèque.
10. Où est la sortie _____ hôpital?

L. *Répondez à ces question:*

1. Fumez-vous? des cigarettes? des cigares? une pipe?
   Fumez-vous beaucoup? Combien de paquets par jour?
   Combien de cigarettes par jour?
2. Aimez-vous cette ville?
3. Savez-vous danser? cuisiner? nager?
4. Étudiez-vous beaucoup?
5. À qui téléphonez-vous souvent? de temps en temps? à vos parents? à des amis?
6. Habitez-vous loin d'ici? près d'ici?
7. Aimez-vous parler français? voyager? chanter? prendre le métro?

EXPANSION: Où habitez-vous? *Where do you live?*

J'habite **20 rue Manin**	*I live at 20 Manin Street*
. . . **près de l'autoroute 22**	*. . . near highway 22*
. . . **juste en face de l'hôpital**	*. . . just opposite the hospital*
. . . **pas loin du centre commercial**	*. . . not far from the shopping center*
. . . **de l'autre côté du parc**	*. . . on the other side of the park*
. . . **dans un vieux quartier**	*. . . in an old neighborhood*
. . . **tout à côté de la route 100**	*. . . right next to Route 100*
. . . **à cinq minutes d'ici**	*. . . five minutes from here*
. . . **à deux pas d'ici**	*. . . close by (literally: two steps from here)*
. . . **loin d'ici**	*. . . far from here*
. . . **tout près d'ici**	*. . . very close by*
. . . **à un kilomètre d'ici**	*. . . 1 kilometer from here*
. . . **à un mille d'ici**	*. . . 1 mile from here*
. . . **en ville**	*. . . in town / downtown*
. . . **dans la banlieue**	*. . . in the suburbs*
. . . **à la campagne**	*. . . in the country*

Exercice: Répondez: **Où habitez-vous?**

PRONONCIATION

1.   Sound (Phonetic Symbol): [i]

SPELLING: **i, ï, î, y**

ENGLISH SOUND RESEMBLED: Vowel sound in word *tea*

PRONUNCIATION: Smile. Pull the corners of the mouth back tightly. Do
                                   not let the sound glide as in English. Keep it short and
                                   abrupt. Also, do not slip into the English short **i** sound
                                   as in the word *hit*.

EXAMPLES FROM THIS CHAPTER: i̱l   sui̱vez
                               ci̱néma   voici̱
                               sorti̱e   merci̱
                               universi̱té   taxi̱
                               i̱ci̱   oui̱
                               pui̱s

2.   Syllabication

Knowing how to break French words into syllables facilitates correct pronunciation.
Here are some general rules:

a. French syllables tend to end in vowel sounds.

b. Single consonants between two vowels go with the following vowel. **(ci-né-ma)**

c. Double consonants between two vowels are generally treated as one and go with
the following vowel sound. **(co-mment)**

d. Two different consonants in a row are usually divided between syllables **(u-ni-ver-si-
té)**, except for the consonant groups **bl, br, cl, cr, dr, fl, fr, gl, gr, pl, tr, vr,** which
remain intact and go with the following vowel sound **(bi-bli-o-thèque, é-glise, ca-thé-
drale**

Breaking French words into syllables also promotes authentic-sounding stress patterns,
with each French syllable receiving the same even stress. In the following list, consider
why each word taken from this chapter has been broken into syllables as it has. Then
practice each one for pronunciation and stress.

par-don	**cher-che**	**es-ca-lier**
pou-vez	**Ei-ffel**	**û-ni-ver-si-té**
ai-der	**sor-tie**	**bi-bli-o-thèque**

toi-lettes	**co-mment**	**tour-nez**
jar-dins	**a-ller**	**con-ti-nu-ez**
pu-blics	**pre-nez**	**de-vant**
ci-né-ma	**mé-tro**	**é-glise**
thé-â-tre	**ta-xi**	**en-trée**
sa-vez	**au-to-bus**	**voi-ci**

IMPROVISATION

Complétez ce dialogue. Employez le vocabulaire et les structures de la leçon:

Vous: Pardon, Monsieur / Madame. Pouvez-vous m'aider?
Un Monsieur / Une Dame: _____
Vous: _____
Le Monsieur / La Dame: _____
Vous: _____
Le Monsieur / La Dame: _____
Vous: Au revoir, Monsieur / Madame.

PROJET

You are giving a party. Give directions to your place (house, apartment, dormitory, etc.) Start from the location of your French class. (Include a simple illustrative map, if possible.)

ACTIVITÉ

Try out asking, giving, and taking directions in the classroom. Ask:

Où est la fenêtre *(window)?*
Où est la porte *(door)?*
Où est le professeur *(professor)?*
Où est le tableau noir *(blackboard)?*
Où est la table *(table)?*
Où est le bureau du professeur *(professor's desk)?*

Now direct your classmates around the classroom, to the window, to the door, to the blackboard, etc. Use these expressions and remember to say please (**s'il vous plaît**)**:**

Levez-vous.	*Get up.*
Tournez à gauche.	*Turn left.*
Encore une fois à gauche.	*Again / Once more to the left.*
Maintenant tournez à droite.	*Now turn right.*
Bien! Oui, c'est ça.	*Good! Yes, that's right.*
Allez tout droit.	*Go straight ahead.*
Continuez tout droit.	*Continue (going) straight ahead.*
Avancez.	*Go forward.*
Encore.	*More / Still further / Again.*
Arrêtez! / Stop!	*Stop!*

If you are taking directions, you may need the following expressions:

Pardon?	*Pardon? Excuse me? I didn't quite hear you.*
Je ne vous comprends pas très bien.	*I don't understand you very well.*
Parlez un peu plus lentement, s'il vous plaît.	*Speak a little more slowly please.*
Zut! / Flûte! (milder expletive)	*Darn it!*
Merci.	*Thank you.*

ALOUETTE, GENTILLE ALOUETTE

2. Je te plumerai le bec,
   Je te plumerai le bec.
   Et le bec. Et le bec.
   Et la tête. Et la tête.
   Alouette. Alouette.
   Oh!

3. Je te plumerai les pattes, etc.

4. Je te plumerai le cou, etc.

5. Je te plumerai le dos, etc.

NUMBERS

Quel âge avez-vous?
—J'ai _____ ans.

0	zéro	20	vingt	80	quatre-vingts
1	un	21	vingt et un	81	quatre-vingt-un
2	deux	22	vingt-deux	82	quatre-vingt-deux
3	trois	23	vingt-trois	90	quatre-vingt-dix
4	quatre	30	trente	91	quatre-vingt-onze
5	cinq	31	trente et un	92	quatre-vingt-douze
6	six	32	trente-deux	100	cent
7	sept	40	quarante	101	cent un
8	huit	41	quarante et un	102	cent deux
9	neuf	42	quarante-deux	200	deux cents
10	dix	50	cinquante	201	deux cent un
11	onze	51	cinquante et un	300	trois cents
12	douze	52	cinquante-deux	1000	mille (invariable)
13	treize	60	soixante	2000	deux mille
14	quatorze	61	soixante et un	5000	cinq mille
15	quinze	62	soixante-deux	10.000	dix mille
16	seize	70	soixante-dix	100.000	cent mille
17	dix-sept	71	soixante et onze	1.000.000	un million (de . . .)
18	dix-huit	72	soixante-douze	1.000.000.000	un milliard (de . . .)
19	dix-neuf				

Notes:

1. **et** is used only in 21, 31, 41, 51, 61, 71. Otherwise a hyphen is used in compound numbers under 100.

2. **vingt** and **cent** take **s** when a multiplying number precedes them and no other number follows them:

   quatre-vingts / quatre-vingt-un
   deux cents / deux cent un

3. **un** is *not* used in front of **cent** and **mille:**

   one hundred / a hundred = **cent**

4. From 1100–1900 **mille** may be used:

   mille cent = onze cents
   mille deux cents = douze cents

   Beginning with 2,000, **mille** must be used:

   deux mille cent = two thousand one hundred / twenty-one hundred

5. Periods are used instead of commas, and vice versa.

   EXAMPLE: 10,820.08 = 10.820,08 (**dix mille huit cent vingt virgule zéro huit**)

6. Pronunciation

   THE DIGITS 2 AND 3:

   The final consonants of **deux** and **trois** are not pronounced. When followed by a word beginning with a vowel, however, the final **x** and **s** join up with the following vowel and are pronounced **z: deux ans, trois ans**

   THE DIGITS 5 AND 8:

   The final consonants of **cinq** and **huit** are pronounced except when followed by a word beginning with a consonant: **cinq livres, huit livres.**

   THE DIGIT 7:

   The final **t** of **sept** is always pronounced. The letter **p** in **sept,** however, is silent: **sept.**

   THE DIGITS 6 AND 10:

   Six and **dix** are pronounced /sis/, /dis/. When followed by a word beginning with a consonant, they are pronounced /si/, /di/: **six livres, dix livres.** When followed by a word beginning with a vowel, the **x** is pronounced **z** and joins up with the following vowel: **six ans, dix ans.**

THE DIGIT 9:

The **f** of **neuf** is pronounced. However, the **f** is pronounced as a **v** when followed by the words **ans** *(years)* and **heures** *(hours, o'clock)*. **Neuf ans** is pronounced [nœvɑ̃]. **Neuf heures** is pronounced [nœvœr].

Note these pronunciations:

17   [disset]
18   [dizyit]
19   [diznœf]
20   [vɛ̃]
21   [vɛ̃teœ̃]

SPRINGBOARDS FOR CONVERSATION

1. Quel âge avez-vous?
   J'ai _____ ans.
2. Quel âge a le professeur? Monsieur . . .? Madame . . .? Mademoiselle . . .? etc. (Devinez.)
   Il / Elle a _____ ans.
3. Quel âge a votre mère? votre père? votre femme? votre mari? votre frère? votre sœur? votre chien? votre meilleur(e) ami(e)?
4. Quel âge préféreriez-vous avoir? Quel âge avez-vous l'impression d'avoir en ce moment? Vingt ans? cent ans? etc.
5. Combien d'étudiants y a-t-il aujourd'hui dans la classe?
   Il y en a _____.
6. Combien de fenêtres y a-t-il dans la classe? combien de chaises? combien de tables? etc.
   Il y en a _____.
7. Combien de frères avez-vous? combien de sœurs? combien d'enfants?
   J'en ai _____.

PROJET

Make a children's book of numbers using the numbers from 1 to 20. Draw or cut out appropriate illustrations. EXAMPLE: 1 . . . **un stylo,** 2 . . . **deux pommes,** 3 . . . **trois fleurs,** etc.

ACTIVITÉS

1. Play Bingo in French.

2. Play "Go Fish," a simple card game. Vocabulary needed:

un	**six**
deux	**sept**
trois	**huit**
quatre	**neuf**
cinq	**dix**

Avez-vous des. . . ? *(Do you have any . . . ?)*

Voilà un. . . *(Here's a. . .)*

Valet, dame, roi, as *(Jack, queen, king, ace)*

Pardon? *(Excuse me? I didn't hear / understand you.)*

C'est tout? *(Is that all?)*

Tricheur! Tricheuse! *(Cheater!)*

Merci. *(Thanks.)*

À qui le tour? C'est à vous / à moi. *(Whose turn is it? It's yours / mine.)*

Quelle chance! *(What luck!)*

Rules for "Go Fish":

The goal is to accumulate the greatest number of packs of four cards of the same denomination. There are three players per group. Each receives seven cards. The player on the dealer's left goes first. He asks any player in his group for a card to complete a pack of which he has at least one representative card in his hand. This continues until that player receives a negative answer, at which point he draws a card from the pack on the table. If he gets the card he had asked for, he goes again. If not, the turn passes to the player on his left. The winner is the player who has the greatest number of packs of four at the game's end. Players cannot ask for a card unless they have at least one card of that denomination in their hands.

Chapitre

3

À la douane	Customs

Proverbe: Autres pays, autres mœurs. | Proverb: Other countries, other customs.

«Avez-vous quelque chose à déclarer?»

DIALOGUE

Le Douanier / La Douanière: Votre passeport, s'il vous plaît.

Vous: Le voici.

Le Douanier: Combien de temps comptez-vous rester en France?

Vous: **Un jour.**

quelques heures
deux jours
trois jours
quatre jours
cinq jours
six jours
une semaine
deux semaines
trois semaines
un mois
Je ne sais pas encore.

Le Douanier: Avez-vous quelque chose à déclarer?

Vous: Non, rien.

Le Douanier: Pas d'alcool? Pas de cigarettes? Pas de cadeaux?

Vous: Oh pardon. J'ai **dix paquets de cigarettes.**

une boîte de cigares
deux bouteilles de vin
trois bouteilles de whisky
quatre flacons de parfum

Combien dois-je payer?

Le Douanier: **Cent** francs, Monsieur / Madame.

dix
vingt
trente
quarante

The Customs Officer: Your passport, please.

You: Here it is.

The Customs Officer: How long do you intend to stay in France?

You: *One day*.

a few hours
two days
three days
four days
five days
six days
one week
two weeks
three weeks
a month
I don't know yet.

Customs Officer: Do you have anything to declare?

You. No, nothing.

Customs Officer: No alcohol? No cigarettes? No gifts?

You: Oh, excuse me. I have *ten packs of cigarettes*.

a box of cigars
two bottles of wine
three bottles of whisky
four small bottles of perfume

How much do I have to pay?

Customs Officer: *One hundred* francs.

ten
twenty
thirty
forty

cinquante	fifty
soixante	sixty
soixante-dix	seventy
quatre-vingts	eighty
quatre-vingt-dix	ninety

Ouvrez **cette valise,** s'il vous plaît.

Open this *suitcase,* please.

ces bagages	luggage
cette malle	trunk
ce panier	basket
ce paquet	package
ce sac	bag
ce sac à main	handbag / purse

Qu'est-ce que c'est?

Vous: Des affaires personnelles et quelques souvenirs.

LE DOUANIER: Très bien. Vous pouvez passer.

Vous: Merci, Monsieur / Madame. . . . Porteur, s'il vous plaît!

What's this?

YOU: Some personal belongings and a few souvenirs.

CUSTOMS OFFICER: Very well. You can go on through.

YOU: Thank you. . . . Porter!

EXERCICE D'APPLICATION

Répondez. Employez le vocabulaire du dialogue:

LE DOUANIER / LA DOUANIÈRE	VOUS
Votre passeport, s'il vous plaît.	_____
Combien de temps comptez-vous rester?	_____
Avez-vous quelque chose à déclarer?	_____
Qu'est-ce que c'est?	_____
Très bien. Vous pouvez passer.	_____

VERBES IRRÉGULIERS: avoir, ouvrir

avoir	*to have*		
j'ai	*I have*	**nous avons**	*we have*
tu as	*you have*	**vous avez**	*you have*
il / elle a	*he / she has*	**ils / elles ont**	*they have*

«**Avez-vous** quelque chose à declarer?»
— «**J'ai** dix paquets de cigarettes.»

ouvrir	*to open*		
j'ouvre	*I open, I am opening*	**nous ouvrons**	*we open*
tu ouvres	*you open*	**vous ouvrez**	*you open*
il / elle ouvre	*he / she opens*	**ils / elles ouvrent**	*they open*

«**Ouvrez** cette valise, s'il vous plaît.»

STRUCTURES

1. Questions

There are several ways of forming a question in French.

a. In conversational French, simply raise your voice at the end of the sentence:

> **C'est vrai.** *It's true.*
> **C'est vrai?** *It's true?*

b. If you are asking a question to which you expect a "yes" answer, simply put the expression **n'est-ce pas** at the end of the sentence:

> Vous avez deux valises, **n'est-ce pas?**
> *You have two suitcases, don't you?*

> Vous avez quelque chose à déclarer, **n'est-ce pas?**
> *You have something to declare, don't you?*

Depending on the sentence, **n'est-ce pas** has various English equivalents: *isn't that true?, no?, isn't that the case?, don't you?,* etc.

c. A sentence may be turned into a question by placing **est-ce que** at the beginning; **est-ce que** becomes **est-ce qu'** when the following word begins with a vowel or mute **h:**

> Vous avez quelque chose à déclarer. → **Est-ce que** vous avez quelque chose à déclarer?
> *You have something to declare.* → *Do you have something to declare?*

> Je dois payer cent francs. → **Est-ce que** je dois payer cent francs?
> *I have to pay 100 francs.* → *Do I have to pay 100 francs?*

d. Inversion

1. A sentence with a pronoun subject may be made interrogative by placing the subject pronoun after the verb, linking the verb and subject with a hyphen:

> Vous avez quelque chose à déclarer? → **Avez-vous** quelque chose à déclarer?

When the third person singular **(il, elle, on)** form of the verb ends in a vowel, the letter **t** is added in a question:

> Il ouvre la valise. → Ouvre-**t**-il la valise?
> Elle a deux flacons de parfum. → A-**t**-elle deux flacons de parfum?

Avoid inverting the verb with **je.** The form **puis-je** *(can I?),* however, is commonly used instead of **est-ce que je peux?** Note also the form **dois-je:** «Combien **dois-je** payer?»

2. A sentence with a noun subject may be made interrogative by keeping the noun at the beginning of the sentence and by introducing the appropriate subject pronoun **(il, elle, ils, elles)** after the verb:

> Marc est en France. → Marc **est-il** en France?

> Henriette est en France. → Henriette **est-elle** en France?

> Marc et Henriette sont en France. → Marc et Henriette **sont-ils** en France?

3. The interrogative words **à qui** *(to whom),* **avec qui** *(with whom),* **combien** *(how much, how many),* **comment** *(how),* **où** *(where),* **pourquoi** *(why),* and **quand** *(when)* may be followed either by **est-ce que** or by inverted word order:

> «**Combien** de temps **comptez-vous** rester en France?» = **Combien** de temps **est-ce que** vous comptez rester en France?

> **Pourquoi ouvre-t-il** ma valise? = **Pourquoi est-ce qu'**il ouvre ma valise?

> «**Combien dois-je** payer?» = **Combien est-ce que** je dois payer?

The noun subject and verb may be inverted in short questions beginning with **comment** and **où:**

Comment va votre mère? *How is your mother feeling?*
Où habite Pierre? *Where does Pierre live?*
Où est ma valise? *Where's my suitcase?*

2. Demonstrative Adjectives: ce, cet, cette, ces

a. Demonstrative adjectives agree in gender and number with the object pointed out. The singular forms (**ce, cet, cette**) mean either *this* or *that*. The plural form (**ces**) means either *these* or *those*.

Use **ce** before a masculine singular noun beginning with a consonant:

ce paquet	*this package / that package*

Use **cet** before a masculine singular noun beginning with a vowel or a mute **h:**

cet aéroport	*this airport / that airport*
cet hôtel	*this hotel / that hotel*

Use **cette** before any feminine singular noun:

cette valise	*this suitcase / that suitcase*

Use **ces** before any plural noun, masculine or feminine:

ces paquets	*these packages / those packages*
ces aéroports	*these airports / those airports*
ces hôtels	*these hotels / those hotels*
ces valises	*these suitcases / those suitcases*

b. To emphasize the distinction between *this / these* and *that / those*, use **-ci** *(this / these)* or **-là** *(that / those)* after the noun:

Ouvrez votre valise! *Open your suitcase!*
—**Cette valise -ci ou cette valise-là?** *This suitcase or that suitcase?*

3. Expressions of Quantity

Expressions of quantity may be used alone or with a noun preceded by **de; de** becomes **d'** before a noun beginning with a vowel or a mute **h:**

assez	*enough*
beaucoup	*many, a lot, much, very much*
combien	*how much, how many*

peu	*few, little, not much*
un peu	*a little*
tant	*so much, so many*

«**Combien de** temps comptez-vous rester en France?»
Avez-vous **beaucoup de** valises?—Oui, **beaucoup!**

4.   il y a, voilà, voici

a. il y a *(there is, there are)* introduces a statement:

Il y a des livres sur le bureau. *There are books on the desk.*

Interrogative: **Est-ce qu'il y a?** = **y a-t-il?**

Est-ce qu'il y a des livres sur le bureau? = **Y a-t-il** des livres sur le bureau?

b. voilà *(there is, here is, there are, here are)* and **voici** *(here is, here are)* specify particular persons or items. **Voilà** tends to be used in place of **voici:**

Voilà Paul! *There's Paul! / Here's Paul!*

Note these special structures with **voici** and **voilà:**

Voilà Paul! **Le voilà!** *There's Paul! There he is!*

Voilà mon livre! **Le voilà!** *There's my book! There it* (m.) *is!*

Voilà Anne! **La voilà!** *There's Anne! There she is!*

Voilà ma valise! **La voilà!** *There's my suitcase! There it* (f.) *is!*

Les voilà! *There they are!*

EXERCICES DE SYNTHÈSE

A.* *Employez la forme correcte du verbe* **avoir:**

1. _____-vous quelque chose à déclarer?
2. J'_____ quelques souvenirs.
3. Tu _____ beaucoup de valises!
4. Ils _____ des cigarettes.
5. Elle _____ quatre valises.
6. Nous _____ trois bouteilles de vin.

B.* *Employez la forme correcte du verbe* **ouvrir:**

1. J'_____ la bouteille.
2. _____-t-il ma valise?
3. Monsieur, _____ votre malle, s'il vous plaît.
4. Madame, _____ votre sac, s'il vous plaît.
5. Elles _____ leurs valises.
6. _____ ta valise!

C.* *Transformez ces phrases en questions avec* **est-ce que** *et avec l'inversion. Puis traduisez:*

EXEMPLE: Vous avez deux bouteilles de vin.
Est-ce que vous avez deux bouteilles de vin?
Avez-vous deux bouteilles de vin?

1. Vous avez quelque chose à déclarer.
2. Vous avez des cigarettes.
3. Tu as beaucoup de valises.
4. Vous pouvez passer.
5. Nous avons une bouteille de whisky.
6. Vous ouvrez la valise.

D. *Transformez ces phrases en questions avec* **est-ce qu'** *et avec l'inversion. Puis traduisez:*

EXEMPLE: Il a les valises.
Est-ce qu'il a les valises? A-t-il les valises?

1. Elle a la valise.
2. Il ouvre les valises.
3. Il parle français.
4. Elle compte rester deux jours.
5. Il va en France.
6. Elle a quelque chose à déclarer.
7. Il reste deux jours.
8. Elle habite à Montréal.
9. Il aime le parfum.
10. Elle fume.

E.* *Transformez ces phrases en questions. Suivez le modèle. Ensuite traduisez:*

MODÈLE: Pierre est en France.
Pierre est-il en France? Est-ce que Pierre est en France?

1. Marie est à Paris.
2. La fenêtre est ouverte.
3. Le douanier ouvre les valises.
4. Le professeur parle français.
5. Vos parents sont en France.
6. Pierre et Henriette sont en France.

F.* *Posez des questions. Suivez le modèle:*

  MODÈLE: Vous parlez. (Pourquoi?)
            Pourquoi parlez-vous? Pourquoi est-ce que vous parlez?

  1. Vous travaillez. (Où?)   4. Vous parlez. (Avec qui?)
  2. Tu ouvres la valise. (Pourquoi?) 5. Je dois payer. (Combien?)
  3. Vous habitez. (Où?)   6. Vous mangez. (Quand?)

  MODÈLE: Il parle. (Pourquoi?)
            Pourquoi parle-t-il? Pourquoi est-ce qu'il parle?

  1. Elle téléphone. (A qui?)   4. Elle voyage. (Pourquoi?)
  2. Il voyage. (Avec qui?)   5. Il compte rester ici. (Combien de temps?)
  3. Elle mange. (Où?)   6. Il travaille. (Où?)

G.* *Remplacez (replace)* **le, la, las,** *par* **ce, cette,** *ou* **ces.** *Traduisez:*

  EXEMPLE: Ouvrez la bouteille!
             Ouvrez cette bouteille!

  1. Ouvrez la boîte!   4. Elle ouvre la malle.   7. Ouvrez le sac!
  2. Ouvrez le flacon!   5. Il ouvre la bouteille.   8. Ouvrez les paquets!
  3. J'ouvre la valise.   6. Ouvrez les valises!

H.* *Posez des questions. Suivez le modèle:*

  MODÈLE: Ouvrez la valise!
            Cette valise-ci ou cette valise-là?

  1. Fermez la fenêtre!   3. Ouvrez le sac!   5. Fermez la porte!
  2. Prenez le livre!   4. Regardez le monsieur!

I.   *Complete each sentence with* **assez, beaucoup, trop,** *or* **peu** *to describe yourself.*

  1. Je voyage. . . .   4. Je travaille. . . .   6. Je marche. . . .
  2. Je mange. . . .   5. Je téléphone. . . .   7. Je parle. . . .
  3. J'étudie. . . .

EXPANSION: Les Objets de classe

Point at different objects in the classroom and ask: **Qu'est-ce que c'est?** The answers will be: **C'est un . . .** or **C'est une . . .** *(It's a . . .):*

un bloc	pad of paper
un bureau	(large) desk, teacher's desk
un cahier	notebook
une carte	map
une chaise	chair
une corbeille à papier	wastebasket
un crayon	pencil
un dictionnaire	dictionary
un drapeau	flag
un extincteur	fire extinguisher
une fenêtre	window
une feuille de papier	piece of paper
une gomme	rubber eraser
une lampe	lamp
un livre	book
une lumière / la lumière	light
un morceau de craie	piece of chalk
une moquette	carpet
un mur	wall
une pendule électrique	electric clock
un plancher / le plancher	floor
un plafond / le plafond	ceiling
une porte / la porte	door
un pupitre	desk (student's)
un radiateur	radiator
un sac à main	handbag
une serviette	briefcase, book bag
un stylo	pen
une table	table
un tableau	painting, picture
un tableau d'affichage	bulletin board
un tableau noir	blackboard
un tapis	rug

Also:

un étudiant	student (m.)
une étudiante	student (f.)
le professeur	professor / teacher

Exercices

1. Ask the person sitting next to you to point out different objects in the classroom:

   EXEMPLES: Où est la lumière? —La voilà!
               Où est le tableau noir? —Le voilà!
               Où sont les fenêtres? —Les voilà!

2. Make a list of what you see in the classroom.

   EXEMPLE: Dans cette salle de classe il y a quatre fenêtres, un bureau, deux
              portes, etc.

3. Make a statement that is either true or false about what can be seen in the classroom.
   Class members will respond: **C'est vrai!** or **C'est faux!**

   EXEMPLES: Voilà une fenêtre!
              Il y a trois fenêtres dans cette salle de classe.
              Il y a des livres sur le bureau.

PRONONCIATION

1.   Sound (phonetic symbol): [u]

SPELLING:	**ou, oû, où**
ENGLISH SOUND RESEMBLED:	Vowel sound in words *you* and *who*
PRONUNCIATION:	Push lips forward into a little circle. Do not let the sound glide as in English. Keep it short and abrupt.

EXAMPLES FROM THIS CHAPTER:

vous	beauc**ou**p
bouteille	n**ou**s p**ou**vons
ouvrez	v**ou**s p**ou**vez
où	j**ou**r
s**ou**venir	j'**ou**vre

2.   <u>Liaison</u> *(linking)* and <u>Enchaînement</u> *(chaining)*

Liaison and **enchaînement** both reflect the French tendency to have syllables end in a vowel sound (See Chapter 2: Syllabication).

Liaison occurs when a normally silent final consonant is pronounced with the initial vowel sound of a following word. For example, the final consonant **t** in the verb form **ils ont** is not pronounced; however, when inverted, the final consonant **t** is pronounced with the following vowel: **ont-ils?**

In **liaison** some final consonants change pronunciation:

s is pronounced [z]	**(ils ont)**
x is pronounced [z]	**(deux ans)**
d is pronounced [t]	**(quand il parle)**

There are certain times in conversational French when **liaison** must be made and others when it is prohibited. On still other occasions it is considered optional. The best guideline to keep in mind is that **liaison** occurs only between words that are naturally grouped together.

OBLIGATORY LIAISONS:

a. Between articles and following nouns: **les églises, des affaires personnelles**
b. Between adjectives and following nouns: **mon hôtel, ces affaires, quelques heures**
c. Between subject pronouns and verbs: **elles ont, ont-ils**

PROHIBITED LIAISONS:

a. Between a proper name used as subject and the following verb: **Robert // a une valise.**
b. Before **oui: mais // oui**
c. After **et: et // elle a . . .**
d. Between **ils** or **elles** in the interrogative verbal form and the following word: **Ont-ils // une valise?**
e. Before an aspirate **h: les // héros**

Enchaînement occurs when the normally pronounced final consonant of one word is treated as if it were the initial sound of the following word beginning with a vowel sound. For example, from this chapter: **il a** = [i-la]

$$\textbf{sac à main} = [\text{sa-ka-m}\tilde{\text{e}}]$$
$$\textbf{il ouvre} = [\text{i-luvr}\text{ə}]$$

IMPROVISATION

Complétez ce dialogue. Employez le vocabulaire et les structures de la leçon:

LE DOUANIER / LA DOUANIÈRE: Avez-vous quelque chose à déclarer?
VOUS: _____

Le Douanier / La Douanière: _____
Vous: _____
Le Douanier / La Douanière: _____
Vous: _____
Le Douanier / La Douanière: Très bien. Vous pouvez passer.

PROJET

List all the items from this lesson that are found in your own bedroom or dormitory room. For example: **Il y a un radiateur, des livres, des stylos, une porte** etc. You may wish to include a rough sketch showing the location of these items.

ACTIVITÉS

1. Using items you have with you in your pockets, purse, briefcase, etc., go through customs. Use as many phrases and structures as possible from the **Dialogue** of this lesson. Additional useful phrases:

Oh pardon! J'ai oublié. . . .	*Oh, pardon me! I forgot . . . .*
Excusez-moi, je suis vraiment désolé(e)!	*Excuse me, I'm truly sorry!*
C'est tout?	*Is that all?*
Oui. C'est tout!	*Yes. That's all!*
Non. voici un / une. . . .	*No. Here's a. . . .*
Non. Voilà un / une . . .	*No. There's a. . . . .*

   You may also wish to refer to **Entracte 2: Numbers**

2. Referring to **Expansion: Les Objets de classe** in this chapter, make labels for items in the classroom, taping these signs to the items themselves. Examples: **un morceau de craie, un mur, le plancher, le tableau noir,** etc.

SUR LE PONT D'AVIGNON

Sur le pont d'A - vi - gnon,
L'on y dan - se, L'on y dan - se.
Sur le pont d'A - vi - gnon,
L'on y dan - se tout en rond.
Les beaux mes - sieurs font comme ça.
Et puis en - core comme ça.

1. Les beaux messieurs font comme ça. . .   (Geste de saluer)
   Et puis encore comme ça. . .   (Autre salut)

2. Les belles dames font comme ça. . .   (Révérence)
   Et puis encore comme ça. . .   (Autre révérence)

3. Les officiers font comme ça. . .   (Salut militaire)
   Et puis encore comme ça. . .   (Autre salut)

Entracte

3

DATES

Quand êtes-vous né(e)?
—Je suis né(e) _____ .

MODÈLE: Je suis né(e) le vingt et un septembre, dix-neuf cent quarante-cinq.

NOTE: Dates are abbreviated numerically: day first, month second, year last.

EXAMPLE: **le vingt et un septembre dix-neuf cent quarante-cinq = 21 / 9 / 45**

1. Les jours de la semaine

The days of the week are not capitalized in French:

lundi	*Monday*	**vendredi**	*Friday*
mardi	*Tuesday*	**samedi**	*Saturday*
mercredi	*Wednesday*	**dimanche**	*Sunday*
jeudi	*Thursday*		

The article **le** is used with days to express regular occurrence:

Le dimanche elle va chez ses parents.
On Sundays (Sundays) she goes to her parents' house.

Dimanche elle va chez ses parents.
On Sunday (Sunday) she is going (to go) to her parents' house.

2. Les mois de l'année

The months of the year are not capitalized in French:

janvier	*January*	**juillet**	*July*
février	*February*	**août**	*August*
mars	*March*	**septembre**	*September*
avril	*April*	**octobre**	*October*
mai	*May*	**novembre**	*November*
juin	*June*	**décembre**	*December*

NOTE: **en septembre** / **au mois de septembre** = *in (the month of) September*

The cardinal numbers (three, ten, twenty-one, etc.) are used with dates, unlike in English. Exception: **le premier** = *the first*. These numbers directly precede the month; no preposition is used between the number and the month. Dates are preceded by the article **le.**

1. **premier**	11. **onze**	21. **vingt et un**
2. **deux**	12. **douze**	22. **vingt-deux**
3. **trois**	13. **treize**	23. **vingt-trois**
4. **quatre**	14. **quatorze**	24. **vingt-quatre**
5. **cinq**	15. **quinze**	25. **vingt-cinq**
6. **six**	16. **seize**	26. **vingt-six**
7. **sept**	17. **dix-sept**	27. **vingt-sept**
8. **huit**	18. **dix-huit**	28. **vingt-huit**
9. **neuf**	19. **dix-neuf**	29. **vingt-neuf**
10. **dix**	20. **vingt**	30. **trente**
		31. **trente et un**

le premier avril = *April first*
le trois avril = *April third*
le huit avril = *April eighth*
le onze avril = *April eleventh*
(Note: No elision occurs between **le huit** and **le onze** in dates.)

Note that the English preposition *on* is not expressed in French dates:

Je vais partir le douze avril.
I'm going to leave (on) April twelfth.

3. L'année

Unlike in English, the word **cent** *(hundred)* is *not* optional in dates. It must be used.

1890	**dix-huit cent quatre-vingt-dix**
1900	**dix-neuf cents**
1905	**dix-neuf cent cinq**
1910	**dix-neuf cent dix**
1920	**dix-neuf cent vingt**
1930	**dix-neuf cent trente**
1940	**dix-neuf cent quarante**
1950	**dix-neuf cent cinquante**
1960	**dix-neuf cent soixante**
1970	**dix-neuf cent soixante-dix**
1980	**dix-neuf cent quatre-vingts**
1982	**dix-neuf cent quatre-vingt-deux**

Mille may be used with dates. For example: 1984 = **mille neuf cent quatre-vingt-quatre**

Note that **en** means *in* with years:

en dix-neuf cent soixante-seize (en 1976) = *in 1976*

SPRINGBOARDS FOR CONVERSATION

1. Quand êtes-vous né(e)?
   Je suis né(e) _____ .

2. Quel jour est-ce aujourd'hui?

   EXEMPLE: C'est aujourd'hui mardi. / Aujourd'hui c'est mardi.
   C'est aujourd'hui _____ . / Aujourd'hui c'est _____ .

3. Quelle est la date aujourd'hui?

   EXEMPLE: C'est aujourd'hui mercredi le dix octobre, dix-neuf cent quatre-vingt-cinq. / Aujourd'hui c'est. . . .
   C'est aujourd'hui _____ . / Aujourd'hui c'est _____ .

4. Quelle est la date de votre anniversaire *(birthday)?*
   C'est le _____ .

5. En quelle année êtes-vous né(e)?
   En _____ .

6. Quelle est la date de l'anniversaire de votre professeur? de Monsieur . . . ? de Madame . . . ? de Mademoiselle . . . ?
   C'est le _____ .

7. Quelle est la date de l'anniversaire de votre mari? de votre femme? de votre mère? de votre père? de votre meilleur(e) ami(e)? etc.
C'est le _____ .

8. Quelle est la date de Noël? du Thanksgiving? du Nouvel An? etc.
C'est le _____ .

PROJET

Make an engagement calendar for whatever month and year it is now. Write out each day's date (**le premier, le deux, le trois,** etc.) Place **le premier** in the small block directly beneath whatever day of the week the first falls in the month, and then continue numbering consecutively. Note that French calendars generally start with **lundi.** Days and months are not capitalized.

_____ (mois)			_____ (année)			
lundi	mardi	mercredi	jeudi	vendredi	samedi	dimanche

ACTIVITÉ

In France, nearly everybody has a **fête** or Saint's Day (Name Day) celebration in addition to his or her birthday. Find your own Saint's Day next to your name on this list. (If your name is not on this list, select a name that resembles yours.) Find out your classmates' Saint's Days: **Quelle est la date de votre fête? . . .C'est le _____.** Wish anyone whose Name Day is near: **Bonne Fête!**

FÊTES À SOUHAITER

A		B					
Achille	12 Mai	Barbara	4 Décembre	Clotilde	4 Juin	Evelyne	6 Septembre
Adèle	24 Décembre	Bastien	20 Janvier	Colette	6 Mars	Eve	6 Septembre
Adeline	20 Octobre	Baudouin	17 Octobre	Coralie	18 Mai		
Adrien	8 Septembre	Béatrice	13 Février	Corinne	18 Mai	**F**	
Agathe	5 Février	Bénédicte	16 Mars	Cyrille	18 Mars		
Agnès	21 Janvier	Benjamin	31 Mars			Fabien	20 Janvier
Ahmed	1 Juin	Benoît	11 Juillet	**D**		Fabrice	22 Août
Aimé	13 Septembre	Bernadette	18 Février			Fanny	26 Décembre
Alain	9 Septembre	Bernard	20 Août	Damien	21 Février	Félix	12 Février
Alban (e)	22 Juin	Berthe	2 Juillet	Daniel	11 Décembre	Ferdinand	30 Mai
Albert	15 Novembre	Bertrand	6 Septembre	David	29 Décembre	Fernand	27 Juin
Alexandre	22 Avril	Bettina	17 Novembre	Deborah	21 Septembre	Florence	1 Décembre
Alexis	17 Février	Blanche	3 Octobre	Delphine	26 Novembre	Florent	4 Juillet
Alfred	12 Octobre	Blandine	2 Juin	Denis	9 Octobre	France	9 Mars
Alice	16 Décembre	Boris	2 Mai	Denise	15 Mai	Francine	9 Mars
Aline	20 Octobre	Brice	13 Novembre	Didier	23 Mai	Francis	4 Octobre
Alphonse	1 Août	Brigitte	23 Juillet	Dominique	8 Août	Franck	4 Octobre
Amandine	9 Juillet	Bruno	6 Octobre	Donald	15 Juillet	François	4 Octobre
Amélie	19 Septembre			Dorothée	6 Février	Françoise	9 Mars
Anatole	3 Février	**C**				Frédéric	18 Juillet
André(e)	30 Novembre			**E**			
Angèle	27 Janvier	Camille	14 Juillet	Edgard	8 Juillet	**G**	
Angèlique	27 Janvier	Carine	7 Novembre	Edith	16 Septembre	Gabriel	29 Septembre
Annabelle	26 Juillet	Carole	4 Novembre	Edmond	20 Novembre	Gael	16 Octobre
Anne	26 Juillet	Caroline	4 Novembre	Edouard	5 Janvier	Gaston	6 Février
Annick	26 Juillet	Catherine	24 Mars	Edwige	16 Octobre	Geneviève	3 Janvier
Anouck	26 Juillet	Cécile	22 Novembre	Eliane	7 Juillet	Geoffroy	8 Novembre
Anthony	17 Janvier	Cédric	7 Janvier	Elise	17 Novembre	Georges	23 Avril
Antoine	17 Janvier	Céline	21 Octobre	Elisabeth	17 Novembre	Gerald	5 Décembre
Ariane	17 Septembre	Chantal	12 Décembre	Emeric	4 Novembre	Gérard	3 Octobre
Armand	23 Décembre	Charles	4 Novembre	Emile	22 Mai	Germaine	15 Juin
Armelle	16 Août	Charlotte	4 Novembre	Emma	19 Avril	Gervaise	19 Juin
Arnaud	10 Février	Christel	24 Juillet	Emmanuel	25 Décembre	Ghislain	10 Octobre
Arnold	18 Juillet	Christian	12 Novembre	Eric	18 Mai	Gilbert	4 Février
Arthur	15 Novembre	Christine	24 Juillet	Ernest	7 Novembre	Gildas	29 Janvier
Aude	18 Novembre	Christophe	25 Juillet	Ernestine	7 Novembre	Gilles	1 Septembre
Audrey	23 Juin	Claire	11 Août	Estelle	11 Mai	Gisèle	7 Mai
Auguste	29 Février	Claude	6 Juin	Etienne	26 Décembre	Guillaume	10 Janvier
Aurélie	15 Octobre	Claudine	15 Février	Esther	1 Juillet	Guy	12 Juin
Aymeric	4 Novembre	Clément	23 Novembre	Eugène	8 Juillet	Gustave	28 Août
				Eugénie	7 Février	Gwendoline	14 Octobre

H		Linda	28 Août	**O**		Stanislas	11 Avril
		Lionel	10 Novembre			Stéphane	26 Décembre
Harold	14 Mai	Loic	25 Août	Odette	20 Avril	Suzanne	11 Août
Hélène	18 Août	Lolita	25 Décembre	Odile	14 Décembre	Sylvain	4 Mai
Henri	13 Juillet	Louis	25 Août	Olivia	5 Mars	Sylvie	5 Novembre
Henriette	16 Mars	Louise	15 Mars	Olivier	12 Juillet		
Herbert	20 Mars	Luc	18 Octobre	Oswald	5 Août	**T**	
Hervé	17 Juin	Lucie	13 Décembre				
Honoré	16 Mai	Lucien	8 Janvier	**P**		Tania	12 Janvier
Hortense	11 Janvier	Ludovic	25 Août			Teddy	5 Janvier
Hubert	3 Novembre	Lydie	3 Août	Paola	26 Janvier	Tessa	17 Décembre
Hugues	1 Avril			Pascal	17 Mai	Thibaut	8 Juillet
		M		Patrice	17 Mars	Thérèse	15 Octobre
I				Patrick	17 Mars	Thierry	1 Juillet
		Madeleine	22 Juillet	Paul	29 Juin	Thomas	28 Janvier
Igor	5 Juin	Magali	22 Juillet	Paule	26 Janvier		
Ingrid	2 Septembre	Maggy	22 Juillet	Pauline	26 Janvier	**U**	
Isaac	20 Décembre	Maité	7 Juin	Perrine	31 Mai		
Isabelle	22 Février	Manuel	25 Décembre	Philippe	3 Mai	Ursula	9 Juillet
		Marc	25 Avril	Pierre	29 Juin		
J		Marcel	16 Janvier			**V**	
		Marguerite	16 Novembre	**R**			
Jacob	20 Décembre	Marianne	9 Juillet			Valentin	14 Février
Jacques	3 Mai	Marie	15 Août	Raoul	7 Juillet	Valérie	28 Avril
Jacqueline	8 Février	Marina	17 Juillet	Raphaël	29 Septembre	Vera	17 Septembre
Jean	27 Décembre	Marius	19 Janvier	Raymond	7 Janvier	Véronique	4 Février
J.-Baptiste	24 Juin	Marilyne	15 Août	Réginald	12 Février	Victor	21 Juillet
Jeanne	30 Mai	Marjorie	15 Août	Régine	7 Septembre	Vincent	22 Janvier
Jeannine	12 Décembre	Marthe	29 Juillet	Régis	16 Juin	Violette	5 Octobre
Jérôme	30 Septembre	Martine	30 Janvier	Renaud	17 Septembre	Virginie	7 Janvier
Joël	13 Juillet	Marylise	15 Août	Rémi	15 Janvier	Vivien	10 Mars
Josselin	13 Décembre	Mathias	14 Mai	René	19 Octobre		
Joseph	19 Mars	Mathieu	21 Septembre	Richard	3 Avril	**W**	
Josephine	19 Mars	Mathilde	14 Mars	Robert	30 Avril		
Josette	19 Mars	Maud	14 Mars	Rodolphe	21 Juin	Walter	23 Juin
Jules	12 Avril	Maurice	22 Septembre	Roger	30 Décembre	Wilfried	12 Octobre
Julien	2 Août	Maximilien	12 Mars	Roland	15 Septembre	William	10 Janvier
Juliette	30 Juillet	Michel	29 Septembre	Romain	28 Février		
		Micheline	19 Juin	Romuald	19 Juin	**X**	
K		Mireille	15 Août	Roseline	17 Janvier		
		Monique	27 Août			Xavier	3 Décembre
Karen	7 Novembre	Muriel	15 Août	**S**			
Karine	7 Novembre	Myriam	15 Août			**Y**	
Katia	29 Avril			Sabine	29 Août		
Katy	29 Avril	**N**		Sabrina	29 Août	Yan	27 Décembre
				Salomon	25 Juin	Yolande	15 Juin
L		Nadege	18 Septembre	Samuel	20 Août	Yves	19 Mai
		Nadine	18 Septembre	Sandra	22 Avril	Yvonne	19 Mai
Laetitia	18 Août	Natacha	26 Août	Sébastien	20 Janvier		
Laure	10 Août	Nathalie	27 Juillet	Serge	7 Octobre		
Laurence	10 Août	Nelly	18 Août	Séverine	27 Novembre		
Laurent	10 Août	Nicolas	6 Décembre	Sidonie	14 Novembre		
Léa	22 Mars	Nicole	6 Décembre	Simone	28 Octobre		
Léon	10 Novembre	Noël (le)	25 Décembre	Solange	10 Mai		
Liliane	27 Juillet	Norbert	6 Juin	Sophie	25 Mai		

Chapitre
4

Au restaurant	At the Restaurant

Proverbe: L'appétit vient en mangeant.

Proverb: Appetite comes with eating.

DIALOGUE

EXERCICE D'APPLICATION

VERBES IRRÉGULIERS: **boire, vouloir**

STRUCTURES:

1. **-ir** Verbs: Present Tense
2. **-re** Verbs: Present Tense
3. Le Passé composé
4. The Partitive Construction: **du, de la, de l', des**
5. Negative Expressions

EXERCICES DE SYNTHÈSE

EXPANSION: **Au restaurant**

PRONONCIATION: [y]

IMPROVISATION

PROJET

ACTIVITÉ

CHANSON: **Trempe ton pain, Marie**

«À votre santé! À la vôtre!»

DIALOGUE

Vous: J'ai réservé une table pour sept heures.

Le Maître d'Hôtel: Très bien, Monsieur / Madame. Par ici, s'il vous plaît. . . .

Vous: Je voudrais une table **près de la fenêtre.**

dans le coin
dehors / à l'extérieur
sur la terrasse
dans le jardin
là-bas

Le Maître d'Hôtel: Très bien, Monsieur / Madame. Bon appétit!

Vous: La carte, s'il vous plaît.

Le Garçon / La Serveuse: Un apéritif, Monsieur / Madame?

Vous: Non, merci. Mais j'ai soif. Apportez-moi **de l'eau minérale,** s'il vous plaît.

une boisson
du vin rouge
du vin blanc
un Coca
un Perrier (de l'eau gazeuse)
un citron pressé
une bière
une carafe d'eau fraîche

Le Garçon / La Serveuse: Voulez-vous commander maintenant?

Vous: Oui. J'ai faim. Pour commencer je prendrai **une soupe.**

des hors-d'œuvre (*m.*)
des artichauts (*m.*)
des asperges (*f.*)
du caviar
des champignons (*m.*)
des escargots (*m.*)

You: I've reserved a table for seven o'clock.

The Maître D': Very well. This way, please.

You: I would like a table *near the window.*

in the corner
outside
on the terrace
in the garden
over there

The Maître D': Very well. Have a good meal! (Literally: Good appetite.)

You: Menu, please.

Waiter / Waitress: (Would you like) a cocktail?

You: No thanks. But I'm thirsty. Bring me *some mineral water,* please.

a beverage
some red wine
some white wine
a Coke
a Perrier (sparkling water)
a lemonade
a beer
a carafe of water

Waiter / Waitress: Do you want to order now?

You: Yes. I'm hungry. To begin (with) I'll have *soup.*

appetizers
artichokes
asparagus
caviar
mushrooms
snails

du pâté des radis *(m.)* du saucisson	pâté radishes sausage

Puis **un bifteck,** des pommes frites et

Then (I'd like) *a steak,* French fried potatoes

de la viande du jambon du lapin une omelette du poisson du poulet du rosbif du veau	meat ham rabbit omelet fish chicken roastbeef veal

une salade.

and *a salad*.

des légumes *(m.)* des carottes *(f.)* du chou-fleur du concombre des épinards *(m.)* des haricots verts *(m.)* des oignons *(m.)* des petits pois *(m.)* du riz des tomates *(f.)*	vegetables carrots cauliflower cucumber spinach green beans onions peas rice tomatoes

LE GARÇON / LA SERVEUSE: Le bifteck, comment le voulez-vous?

VOUS: **Saignant.**

WAITER / WAITRESS: How do you want the steak?

YOU: *Rare*.

bleu à point bien cuit	very rare medium well done

LE GARÇON / LA SERVEUSE: Et du fromage?

VOUS: Non, pas ce soir. Mais qu'est-ce que vous avez comme dessert?

LE GARÇON / LA SERVEUSE: Nous avons du gâteau au chocolat, **des fruits** et de la glace à la vanille.

WAITER / WAITRESS: And some cheese?

YOU: No, not tonight. But what do you have for dessert?

WAITER / WAITRESS: We have chocolate cake, *fruit* and vanilla ice cream.

des abricots *(m.)*	apricots
des bananes *(f.)*	bananas
des cerises *(f.)*	cherries
des fraises *(f.)*	strawberries
des framboises *(f.)*	raspberries
des marrons *(m.)*	chestnuts
du melon	melon
des noix *(f.)*	nuts, walnuts
des oranges *(f.)*	oranges
des pamplemousses *(m.)*	grapefruit
des pêches *(f.)*	peaches
des poires *(f.)*	pears
des pommes *(f.)*	apples
du raisin	grapes

VOUS: Je prendrai tout simplement **un café.**

YOU: I'll simply have *coffee.*

un café au lait	coffee with milk
un digestif	an after-dinner drink
un express	an espresso
un thé	tea

LE GARÇON / LA SERVEUSE: C'est tout?

VOUS: Oui. C'est tout. Mais puis-je avoir **un autre couteau?**

WAITER / WAITRESS: Is that all?

YOU: Yes. That's all. But may I have another *knife?*

une autre assiette	plate
un autre cendrier	ashtray
une autre cuillère	spoon
une autre fourchette	fork
une autre nappe	tablecloth
une autre serviette	napkin
une autre tasse	cup
un autre verre	glass

EXERCICE D'APPLICATION*

Dites que vous avez réservé une table . . . que vous préférez une table sur la terrasse . . . que vous voulez la carte . . . que vous désirez un apéritif . . . que vous voulez de l'eau minérale . . . que vous voulez commander . . . que vous avez faim . . . que vous

avez soif . . . que vous prendrez une soupe, du poulet, des tomates et des pommes frites
. . . que vous voulez votre bifteck à point . . . que vous prendrez des fraises . . . que
vous voulez un autre verre.

VERBES IRRÉGULIERS: boire, vouloir

boire	*to drink*

je bois	nous buvons
tu bois	vous buvez
il / elle boit	ils / elles boivent

vouloir	*to want, to wish*

je veux	nous voulons
tu veux	vous voulez
il / elle veut	ils / elles veulent

«**Voulez-vous** commander maintenant?»
«Le bifteck, comment le **voulez-vous?**»

je voudrais = *I would like*

«**Je voudrais** une table près de la fenêtre.»

voulez-vous bien + **l'infinitif** = *would you kindly, would you please*

Voulez-vous bien fermer la fenêtre, s'il vous plaît?
Would you please close the window?

STRUCTURES

1.   -ir Verbs: Present Tense

The infinitives of many French verbs end in **-ir.** The present tense of these verbs is
formed by adding the appropriate endings to the base of the verb. The base is formed by
dropping the **-ir** of the infinitive. For example, the base of **finir** *(to finish)* is **fin-:**

je finis	nous finissons
tu finis	vous finissez
il finit	ils finissent
elle finit	elles finissent
on finit	

Some common **-ir** verbs:

applaudir	*to applaud*
atterrir	*to land*
bâtir	*to build*
choisir	*to choose*
désobéir (à)	*to disobey*
finir	*to finish*
maigrir	*to get thin*
obéir (à)	*to obey*
pâlir	*to grow pale*
punir	*to punish*
réfléchir	*to reflect*
remplir	*to fill; to fill up; to fill out (a form)*
réussir	*to be successful, to succeed* (**réussir à un examen** = *to pass an exam*)
rougir	*to blush*
vomir	*to vomit*

2.   -re Verbs: Present Tense

The present tense of **-re** verbs is formed by adding the appropriate endings to the base. The base is formed by dropping the **-re** of the infinitive. For example, the base of **attendre** *(to wait)* is **attend-:**

j'attends	nous attendons
tu attends	vous attendez
il attend	ils attendent
elle attend	elles attendent
on attend	

Some common **-re** verbs:

attendre	*to wait, to wait for*
défendre	*to forbid*
entendre	*to hear*
interrompre	*to interrupt* (except: **il interrompt**)

perdre	*to lose*
rendre	*to give back*
répondre (à)	*to answer*
vendre	*to sell*

3.   Le Passé Composé

This past tense is composed of a conjugated form of **avoir,** which is called the auxiliary or "helping" verb, plus the past participle of the main verb.

a. The past participle of **-er** verbs ends in **-é:**

réser**ver** → réserv**é**	
j'**ai** réservé	nous **avons** réservé
tu **as** réservé	vous **avez** réservé
il **a** réservé	ils **ont** réservé
elle **a** réservé	elles **ont** réservé
on **a** réservé	

J'ai réservé une table.
I have reserved / I reserved / I did reserve a table.

b. The past participle of **-ir** verbs ends in **-i:**

fin**ir** → fin**i**	
j'**ai** fini	nous **avons** fini
tu **as** fini	vous **avez** fini
il **a** fini	ils **ont** fini
elle **a** fini	elles **ont** fini
on **a** fini	

c. The past participle of **-re** verbs ends in **-u:**

atten**dre** → attend**u**	
j'**ai** attendu	nous **avons** attendu
tu **as** attendu	vous **avez** attendu
il **a** attendu	ils **ont** attendu
elle **a** attendu	elles **ont** attendu
on **a** attendu	

d. In negative sentences, the auxiliary verb is made negative:

> j'**ai** réservé → je **n'ai pas** réservé

e. In questions, the subject pronoun follows the auxiliary verb and is joined to it with a hyphen:

> **Vous avez** réservé une table. → **Avez-vous** réservé une table?
>
> **Il a** fini. → **A-t-il** fini?

f. Irregular verbs often have irregular past participles:

Infinitive		Past Participle
apprendre	*to learn*	**appris**
avoir	*to have*	**eu**
boire	*to drink*	**bu**
comprendre	*to understand*	**compris**
connaître	*to know*	**connu**
être	*to be*	**été**
ouvrir	*to open*	**ouvert**
pouvoir	*to be able, can*	**pu**
prendre	*to take*	**pris**
vouloir	*to wish*	**voulu**

g. **Aller** is conjugated with **être** as its auxiliary verb in the **passé composé.** The past participle, **allé,** agrees in gender (masculine or feminine) and in number (singular or plural) with the subject. The letter **e** is added to the past participle when the subject is feminine (**allée**). The letter **s** is added to the past participle when the subject is plural (**allés**). The letters **es** are added when the subject is both plural and feminine (**allées**):

je **suis allé(e)**	nous **sommes allé(e)s**
tu **es allé(e)**	vous **êtes allé(e)(s)**
il **est allé**	ils **sont allés**
elle **est allée**	elles **sont allées**

h. The following **-er** verbs are also conjugated with **être.** They are commonly called
''verbs of coming and going'':

arriver	*to arrive*
entrer	*to enter*
monter	*to climb up, to go up, to come up*
rentrer	*to go in again, to go home, to come home*
rester	*to remain, to stay*
retourner	*to go back, to return*
tomber	*to fall*

4.   The Partitive Construction: du, de la, de l', des

a. Although the words *some* and *any* are often omitted in English, they are rarely left
out in French:

To indicate *some* or *any,* use:

du before masculine singular nouns:

«Je prendrai **du** rosbif».

de la before feminine singular nouns:

«Nous avons **de la** glace à la vanille».

de l' before masculine or feminine singular nouns beginning with a vowel or mute **h:**

«Apportez-moi **de l'**eau minérale, s'il vous plaît».

des before all plural nouns:

«Je prendrai **des** asperges».

---

b. un, une, du, de la, de l', and **des** all become **de (d')** after a negative:

J'ai **un** couteau. → Je n'ai pas **de** couteau.
Je prends **du** fromage. → Je ne prends pas **de** fromage.
Nous avons **des** asperges. → Nous n'avons pas **d'**asperges.

 le, la, and **les** do not change after a negative:

c. Note that the definite article (**le, la, l', les**), is used before nouns that are meant in a
general sense. The definite article is often used after **aimer, adorer, détester,** and
préférer:

Je n'aime pas **le poisson.** *I don't like fish* (in general).
L'eau est bonne quand on a soif. *Water is good when you're thirsty.*

5. Negative Expressions

ne . . . pas	*not*	Je **ne** prends **pas** de dessert ce soir.
ne . . . jamais	*never*	Je **ne** prends **jamais** de café.
ne . . . rien	*nothing*	Il **ne** mange **rien.** Absolument rien!
ne . . . personne	*nobody, no one*	Je **ne** connais **personne** ici. Absolument **personne!**
ne . . . plus	*no longer, not any more*	Je **ne** vais **plus** dans ce restaurant.
ne . . . que	*only*	Je **n**'ai **que** deux dollars.

In the **passé composé** all these expressions replace **ne . . . pas** around the auxiliary verb:

Je **n'ai rien** mangé. Absolument rien!

EXCEPTION: **ne . . . personne.**
Je **n**'ai vu **personne.**

EXERCICES DE SYNTHÈSE

A.* *Donnez la forme correcte du verbe* **boire** *au présent et au passé composé. Ensuite, traduisez:*

1. Vous _____ de l'eau.
2. Il _____ du vin.
3. Nous _____ du lait.
4. Je _____ de la bière.
5. Elle _____ du café.
6. Est-ce que tu _____ du vin?

B.* *Donnez la forme correcte du verbe* **vouloir** *au présent. Ensuite, traduisez:*

1. Que _____ -tu?
2. Que _____ -vous?
3. Il _____ manger quelque chose.
4. Nous _____ une table près de la fenêtre.
5. _____ -vous bien fermer la fenêtre?
6. Je _____ manger.

C.* *Transformez. Remplacez les verbes en italique:*

EXEMPLE: Pourquoi *applaudissez*-vous? (désobéir)
Pourquoi désobéissez-vous?

1. finir	4. réfléchir	7. applaudir
2. maigrir	5. rougir	8. désobéir
3. pâlir	6. vomir	

EXEMPLE: Je ne *rougis* pas. (finir)
           Je ne finis pas.

1. choisir	3. applaudir	5. pâlir
2. désobéir	4. obéir	6. rougir

D.   *Mettez le verbe entre parenthèses au présent. Ensuite, traduisez:*

1. Je n' _____ rien. (entendre)
2. J' _____ devant le restaurant. (attendre)
3. Tu _____ ton temps. (perdre)
4. Qu'est-ce qu'il _____? (vendre)
5. _____ à la question! (répondre)
6. J' _____ mon ami. (attendre)

E.*   *Répondez par «oui» ou par «non» selon le cas:*

EXEMPLE: Avez-vous étudié?
           Oui, j'ai étudié. *Ou,*
           Non, je n'ai pas étudié.

a
1. Avez-vous regardé la télévision hier soir *(last night)*?
2. Avez-vous écouté la radio aujourd'hui?
3. Avez-vous fumé aujourd'hui?
4. Avez-vous parlé français aujourd'hui?
5. Avez-vous étudié hier soir?
6. Avez-vous oublié quelque chose aujourd'hui? (ne . . . rien)

b
1. Avez-vous applaudi récemment *(recently)*?
2. Avez-vous fini la leçon?
3. Avez-vous rougi récemment?
4. Avez-vous maigri récemment?
5. Avez-vous réussi à un examen récemment?
6. Avez-vous obéi à votre professeur de français?

c
1. Avez-vous répondu correctement à la question?
2. Avez-vous perdu quelque chose récemment? (ne . . . rien)

3. Avez-vous attendu quelqu'un récemment? (ne . . . personne)
4. Avez-vous entendu votre professeur?
5. Avez-vous vendu quelque chose récemment? (ne . . . rien)

d
1. Avez-vous ouvert la fenêtre de la classe?
2. Avez-vous bu quelque chose récemment? (ne . . . rien)
3. Avez-vous bien compris cet exercice?
4. Avez-vous appris la leçon?
5. Avez-vous eu assez de temps pour étudier hier soir?

F.* *Mettez l'article partitif* (**du, de la, de l', des**). *Traduisez:*

1. Je voudrais _____ vin rouge.
2. Apportez-moi _____ eau minérale, s'il vous plaît.
3. Je prendrai _____ artichauts.
4. Je voudrais _____ pâté.
5. Voulez-vous _____ carottes?
6. Je prends _____ escargots.
7. Avez-vous _____ pommes frites?
8. Je prendrai _____ rosbif.
9. Elle prendra _____ poulet.
10. Voulez-vous _____ veau?
11. Y a-t-il _____ tomates dans la soupe?
12. Voulez-vous _____ riz?
13. Prenez-vous _____ café ou _____ thé?

G. *Mettez l'article défini* (**le, la, l', les**). *Puis traduisez:*

1. Je n'aime pas _____ vin rouge.
2. _____ eau minérale est très bonne quand on a soif.
3. Je n'aime pas _____ artichauts.
4. _____ pâté est bon.
5. Pourquoi n'aimez-vous pas _____ carottes?
6. Je déteste _____ escargots.
7. Aimez-vous _____ pommes frites?
8. J'adore _____ rosbif et _____ riz.
9. _____ poulet est prêt.
10. Aimez-vous _____ veau?
11. Vous n'aimez pas _____ asperges?
12. Je n'aime pas _____ pommes.
13. J'aime _____ café.

H. *Répondez par «oui» ou par «non» selon le cas. Attention:* **du, de la, des** → **de** *(aù négatif)*:

EXEMPLE: Est-ce qu'il y a du rosbif dans votre réfrigérateur?
Oui, il y a du rosbif dans mon réfrigérateur. *Ou,*
Non, il n'y a pas de rosbif dans mon réfrigérateur.

1. du vin?   5. du pâté?   9. des carottes?
2. de la bière?   6. du poulet?   10. du riz?
3. des artichauts?   7. du veau?   11. des petits pois?
4. des champignons?   8. des légumes?   12. de la glace?

I. *Répondez par «oui» ou par «non» selon le cas:*

EXEMPLE: Oui, je bois du / de la / de l' _____ . *Ou*
Non, je ne bois jamais de / d' _____ .

1. Bois-tu du café?   3. Buvez-vous du vin rouge?   5. Buvez-vous de l'eau?
2. Bois-tu de la bière?   4. Buvez-vous du vin blanc?   6. Bois-tu du thé?

J. *Répondez à ces questions:*

1. Avez-vous pris du café ce matin?
2. Mangez-vous de la viande tous les jours?
3. Aimez-vous les légumes? lesquels?
4. Aimez-vous le vin? la bière? le café? le thé? etc.
5. Aimez-vous le rosbif saignant?
6. Qu'est-ce que vous détestez? les épinards? les carottes? le poisson? etc.
7. Quelle est votre boisson préférée? le café? l'eau? etc.
8. Buvez-vous de la bière?
9. Prenez-vous du vin avec vos repas?
10. Avez-vous soif maintenant? Avez-vous faim?
11. Qu'est-ce que vous avez envie de manger en ce moment?
12. Que mangez-vous [grignotez-vous *(snack on)*] pendant que vous regardez la télévision? Que buvez-vous?
13. D'habitude prenez-vous vos repas seul(e)? avec des amis? en famille?
14. Qu'avez-vous acheté au supermarché cette semaine?
15. D'habitude qu'est-ce qu'il y a dans votre réfrigérateur?
16. Quel est votre menu préféré?

K. *Répondez à ces questions:*

1. Quels restaurants recommandez-vous dans la région?
2. Allez-vous souvent au restaurant? à quels restaurants? avec qui?

3. Quel est votre restaurant préféré?
   a. Y êtes-vous allé(e) récemment? avec qui? quand?
   b. Avez-vous réservé une table? pour quelle heure? pour combien de personnes?
   c. Comment est le service? bon? mauvais? (trop) lent? (trop) rapide?
   d. Avez-vous pris un apéritif?
   e. Qu'est-ce que vous avez commandé?
   f. Comment sont les prix? raisonnables? élevés? bas?

EXPANSION: Au restaurant

1. **Ce n'est pas ce que j'ai commandé.** — *That's not what I ordered. / This isn't what I ordered.*

2. **Quelle est la spécialité de la maison?** — *What's the specialty of the house?*

3. **Que me recommandez-vous?** — *What do you recommend?*

4. **À votre santé . . . à la vôtre!** — *To your health! . . . to yours!*

5. **Le sel / le poivre / le beurre / la moutarde, s'il vous plaît.** — *The salt / pepper / butter / mustard, please.*

6. **Encore un peu de pain, s'il vous plaît.** — *A little more bread, please.*

7. **C'est trop cuit / dur / sucré / amer / salé / gras.** — *It's too well done / hard / sweet / bitter / salty / greasy.*

8. **C'est délicieux / bon / affreux / immangeable!** — *It's delicious / good / horrible / inedible!*

9. **Ça sent bon / mauvais.** — *That smells good / bad.*

10. **Ça n'a pas de goût.** — *That has no taste.*

11. **Faites mes compliments au chef.** — *Give my compliments to the chef.*

12. **L'addition, s'il vous plaît.** — *Check, please.*

13. **Est-ce que le service est compris?** — *Is the service charge included?*

14. **Quelles cartes de crédit acceptez-vous?** — *What credit cards do you accept?*

15. **Pas de pourboire pour vous!** — *No tip for you!*

16. **C'est ma tournée.** — *Drinks are on me. (Literally: It's my turn / round.)*

17. **Où sont les toilettes, s'il vous plaît?** — *Where's the restroom, please?*

18. **Je voudrais un ouvre-boîtes / un ouvre-bouteilles / un tire-bouchon.** — *I would like a can opener / a bottle opener / a corkscrew.*

19. **Le petit déjeuner, le déjeuner, le goûter, le dîner, le souper, le casse-croûte, la pause-café.** — *Breakfast, lunch, afternoon snack (tea), dinner, supper, snack, coffee break.*

Exercices

1. Vous terminez votre repas. Vous dites au garçon: _____
2. Le garcon vous apporte du rosbif mais vous avez commandé du poulet. Vous dites: _____
3. Le garçon apporte l'addition. Vous demandez: _____
4. Il y a trop de sucre dans votre café. Vous dites: _____
5. Le café sent bon. Vous dites: _____
6. Vous voulez le sel. Vous dites: _____
7. Votre ami vous dit, «À votre santé!». Vous répondez: _____
8. D'habitude est-ce que vous donnez un pourboire au garçon / à la serveuse?
9. Vous avez commandé du rosbif saignant. Le garçon vous apporte le rosbif bien cuit. Vous dites: _____
10. Vous voulez la moutarde. Vous dites: _____
11. Vous voulez encore un peu de pain. Vous dites: _____
12. Vous préférez payer avec une carte de crédit. Vous demandez: _____
13. Vous mangez un excellent bifteck. Vous dites: _____
14. À quelle heure prenez-vous le petit déjeuner? le déjeuner? le dîner? en semaine? le dimanche?
15. Où déjeunez-vous en semaine? chez vous? à la cantine? sur votre lieu de travail? au restaurant? chez des amis? Où dînez-vous?
16. Que prenez-vous après le dîner? un digestif? du café? du thé?
17. Qu'est-ce que vous avez pris au dîner hier soir? au déjeuner hier? au déjeuner aujourd'hui?
18. Que prenez-vous d'habitude au déjeuner? du yaourt? du café? un sandwich? un bifteck? etc.
19. Que prenez-vous d'habitude au casse-croûte? à la pause-café? des fruits? du café? du gâteau? de la glace? un sandwich? des restes *(leftovers)?* etc.

PRONONCIATION

1.   Sound (Phonetic Symbol): [y]

SPELLING:	**u, û** (also **eu** in past participle of **avoir**)
PRONUNCIATION:	Round and protrude lips while attempting to say the sound [i].
EXAMPLES FROM THIS CHAPTER:	**une** **punir**
	du **vu**
	tu **bu**

l<u>é</u>gumes	pl<u>u</u>s
b<u>u</u>vons	atten<u>du</u>
b<u>u</u>vez	r<u>é</u>ussir
	j'ai <u>eu</u>

Contrast the vowel sound [u] (see Chapter 3) with the vowel sound [y] using the following examples from this chapter:

[u]   [y]

n<u>ou</u>s	b<u>u</u>vons
v<u>ou</u>s	b<u>u</u>vez
n<u>ou</u>s	avons <u>eu</u>
v<u>ou</u>s	avez b<u>u</u>
n<u>ou</u>s	avons v<u>u</u>
avez-v<u>ou</u>s	v<u>u</u>?
v<u>ou</u>s	r<u>é</u>ussissez

IMPROVISATION

Complétez ce dialogue. Employez le vocabulaire et les structures de la leçon:

(Vous êtes au restaurant. Commandez votre repas.)

Vous: J'ai très faim! Que me recommandez-vous?
Le Garçon / La Serveuse: _____
Vous: _____
Le Garçon / La Serveuse: _____
Vous: _____
Le Garçon / La Serveuse: _____
Vous: _____

PROJET

Design a menu for your own restaurant. Choose an appropriate name. Then, list all the items you yourself would actually be willing or able to prepare for your clients. Include your specialties: **Bifteck, Hamburger avec de la sauce tomate, Sandwich au beurre de cacahuètes, Salade de thon, Hot-dog,** etc. Price each item. Include as many of the following categories as possible: **Hors d'œuvre, Soupes / Potages, Entrées, Salades, Desserts, Boissons.**

ACTIVITÉ

Have an in-class restaurant. Everyone should bring in food. A few students will serve as chefs, maître d', and waiters. Everyone else will be diners. Be sure to use as many phrases and structures from the **Dialogue, Structures** and **Expansion** sections of this chapter as possible.

TREMPE TON PAIN, MARIE

4

BREAKFAST FOODS

Qu'est-ce que vous avez pris au petit déjeuner ce matin?

JUS DE FRUITS	FRUIT JUICES
un jus d'ananas	*pineapple juice*
un jus d'orange	*orange juice*
un jus de pamplemousse	*grapefruit juice*
un jus de pomme	*apple juice*
un jus de tomate	*tomato juice*

FRUITS	FRUITS
des abricots *(m.)*	*apricots*
une banane	*a banana*
des cerises *(f.)*	*cherries*
des fraises *(f.)*	*strawberries*
des framboises *(f.)*	*raspberries*
du melon	*melon*
des noix *(f.)*	*nuts, walnuts*
une orange	*an orange*
un (demi-) pamplemousse	*(half) grapefruit*
une pêche	*a peach*

79

une poire	*a pear*
une pomme	*an apple*
une prune	*a plum*
des pruneaux *(m.)*	*prunes*
du raisin	*grapes*
des raisins secs	*raisins*

PAINS, GÂTEAUX, PÂTISSERIE	BREADS, CAKES, PASTRY
des biscottes *(f.)*	*zwieback*
des biscuits *(m.)*	*biscuits, crackers, cookies*
des crêpes *(f.)*	*thin pancakes, crepes*
des croissants *(m.)*	*croissants*
un gâteau	*a piece of pastry*
du gâteau	*cake*
des gâteaux secs	*cookies*
des gaufres *(f.)*	*waffles*
du pain	*bread*
du pain grillé	*toast*
du pain perdu	*French toast*
de la pâtisserie	*pastry*
une pâtisserie danoise	*a Danish*
des petits pains	*rolls*

avec:

du beurre	*butter*
du beurre de cacahuètes	*peanut butter*
de la confiture	*jam*
de la gelée	*jelly*
de la margarine	*margarine*
de la marmelade	*marmalade*
du miel	*honey*
du sirop d'érable	*maple syrup*

CÉRÉALES	CEREALS
des céréales	*cereal*
des cornflakes, Wheaties, Cheerios, etc.	*cornflakes, etc.*
de la crème de blé	*cream of wheat*
des flocons d'avoine	*oatmeal*

avec:

des fruits	*fruit*
du lait	*milk*
du sucre	*sugar*

VIANDES, POISSONS, FROMAGE, ŒUFS   MEAT, FISH, CHEESE, EGGS

du bacon   *bacon*
un bifteck   *steak*
du caviar   *caviar*
du fromage   *cheese*
du jambon   *ham*
des œufs   *eggs*
. . . brouillés   *. . . scrambled*
. . . à la coque   *. . . soft-boiled*
. . . durs   *. . . hard-boiled*
. . . sur le plat   *. . . fried*
. . . pochés   *. . . poached*
une omelette   *an omelet*
. . . aux champignons   *. . . with mushrooms*
. . . au fromage   *. . . cheese*
. . . aux fines herbes   *. . . with herbs*
. . . au jambon   *. . . ham*
. . . nature   *. . . plain*
des saucisses   *sausages*
du saumon fumé   *smoked salmon, lox*
de la viande froide   *cold cuts*
du yaourt, du yogourt   *yogurt*

      avec:

des frites   *French fries*
des pommes de terre sautées   *home-fried potatoes*
du poivre   *pepper*
du sel   *salt*

  BOISSONS   BEVERAGES

du café   *coffee*
un café au lait   *coffee with (boiled) milk*
un café crème   *coffee with cream*
du chocolat   *hot chocolat*
du lait   *milk*
du thé   *tea*

  avec:

du citron   *lemon*
du lait   *milk*
du sucre   *sugar*

Rien. Je ne déjeune jamais le matin.   *Nothing. I never have breakfast.*

SPRINGBOARDS FOR CONVERSATION

1. Qu'est-ce que vous avez pris au petit déjeuner ce matin?
2. Qu'est-ce que le professeur a pris au petit déjeuner ce matin? votre mère? votre père? votre mari? votre femme? votre fils? votre fille? Monsieur . . . ? Madame . . . ? Mademoiselle . . . ? etc.
3. De quoi se compose votre petit déjeuner préféré?
4. D'habitude que prenez-vous au petit déjeuner en semaine? le dimanche? en hiver? en été? en voyage? en vacances?
5. Buvez-vous du café au petit déjeuner? À quel âge avez-vous commencé à boire du café?
6. Quand vous étiez jeune, que preniez-vous au petit déjeuner? Qui vous préparait le petit déjeuner? votre mère? votre père? vous-même?
7. Préparez-vous vous-même votre petit déjeuner?
8. Qu'est-ce que vous ne prenez jamais au petit déjeuner? Pourquoi?
   Je ne prends jamais de / d' _____.
9. Avez-vous faim au petit déjeuner? Prenez-vous votre petit déjeuner chaque matin?
10. Aimez-vous les pruneaux? les pamplemousses?
    les œufs? le saumon fumé? les crêpes? Qu'est-ce que vous n'aimez pas?
    Oui, j'aime les _____.
    Non, je n'aime pas les _____.
11. D'habitude où prenez-vous le petit déjeuner? à la maison? au travail? à la cafétéria? au restaurant?
12. Avez-vous déjà pris le petit déjeuner au lit? À quelle occasion? Qui vous l'a préparé?
13. Avec qui avez-vous pris votre petit déjeuner ce matin? avec votre famille? avec un(e) ami(e)? avec un(e) collègue? seul(e)? D'habitude avec qui prenez-vous votre petit déjeuner?
14. À quelle heure avez-vous pris votre petit déjeuner ce matin? D'habitude à quelle heure prenez-vous votre petit déjeuner en semaine? le dimanche?
15. En prenant votre petit déjeuner, écoutez-vous la radio? regardez-vous la télévision? lisez-vous le journal? Aimez-vous parler en prenant votre petit déjeuner?

PROJETS

1. Order your breakfast on the hotel forms on the opposite page.
2. You are having a breakfast party or brunch. Indicate what you would like to serve at this gathering. Design your own menu.

ACTIVITÉ

Bring to class as many as possible of the breakfast foods of this lesson. Have breakfast in class. Use the vocabulary and structures presented here for serving each other and for table talk.

HÔTEL BAKOUA

SUSPENDRE
AVANT
6 HEURES
DU MATIN

AU
BOUTON
EXTÉRIEUR
DE LA PORTE

COMMANDE DU PETIT-DÉJEUNER

mettre une croix ou un chiffre dans la case correspondante

SERVEZ   entre   h. et   h.

CHAMBRE N°

POUR   PERSONNES

PETIT-DÉJEUNER

AU CHOIX

SERVI AVEC

CAFÉ

CAFÉ AU LAIT

THÉ AU LAIT

THÉ AU CITRON

CHOCOLAT

○ Beurre, confiture et marmelade
ou
○ Beurre et miel
et avec
○ Croissant, petit-pain et brioche
ou
○ Toasts

○ Jus Maracoudja
○ Jus d'orange frais
○ Jus Goyave
○ Jus de pamplemousse
○ Jus d'ananas
○ Jus de tomate
○ 1/2 Pamplemousse
○ Fruits frais
○ Compotes
○ Eau minérale
○ Toasts

○ Corn flakes
○ Rice Crisprie
○ Œuf à la coque
○ Œufs au plat
○ Œufs au plat jambon
○ Œufs au plat bacon
○ Œufs brouillés
○ Omelette
○ Jambon
○ Crêpes

COMMANDE SPÉCIALE

DATE

Signature du Client :

Imp. Ferrez ELISABETH

Hôtel Plaza Athénée - Paris

POUR VOTRE PETIT DÉJEUNER
SI VOUS ETES PRESSÉ
VEUILLEZ NOTER VOTRE
COMMANDE CE SOIR
SUR VOTRE FICHE ET
L'ACCROCHER AU
...
DE VOTRE PORTE
SINON APPELEZ LE
SERVICE D'ETAGE
DEMAIN MATIN
COMME D'HABITUDE
MERCI

SHOULD YOU BE IN A HURRY FOR
YOUR BREAKFAST KINDLY FILL
IN THIS FORM TONIGHT AND
HANG IT OUTSIDE YOUR
DOOR IF NOT PLEASE
CALL ROOM SERVICE
AS USUAL
THANK YOU.

NOMBRE
DE PERSONNES
NUMBER
OF PERSONS

N° DE CHAMBRE
ROOM NUMBER

NOM
NAME

SERVEZ ENTRE   H. ET   H.
TO BE SERVED BETWEEN

PARAGON B

PETIT DÉJEUNER		CONTINENTAL BREAKFAST	
SIMPLE	COMPLET	SIMPLE	COMPLET
CAFÉ		THÉ	
NESCAFÉ		CHOCOLAT	
AMÉRICAIN		LAIT CHAUD	
SANKA		LAIT FROID	

SUPPLÉMENTS - EXTRAS

ŒUFS COQUE / BOILED EGGS	2'	3'	4'	5'	6'

RICE CRISPIES		PORRIDGE		CORN FLAKES	

ŒUFS	AU PLAT FRIED	BROUILLÉS SCRAMBLED	POCHÉS POACHED	OMELETTE OMELET	EGGS
NATURE					PLAIN
JAMBON					HAM
FROMAGE					CHEESE
TOMATE					TOMATO
BACON					BACON
FINES HERBES					HERBS

JAMBON - COLD HAM		JAMBON GRILLÉ	
BACON GRILLÉ		PRUNE JUICE	
YOGOURTH		GRAPE FRUIT	
COMPOTES			
FRUIT SALAD			
FROMAGES - CHEESE			

JUS DE FRUITS FRAIS - FRESH FRUIT JUICES

ORANGE   GRAPEFRUIT

EAUX MINÉRALES - MINERAL WATER

ÉVIAN   VITTEL   VICHY   BADOIT

PERRIER   JUS TOMATE   JUS ANANAS   COCA-COLA

N° DE CHAMBRE

S/TOTAL

SERVICE

DATE   TOTAL

Chapitre

5

Les Achats

Shopping

Proverbe: Les bons comptes font les bons amis.

Proverb: Short reckonings make long friends.
(*Literally:* Good accounts make good friends.)

«Je voudrais un souvenir.»

DIALOGUE

(Dans un grand magasin)	*(In a department store)*
LE VENDEUR / LA VENDEUSE: Vous désirez, Monsieur / Madame?	THE SALESPERSON: May I help you?
VOUS: Je voudrais **un souvenir.**	YOU: I would like *a souvenir.*

un cadeau pour . . . des cartes *(f.)* postales un dictionnaire anglais-français un disque un jouet un journal un livre un parapluie du parfum un porte-clés un portefeuille un porte-monnaie une poupée une revue ceci cela (ça)	a present for . . . some post cards an English-French dictionary a record a toy a newspaper a book an umbrella some perfume a keychain, key ring a wallet a change purse a doll a magazine this that

LE VENDEUR: Un mouchoir, peut-être? Que pensez-vous de celui-ci? Il est très joli, n'est-ce pas?	THE SALESPERSON: A handkerchief, perhaps? What do you think of this one? It's very pretty, isn't it?
VOUS: L'avez-vous en **rouge?**	YOU: Do you have it in *red?*

beige blanc bleu brun gris jaune noir orange pourpre rose vert violet	beige white blue brown gray yellow black orange purple pink green violet

LE VENDEUR: Certainement, Monsieur / Madame.	THE SALESPERSON: Certainly.

VOUS: C'est combien?

LE VENDEUR: **Cent** francs

dix
vingt
trente
quarante
cinquante
soixante
soixante-dix
quatre-vingts
quatre-vingt-dix

VOUS: C'est trop **cher**. Avez-vous quelque chose

lourd	léger
grand	petit
solide	fragile
foncé	clair
épais	fin
large	étroit

de meilleur marché?

LE VENDEUR: Mais oui, Monsieur / Madame, Celui-ci est en solde aujourd'hui.

VOUS: Parfait. Je le prends.

LE VENDEUR: Désirez-vous autre chose, Monsieur / Madame?

VOUS: Non, merci. C'est tout.

LE VENDEUR: À votre service.

YOU: How much is it?

THE SALESPERSON: *One hundred* francs

ten
twenty
thirty
forty
fifty
sixty
seventy
eighty
ninety

YOU: That's too *expensive*. Do you have some-

heavy	light (in weight)
big	little
solid	fragile
dark	light (in color)
thick	thin
wide	narrow

thing less expensive?

THE SALESPERSON: Yes. (*Literally:* But yes.) This one is on sale today.

YOU: Perfect. I'll take it.

THE SALESPERSON: Do you want something else?

YOU: No, thank you. That's all.

THE SALESPERSON: Glad to have helped you. (*Literally:* At your service.)

EXERCICES D'APPLICATION

1. Dites que vous voulez un souvenir . . . que vous voulez des cartes postales . . . que vous voulez un dictionnaire anglais-français . . . que vous voulez un journal . . . que le mouchoir est très joli . . . que vous le prenez.
2. Demandez à la vendeuse si elle a des mouchoirs . . . si elle a le mouchoir en rouge

. . . si elle l'a en bleu . . . si le mouchoir est en solde . . . combien c'est . . . si elle
a quelque chose de meilleur marché.

3. *Ask other class members:* «**Quelle est votre couleur préférée**»? «**C'est le** _____.»
4. De quelle couleur est votre portefeuille? votre porte-clés? votre livre de français?
   votre stylo? votre sac? «**Il est** _____.»
5. *Point to various objects around you and describe their color.* EXEMPLES: **C'est bleu.**
   C'est vert. C'est rouge. etc.
6. *Now describe the objects around you, using* «**C'est . . .** » *or* «**C'est très. . . .** »
   Employ the adjectives of this **Dialogue: joli, cher, bon marché, lourd, léger, grand,**
   petit, solide, fragile, clair, foncé, épais, fin, large, étroit.

VERBE IRRÉGULIER: croire

croire	*to believe*	
Le présent:	**je crois**	**nous croyons**
	tu crois	**vous croyez**
	il / elle croit	**ils / elles croient**
Le participe passé:	**cru**	

Je **crois** qu'il y a une erreur dans la facture.
I think that there is an error in the bill.

Je **crois** au Père Noël!
I believe in Santa Claus!

STRUCTURES

1.   Future Tense

a. To form the future tense of **-er** and **-ir** verbs, add the future endings to the infinitive.
To form the future tense of **-re** verbs, drop the final **e** from the infinitive and add the
future endings to this base. The future endings are: **-ai, -as, -a, -ons, -ez, -ont.** The
usual English equivalent of the future is *shall* or *will.*

Verbes en **-er**	Verbes en **-ir**	Verbes en **-re**
téléphoner	**finir**	**vendre**
je téléphoner**ai**	je finir**ai**	je vendr**ai**
tu téléphoner**as**	tu finir**as**	tu vendr**as**
il téléphoner**a**	il finir**a**	il vendr**a**
elle téléphoner**a**	elle finir**a**	elle vendr**a**
on téléphoner**a**	on finir**a**	on vendr**a**
nous téléphoner**ons**	nous finir**ons**	nous vendr**ons**
vous téléphoner**ez**	vous finir**ez**	vous vendr**ez**
ils téléphoner**ont**	ils finir**ont**	ils vendr**ont**
elles téléphoner**ont**	elles finir**ont**	elles vendr**ont**

b. Some irregular verbs have irregular future bases. These bases must be learned individually. The future endings, however, remain the same:

L'Infinitif	La Base du futur	
aller	**ir-**	*to go*
avoir	**aur-**	*to have*
être	**ser-**	*to be*
pouvoir	**pourr-**	*to be able, can*
savoir	**saur-**	*to know*
vouloir	**voudr-**	*to want*

Other irregular verbs follow the pattern of **-ir** and **-re** verbs:

L'Infinitif	La Base du futur	
apprendre	**apprendr-**	*to learn*
boire	**boir-**	*to drink*
comprendre	**comprendr-**	*to understand*
connaître	**connaîtr-**	*to know*
croire	**croir-**	*to believe*
ouvrir	**ouvrir-**	*to open*
prendre	**prendr-**	*to take*

2. Future with <u>aller</u> + Infinitive

To express an idea in the near future, use **aller** + infinitive. We have the same construction in English:

> **Je vais acheter** un cadeau pour mon ami.
> *I am going to buy / I will buy a gift for my friend.*

3. Interrogative Pronouns: lequel? laquelle? lesquels? lesquelles?

These pronouns ask the question *which one?* or *which ones?* They agree in gender and in number with the noun to which they refer. They are used in order to designate persons, animals, or things:

> Voilà deux portefeuilles. **Lequel** préférez-vous?
> *Here are two wallets. Which one do you prefer?*

> Voici des livres. **Lesquels** voulez-vous?
> *Here are some books. Which ones do you want?*

> **Laquelle** de ces revues désirez-vous?
> *Which (one) of these magazines do you want?*

4. Interrogative Adjectives: quel, quelle, quels, quelles

a. Interrogative adjectives ask the question *which?* or *what?* They may be followed directly by the noun they modify or separated from the noun by **être.** Interrogative adjectives agree in gender and number with the noun they modify:

> **Quel** livre voulez-vous? *Which book do you want?*
> **Quelle** couleur désirez-vous? *What color do you want?*
> **Quelle** est votre couleur préférée? *What is your favorite color?*

b. The forms of **quel** are placed before nouns to mean *What a . . . !* or *What . . . . . s!*

> **Quel** vendeur! **Quels** vendeurs!

5. Demonstrative Pronouns: celui, celle, ceux, celles

Demonstrative pronouns agree in gender and number with the nouns they replace.

a. Used with **-ci** and **-là,** they mean *this one, that one, these, those:*

	Demonstrative Adjective + Noun		Demonstrative Pronoun	
Masculine Singular	**ce** disque-**ci** **ce** disque-**là**	*this record* *that record*	**celui-ci** **celui-là**	*this one* *that one*
Feminine Singular	**cette** revue-**ci** **cette** revue-**là**	*this magazine* *that magazine*	**celle-ci** **celle-là**	*this one* *that one*

The plurals of **celui** and **celle** are **ceux** and **celles,** respectively:

Plural	**ces** disques-**ci** **ces** revues-**là**	*these records* *those magazines*	**ceux-ci** **celles-là**	*these* *those*

«**Celui-ci** est en solde aujourd'hui.»
«Que pensez-vous de **celui-ci?**»

Ces cartes-**ci** sont plus jolies que **celles-là.**
These cards are prettier than those.

Ces livres-**ci** sont plus chers que **ceux-là.**
These books are more expensive than those.

Although **celui-ci** / **celle-ci** designate the object or person closer to you and **celui-là** / **celle-là** the object or person farther from you, it is common to use **celui-là** / **celle-là** in both cases to mean *this one* as well as *that one.*

b. When used with **qui** and **que,** they mean *the one, the ones:*

Ceux qui sont en solde sont moins chers.
The ones which are on sale are less expensive.

Celui que vous avez acheté est très joli.
The one you bought is very pretty.

c. When used with **de,** they show possession *(the one of):*

J'aime ce portefeuille mais je préfère **celui de** mon père.
I like this wallet but I prefer my father's (the one of my father).

EXERCICES DE SYNTHÈSE

A.* *Donnez la forme correcte du verbe* **croire** *au présent. Ensuite, traduisez:*

1. Je _____ qu'il y a une erreur dans cette facture.
2. _____-vous au Père Noël?
3. Elle _____ que je préfère celui-ci.
4. Oui, je _____.
5. Ils ne vous _____ pas.
6. Nous _____ que c'est trop cher.

B.* *Donnez le contraire. Suivez le modèle:*

MODÈLE: C'est trop cher.
Mais non, ce n'est pas trop cher. C'est bon marché.

1. C'est trop lourd.
2. C'est trop clair.
3. C'est trop grand.
4. C'est trop fragile.
5. C'est trop étroit.
6. C'est trop épais.

C.* *Transformez selon le modèle.*

MODÈLE: C'est trop cher.
Je voudrais quelque chose de moins cher.

1. C'est trop foncé.
2. C'est trop clair.
3. C'est trop large.
4. C'est trop fragile.
5. C'est trop fin.
6. C'est trop lourd.
7. C'est trop léger.
8. C'est trop grand.

D.* *Mettez les phrases suivantes au futur. Ensuite, traduisez:*

1. Je prends le portefeuille.
2. Tu réserves une table, n'est-ce pas?
3. L'avez-vous en rouge?
4. Il mange bien.
5. À quelle heure finit la classe?
6. Je ne vais plus dans ce magasin.
7. Je suis fatigué(e).
8. Il vous croit.
9. Vous ouvrez le cadeau, n'est-ce pas?
10. Je ne peux pas téléphoner.
11. Je n'ai pas assez de temps pour acheter des souvenirs.

12. Elle le sait, n'est-ce pas?
13. Il comprend, n'est-ce pas?
14. Elle boit beaucoup de bière!
15. Quand commencez-vous?
16. Où allez-vous?

E.*   *Mettez les phrases au futur avec **aller** + l'infinitif. Ensuite, traduisez:*

EXEMPLE: Je prends le portefeuille.
                     Je vais prendre le portefeuille.

1. Je téléphone au magasin.
2. Tu manges quelque chose, n'est-ce pas?
3. Il commence.
4. Elle ouvre le cadeau.
5. Nous prenons le dictionnaire.
6. Vous achetez des souvenirs, n'est-ce pas?
7. Ils finissent la leçon.

F.*   *Remplacez les mots en italique par un pronom démonstratif:*

EXEMPLE: *Ces livres*-ci sont en solde.
                     Ceux-ci sont en solde.

1. Prenez *cette revue*-ci.
2. Préférez-vous *le livre* qui est en solde?
3. J'aime beaucoup ce portefeuille mais je préfère *le portefeuille* que vous avez acheté.
4. Préférez-vous *ce disque*-ci ou *ce disque*-là?
5. Puis-je avoir un autre journal? Je n'aime pas *ce journal*.
6. *Ce parfum*-ci sent bon.
7. Avez-vous acheté *ce journal*-ci?
8. Mon portefeuille est noir. *Le portefeuille* de mon ami est brun.

G.   *Changez en exclamations en vous servant de la forme correcte de **quel**. Puis traduisez.*

EXEMPLE: beau cadeau
                     Quel beau cadeau!

1. jolie carte   5. vendeuse   8. jolies cartes postales
2. professeur   6. revue   9. beau paquet
3. question   7. joli mouchoir   10. souvenir
4. vendeur

H.   *Draw up your own list of exclamative phrases using the correct form of* **quel:**

EXEMPLES: Quelle classe! Quel professeur! Quelles voitures! Quels livres!

EXPANSION: Les Achats

1. **Quelle taille faites-vous?**   *What's your size?* (Shirts, dresses, suits,
   Du _____ .   coats) *(I wear a)* _____ .
2. **Quelle pointure faites-vous?**   *What's your size?* (gloves, hats, shoes, socks,
   Du _____ .   stockings) *(I wear a)* _____ .

For your reference when traveling:

EUROPEAN-AMERICAN SIZE CHART					
Women's Dresses and Suits		**Women's Shoes**			
U.S.	Continental Europe	U.S.	Continental Europe		
6	34	6	36		
8	36	6$^1/_2$	37		
10	38	7	38		
12	40	7$^1/_2$	38		
14	42	8	38$^1/_2$		
16	44	8$^1/_2$	39		
18	46	9	40		
20	48				
Men's Suits and Coats		**Men's Shirts**		**Men's Shoes**	
U.S.	Continental Europe	U.S.	Continental Europe	U.S.	Continental Europe
36	46	14	36	5	38
38	48	15	38	6	39
40	50	16	41	7	41
42	52	17	43	8	42
44	54			9	43
46	56			10	44
				11	45

3. **Où puis-je l'essayer?**	*Where can I try it on?*
4. **Où se trouve le rayon des chaussures?**	*Where's the shoe department?*
5. **Il y a une erreur dans la facture.**	*There's an error in the bill.*
6. **Je voudrais rendre / échanger ceci.**	*I would like to return / exchange this.*
7. **Je voudrais être remboursé(e).**	*I would like my money back.*
8. **Je ne fais que regarder.**	*I'm only looking.*
9. **Je vais réfléchir.**	*I'll think about it.*
10. **Cela coûte très cher. C'est exorbitant!**	*That costs a lot. It's exorbitant!*
11. **C'est une affaire.**	*It's a bargain.*
12. **À quelle heure ouvre / ferme le magasin?**	*What times does the store open / close?*
13. **Je vais faire des achats.**	*I'm going to do some shopping.*
14. **J'aime faire du lèche-vitrines.**	*I like window shopping.*
15. **Acceptez-vous les chèques de voyage? les cartes de crédit?**	*Do you accept travelers checks? credit cards?*
16. **Puis-je payer par chèque?**	*Can I pay with a check?*
17. **Je préfère payer comptant.**	*I prefer to pay cash.*

Exercices

1. Vous avez trouvé quelque chose de joli. Vous voulez l'essayer. Vous demandez à la vendeuse: _____

2. Vous n'aimez pas le porte-clés que votre ami vous a offert. Vous allez au magasin où il l'a acheté et vous dites: _____

3. Vous ne voulez rien acheter. Quand la vendeuse vous dit, «Vous désirez?», vous répondez: _____

4. Que dites-vous quand il y a une erreur dans la facture? _____

5. Vous cherchez le rayon des chaussures. Vous demandez: _____

6. Vous voulez acheter des chaussures. Le vendeur vous demande: _____

7. Vous achetez un porte-monnaie. Vous voulez payer avec des chèques de voyage. Vous demandez: _____

8. Vous êtes dans un grand magasin. Il est six heures du soir et vous ne savez pas à quelle heure ferme le magasin. Vous demandez au vendeur: _____

9. Votre ami vous demande ce que vous allez faire aujourd'hui. Vous répondez: _____

10. Un article n'est pas cher. Vous dites: _____

PRONONCIATION

Sound (Phonetic Symbol): [ɑ̃]

SPELLING:	**an, en, am, em**
ENGLISH SOUND RESEMBLED:	Vowel sound in words *Tom* and *John*
PRONUNCIATION:	Slightly round lips. Constrict throat slightly. Do not pronounce the final /n/ or /m/ as in English. Mouth remains open throughout entire sound.

EXAMPLES FROM THIS CHAPTER:

dans	**en**
grand	**blanc**
vendeur	**orange**
anglais	**cent**
français	**trente**

Contrast the nasal vowel sound [ɑ̃] with the nasal vowel sound [ɔ̃] (see Chapter 1), using the following examples from this chapter:

[ɑ̃]	[ɔ̃]	[ɔ̃, ɑ̃]
blanc	**bon**	**comprendre**
cent	**comptes**	**comptant**
grand	**non**	
trente	**font**	
quarante	**rayon**	
orange	**foncé**	

NOTES:

1. The spellings **en, em, am,** or **an,** when followed by a vowel or by another **n** or **m,** lose their nasal quality. Examples from this chapter:

   madame   amis   exclamation   ils comprennent   elles prennent

2. The spellings **en** or **em,** preceded by the letter **i,** are pronounced [ɛ̃] (see Chapter 6).

   EXAMPLES: **bien   combien   rien**

IMPROVISATION

Complétez ce dialogue. Employez le vocabulaire et les structures de cette leçon:

Le Vendeur / La Vendeuse: Vous désirez, Monsieur / Madame?
Vous: _____
Le Vendeur / La Vendeuse: _____
Vous: _____
Le Vendeur / La Vendeuse: _____
Vous: _____
Le Vendeur / La Vendeuse: _____
Vous: Très bien. Je le prends.

PROJET

Using the colors given in the **Dialogue** of this chapter, make a children's book of colors. Limit it to one color per page. Name the color and then have some sort of illustration or example. Colored paper, colored pens and pencils, crayons, magazine cutouts, scraps of colored fabric, color photographs, etc. can all be used effectively.

ACTIVITÉ

Have a flea market in class. Students can bring to class four or five items (such as old magazines, books, records, pencils, etc.) to be actually sold to each other for play money. Students keep what they buy. Use as many phrases from the **Dialogue** and **Expansion** sections of this chapter as possible. Class can end with an auction (**une vente aux enchères**) to dispose of any unsold items.

IL ÉTAIT UNE BERGÈRE

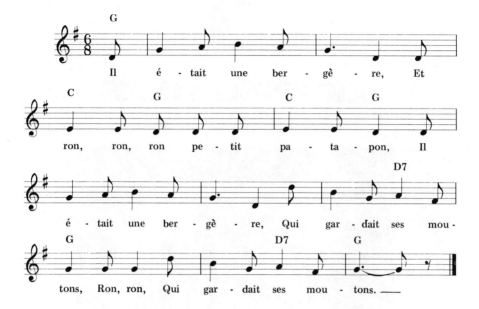

Il é - tait une ber - gè - re, Et ron, ron, ron pe - tit pa - ta - pon, Il é - tait une ber - gè - re, Qui gar - dait ses mou - tons, Ron, ron, Qui gar - dait ses mou - tons. ___

2. Elle fit un fromage
   Et ron, ron, ron, petit patapon,
   Elle fit un fromage,
   Du lait de ses moutons, ron, ron
   Du lait de ses moutons.

3. Le chat qui la regarde
   Et ron, ron, ron, petit patapon,
   Le chat qui la regarde,
   D'un petit air fripon, ron, ron
   D'un petit air fripon.

4. Si tu y mets la patte
   Et ron, ron, ron petit patapon,
   Si tu y mets la patte
   Tu auras du bâton, ron, ron
   Tu auras du bâton.

5. Il n'y mit pas la patte
   Et ron, ron, ron, petit patapon,
   Il n'y mit pas la patte
   Il y mit le menton, ron, ron
   Il y mit le menton.

Entracte

5

SHOPPING ITEMS

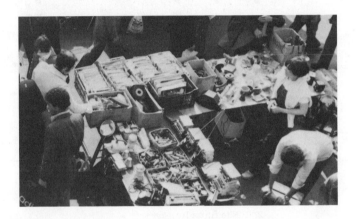

Qu'est-ce que vous avez acheté cette semaine?
—Cette semaine j'ai acheté _____ .

des allumettes	*matches*
un appareil photo	*camera*
de l'aspirine	*aspirin*
des bonbons	*candy*
un briquet	*cigarette lighter*
une brosse à dents	*toothbrush*
un cadeau pour . . .	*gift for . . .*
des cartes postales	*postcards*
des cigares	*cigars*
des cigarettes	*cigarettes*
un crayon	*pencil*
de la crème à raser	*shaving creme*
du dentifrice	*toothpaste*
du déodorant	*deodorant*

des élastiques	rubber bands
des enveloppes	envelopes
de l'essence	gasoline
de la ficelle	string
un film	movie film
un journal	newspaper
des lames de rasoir	razor blades
un livre	book
du maquillage	make-up
des mouchoirs en papier / des Kleenex	tissues / Kleenex
du papier à lettres	stationery
du papier hygiénique	toilet paper / bathroom tissue
des pastilles contre la toux	coughdrops
une pellicule	roll of film (slides, prints)
une pipe	pipe
une plante	plant
des provisions	food
une revue / un magazine	magazine
du savon	soap
un sandwich	sandwich
du scotch	Scotchtape
du shampooing	shampoo
un stylo	pen
du talc	talcum powder
des timbres	stamps
des vitamines	vitamins

SPRINGBOARDS FOR CONVERSATION

1. Qu'est-ce que vous avez acheté cette semaine? Pour qui? Quand? Où? C'est tout? Quoi d'autre?
2. Qu'est-ce que le professeur a acheté cette semaine? Monsieur . . . ? Madame . . . ? Mademoiselle . . . ? etc.
   Il / Elle a acheté _____. C'est tout? Quoi encore?
3. Vous avez acheté un livre? lequel?
   un journal? lequel?
   des cigarettes? quelle marque (brand)?
   un stylo? de quelle couleur?
   une revue? laquelle?
   une brosse à dents? de quelle couleur? etc.
4. Qui dans la classe a acheté de l'aspirine? des cigarettes? un journal? etc.

5. Qu'est-ce qui coûte le plus cher? les allumettes? les cigarettes? les timbres? etc.
6. Qu'est-ce que votre mari / femme / ami(e) / fils / fille, etc. vous a demandé de lui acheter cette semaine?
7. Que vous faut-il acheter aujourd'hui?
8. Qu'est-ce que vous achetez presque tous les jours? Quelles sont les choses que vous n'achetez que rarement?
9. De quoi avez-vous besoin? D'un journal? D'une nouvelle brosse à dents? De dentifrice? D'aspirine? De timbres?

> NOTE: **avoir besoin de** = *to need*. For example: **J'ai besoin d'un journal. J'ai besoin d'une pellicule.** But: **J'ai besoin de dentifrice, d'aspirine, de ficelle, de timbres.** In other words, with the expression **avoir besoin, de** and **d'** replace **du, de l', de la** and **des.**

PROJET

Using the list of items from this **Entracte** as a guideline, make up your own **liste d'achats à faire** *(shopping list)*.

Chapitre

6

À l'hôtel (Arrivée et Départ)	At the Hotel (Arrival and Departure)

Proverbe: Tout est bien qui finit bien.

Proverb: All's well that ends well.

DIALOGUE
EXERCICES D'APPLICATION
VERBES IRRÉGULIERS: **dire, suivre, voir**
STRUCTURES:
1. Conditional Tense
2. Relative Pronouns: **qui, que, dont**
EXERCICES DE SYNTHÈSE
EXPANSION: **À l'hôtel (Arrivée et Départ)**
PRONONCIATION: [ɛ̃], [œ̃]
IMPROVISATION
PROJET
ACTIVITÉ
CHANSON: **Quand trois poules vont aux champs**

«Quel est le numéro de ma chambre?»

DIALOGUE

VOUS: Je voudrais une chambre **pour une personne.**

à un lit
pour deux personnes
à deux lits
avec un grand lit / avec un lit à deux places
avec un lit supplémentaire

LE GÉRANT / LA GÉRANTE: Avez-vous une réservation?

VOUS: Oui. Voici la confirmation. Et je voudrais une chambre qui donne sur **la mer.**

la cour
le square
le jardin
le lac
la plage
la rue

LE GÉRANT: Très bien, Monsieur / Madame. Une petite minute. Je vais voir. . . . J'ai encore une chambre avec **salle de bains** au

téléphone
télévision
douche seulement
lavabo

troisième étage.[1]

quatrième
cinquième
sixième
septième
huitième
neuvième
dixième

YOU: I would like a room *for one person.*

with one bed
for two people
with two beds
with a double bed
with an extra bed

THE HOTEL MANAGER: Do you have a reservation?

YOU: Yes. Here's the confirmation. And I would like a room which looks out onto the *sea.*

courtyard
square
garden
lake
beach
street

MANAGER: Very well. One moment. I'll see. . . . I still have a room with a *bath* on the

telephone
television
shower only
sink

fourth floor.[1]

fifth
sixth
seventh
eighth
ninth
tenth
eleventh

1. In Europe, the American *first floor* or *ground floor* is called **le rez-de-chaussée.** The American *second floor* is called **le premier étage,** the American *third floor* is called **le deuxième étage,** etc.

Vous: Quel est le prix par nuit?

Le Gérant: Cent francs, service et taxes compris. Combien de temps pensez-vous rester?

Vous: **Une nuit.**

deux jours
une semaine
quelques jours
un mois
jusqu'à lundi
jusqu'à mardi
jusqu'à mercredi
jusqu'à jeudi
jusqu'à vendredi
jusqu'à samedi
jusqu'à dimanche

Le Gérant: Voudriez-vous remplir cette fiche?[2] Vous avez la chambre trente-huit. Voilà la clé.

Vous: Puis-je voir la chambre?

Le Gérant: Mais bien sûr. Veuillez me suivre.[2]

You: How much is it per night?

Manager: One hundred francs, service charge and tax included. How long do you intend to stay?

You: *One night*.

two days
a week
a few days
a month
until Monday
until Tuesday
until Wednesday
until Thursday
until Friday
until Saturday
until Sunday

Manager: Would you please fill out this form?[2] You have room number 38. Here's the key.

You: Can I see the room?

Manager: But of course. Please follow me.[2]

EXERCICES D'APPLICATION

1. Dites que vous voulez une chambre pour une personne . . . que vous voulez une chambre pour deux personnes . . . que vous avez une réservation . . . que vous voulez une chambre qui donne sur la cour . . . que vous voulez une chambre avec salle de bains . . . que vous pensez rester quelques jours . . . que vous allez rester une semaine . . . que vous voulez voir la chambre.

2. Demandez si la chambre donne sur la rue . . . si elle donne sur la mer . . . si elle donne sur le jardin . . . à quel étage est la chambre . . . s'il y a le téléphone . . . combien est-ce par nuit . . . si vous pouvez voir la chambre.

3. What do you say to ask for a hotel room for one person? for two people? How do you ask for a room with an extra bed? with a bath? with a telephone? with a television set? with two beds?

2. **Voudriez-vous** + l'infinitif / **Veuillez** + l'infinitif = *please* (used for polite commands).

VERBES IRRÉGULIERS: dire, suivre, voir

dire	to say, to tell

Le présent:	je dis	nous disons
	tu dis	vous dites
	il / elle dit	ils / elles disent

Le participe passé: **dit**
La base du futur: **dir-**

vouloir dire = *to mean*

    Que **voulez-vous dire?** *What do you mean?*
    Qu'est-ce que cela **veut dire?** *What does that mean?*
    Que **veut dire** le mot «fiche»? *What does the word ''fiche'' mean?*

Comment **dit-on** _____ en français? *How do you say _____ in French?*

suivre	to follow

Le présent:	je suis	nous suivons
	tu suis	vous suivez
	il / elle suit	ils / elles suivent

Le participe passé: **suivi**
La base du futur: **suivr-**

    «Veuillez me **suivre.**»

suivre un cours = *to take a course*
suivre un régime = *to be on a diet*

voir	to see

Le présent:	je vois	nous voyons
	tu vois	vous voyez
	il / elle voit	ils / elles voient

Le participe passé: **vu**
La base du futur: **verr-**

    «Une petite minute. Je vais **voir.** . . .»
    «Puis-je **voir** la chambre?»

STRUCTURES

1. The Conditional Tense

a. To form the conditional tense of **-er** and **-ir** verbs, add the conditional endings to the infinitive. To form the conditional tense of **-re** verbs, drop the final **e** from the infinitive and add the conditional endings to this base. The conditional endings are: **-ais, -ais, -ait, -ions, -iez, -aient.** The usual English equivalent of the conditional is *would*.

Verbes en **-er**	Verbes en **-ir**	Verbes en **-re**
donner	**remplir**	**attendre**
je donne**rais**	je rempli**rais**	j'attend**rais**
tu donne**rais**	tu rempli**rais**	tu attend**rais**
il donne**rait**	il rempli**rait**	il attend**rait**
elle donne**rait**	elle rempli**rait**	elle attend**rait**
on donne**rait**	on rempli**rait**	on attend**rait**
nous donne**rions**	nous rempli**rions**	nous attend**rions**
vous donne**riez**	vous rempli**riez**	vous attend**riez**
ils donne**raient**	ils rempli**raient**	ils attend**raient**
elles donne**raient**	elles rempli**raient**	elles attend**raient**

b. Some irregular verbs have irregular conditional bases. These bases (which are the same as the future bases) must be learned individually. The conditional endings, however, remain the same:

L'Infinitif	La Base du Conditionnel	
aller	**ir-**	*to go*
avoir	**aur-**	*to have*
être	**ser-**	*to be*
pouvoir	**pourr-**	*to be able, can*
savoir	**saur-**	*to know*
voir	**verr-**	*to see*
vouloir	**voudr-**	*to want*

«**Je voudrais** une chambre pour une personne.»
«Et **je voudrais** une chambre qui donne sur la mer.»
«**Voudriez-vous** remplir cette fiche?»

The conditional of **pouvoir** (*to be able, can*) means *could:*

> **Pourriez-vous** m'aider, s'il vous plaît?
> *Could you help me, please?*

c. Other irregular verbs follow the pattern of **-ir** and **-re** verbs:

L'Infinitif	La Base du Conditionnel	
apprendre	**apprendr-**	*to learn*
boire	**boir-**	*to drink*
comprendre	**comprendr-**	*to understand*
connaître	**connaîtr-**	*to know*
croire	**croir-**	*to believe*
dire	**dir-**	*to say, to tell*
ouvrir	**ouvrir-**	*to open*
prendre	**prendr-**	*to take*
suivre	**suivr-**	*to follow*

2. Relative Pronouns: qui, que, dont

a. **qui** means *who, that, which*. **Qui** immediately precedes the verb of which it is the subject. It may refer to persons or things.

> «Je voudrais une chambre **qui** donne sur la mer.»

> Le monsieur **qui** parle est le gérant de l'hôtel.
> *The gentleman who is speaking is the hotel manager.*

b. **que** (**qu'** before a vowel or a mute **h**) means *whom, which, that*. It is the object of a verb and may refer to persons or things.

> Le monsieur **que** vous voyez est le gérant de l'hôtel.
> *The gentleman whom you see is the hotel manager.*

> La chambre **que** vous voulez donne sur la mer.
> *The room that you want looks out onto the sea.*

c. **dont** means *of whom, of which, whose, about whom, about which:*

> Où est le monsieur **dont** vous avez parlé?
> *Where is the man whom you spoke about?* (Literally: . . . *about whom* or *of whom you spoke.*)

> Puis-je voir la chambre **dont** vous parlez?
> *Can I see the room that you are talking about?* (Literally: . . . *about which* or *of which you are talking*)

d. à qui *(to whom)*, **pour qui** *(for whom)*, **avec qui** *(with whom):*

Le monsieur **à qui** je parle est le gérant.
The gentleman to whom I am speaking is the manager.

EXERCICES DE SYNTHÈSE

A.* *Donnez la forme correcte du verbe* **suivre** *au présent. Puis traduisez la phrase en anglais:*

1. Je _____ un cours de français.
2. _____ -tu un régime?
3. Pourquoi _____ -vous le gérant?
4. Elle _____ un régime.
5. _____ -moi, s'il vous plaît.
6. Veuillez me _____.
7. Nous _____ un cours de français.
8. Ils _____ la conversation.

B.* *Employez le verbe* **voir** *au présent et au passé composé dans les phrases suivantes. Puis traduisez:*

1. Je _____ le gérant de l'hôtel.
2. Tu _____ l'hôtel, n'est-ce pas?
3. Vous _____ ?
4. Ils _____ la mer.
5. Qu'est-ce qu'elle _____ ?
6. Nous _____ l'hôtel.

C.* *Transformez selon le modèle. Puis traduisez:*

MODÈLE: À votre place *(If I were you)*, je suivrais un autre cours. (finir)
          À votre place, je finirais.

1. aller à la maison
2. voir le film
3. dire la vérité
4. fumer moins
5. boire moins
6. téléphoner
7. attendre
8. vendre l'hôtel
9. dire «non»
10. choisir l'autre chambre

D. *Mettez les verbes entre parenthèses au conditionnel. Puis traduisez la phrase:*

1. Où _____ -vous? (aller)
2. _____ -vous m'aider? (pouvoir)

3. Je _____ voir la chambre. (vouloir)

4. _____ -vous une autre chambre? (avoir)

5. Nous _____ voir la chambre. (aimer)

6. _____ -vous remplir la fiche? (vouloir)

7. Il a dit qu'il _____ absent. (être)

8. À sa place je _____ tout de suite. (commencer)

9. J' _____ vous inviter à dîner. (aimer)

10. _____ -ils en France? (aller)

11. _____ -elle téléphoner demain? (pouvoir)

12. _____ -tu aller en France? (vouloir)

E.   *Remplacez les tirets par* **qui, que,** *ou* **dont:**

1. Je voudrais une chambre _____ donne sur le jardin.

2. Voici la chambre _____ il a parlé.

3. La fiche _____ vous remplissez est pour la police.

4. Où est l'hôtel _____ il parle?

5. Elle veut une chambre _____ donne sur la mer.

6. Je voudrais la clé _____ vous avez dans votre sac.

7. C'est le monsieur avec _____ j'ai parlé.

8. J'ai dit _____ je voudrais une chambre pour une personne.

EXPANSION: À l'hôtel (Arrivée et Départ)

1. **Nous sommes quatre.**	*There are four of us.*
2. **Y a-t-il une réduction pour un long séjour?**	*Is there a reduced rate for a long stay?*
3. **Je voudrais deux chambres communicantes.**	*I would like two adjoining rooms.*
4. **Je ne veux pas de chambre près de l'ascenseur.**	*I don't want a room near the elevator.*
5. **Quel est le numéro de ma chambre?**	*What's my room number?*
6. **Où puis-je garer (laisser) ma voiture?**	*Where can I park (leave) my car?*
7. **Veuillez faire monter / descendre mes bagages.**	*Please have my luggage brought up / brought down.*
8. **Réveillez-moi demain matin à six heures, s'il vous plaît.**	*Wake me tomorrow morning at six o'clock, please.*
9. **Je pars maintenant. Puis-je avoir la note, s'il vous plaît?**	*I'm leaving now. Can I have the bill, please?*
10. **Je crois qu'il y a une erreur dans cette note.**	*I think there's a mistake in this bill.*
11. **Pouvez-vous m'appeler un taxi? Je suis pressé(e).**	*Can you call me a taxi? I'm in a hurry.*

Que dites-vous quand:

1. on vous montre une chambre près de l'ascenseur?
2. vous voyagez avec trois amis?
3. vous ne savez pas où laisser votre voiture?
4. vous voulez une réduction parce que vous allez rester deux mois à l'hôtel?
5. vous avez oublié le numéro de votre chambre?
6. votre avion part à huit heures et vous voulez arriver à l'aéroport vers sept heures. Vous téléphonez à la réception et vous dites: _____
7. vous quittez l'hôtel et vous voulez la note?
8. il y a une erreur dans la note?
9. vous voulez un taxi?
10. vous êtes pressé(e)?

PRONONCIATION

1. **Sound (Phonetic Symbol): [ɛ̃]**

SPELLING:	**in, im, ain, aim, ein, eim, en** (after **i** or **é**)
ENGLISH SOUND RESEMBLED:	Vowel sound in words *A*nne and *h*am
PRONUNCIATION:	Open lips. Slightly constrict throat. Do not pronounce the final **n** or **m** as in English. Mouth remains open throughout entire sound.

EXAMPLES FROM THIS CHAPTER:	**b<u>ien</u>**	**jar<u>din</u>**	**dema<u>in</u>**	**ba<u>ins</u>**
NOTES:	**comb<u>ien</u>**	**ma<u>in</u>tenant**	**mat<u>in</u>**	**c<u>in</u>quième**

1. The spellings **in, im, ain, aim** change pronunciation when followed by a vowel or by another **n** or **m**, as in: **a<u>im</u>er, <u>im</u>age, v<u>in</u>aigre** and **douza<u>in</u>e.** Example from this chapter: **une sema<u>in</u>e**

2. American speakers will have to pay particular attention to the fact that the spelling **in** is pronounced [ɛ̃], especially in such words as: **v<u>in</u>, v<u>in</u>gt, l<u>in</u>gerie,** etc.

2. **Sound (Phonetic Symbol): [œ̃]**

SPELLING:	**un, um**
PRONUNCIATION:	This nasal vowel sound [œ̃], similar to the nasal vowel sound [ɛ̃], is produced by rounding the lips a little more. The [œ̃] sound, however, is gradually disappearing from current usage. Many French-speaking people actually use only the one sound [ɛ̃] for both cases. For this reason, you will hear **un** pronounced either [œ̃] or [ɛ̃], **l<u>un</u>di** pronounced either [lœ̃di] or [lɛ̃di], and so forth.

IMPROVISATION

Complétez ce dialogue. Employez le vocabulaire et les structures de la leçon:

VOUS: Bonjour, Monsièur / Madame. Je voudrais une chambre.
LE GÉRANT / LA GÉRANTE: Très bien . . . .
VOUS: _____
LE GÉRANT / LA GÉRANTE: _____
VOUS: _____
LE GÉRANT / LA GÉRANTE: _____
VOUS: _____
LE GÉRANT / LA GÉRANTE: Veuillez me suivre.

PROJET

Fill out this **Fiche de Voyageur** for another class member. Obtain the necessary information by asking these simple questions:

1. Quel est votre nom, s'il vous plaît?
2. Quels sont vos prénoms?
3. Quand êtes-vous né(e)?
   Où êtes-vous né(e)?
4. Quelle est votre profession?
   (see Entracte 19A: **Professions**)
5. Quelle est votre adresse?
   Où habitez-vous?
6. Quelle est votre nationalité?
   (see Entracte 15: **Nationalities**)

Nom et adresse de l'hôtel

FICHE DE VOYAGEUR

HÔTEL BAKOUA MARTINIQUE

Ch. Nº

NOM _____
(Écrire en majuscules)

Nom de jeune fille: _____

Prénoms: _____

Né le _____ à _____

Département (ou Pays pour l'Étranger): _____

Profession: _____

Domicile habituel: _____

NATIONALITÉ: [_____]

T.S.V.P.

ACTIVITÉ

Check into a hotel, using this registration form. Then check out, paying your bill. Students acting as desk clerks can supervise registration activities and may prepare appropriate hotel bills. Use as many phrases and structures from the **Dialogue** and **Expansion** portions of this lesson as possible.

BIENVENUE À L'HÔTEL BAKOUA

En caractère d'imprimerie

NOM _____ Personnes _____
          Nom de famille   Prénoms

ADRESSE _____ Ville _____ Dépt _____ Pays _____

PROFESSION _____

Date de naissance _____ CARTE D'IDENTITÉ _____

Nationalité _____ Passeport Nº _____ Délivre lé _____

Nº Carte de Crédit _____ Émise par _____

Vous pouvez charger votre compte a Diner's Club, Carte Blanche, American Express, Eurocard et Master Charge. Des coffres–forts sont à votre disposition à la réception, pour déposer vos valeurs. L'hôtel n'est pas responsable pour les objets de valeur laissés dans les chambres.

HEURE DE DÉPART 12.00

DÉPART PRÉVU LE

Signature _____

CHAMBRE	PRIX	INITIALES	AR	O	ARRANGEMENT	
			SR	O		
						O

GRAND HOTEL du PALAIS ROYAL
MAISON des UNIVERSITAIRES

SOCIÉTÉ COOPÉRATIVE · CAPITAL ET PERSONNEL VARIABLES · SIREN 58 206 25 68

4, RUE DE VALOIS
75001 PARIS

C.C.P. 16957-00 PARIS

TÉL. 261.35.51
    261.32.28

M. _____

DOIT

SÉJOUR DU _____ AU _____ CHAMBRE Nº _____

NOMBRE NUITS	TARIF	LIT SUP.	OCCUP-ATION	TOTAL

CHAMBRE _____

PETIT DÉJEUNER _____ à _____

PETITS DÉJEUNERS _____

DATE	REPAS		BAR	TÉLÉPHONE ET DIVERS
	MIDI	SOIR		

RESTAURANT _____

BAR _____

DIVERS ET TÉL _____

RÈGLEMENT

CAISSE ☐   C.C.P. ☐   BANQUE ☐

TOTAL T.T.C. _____

Imp. BERNAYENNE

QUAND TROIS POULES VONT AUX CHAMPS

Quand trois pou - les vont aux champs,
La pre - miè - re va de - vant.
La se - conde suit la pre - miè - re,
La troi - sième vient la der - niè - re.
Quand trois pou - les vont aux champs,
La pre - miè - re va de - vant.

Alternate words to same tune:

Ah! vous dirais-je, maman!
Ce qui cause mon tourment.
Papa veut que je raisonne
Comme une grande personne
Moi, je dis que les bonbons
Valent mieux que la raison.

Entracte

6

TELLING TIME

Quelle heure est-il?
—Il est _____ **.**

une heure	*1 o'clock*	huit heures	*8 o'clock*
deux heures	*2 o'clock*	neuf heures	*9 o'clock*
trois heures	*3 o'clock*	dix heures	*10 o'clock*
quatre heures	*4 o'clock*	onze heures	*11 o'clock*
cinq heures	*5 o'clock*	midi	*noon*
six heures	*6 o'clock*	minuit	*midnight*
sept heures	*7 o'clock*		

du matin	*A.M.*
de l'après-midi	*P.M. (afternoon)*
de soir	*P.M. (evening)*

Il est trois heures du matin.
It's 3 A.M.

Quarter past:	add **et quart** 3:15 = **trois heures et quart**
Half past:	add **et demie** 3:30 = **trois heures et demie** EXCEPTION: **midi et demi, minuit et demi**
Quarter to / of:	use **moins le quart** and measure back from the next hour 2:45 = **trois heures moins le quart**
Minutes after:	add the number of minutes past 3:10 = **trois heures dix**
Minutes before:	use **moins** and measure back from the next hour 2:50 = **trois heures moins dix**

1. un	11. onze	21. vingt et un
2. deux	12. douze	22. vingt-deux
3. trois	13. treize	23. vingt-trois
4. quatre	14. quatorze	24. vingt-quatre
5. cinq	15. quinze	25. vingt-cinq
6. six	16. seize	26. vingt-six
7. sept	17. dix-sept	27. vingt-sept
8. huit	18. dix-huit	28. vingt-huit
9. neuf	19. dix-neuf	29. vingt-neuf
10. dix	20. vingt	

NOTES:

1. The twenty-four hour clock is used for official purposes such as transportation schedules, business hours, theater schedules, announcements, etc.:

   1 A.M. = **une heure** (1 **h.**)
   1 P.M. = **treize heures** (13 **h.**)
   8:30 A.M. = **huit heures trente** (8 **h.** 30)
   8:30 P.M. = **vingt heures trente** (20 **h.** 30)

2. Pronunciation: When followed by **heures** *(o'clock),* the final **x** and **s** in **deux, trois, six** and **dix** are pronounced [z]; the final **q** of **cinq** is pronounced [k]; the final **t** of **sept** and **huit** are pronounced [t]; and the final **f** of **neuf** is pronounced [v].

SPRINGBOARDS FOR CONVERSATION

1. Quelle heure est-il?
   Il est _____.
2. À quelle heure commence la classe de français?
   Elle commence à _____.
3. À quelle heure se termine la classe de français?
   Elle se termine à _____.
4. D'habitude à quelle heure vous couchez-vous?
   À *(at)* / Vers *(around)* _____. Entre *(between)* _____ et _____
   heures.
5. À quelle heure vous êtes-vous couché(e) hier soir?
   À / Vers _____.
6. D'habitude à quelle heure vous levez-vous le matin *(in the morning)?* en semaine? le
   dimanche?
7. À quelle heure vous êtes-vous levé(e) ce matin?
8. À quelle heure dînez-vous d'habitude?
9. À quelle heure avez-vous dîné hier soir?
10. D'habitude à quelle heure prenez-vous le petit déjeuner? en semaine? de dimanche?
11. À quelle heure avez-vous pris votre petit déjeuner ce matin?
12. À quelle heure est-ce que le professeur s'est levé ce matin? Madame . . . ?
    Monsieur . . . ? Mademoiselle . . . ? etc.
13. À quelle heure est-ce que le professeur s'est couché hier soir? Madame / Monsieur /
    Mademoiselle . . . ? etc.
14. Portez-vous *(are you wearing)* une montre *(watch)?* Quelle heure avez-vous? Est-ce
    que votre montre avance? *(Is your watch fast?* Literally: *Does your watch advance /
    gain time?)* De combien? de cinq minutes? Est-ce qu'elle retarde? *(Is it slow?)* De
    combien? de trois minutes?
15. D'habitude à quelle heure rentrez-vous *(get home)* le soir *(in the evening)?*
16. À quelle heure êtes-vous rentré(e) hier soir? Avant *(before)* dix heures? Après *(after)*
    huit heures? etc.

PROJET

Using scenes clipped from magazines, assign a time of day to each one. For example:
A scene depicting people eating breakfast may be captioned: «**Il est huit heures du
matin.**»

ACTIVITÉ

Circulate around the classroom, asking classmates for the exact time according to their watches, or, if need be, according to the classroom clock. «**Pardon, Monsieur / Madame / Mademoiselle. Avez-vous l'heure, s'il vous plaît?**»—«**Il est huit heures précises. / Il est deux heures justes. / Il est cinq heures dix.**» etc.

Chapitre
7

À l'hôtel (Séjour)

Staying at the Hotel

Proverbe: Comme on fait son lit on se couche.

Proverb: You've made your bed, now lie in it. (*Literally:* As one makes one's bed, one goes to bed.)

DIALOGUE
EXERCICES D'APPLICATION
VERBES IRRÉGULIERS: **dormir, faire**
STRUCTURES:
1. Adjective Agreement
2. Comparisons with Adjectives
3. Position of Adjectives
4. Direct and Indirect Object Pronouns
5. Causal **faire**
EXERCICES DE SYNTHÈSE
EXPANSION: **Entretien des vêtements, Chez le coiffeur**
PRONONCIATION: [e], [ɛ]
IMPROVISATION
PROJET
ACTIVITÉS
CHANSON: **Fais dodo**

«Et où sont mes valises?»

DIALOGUE

(Toc. Toc.)

VOUS: Qui est-ce?

LE VALET DE CHAMBRE: C'est le valet de chambre, avec votre petit déjeuner.

VOUS: Un instant! . . . Entrez!

LE VALET: Bonjour, Monsieur / Madame. Avez-vous bien dormi?

VOUS: Non. Cette chambre est trop **bruyante.**

chaude
claire
froide
grande
petite
sombre

J'en voudrais une autre. Et où sont mes valises?

LE VALET: Elles sont en bas. Je vais les monter tout de suite.

VOUS: Merci. Et il me faudrait **une serviette de bain.**

une ampoule pour la lampe
une bouteille d'eau minérale
un cendrier
une autre chaise
des cintres *(m.)*
une couverture supplémentaire
des draps *(m.)*
un autre oreiller
une savonnette
un tapis de bain

LE VALET: Je vais appeler la femme de chambre.

VOUS: Ce n'est pas tout. Je ne peux pas fermer / ouvrir **la fenêtre**

le lit pliant
le placard

(Knock. Knock.)

YOU: Who is it?

THE VALET: It's the valet, with your breakfast.

YOU: One moment! . . . Come in!

VALET: Hello. Have you slept well? / Did you sleep well?

YOU: No. This room is too *noisy.*

hot
bright
cold
big
little
dark

I would like another. And where are my suitcases?

VALET: They're downstairs. I'll bring them up right away.

YOU: Thank you. And I need *a bath towel*

a light bulb for the lamp
a bottle of mineral water
an ashtray
another chair
some hangers
an extra blanket.
some sheets
another pillow
a cake of soap
a bathmat

VALET: I'll call the chambermaid.

YOU: That's not all. I can't close / open the *window*

folding bed
cupboard / closet

la porte	door
le rideau	curtain
le tiroir	drawer
les volets	shutters

et **le chauffage** ne fonctionne pas.   and the *heat* doesn't work.

le climatiseur	air conditioner
la douche	shower
l'interrupteur	(light) switch
la lampe de chevet	bedside lamp
le lavabo	sink
la lumière	light
la prise de courant	electric outlet
le robinet	faucet
le téléphone	telephone
la télévision	television
le ventilateur	fan, ventilator

Pouvez-vous le (la / les) faire réparer?   Can you have it (them) fixed?

LE VALET: Certainement. Vous pouvez compter   VALET: Certainly. You can count on me. Have a
sur moi. Bonne journée, Monsieur / Madame.   good day.

EXERCICES D'APPLICATION

*1. Dites que vous n'avez pas bien dormi . . . que la chambre est trop bruyante . . . qu'elle est trop grande . . . qu'elle est trop sombre . . . que vous voulez une autre chambre . . . que les valises sont en bas . . . que vous allez les monter . . . qu'il vous faut une serviette de bains . . . qu'il vous faut des cintres . . . que vous allez appeler la femme de chambre . . . que vous ne pouvez pas fermer la fenêtre . . . que vous ne pouvez pas ouvrir le placard . . . que le climatiseur ne fonctionne pas . . . que la télévision ne fonctionne pas.

2. Comment est la salle de classe? Est-elle froide? chaude? sombre? claire? etc. Comment est votre chambre?

3. Qu'est-ce qu'il y a dans la salle de classe? des cendriers? un climatiseur? des placards? etc.

4. Qu'est-ce qui ne fonctionne pas dans la salle de classe? le ventilateur? la prise de courant? etc. Qu'est-ce qui ne fonctionne pas chez vous? dans votre chambre?

5. In the classroom, go up to the window, to the door, to a closet, to a desk drawer, etc. Pretend that you cannot get it opened: «**Je ne peux pas ouvrir. . . .**» When a classmate helps you, then pretend that you cannot get it closed again!: «**Je ne peux pas fermer. . . .**» Use the vocabulary from the **Dialogue** above.

VERBES IRRÉGULIERS: dormir, faire

dormir	to sleep

Le présent:	**je dors**	**nous dormons**
	tu dors	**vous dormez**
	il / elle dort	**ils / elles dorment**

Le participe passé: **dormi**
La base du futur et du conditionnel: **dormir-**

«Avez-vous bien **dormi?**»

faire	to do, to make

Le présent:	**je fais**	**nous faisons**
	tu fais	**vous faites**
	il / elle fait	**ils / elles font**

Le participe passé: **fait**
La base du futur et du conditionnel: **fer-**

«Comme **on fait** son lit, on se couche.»
«Pouvez-vous le **faire** réparer?»

STRUCTURES

1. Adjective Agreement

Adjectives agree with the nouns they describe both in gender (masculine / feminine) and in number (singular / plural):

a. The letter **e** must be added to the masculine form of the following adjectives to derive the feminine form. The letter **s** is added to make the adjective plural.

> MODÈLE:
> masculine singular: **bruyant**
> feminine singular: **bruyante**
> masculine plural: **bruyants**
> feminine plural: **bruyantes**

bleu	*blue*	**fin**	*fine, thin*
brun	*brown*	**foncé**	*dark* (in color)
bruyant	*noisy*	**froid**	*cold*
carré	*square*	**grand**	*big*
cassé	*broken*	**intelligent**	*intelligent*
charmant	*charming*	**joli**	*pretty*
chaud	*warm, hot*	**laid**	*ugly*
chiffonné	*wrinkled, rumpled, crumpled*	**lourd**	*heavy*
clair	*light* (in color), *bright*	**ouvert**	*opened*
content	*happy*	**parfait**	*perfect*
court	*short* (in length), *brief*	**petit**	*little, small*
déchiré	*torn*	**prêt**	*ready*
dur	*hard*	**rond**	*round*
étroit	*narrow*	**usé**	*worn-out*
fatigué	*tired*	**vert**	*green*
fermé	*closed, shut*		

«Cette chambre est trop **bruyante** / **froide** / **chaude** / **claire** / **petite** / **grande.**»

Some adjectives, like **anglais** *(English)*, **assis** *(seated, sitting down)*, **français** *(French)*, **gris** *(gray)*, and **mauvais** *(bad)*, already have an **s** in the masculine singular. Consequently, the masculine plural and the masculine singular forms of these adjectives are identical.

b. The following adjectives already have the letter **e** in the masculine form. Consequently, the masculine singular and feminine singular forms are identical. The letter **s** is added to make the adjective plural.

> MODÈLE:
> masculine singular: **sombre**
> feminine singular: **sombre**
> masculine plural: **sombres**
> feminine plural: **sombres**

agréable	*pleasant*	**étrange**	*strange*
autre	*other*	**fragile**	*fragile*
beige	*beige*	**inutile**	*useless*
calme	*calm, peaceful*	**jaune**	*yellow*
chaque	*each*	**jeune**	*young*
confortable	*comfortable*	**large**	*wide*
énorme	*enormous*	**libre**	*free*

magnifique	*magnificent*	**riche**	*rich*
mince	*thin, slim*	**rose**	*pink*
moderne	*modern*	**rouge**	*red*
orange	*orange*	**sale**	*dirty*
ovale	*oval*	**solide**	*solid, sturdy*
pourpre	*purple*	**sombre**	*dark, gloomy*
pratique	*practical*	**tranquille**	*quiet, peaceful*
propre	*clean*	**utile**	*useful*
rectangulaire	*rectangular*	**vide**	*empty*

«Cette chambre est trop **sombre.**»
«Et il me faudrait une **autre** chaise / un **autre** oreiller.»

c. Adjectives with the masculine singular form ending in **-eux** have the feminine singular form ending in **-euse:**

> Mᴏᴅᴇ̀ʟᴇ:
> masculine singular: **heureux**
> feminine singular: **heureuse**
> masculine plural: **heureux**
> feminine plural: **heureuses**

affreux	*horrible*	**heureux**	*happy*
curieux	*curious, strange*	**joyeux**	*merry, joyous*
dangereux	*dangerous*	**malheureux**	*unhappy, unfortunate*
délicieux	*delicious*	**merveilleux**	*marvelous*
fameux	*famous*	**sérieux**	*serious*

d. Adjectives with the masculine singular form ending in **-er** have the feminine singular form ending in **-ère:**

> Mᴏᴅᴇ̀ʟᴇ:
> masculine singular: **premier**
> feminine singular: **première**
> masculine plural: **premiers**
> feminine plural: **premières**

cher	*expensive, dear*	**entier**	*entire*
dernier	*last*	**léger**	*light (in weight)*
étranger	*foreign*	**premier**	*first*

e. Some irregular adjectives:

IRREGULAR ADJECTIVES				
SINGULAR		PLURAL		
Masculine	Feminine	Masculine	Feminine	
beau (bel)*	belle	beaux	belles	*pretty, beautiful*
blanc	blanche	blancs	blanches	*white*
bon	bonne	bons	bonnes	*good*
épais	épaisse	épais	épaisses	*thick*
favori	favorite	favoris	favorites	*favorite*
frais	fraîche	frais	fraîches	*fresh, cool*
gentil	gentille	gentils	gentilles	*nice, kind*
gros	grosse	gros	grosses	*big, fat*
long	longue	longs	longues	*long*
nouveau (nouvel)*	nouvelle	nouveaux	nouvelles	*new*
tout	toute	tous	toutes	*all*
vieux (vieil)*	vieille	vieux	vieilles	*old*

*__Beau, nouveau,__ and **vieux** become **bel, nouvel,** and **vieil** before masculine nouns beginning with a vowel or a mute **h: un nouvel hôtel.**

«**Bonne** journée, Monsieur / Madame.»

2. Comparisons with Adjectives

a. plus . . . que   *more . . . than*   Cette chambre est **plus** grande **que** l'autre.
This room is larger than the other.

moins . . . que   *less . . . than;*   Cet hôtel est **moins** joli **que** l'autre.
not as . . . as   *This hotel isn't as pretty as the other.*

aussi . . . que   *as . . . as,* with   Ce lit est **aussi** confortable **que** l'autre.
positive verbs   *This bed is as comfortable as the other.*

b. The comparative of **bon / bonne** is **meilleur / meilleure:**

Cette chambre est **meilleure** que l'autre.
This room is better than the other.

The comparative of **mauvais / mauvaise** is **pire / pire,** *or* **plus mauvais / plus mauvaise:**

Cet hôtel est **pire** que l'autre.
This hotel is worse than the other.

c. The superlative is formed by placing **le, la,** or **les** before the comparative form:

> C'est **le** meilleur lit.
> *It's the best bed.*

NOTE: **de** is equivalent to *in* after superlatives:

> C'est la plus belle chambre **de** l'hôtel.
> *It's the most beautiful room in the hotel.*

3. Position of Adjectives

a. French adjectives usually come after the noun they describe:

un hôtel agréable   **une chambre bruyante**

b. The following adjectives, however, generally precede the noun they modify:

autre	joli	petit
beau	long	premier
bon	mauvais	tout
chaque	le meilleur	vieux
jeune	nouveau	

«Et il me faudrait **un autre oreiller / une autre chaise.**»
«**Bonne journée,** Monsieur / Madame.»

c. Certain adjectives vary in meaning depending on whether they precede or follow the noun:

un **grand** homme	*a great man / a big man*	un homme **grand**	*a tall man*
mon **cher** ami	*my dear friend*	un hôtel **cher**	*an expensive hotel*
la **dernière** semaine	*the final week*	la semaine **dernière**	*last week*
la **pauvre** femme	*the poor woman* (to be pitied)	la femme **pauvre**	*the poor woman* (without money)
ma **propre** chambre	*my own room*	une chambre **propre**	*a clean room*
un **gros** pourboire	*a big tip*	un homme **gros**	*a fat man*
le **même** hôtel	*the same hotel*	l'hôtel **même**	*the very hotel / the hotel itself*

4. Direct and Indirect Object Pronouns

a. Object pronouns precede the verb except in positive commands:

Connaissez-vous Mademoiselle . . . ?	*Do you know Miss . . . ?*
—Oui, je **la** connais très bien.	*Yes, I know her very well.*

Voyez-vous mes valises?	*Do you see my suitcases?*
—Non, je ne **les** vois pas.	*No, I don't see them.*
Il **vous** connaît, n'est-ce pas?	*He knows you, doesn't he?*
—Non, il ne **me** connaît pas.	*No, he doesn't know me.*

b. Note that when a sentence ends with a number or an expression of quantity, **en** must precede the verb. In English the equivalent *of it* or *of them* is usually dropped:

Avez-vous des valises?	*Do you have any suitcases?*
—Oui, j'**en** ai deux.	*Yes, I have two (of them).*
—Oui, j'**en** ai plusieurs.	*Yes, I have several (of them).*

c. When there is a conjugated verb and an infinitive, the object pronouns precede the infinitive:

«Je vais **les** monter tout de suite.»	
Je voudrais **la** voir.	*I would like to see it.*
Je vais **en** prendre deux.	*I'm going to take two of them.*
Je pense **y** aller.	*I'm thinking of going there.*

d. The following chart shows how to determine the order and position of object pronouns when there are more than one in the sentence. First person pronouns (**me, nous**) precede second person pronouns (**te, vous**), and these come before third person pronouns (**la, le, les, leur, lui**); **y** and **en** are placed directly before the conjugated verb. When both object pronouns are third person, **la, le, les** come before **leur, lui** (in other words, in alphabetical order):

1 First Person Pronouns	2 Second Person Pronouns	3 Third Person Pronouns	y	en	Conjugated Verb
me *(me, to me)* **nous** *(us, to us)*	**te** *(you, to you)* **vous** *(you, to you)*	**la** *(her, it)* **le** *(him, it)* **les** *(them)* **leur** *(to them)* **lui** *(to him, to her)*	*(there, to that place)*	*(some, some of it, some of them, of it, of them, any, any of it,* *any of them, about it, about them)*	All precede conjugated verb

RULE: Object Pronoun Order = 1 - 2 - 3 - **y** - **en** - Verb, except in positive commands

EXEMPLES:

The first person pronoun **me** comes before the third person pronoun **les:**

> Elle **me les** donne toujours. *She always gives them to me.*
> 1 3

The second person pronoun comes before **en:**

> Je **vous en** ai parlé. *I spoke to you about it / about them.*
> 2

When both pronouns are third person, they are placed in alphabetical order:

> Je **le lui** ai montré. *I showed it to him / to her.*
> 3 3

Note the positions of pronouns in the following examples:

> Elle **vous l**'a montré.
> 2 3
>
> Ne **me le** donnez pas.
> 1 2
>
> Je **leur en** ai parlé.
> 3
>
> Je vais **vous le** donner.
> 2 3
>
> Je voudrais **lui en** parler.
> 3

e. With positive commands, direct and indirect object pronouns are placed after the verb; **me** and **te** become **moi** and **toi** except before **en.** Pronoun order in positive commands:

Conjugated Verb	3	2	1	y	en
	la **le** **les** **leur** **lui**	**toi / te** **vous**	**moi / me** **nous**		

RULE: Object Pronoun Order with positive commands = Verb -3 - 2 - 1 - **y** - **en**

EXEMPLES:

Donnez-**le-moi,** s'il vous plaît.
Téléphonez-**moi.**
Montrez-**le-lui.**
Donnez-**m'en.**
Ouvrez-**le.**

f. Object pronouns are used with the expressions **il faut** *(to need)* and **il manque** *(to be missing, to be lacking, to be short)*:

Il me faut une serviette de bain. *I need a bath towel.*

Il me faut. . . .	*I need.* . . .
Il te faut. . . .	*You need.* . . .
Il lui faut. . . .	*He / She needs.* . . .
Il nous faut. . . .	*We need.* . . .
Il vous faut. . . .	*You need.* . . .
Il leur faut. . . .	*They need.* . . .

It is more polite to say **il me faudrait** (conditional tense) to mean *I need* when addressing a person who will perform a service as a result of your request. For example, in the **Dialogue:** «Et **il me faudrait** une serviette de bain.»

Il me manque une valise. *I'm missing a suitcase.*

Il me manque. . . .	*I'm missing.* . . .
Il te manque. . . .	*You're missing.* . . .
Il lui manque. . . .	*He / She is missing.* . . .
Il nous manque. . . .	*We're missing.* . . .
Il vous manque. . . .	*You're missing.* . . .
Il leur manque. . . .	*They're missing.* . . .

5.   Causal <u>faire</u>

The verb **faire** followed directly by an infinitive is used when an action is to be done by someone else. In English we use *to have* plus a past participle *(I had the radio fixed)* or *to make (He makes us laugh)*:

«Pouvez-vous le (la / les) **faire réparer?**»

Pouvez-vous **faire réparer** le ventilateur?
Can you have the fan fixed?

EXERCICES DE SYNTHÈSE

A.* *Donnez le contraire:*

EXEMPLE: ouvert → fermé

1. bon	8. clair	14. premier
2. bruyant	9. jeune	15. grand
3. lourd	10. content	16. propre
4. carré	11. mince	17. joli
5. fragile	12. étroit	18. riche
6. chaud	13. fermé	19. long
7. inutile		

B.   *Complétez ces phrases. Employez les adjectifs de la leçon:*

MODÈLE: Je n'aime pas ce lit. Il est **trop dur.**

1. Je n'aime pas cet hôtel. Il est. . . .
2. Je n'aime pas cette chambre. Elle est. . . .
3. Je n'aime pas cette couverture. Elle est. . . .
4. Je n'aime pas ce cendrier. Il est. . . .
5. Je n'aime pas cette valise. Elle est. . . .
6. Je n'aime pas cette chaise. Elle est. . . .

C.   *Donnez la forme correcte de l'adjectif qui convient. Employez les adjectifs de la leçon. Puis traduisez:*

1. La rue est trop _____ pour cette voiture.
2. Un instant, s'il vous plaît. La chambre n'est pas _____.
3. Où est la lumière? Cette chambre est trop _____.
4. Où est le climatiseur? Cette chambre est trop _____.
5. Les hôtels à New-York sont grands. À Paris les hôtels sont plus _____.
6. Elle est contente mais ses amis sont _____.
7. Ma chambre est jolie mais votre chambre est très _____.
8. Les draps sont propres mais les serviettes de bain sont _____.
9. Elle est toujours la première; il est toujours le _____.
10. Cette valise n'est pas lourde. Elle est _____.
11. Ce lit n'est pas très _____.
12. Cette chambre est trop bruyante. Je voudrais une chambre plus _____.

D.   *Répondez. Employez* **plus . . . que, moins . . . que** *ou* **aussi . . . que,** *selon le cas:*

1. Êtes-vous aussi grand(e) que votre mère?
2. Êtes-vous aussi grand(e) que votre père? ·

3. Êtes-vous aussi intelligent(e) que votre professeur de français?
4. Êtes-vous aussi charmant(e) que votre chien?
5. Êtes-vous aussi fatigué(e) que le président?

E.* *Transformez selon le modèle. Attention à la position des adjectifs:*

MODÈLES: Le valet est intelligent.   L'hôtel est mauvais.
               C'est un valet intelligent.   C'est un mauvais hôtel.

1. Le lit est petit.   6. La chambre est jolie.
2. Le petit déjeuner est très bon.   7. La lampe est nouvelle.
3. La chambre est froide.   8. Le lit est confortable.
4. La valise est chère.   9. L'hôtel est très agréable.
5. La rue est longue.   10. Le monsieur est riche.

F.* *Employez* **en.** *Ensuite, traduisez:*

EXEMPLE: Voilà un cendrier.
               En voilà un.

1. Voilà deux cintres.   3. Voilà une télévision.   5. Voilà une autre chaise.
2. Voilà quatre valises.   4. Voilà un téléphone.

EXEMPLE: Avez-vous des valises? (deux)
           J'**en** ai deux.

1. Avez-vous des serviettes? (deux)
2. Avez-vous réservé des chambres? (trois)
3. Y a-t-il un lit? (deux)
4. Y a-t-il des cintres? (quatre)
5. Y a-t-il des chaises dans la chambre? (deux)

EXEMPLE: Je n'aime pas cette chambre.
               J'**en** voudrais une autre.

1. Je n'aime pas cette couverture.   5. Je n'aime pas cette serviette de bain.
2. Je n'aime pas cette chaise.   6. Je n'aime pas ce cendrier.
3. Je n'aime pas cette lampe.   7. Je n'aime pas ce lit pliant.
4. Je n'aime pas cette valise.

G.   *Répondez aux questions suivantes en employant* **en** *dans les réponses:*

EXEMPLE: Avez-vous des enfants?
               Oui, j'**en** ai un. *Ou,*

Oui, j'**en** ai deux. *Ou,*
Non, je n'**en** ai pas.

1. Avez-vous des frères? Combien?
2. Avez-vous des sœurs? Combien?
3. Avez-vous un chien? un chat? des plantes?
4. Est-ce que vous fumez des cigarettes? Combien par jour?
5. Avez-vous une voiture? deux voitures?
6. Avez-vous une bicyclette? une moto?
7. Avez-vous beaucoup d'amis?
8. Avez-vous fait beaucoup de voyages?

H.* *Remplacez les mots en italique par* **le, la, les, lui** *ou* **leur:**

EXEMPLE: Je connais *cette dame.*
            Je **la** connais.

1. Je connais *le professeur.*
2. Vous connaissez *ce monsieur,* n'est-ce pas?
3. Je téléphone *à mon ami* chaque jour.
4. Est-ce que vous connaissez *cette dame?*
5. Je ne vois pas *mes valises.*
6. Je ferme *la fenêtre.*
7. Il monte *les valises.*
8. Je parle souvent *à mes amis.*

EXEMPLE: Je vais fermer *la fenêtre.*
            Je vais **la** fermer.

1. Il va monter *les valises* tout de suite.
2. Je voudrais voir *la chambre.*
3. Je ne peux pas fermer *la fenêtre.*
4. Je vais téléphoner *à mon ami.*
5. Je vais téléphoner *à Pierre.*
6. Je vais téléphoner *à Henriette.*
7. Je vais fermer *les fenêtres.*
8. Je vais ouvrir *les valises.*

I.* *Remplacez les mots en italique par un pronom:*

1. Elle m'a montré *le livre.*
2. Elle va me montrer *le livre.*
3. Elle voudrait me montrer *le livre.*
4. Elle va en parler *à Pierre.*
5. Elle vous a déjà donné *le livre.*
6. Elle a déjà donné *le livre à Pierre.*
7. Elle a déjà donné *le livre à Henriette.*
8. Elle a déjà donné *le livre à ses parents.*

9. Il va vous parler *de ses problèmes*.
10. Il vous a déjà parlé *de ses problèmes*, n'est-ce pas?
11. Je voudrais vous montrer *la chambre*.
12. Je vais montrer *la chambre à Henriette* tout de suite.

J.*   *Suivez le modèle. Employez les pronoms* **le, la** *ou* **les**. *Ensuite, traduisez:*

MODÈLE: Ces volets? Pouvez-vous **les** faire réparer?

1. Ce tiroir?	5. Cette fenêtre?	9. Ces lampes?
2. Ce placard?	6. Ces volets?	10. Ce lavabo?
3. Ce lit pliant?	7. Cette porte?	11. Cette télévision?
4. Cette lumière?	8. Ce climatiseur?	12. Ce téléphone?

K.   *Répondez à ces questions:*

1. Votre chambre donne-t-elle sur la rue? sur un jardin? etc.
2. À quel étage est votre chambre?
3. Avez-vous le téléphone dans votre chambre?
4. Avez-vous la télévision dans votre chambre?
5. Y a-t-il un grand lit dans votre chambre? deux lits? un lit d'une place? etc.
6. Préférez-vous les hôtels ou les motels? Pourquoi?
7. Combien d'hôtels et de motels y a-t-il dans votre ville? un? cinq? dix?
8. Avez-vous déjà séjourné dans un hôtel? Où? Quand? Avez-vous réservé la chambre?

EXPANSION: Entretien des vêtements, Chez le coiffeur

1. **Je voudrais faire nettoyer (à sec) et repasser ceci.**   *I would like to have this (dry) cleaned and pressed.*
2. **J'ai du linge à faire laver.**   *I have some laundry to be washed.*
3. **Il me le / la / les faut le plus vite possible.**   *I need it / them as soon as possible.*
4. **Je voudrais me faire raser.**   *I would like a shave.*
5. **Je voudrais une coupe / un shampooing / un rinçage / une manucure.**   *I would like a haircut / shampoo / (color) rinse / manicure.*
6. **Ensuite faites-moi une mise en plis / une décoloration / une permanente.**   *Then, give me a set / dye / permanent.*

Exercices:

1. Vous ouvrez votre valise. Vous trouvez que tous vos vêtements sont sales et chiffonnés. Vous appelez le valet de chambre et vous dites: _____
2. Vous voulez vos vêtements le plus vite possible. Vous dites: _____

3. Vous avez du linge à faire laver. Vous dites: _____
4. Vos cheveux sont trop longs. Vous allez chez le coiffeur et vous dites: _____
5. Vos cheveux sont sales après un long voyage. Vous allez chez le coiffeur et vous dites: _____
6. Vous voulez changer la couleur de vos cheveux. Vous dites au coiffeur: _____
7. Il vous faut aussi une manucure. Vous dites: _____

PRONONCIATION

1. **Sound (Phonetic Symbol): [e] (referred to as "closed e")**

SPELLING:	**é, ée, er, ez** **ai** in verb ending (future tense, **j'ai,** etc.) conjunction **et** (and) the words **les, des, ces, mes, tes, ses** verb forms: **je sais, tu sais, il sait, je vais**
ENGLISH SOUND RESEMBLED:	Vowel sound in word *day*
PRONUNCIATION:	Smile. Pull the corners of the mouth back. Slightly open lips. Do not let the sound glide as in English. Keep it short and abrupt.

EXAMPLES FROM THIS CHAPTER:

déjeuner	**télévision**
entrez	**téléphone**
téléphoner	**chez**
monter	**léger**
les	**réparer**

2. **Sound (Phonetic Symbol): [ɛ] (referred to as "open e")**

SPELLING:	**e, è, ê, et, êt, ei, ai, aî, ais, ait**
ENGLISH SOUND RESEMBLED:	Vowel sound in word *set*
PRONUNCIATION:	Open lips wider than for vowel sound [e]. Do not let the sound glide as in English. Keep it short and abrupt.

EXAMPLES FROM THIS CHAPTER: ser͟viette   cha͟ise
                             e͟lle   fer͟mer
                             savon͟ette   fa͟ites
                             v͟ert   bou͟teille

NOTES:

1. The word endings **ais, ait, es, est, et,** and **êt** are pronounced either [e] or [ɛ], depending on the speaker and the region. For example:

tu es	**c'est**	**je voudrais**	**valet**
il est	**je fais**	**anglais**	**prêt**
elle est	**il fait**	**français**	

2. Notice these pronunciations: **nous faisons** [nufəzɔ̃]
                                   vous faites   [vufɛt]

IMPROVISATION

Complétez ce dialogue. Employez le vocabulaire et les structures de la leçon:

Vous: Je voudrais voir une autre chambre.
Le Gérant / La Gérante: _____
Vous: _____
Le Gérant / La Gérante: _____
Vous: _____
Le Gérant / La Gérante: _____
Vous: _____
Le Gérant / La Gérante: _____

PROJET

Describe all the items in your bedroom using the vocabulary and structures from the **Dialogue** and **Structures** sections of this chapter. Adjectives should agree in gender (masculine / feminine) and in number (singular / plural) with the objects they describe. For example: **Le lit est grand et dur. La table est ronde. La lampe est petite et fragile,** etc.

ACTIVITÉS

1. Using as many adjectives as possible from this lesson, make descriptive labels for every item in the classroom (see Chapter 3, **Expansion: Les Objets de Classe.**) Indicate

color, size, shape, condition, etc. Make sure adjectives agree in gender (masculine / feminine) and in number (singular / plural) with the objects they describe. Tape the labels to the items. For example: **Le tableau noir est rectangulaire. Le bureau du professeur est brun, solide et laid. La porte est ouverte,** etc.

2. At least one possession of each class member should be placed in a central area (such as the instructor's desk), labeled: **Bureau des Objets trouvés** *(Lost and Found).* To reclaim these possessions, tell the person in charge of this area: **«J'ai perdu mon / ma / mes . . .»** *(I lost my. . . .)* and thoroughly describe the missing object, using as many adjectives as possible from this lesson. For example: **Il est rouge. Elle est très petite. Ils sont déchirés. Elles sont vertes,** etc.

FAIS DODO

Entracte

7

ADJECTIVES: PERSONAL ATTRIBUTES

Êtes-vous ridicule?
—Non! Je ne suis pas ridicule! Je suis _____ .

In French, adjectives agree with the nouns they describe both in gender (masculine / feminine) and in number (singular / plural). On the following list the masculine form is given first.

adorable	*adorable*
agréable	*pleasant*
agressif / agressive	*aggressive*
aimable	*amiable, nice, pleasant*
amical / amicale	*friendly*
amusant / amusante	*fun to be with*
autoritaire	*bossy*
avenant / avenante	*gracious, charming*
beau / belle	*handsome, beautiful*

140

blagueur / blagueuse	*a kidder, a joker*
brillant / brillante	*brilliant*
capable	*capable*
capricieux / capricieuse	*capricious*
chaleureux / chaleureuse	*warm*
charmant / charmante	*charming*
compétent / compétente	*competent*
complexé / complexée	*having complexes, withdrawn*
content / contente	*happy*
courageux / courageuse	*courageous*
cruel / cruelle	*cruel*
décontracté / décontractée	*relaxed, easygoing*
désagréable	*disagreeable*
difficile	*difficult to be with*
doux / douce	*sweet, kind, gentle*
drôle	*funny*
dynamique	*dynamic*
éblouissant / éblouissante	*dazzling*
effacé / effacée	*self-effacing, quiet*
énergique	*energetic*
équilibré / équilibrée	*well-balanced, well-adjusted*
enthousiaste	*enthusiastic*
exigent / exigente	*exacting, demanding*
exquis / exquise	*exquisite*
fascinant / fascinante	*fascinating*
formidable	(slang) *great, terrific*
fou / folle	*crazy*
franc / franche	*frank, honest, open*
généreux / généreuse	*generous, noble*
gentil / gentille	*kind, good, nice*
heureux / heureuse	*happy*
idéaliste	*idealistic*
idiot / idiote	*idiotic*
impulsif / impulsive	*impulsive*
intelligent / intelligente	*intelligent*
jaloux / jalouse	*jealous*
joli / jolie	*pretty*
maladroit / maladroite	*clumsy*
malheureux / malheureuse	*unhappy*
méchant / méchante	*evil, wicked, naughty*
mignon / mignonne	*cute*
méthodique	*methodical*

optimiste	*optimistic*
ouvert / ouverte	*open*
parfait / parfaite	*perfect*
patient / patiente	*patient*
paresseux / paresseuse	*lazy*
perfectionniste	*(a) perfectionist*
pessimiste	*pessimistic*
poli / polie	*polite*
prévenant / prévenante	*attentive, considerate*
ràvissant / ravissante	*ravishing*
réaliste	*realistic*
riche	*rich*
sage	*wise, well-behaved*
séduisant / séduisante	*seductive*
sensationnel / sensationnelle	*sensational*
sincère	*sincere*
sociable	*sociable*
sportif / sportive	*athletic*
stupide	*stupid*
spirituel / spirituelle	*witty, clever*
sympathique	*nice, appealing*
timide	*timid, shy*
triste	*sad*
unique	*unique*
vilain / vilaine	*mean, nasty*

SPRINGBOARDS FOR CONVERSATION

1. Êtes-vous ridicule? toujours? souvent? jamais? de temps en temps? rarement?
2. Comment est le professeur? votre mère? votre frère? votre meilleur(e) ami(e)? Monsieur . . . ? Madame. . . . ? Mademoiselle . . . ? etc.
   Il / Elle est _____.
3. Qui dans la classe est drôle? énergique? sympathique? etc.
4. Êtes-vous sincère? optimiste? agréable? etc. Toujours? souvent? etc.
5. Pourquoi aimez-vous votre professeur? Monsieur. . . ? Madame. . . ? Mademoiselle . . . ? votre mari? votre femme? votre ami(e)? votre camarade de chambre? votre fiancé(e)? etc.
   Je l'aime parce qu'il / qu'elle est _____.

PROJETS

1. Using these adjectives, describe your three favorite people and your three least favorite people.

2. Make captions for photos of people. Use cutouts from magazines or newspapers or use photographs you may have on hand. For example: **Il est vilain. Elle est agréable. Ils sont ridicules,** etc.

ACTIVITÉ

Using the adjectives presented here, write a **billet doux** *(love letter)* to at least two other class members. These letters may be collected and delivered by an appointed **Cupidon.**

For example: «**Cher** _____ / **Chère** _____ . **Je vous aime (Je t'aime) parce que vous êtes (tu es)** . . . . . . (Signature).» Complete this phrase by employing as many descriptive terms as possible from the above list.

(Alternatives to «**Cher / Chère** _____» include: **Amour de mon cœur, Amour de ma vie, Mon ange, Chéri(e), Mon trésor, Mon amour,** etc. Alternatives to ''Signature'' include: **Un admirateur anonyme, Une admiratrice anonyme,** or **Devinez que vous écrit!**)

Chapitre

8

La Santé: Chez le docteur

Health: At the Doctor's

Proverbe: Mieux vaut prévenir que guérir.

Proverb: An ounce of prevention is worth a pound of cure. (*Literally:* It is better to prevent than to cure.)

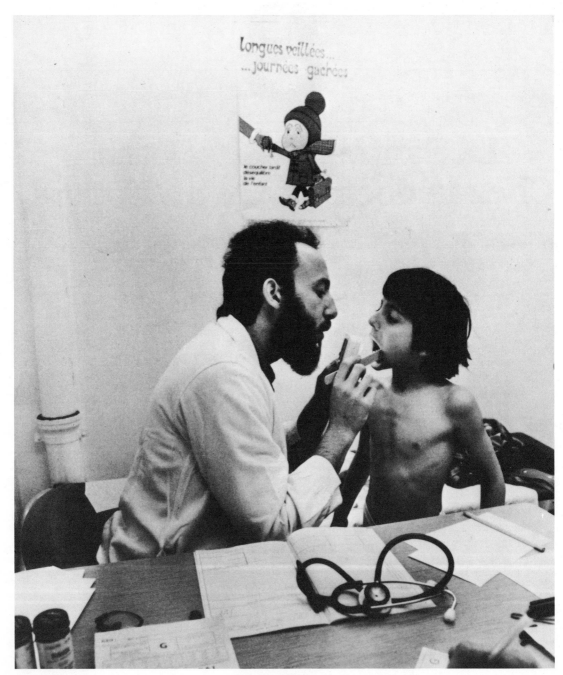

«Dites: Ahhh . . .»

DIALOGUE

LE DOCTEUR / LA DOCTORESSE: Alors, qu'est-ce qui ne va pas?

VOUS: Je me sens un peu **fatigué(e)** aujourd'hui.

agité(e)
déprimé(e)
énervé(e)
épuisé(e)
étourdi(e)
faible
malade

THE DOCTOR: What's wrong?

YOU: I feel a little *tired* today.

nervous, restless
depressed
on edge
exhausted
dizzy
weak
sick

LE DOCTEUR / LA DOCTORESSE: Avez-vous **de la fièvre?**

de l'appétit
des courbatures
la diarrhée
des élancements
des essoufflements
des étourdissements

THE DOCTOR: Do you have *a fever?*

any appetite
aches, pains
diarrhea
shooting pains
shortness of breath
dizziness

VOUS: Non.

LE DOCTEUR: Où avez-vous mal exactement?

VOUS: J'ai mal à la **gorge.** J'ai mal au **dos.**

bouche	bras
cheville	cou
figure	coude
jambe droite	doigt
jambe gauche	front
joue	genou
main	menton
poitrine	nez
tête	pied
	sein
	ventre
	visage

YOU: No.

DOCTOR: Where does it hurt you, exactly?

YOU: My *throat* hurts. My *back* hurts.

mouth	arm
ankle	neck
face	elbow
right leg	finger
left leg	forehead
cheek	knee
hand	chin
chest	nose
head	foot
	breast
	stomach, belly
	face

Et j'ai mal **ici**.   And I hurt *here*.

aux oreilles
aux yeux
à l'épaule
à l'estomac
à l'œil
partout

ears (earache)
eyes
shoulder
stomach (stomach ache)
eye
everywhere (ache all over)

LE DOCTEUR: Depuis combien de temps?   DOCTOR: For how long?

VOUS: Depuis **un jour ou deux**.   YOU: For *a day or two*.

vingt minutes
quelques jours
une semaine
un mois
à peu près un mois
un an
à peu près cinq ans
des années
longtemps

twenty minutes
a few days
a week
a month
about a month
a year
about five years
years
a long time

LE DOCTEUR: Avez-vous déjà eu **les oreillons?**   DOCTOR: Have you ever had *mumps?*

l'appendicite
de l'arthrite
une bronchite
la coqueluche
une crise cardiaque
la diphtérie
la grippe
la poliomyélite
une pneumonie
des rhumatismes
la rougeole
la rubéole
la scarlatine
le tétanus
la typhoïde
la varicelle
la variole

appendicitis
arthritis
bronchitis
whooping cough
a heart attack
diphtheria
influenza
polio
pneumonia
rheumatism
measles
German measles
scarlet fever
tetanus
typhoid
chicken pox
small pox

VOUS: Oui. Il y a très longtemps.   YOU: Yes. A very long time ago.

LE DOCTEUR: Êtes-vous allergique **à la pénicilline?**   DOCTOR: Are you allergic to *penicillin?*

| aux antibiotiques |
| au chocolat |
| au foin |
| à la fumée |
| à l'herbe |
| à la laine |
| au moisi |
| au poil des animaux |
| au pollen |
| à la pollution |
| à la poussière |

| antibiotics |
| chocolate |
| hay |
| smoke |
| grass |
| wool |
| mold |
| animal fur |
| pollen |
| pollution |
| dust |

Vous: Non.

Le Docteur: Je vais vous examiner. Déshabillez-vous. **Étendez-vous là,** s'il vous

| Ouvrez la bouche |
| Tirez la langue |
| Dites: Ahhh. . . . |
| Respirez profondément |
| Toussez |
| Avalez |

| Open your mouth |
| Stick out your tongue |
| Say: Ahhh. . . . |
| Breathe deeply |
| Cough |
| Swallow |

plaît. Est-ce que ça vous fait mal?

Vous: Non. . . . Alors, est-ce grave? Docteur, faut-il m'opérer?

Le Docteur: Non. Pas du tout. Vous avez un rhume. Il vous faut du repos. Vous vous sentirez beaucoup mieux dans quelques jours. Voici **une ordonnance.** Revenez me voir dans

| un antibiotique |
| de l'aspirine (f.) |
| un calmant |
| des gouttes (f.) |
| un laxatif |
| un médicament |
| des pastilles (f.) contre la toux |
| des pastilles (f.) pour la gorge |
| des pilules (f.) |
| un sédatif |
| des somnifères (m.) |
| des vitamines (f.) |

une semaine.

YOU: No.

DOCTOR: I'm going to examine you. Get undressed. *Lie down there,* please. Does that

hurt you?

YOU: No . . . Well, is it serious? Doctor, will I need an operation?

DOCTOR: No. Not at all. You have a cold. You need rest. You will feel much better in a few days. Here is *a prescription.* Come back to

| an antibiotic |
| some aspirin |
| a sedative / pain killer |
| some drops |
| a laxative |
| some medicine / medication |
| some coughdrops |
| some throat lozenges |
| some pills |
| a sedative / tranquilizer |
| sleeping pills |
| some vitamins |

see me in a week.

EXERCICES D'APPLICATION

1. Dites que vous vous sentez un peu fatigué(e) aujourd'hui . . . que vous n'avez pas de fièvre . . . que vous avez mal à la gorge . . . que vous avez mal à la tête . . . que vous avez mal partout . . . que vous avez eu les oreillons il y a très longtemps . . . que vous êtes allergique à la pénicilline . . . que vous toussez . . . que vous avez un rhume . . . que vous vous sentez beaucoup mieux.

2. Répondez:
   a. Qu'est-ce qui ne va pas aujourd'hui?
   b. Est-ce que vous vous sentez un peu fatigué(e) aujourd'hui? déprimé(e)? agité(e)? etc.
   c. Avez-vous de la fièvre aujourd'hui?
   d. Où avez-vous mal exactement? à la tête? à la gorge? à l'estomac? etc.
   e. Avez-vous déjà eu les oreillons? la rougeole? la varicelle? la grippe? etc. Quand?
   f. À quoi êtes-vous allergique? à l'herbe? au pollen? etc. À rien?
   g. Avez-vous un rhume?
   h. Est-ce qu'il vous faut du repos?
   i. Prenez-vous des vitamines?

VERBE IRRÉGULIER: se sentir

se sentir	*to feel, to be* (in relation to health)	
Le présent:	**je me sens**	**nous nous sentons**
	tu te sens	**vous vous sentez**
	il / elle se sent	**ils / elles se sentent**
Le participe passé: **senti**		
La base du futur et du conditionnel: **sentir-**		

Je me sens un peu fatigué(e) aujourd'hui.»
«**Vous vous sentirez** beaucoup mieux dans quelques jours.»

Like **se sentir: sentir**   *to feel; to smell*

J'ai senti une douleur à l'épaule.
I felt a pain in my shoulder.

Ça sent bon!
That smells good!

STRUCTURES

1.   avoir mal à

To say that you have an ache or pain somewhere, use **j'ai mal à . . .** (literally: *I have pain at . . .*) followed by the part of the body that hurts. Remember that **à** + **le** = **au, à** + **les** = **aux:**

> **«Où avez-vous mal?»**
> **«J'ai mal à la tête».**
> **«J'ai mal au dos».**

2.   Special Uses of the Present Tense

Depuis *(for, since)* followed by a period of time is used with the present tense to express an action or a condition that started in the past and is still going on in the present.

a. The question **Depuis combien de temps?** asks how long something has been going on.

> «Et j'ai mal ici . . .» «—**Depuis combien de temps?**»

> **Depuis combien de temps** êtes-vous malade?
> *For how long have you been sick?*

As seen in the Dialogue above, answers can include: **depuis vingt minutes, depuis un jour, depuis quelques jours,** etc.

The question **Depuis combien de temps?** is answered in the present tense:

depuis	Je suis malade **depuis** trois jours.
Ça fait . . . que . . .	**Ça fait** trois jours **que** je suis malade.
Voilà . . . que . . .	**Voilà** trois jours **que** je suis malade.
Il y a . . . que . . .	**Il y a** trois jours **que** je suis malade.

All four sentences = *I've been sick for three days.*

b. The question **Depuis quand?** asks for information about a specific starting point in time:

> **Depuis quand** êtes-vous malade?   *Since when have you been sick?*

Possible answers include:

depuis ce matin	*since this morning*
depuis hier soir	*since yesterday evening*
depuis lundi, mardi, etc.	*since Monday, Tuesday,* etc.

depuis deux heures	*since two o'clock*
depuis mon arrivée	*since my arrival*
depuis la semaine passée	*since last week*
depuis le mois passé	*since last month*
depuis l'année dernière	*since last year*
depuis janvier, février, etc.	*since January, February,* etc.
depuis le dix mars	*since March 10*
depuis 1980	*since 1980*
depuis mon enfance	*since my childhood*
depuis l'âge de cinq ans	*since the age of five*

The question **Depuis quand?** is answered with **depuis** and the present tense:

> **Depuis quand** êtes-vous malade?
> —Je **suis** malade **depuis** lundi.
> *I've been sick since Monday.*

c. With completed actions, **il y a** followed by an expression of time means *ago:*

> «Avez-vous déjà eu les oreillons?»
> «—Oui. **Il y a** longtemps.»

EXERCICES DE SYNTHÈSE

A.   *Répondez à la question. Suivez le modèle:*

MODÈLE: Depuis combien de temps êtes-vous malade? (deux jours)
              Je suis malade depuis deux jours.
              Ça fait deux jours que je suis malade.
              Voilà deux jours que je suis malade.
              Il y a deux jours que je suis malade.

1. Depuis combien de temps êtes-vous allergique aux antibiotiques? (cinq ans)
2. Depuis combien de temps avez-vous mal partout? (une semaine)
3. Depuis combien de temps attendez-vous le médecin? (deux heures)
   (le médecin = le docteur / la doctoresse)
4. Depuis combien de temps vous sentez-vous fatigué(e)? (quelques jours)

B.   *Répondez aux questions suivantes:*

1. Depuis combien de temps étudiez-vous le français?
2. Depuis combien de temps habitez-vous dans cette ville?
3. Depuis combien de temps habitez-vous ici?
4. Êtes-vous marié(e)? fiancé(e)? divorcé(e)? Depuis combien de temps? Depuis

combien de temps connaissez-vous votre mari? votre femme? votre fiancé(e)? votre meilleur(e) ami(e)?

5. Fumez-vous? Depuis combien de temps?
6. Travaillez-vous? Depuis combien de temps travaillez-vous dans le même établissement?
7. Êtes-vous en retraite? Depuis combien de temps?
8. Savez-vous conduire? Depuis combien de temps?
9. Depuis combien de temps connaissez-vous le professeur de français? Monsieur . . . ? Madame . . . ? Mademoiselle . . . ?
10. Depuis combien de temps allez-vous chez le même docteur?
11. Faites-vous partie d'un club? lequel? d'une équipe? laquelle? Depuis combien de temps?
12. Jouez-vous au tennis? au golf? Faites-vous du sport? Depuis combien de temps?
13. Buvez-vous du café? du vin? Depuis combien de temps?
14. Jouez-vous d'un instrument de musique? du piano? de la guitare? etc. Depuis combien de temps?
15. Fait-il beau aujourd'hui? Pleut-il? Neige-t-il? Depuis combien de temps?
16. Vous sentez-vous fatigué(e)? Depuis combien de temps?
17. Depuis combien de temps travaillez-vous sur les questions de cet exercice?

C. *Transformez les questions de l'Exercice B en employant* **Depuis quand.** *Ensuite, répondez aux questions:*

EXEMPLE: Depuis combien de temps étudiez-vous le français?
          Depuis quand étudiez-vous le français?

EXPANSION: Chez le docteur, À l'hôpital

1. **Quelles maladies infantiles avez-vous eues? Quand?**	*Which childhood diseases have you had? When?*
2. **Avez-vous mal au cœur? Avez-vous des nausées?**	*Do you feel sick to your stomach? nauseated?*
3. **Avez-vous peur quant le médecin / l'infirmier (l'infirmière) vous fait une piqûre?**	*Are you afraid when the doctor / nurse gives you an injection?*
4. **Est-ce que votre tension est normale / élevée / basse?**	*Is your blood pressure normal / high / low?*
5. **Quel est votre groupe sanguin? O/AB/A/B Rhésus positif / négatif?**	*What is your blood type? O / AB / A / B Rh positive / negative?*
6. **Avez-vous de la fièvre? 37°C / 38°C / 39°C / 40°C**	*Do you have a fever? 98.6°F / 100.4°F / 102.2°F / 104°F*
J'ai 37.	*My temperature is 98.6°F.*

7. **Êtes-vous souvent enrhumé(e)?**	*Do you often have colds?*
8. **Est-ce que votre professeur de français a bonne / mauvaise mine aujourd'hui?**	*Does your French teacher look healthy / ill today?*
9. **Atchoum! . . . Qui a éternué pendant la classe?**	*Achoo! . . . Who sneezed during class?*
À vos (tes) souhaits / Que Dieu vous (te) bénisse / À vos (tes) amours.	*God bless you!* (Literally: *To your wishes / [Let] God bless you / To your loves.*)
10. **Avez-vous passé une visite médicale cette année?**	*Have you had a physical examination this year?*
11. **Avez-vous déjà été hospitalisé(e)? Quand?**	*Have you ever been hospitalized? When?*
12. **Êtes-vous enceinte?**	*Are you pregnant?*
13. **Avez-vous eu un rhume récemment? Allez-vous mieux?**	*Have you had a cold recently? Are you feeling better?*
14. **Avez-vous subi une opération? Quand?**	*Have you undergone an operation? When?*
15. **Êtes-vous cardiaque?**	*Do you have a heart condition?*
16. **Êtes-vous en bonne santé?**	*Are you in good health?*
17. **Appelez un médecin! Vite!**	*Call a doctor! Quickly!*

Exercices:

1. Répondez aux questions 1–16 posées ci-dessus.
2. Il vous faut un médecin vite. C'est un cas d'urgence. Vous dites: _____ .
3. Racontez votre dernière visite chez le médecin. Qu'a-t-il / elle dit? Qu'avez-vous répondu? Que vous a-t-il / elle fait? etc.

PRONONCIATION

1. Sound (Phonetic Symbol): [o] (referred to as "closed o")

SPELLING:	**o, ô, au, eau**
ENGLISH SOUND RESEMBLED:	Vowel sound in words *sn<u>o</u>w* or *g<u>o</u>*
PRONUNCIATION:	Tightly round and protrude lips. Do not let the sound glide as in English. Keep it short and abrupt.

EXAMPLES FROM THIS CHAPTER:	<u>au</u>	be<u>au</u>coup
	<u>au</u>x	il v<u>au</u>t
	rep<u>o</u>s	il f<u>au</u>t
	d<u>o</u>s	v<u>o</u>s

2. **Sound (phonetic symbol): [ɔ] (referred to as "open o")**

SPELLING:	**o, au**
ENGLISH SOUND RESEMBLED:	Vowel sound in words *love* or *cup*
PRONUNCIATION:	Open mouth wider than for vowel sound [o]. Lips are more rounded than for English sound. Do not let the sound glide as in English. Keep it short and abrupt.

EXAMPLES FROM THIS CHAPTER:

docteur	**pollution**	**professeur**
proverbe	**ordonnance**	**normale**
opération	**bonne**	
chocolat	**votre**	

NOTES:

1. The letter **o** is pronounced [o] when it is the final sound of a word, as in **piano, repos, vos;** when it precedes the spelling **-tion,** as in **émotion;** when it is followed by the sound [z], as in **rose, chose.** The letter **o** is pronounced [ɔ] in nearly all other positions, (that is, other than in the final sound of a word), as in **docteur** [dɔktœr], **oreille** [ɔrɛj].

2. The letter **ô (accent circonflexe)** is pronounced [o] as in **hôtel, bientôt,** etc. Exception: **hôpital** [ɔ].

3. The spellings **eau** and **au** are pronounced [o] when they are the final pronounced sound of a word, (as in **beau, il faut),** or when they end a syllable, (as in **beaucoup**). In many words, however, when the spelling **au** ends a syllable, the tendency these days is to pronounce the spelling **au** as [ɔ], as in the words **mauvais, j'aurai.**

4. In syllables ending in a consonant sound, **au** is pronounced [ɔ], as in **augmenter.**

5. The nasal sound [õ] loses its nasal quality when it is followed by a double consonant or by a vowel (see Chapter 1). The letter **o** at this time becomes [ɔ].

EXAMPLES:

bonne [bɔn]	**bon anniversaire** [bɔnanivɛrsɛr]
comment [kɔmã]	**bon appetit** [bɔnapeti]

IMPROVISATION

Vous ne vous sentez pas bien. Vous allez voir un médecin. Il (ou elle) vous pose quelques questions et veut vous examiner:

Vous: _____

Le Médecin: _____

Vous: _____
Le Médecin: _____
Vous: _____
Le Médecin: _____
Vous: _____
Le Médecin: _____

PROJETS

1. To the best of your abilities draw a human body (a photo or magazine cutout may be substituted), labeling as many parts as possible: **la main, la tête, le pied,** etc.
2. Prepare your own medical history: illnesses and dates, allergies, vaccinations, medications, broken bones, hospitalizations, operations, etc.

ACTIVITÉS

1. Assume you are a health officer or a medical assistant. Using the **Dialogue** and **Expansion** sections of this chapter, prepare a list of as many health-related questions as possible. Then obtain a very complete medical history from a classmate. Keep track of the answers. Try to be discrete. For example: **Avez-vous déjà eu les oreillons? Quand? Et la rougeole? Êtes-vous allergique à la pénicilline? à la poussière? Prenez-vous des médicaments? lesquels?** etc.
2. Here is a variation on "Simon says" («**Jacques a dit**» in French), that uses the vocabulary of this lesson. Everyone plays while one person gives orders: «**Jacques a dit: Mettez la main gauche sur la bouche!**» or, «**Jacques a dit: Mettez les mains sur la tête!**» etc. When the expression «**Jacques a dit**» is omitted before the command (for example: «**Croisez les bras!**»), students who perform the action anyhow are consequently disqualified. For greater challenge, the person giving the orders may occasionally try to mislead the other players by giving one command (such as, «**Jacques a dit: Avancez le pied gauche!**»), while acting out another action (such as waving his or her right hand). Players who mistakenly imitate the action rather than following the spoken command are disqualified. The game is played until there is a winner.

SAVEZ-VOUS PLANTER LES CHOUX?

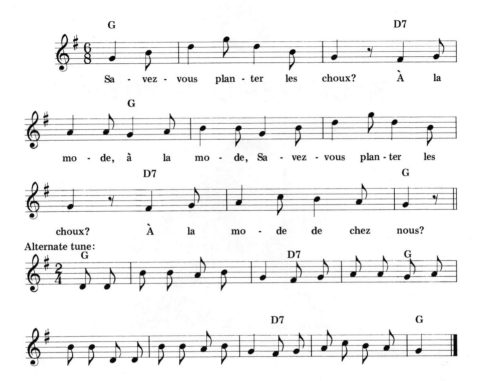

Sa - vez - vous plan - ter les choux? À la

mo - de, à la mo - de, Sa - vez - vous plan - ter les

choux? À la mo - de de chez nous?

Alternate tune:

2. On les plante avec le pied,
   À la mode, à la mode,
   On les plante avec le pied,
   À la mode, de chez nous.

3. *Continue this song, each time
   substituting a different part
   of the body:* **la main, le nez,
   le coude, l'index, la tête,** etc.

Entracte

8

SELF-DESCRIPTION

Faites votre autoportrait.
—**J'ai** _____ .

une barbe	*a beard*
un beau sourire	*a nice smile*
un chignon	*a chignon / bun*
une envie	*a birthmark*
les épaules larges et musclées	*broad, muscular shoulders*
une fossette	*a dimple*
une frange	*bangs*
un grain de beauté	*beauty spot, mole*
de longs cils	*long eyelashes*
des ongles longs	*long finger-nails*
une moustache	*a moustache*
des nattes	*braids*
le nez aquilin / courbé / court / droit / long / retroussé	*an aquiline / curved / short / straight / long / turned-up nose*
des pattes / des favoris	*sideburns / whiskers*
la peau délicate / lisse	*delicate / smooth skin*

les sourcils épais	*thick eyebrows*
des taches de rousseur	*freckles*
la taille fine	*a slender waist*

—J'ai les cheveux _____. (Mes cheveux sont _____.)

bouclés	*curly*
courts	*short*
dépeignés / en désordre	*tousled, mussed up*
emmêlés	*tangled*
fins	*fine*
frisés	*curly, very curly*
gras	*oily*
longs	*long*
ondulés	*wavy*
raides	*straight*
secs	*dry*

argentés	*silver*
blancs	*white*
blonds	*blonde*
bruns	*brown, dark brown*
châtains	*chestnut*
châtain clair *(invariable)*	*light brown*
châtain foncé *(invariable)*	*dark brown*
gris	*gray*
noirs	*black*
roux	*red*

(je suis) chauve	*(I'm) bald*

—Je porte _____.

des lunettes	*glasses*
une perruque	*a wig*
un postiche	*a hairpiece, a toupee*
la raie à droite / à gauche / au milieu	*a part on the right / left / in the middle*
des verres de contact	*contact lenses*

—J'ai les yeux _____. (Mes yeux sont _____.)

bleus	*blue*
bruns	*brown*
brun clair *(invariable)*	*hazel*
brun foncé *(invariable)*	*dark brown*
gris	*gray*
marron *(invariable)*	*chestnut*

noirs	*black*
verts	*green*
(J'ai de grands yeux bleus / bruns.)	*(I have big blue / brown eyes.)*

—Je suis _____ .

beau / belle	*handsome / beautiful*
bien proportionné(e)	*well-proportioned*
bien habillé(e)	*well-dressed*
bien soigné(e)	*well-groomed*
costaud	*husky, strapping, very solid* *(masc. only)*
élégant(e)	*elegant*
grand(e)	*big, tall*
gros(se)	*fat*
joli(e)	*pretty*
laid(e)	*ugly*
maigre	*skinny*
mignon(ne)	*cute, adorable*
mince	*slim*
petit(e)	*small,* also *short*
potelé(e)	*chubby, pleasantly plump*
de taille moyenne	*of average height*

—Je pèse à peu près _____ **kilos / livres.**[1]
I weigh about _____ *kilos / pounds.*[1]

> EXEMPLE: Je pèse à peu près cent livres. =
> Je pèse à peu près quarante-cinq kilos.

—Je fais / Je mesure _____ **mètres** _____ (_____ **pieds** _____ **pouces).**[1]
I am _____ *meters* _____ *centimeters (* _____ *feet* _____ *inches) tall.*[1]

> EXEMPLE: Je fais / Je mesure cinq pieds trois pouces. =
> Je fais / Je mesure un mètre soixante.

1. CONVERSION TABLE

1 **centimètre** = .39 *inches*
1 **mètre** = 39.36 *inches*
1 *inch* = 2.54 **centimètres** = .0254 **mètres**
1 *foot* = .3 **mètres**
1 **kilogramme** = 2.2 *pounds*
1 *pound* = .45 **kilogrammes**

USEFUL FORMULAS

$$\frac{1 \text{ inch}}{2.54 \text{ centimètres}} = \frac{\text{Your height (in inches)}}{\text{Your height (in centimeters)}}$$

$$\frac{1 \text{ pound}}{.45 \text{ kilos}} = \frac{\text{Your weight (in pounds)}}{\text{Your weight (in kilos)}}$$

SPRINGBOARDS FOR CONVERSATION

1. Faites votre autoportrait.
   J'ai les cheveux _____.
   J'ai les yeux _____, etc.
2. Faites votre autoportrait lorsque vous aviez cinq ans, dix ans, quinze ans, vingt ans, etc.
   J'avais _____.
   Je portais _____.
   J'étais _____.
   Je pesais _____.
   Je faisais / Je mesurais_____, etc.
3. Faites le portrait du professeur.
   Il / Elle a les cheveux _____.
   Il / Elle a les yeux _____, etc.
4. Faites le portrait de votre voisin(e) de gauche / de droite (classmate on your left / right).
5. Qui dans la classe a les cheveux bruns? blonds? longs? courts? etc.
6. Qui dans la classe a les yeux bleus? marron? etc. Qui a de grands yeux bleus? de grands yeux bruns? etc.
7. Qui dans la classe porte des lunettes? des verres de contact?
8. Y a-t-il des absents aujourd'hui? Qui? Faites le portrait de Monsieur / Madame / Mademoiselle. . . .
   Il / Elle a les cheveux _____, etc.
9. Faites le portrait de votre mère. De votre père. De votre mari / femme / meilleur(e) ami(e). De votre sœur. De votre frère. De vos enfants. etc.
10. Comment êtes-vous? grand(e)? petit(e)? de taille moyenne? Êtes-vous plus grand(e) que votre mère? que votre père? que votre mari / femme / meilleur(e) ami(e)? que votre fille / fils? etc.
11. Combien faites-vous en pieds et en pouces? en mètres et en centimètres?
12. Combien pesez-vous? En kilos? En livres?
13. Comment est votre nez?
14. Faites-vous une raie? De quel côté (on which side)?
15. À qui ressemblez-vous? À votre mère? À votre père? Avez-vous le nez de votre mère? les yeux de votre père? etc.
    Je ressemble à mon / ma _____.
16. Portez-vous les cheveux longs ou courts? Avez-vous déjà porté les cheveux longs? les cheveux courts?
17. Portez-vous la barbe? la moustache? Avez-vous déjà porté la barbe? la moustache?
18. De quelle couleur sont vos yeux?
19. De quelle couleur sont vos cheveux?
20. Comment voudriez-vous être?
21. Vous trouvez-vous trop mince? trop gros(se)? etc.

PROJETS

1. Employ the vocabulary of this lesson to describe a picture of someone in detail. You may wish to use a magazine or newspaper photo, a snapshot you may have on hand, or even a picture you yourself have drawn.
2. Using the vocabulary and structures of this lesson describe your three favorite people. These may include friends, relatives, acquaintances, celebrities, etc.

ACTIVITÉS

1. The class is divided into small groups, who then use the vocabulary of this lesson to prepare a detailed description of another class member (present or absent). These descriptions are then presented before the whole class, while everyone tries to guess the identity of the person being described.
2. Everyone has a partner for this variation of the guessing game Twenty Questions. One person thinks of a mystery person. (It can be a classmate, a celebrity, a local personage, etc.) The second partner now tries to guess the identity of the mystery person by using the vocabulary and structures of this lesson. For example: **Est-il chauve? Est-elle belle? A-t-il les yeux bleus? Porte-t-elle des lunettes?** etc.

La Santé: Chez le dentiste	Health: At the Dentist's
Proverbe: Tout ce qui brille n'est pas or.	Proverb: All that glitters is not gold.

«J'ai perdu mon plombage.»

DIALOGUE

LE DENTISTE: Asseyez-vous dans le fauteuil, je vous prie. Alors, que puis-je faire pour vous?

VOUS: J'ai très mal aux dents.

LE DENTISTE: Où avez-vous mal, exactement?

VOUS: J'ai une violente douleur du côté gauche / droit du visage.

LE DENTISTE: Je vais regarder. Ouvrez la bouche, s'il vous plaît. C'est cette dent en haut / en bas qui vous fait mal?

VOUS: Aïe! Vous me faites mal!

LE DENTISTE: Cette dent est trop cariée pour être plombée.

VOUS: Faudra-t-il l'arracher?

LE DENTISTE: Malheureusement, je dois vous l'arracher. Mais d'abord il me faut une radio des dents voisines.

VOUS: Vous ne pouvez pas la plomber?

LE DENTISTE: N'ayez pas peur. Je vais vous faire une anesthésie locale. Êtes-vous allergique à la novocaïne?

THE DENTIST: Sit down in the chair, please. Well, what can I do for you?

YOU: I have a bad toothache.

DENTIST: Where does it hurt you, exactly?

YOU: I have a terrible pain in the left / right side of my face.

DENTIST: I'll take a look. Open your mouth, please. Is it this tooth up here / down here which hurts?

YOU: Ow! You're hurting me!

DENTIST: This tooth is too decayed to be filled.

YOU: Must it be pulled?

DENTIST: Unfortunately I have to pull it. But first I need an X-ray of the teeth next to it.

YOU: You can't fill it?

DENTIST: Don't be afraid. I'll give you a local anesthetic. Are you allergic to novocaine?

EXERCICE D'APPLICATION*

Dites au dentiste que vous avez mal aux dents . . . que vous avez une violente douleur du côté droit du visage . . . que c'est cette dent qui vous fait mal. Demandez au dentiste si la dent est trop cariée pour être plombée . . . s'il faut l'arracher. . . . s'il / si elle peut la plomber. Dites au dentiste qu'il / elle vous fait mal . . . que vous voulez une anesthésie locale . . . que vous n'êtes pas allergique à la novocaïne.

VERBE IRRÉGULIER: s'asseoir

s'asseoir	*to sit down*

Le présent: **je m'assieds**   **nous nous asseyons**
                        tu t'assieds   **vous vous asseyez**
             il / elle s'assied   **ils / elles s'asseyent**
                            ou
                        je m'assois   **nous nous assoyons**
                        tu t'assois   **vous vous assoyez**
             il / elle s'assoit   **ils / elles s'assoient**
Le participe passé: **assis** *(seated)*
La base du futur et du conditionnel: **assiér-**

Il est **assis.**   *He is seated.*
Il s'est assis.   *He sat down.*

«**Asseyez-vous** dans le fauteuil, je vous prie.»

STRUCTURES

Reflexive Constructions

a. When the subject of a verb performs an action upon itself, *(he cut himself),* or when a reciprocal action occurs, *(they talk to each other,* or *they talk to one another),* the reflexive pronouns **me, te, se, nous, vous, se** are used.

Any verb may be made reflexive:

(nonreflexive)   Je connais le dentiste. Je le connais.
                                    I know the dentist. I know him.

(reflexive)   Je **me** connais bien.
                                      I know myself well.

(nonreflexive)   J'aime mon ami(e). Il / elle m'aime.
                                    I love my friend. He / she loves me.

(reflexive; reciprocal action) Nous **nous** aimons.
                                    We love each other (one another).

b. Certain verbs are reflexive in French; their English equivalents are not. Many reflexive verbs correspond to the English *get (to get nervous, to get married,* etc.). A large number of reflexive verbs are **-er** verbs:

s'en aller	*to leave, to go away*
s'arrêter	*to stop*
s'asseoir	*to sit (down)*
se brosser les dents, les cheveux	*to brush one's teeth, one's hair*
se coucher	*to go to bed, to lie down*
se dépêcher	*to hurry (up)*
se déshabiller	*to get undressed*
se doucher	*to shower*
s'endormir	*to fall asleep*
s'énerver	*to get nervous, to be exasperated*
s'enrhumer	*to get a cold, to catch cold*
s'étendre	*to stretch out, to lie down*
se fâcher (avec)	*to get angry (with)*
se fiancer	*to get engaged*
s'habiller	*to get dressed*
s'habituer à	*to get used to*
s'impatienter	*to get impatient, to grow impatient*
s'intéresser à	*to be interested in*
se laver	*to wash oneself*
se laver la tête, les mains, etc.	*to wash one's hair, hands, etc.*
se lever	*to get up*
se maquiller	*to put on makeup*
se marier (avec)	*to get married (to)*
se moquer de	*to make fun of*
se moucher	*to wipe one's nose*
s'occuper (de)	*to keep busy, to take care of*
se peigner	*to comb one's hair*
se presser	*to hurry*
se promener	*to take a walk*
se raser	*to shave*
se rencontrer	*to meet, to get together*
se renseigner	*to get information*
se reposer	*to rest*
se réveiller	*to wake up*
se souvenir de	*to remember*

c. Some verbs change in meaning when they are reflexive:

acheter	*to buy*	**s'acheter**	*to buy for oneself*
amuser	*to amuse*	**s'amuser**	*to have a good time*

appeler	to call	s'appeler	to be named
demander	to ask, ask for	**se demander**	to wonder
disputer	to dispute	**se disputer**	to argue, quarrel
ennuyer	to bore, annoy	**s'ennuyer**	to get bored
entendre	to hear	**s'entendre**	to get along
faire	to do, make	**se faire mal**	to hurt oneself, get hurt
passer	to pass	**se passer**	to happen
perdre	to lose	**se perdre**	to get lost
porter	to carry, wear	**se porter**	to be (health)
préparer	to prepare	**se préparer**	to get ready
rappeler	to call back	**se rappeler**	to remember
sentir	to smell	**se sentir**	to feel, to be (health)
tromper	to deceive	**se tromper**	to be mistaken
trouver	to find	**se trouver**	to be located

Ça sent bon!   *That smells good!*
Je me sens bien.   *I feel well.*

J'appelle le docteur.   *I'm calling the doctor.*
Je m'appelle . . .   *My name is. . . .*

d. Reflexive pronouns precede the conjugated verb except in positive commands, when **te** becomes **toi:**

   Amuse-**toi** bien!   Amusez-**vous** bien!   *Have a good time!*
   Assieds-**toi.**   Asseyez-**vous.**   *Sit down.*

e. Reflexive verbs are conjugated with **être** in compound tenses. The past participle agrees in gender and number with the preceding direct object:

je me suis amusé(e)	nous nous sommes amusé(e)s
tu t'es amusé(e)	vous vous êtes amusé(e)(s)
il s'est amusé	ils se sont amusés
elle s'est amusée	elles se sont amusées

There are situations where the reflexive pronoun is not the *direct* object of the verb but rather the *indirect* object. For example, in the sentence **Ils se sont parlé au télé-phone** *(They spoke to each other on the phone),* the reflexive functions as an *indirect* object. Consequently the past participle does not agree.

f. In reflexive constructions, parts of the body are preceded by the definite article (**le, la, les**) rather than by the possessive adjective (**mon, ma, mes,** etc.). This usage is different from English. Since the reflexive pronoun now functions as a preceding indirect object, there is no past-participle agreement:

Je me suis cassé le bras.	*I broke my arm.*
Je me suis fouillé la cheville.	*I sprained my ankle.*
Elle s'est brossé les dents.	*She brushed her teeth.*
Je me suis fait mal à la jambe.	*I hurt my leg.*

g. When the reflexive verb is in the infinitive form, the reflexive pronoun changes from **se** to **me, te, nous** or **vous** depending on the subject of the verb and comes directly before the infinitive:

Je vais me reposer.	**Nous allons nous reposer.**
Tu vas te reposer.	**Vous allez vous reposer.**
Il / elle va se reposer.	**Ils / elles vont se reposer.**

EXERCICES DE SYNTHÈSE

A.*   *Suivez le modèle. Ensuite, traduisez:*

MODÈLE: Où puis-je . . . (s'arrêter)?
              Où puis-je m'arrêter?

1. se doucher	5. se raser	9. se laver les mains
2. s'habiller	6. se brosser les dents	10. se reposer
3. se promener	7. se déshabiller	11. s'asseoir
4. se renseigner	8. se coucher	12. se peigner

B.*   *Suivez le modèle. Ensuite traduisez:*

MODÈLE: Pourquoi . . . (s'arrêter)?
              Pourquoi vous arrêtez-vous?

1. se laver	6. s'impatienter	11. se moucher
2. se fâcher	7. se moquer	12. se maquiller
3. se lever	8. s'ennuyer	13. se préparer
4. se disputer	9. s'énerver	14. se presser
5. se dépêcher	10. se marier	

C.   *Suivez le modèle. Ensuite, répondez aux questions:*

MODÈLE: À quelle heure . . . (s'arrêter)?
              À quelle heure vous arrêtez-vous?

1. se coucher	4. se réveiller	7. se reposer
2. se déshabiller	5. s'habiller	8. se doucher
3. se lever	6. se laver	

D.*   *Donnez un ordre. Suivez le modèle. Puis traduisez:*

MODÈLE: (s'arrêter)
     Arrêtez-vous!
     Arrête-toi!

1. se coucher	6. se reposer	10. se préparer
2. se laver	7. s'habiller	11. se fiancer
3. se renseigner	8. se réveiller	12. se marier
4. se dépêcher	9. se peigner	13. s'asseoir
5. se lever		

E.*   *Transformez les phrases suivantes. Suivez le modèle. Puis répondez par des phrases complètes:*

MODÈLE: Est-ce que vous vous êtes levé(e) de bonne heure *(early)* ce matin?
     Vous êtes-vous levé(e) de bonne heure ce matin?

1. Est-ce que vous vous êtes bien reposé(e) hier soir?
2. Est-ce que vous vous êtes couché(e) de bonne heure hier soir?
3. Est-ce que vous vous êtes lavé(e) le visage ce matin?
4. Est-ce que vous vous êtes fiancé(e)?
5. Est-ce que vous vous êtes marié(e)?
6. Est-ce que vous vous êtes ennuyé(e)?
7. Est-ce que vous vous êtes promené(e) hier?

F.*   *Mettez les questions suivantes au passe composé. Suivez le modèle:*

MODÈLE: À quelle heure vous couchez-vous?
     À quelle heure vous êtes-vous couché(e)?

1. À quelle heure vous levez-vous?
2. À quelle heure vous déshabillez-vous?
3. À quelle heure vous réveillez-vous?
4. À quelle heure vous douchez-vous?
5. À quelle heure vous lavez-vous?
6. À quelle heure vous habillez-vous?
7. À quelle heure vous reposez-vous?

G.   *Répondez à ces questions par des phrases complètes:*

1. Comment vous sentez-vous aujourd'hui?
2. Vous intéressez-vous à la politique? aux sports? au théâtre? à la musique? à la médecine?

3. À quelle heure vous couchez-vous en semaine? le samedi soir? le dimanche soir? pendant les vacances?

4. À quelle heure vous levez-vous en semaine? le samedi matin? le dimanche matin? pendant les vacances?

5. À quelle heure vous réveillez-vous le matin?

6. Quand vous ennuyez-vous? en classe? à la maison? pendant les vacances?

7. Vous disputez-vous avec vos amis? souvent? rarement? de temps en temps? et avec votre mari / femme? et avec vos parents / enfants?

8. Avec qui vous entendez-vous très bien? avec votre femme / mari? avec votre meilleur(e) ami(e)? avec vos parents / enfants?

9. Combien de fois par jour vous brossez-vous les dents? une fois? deux fois? après chaque repas?

10. Préférez-vous vous doucher le matin ou le soir? Ou, préférez-vous prendre un bain *(take a bath)?*

11. Aimez-vous vous promener? vous lever de bonne heure? Qu'est-ce que vous n'aimez pas faire? vous coucher tard? vous raser? etc.

12. Comment s'appelle votre meilleur(e) ami(e)? votre mère? votre père? votre professeur de français? votre mari / femme? votre fiancé(e)? votre dentiste?

13. Vous fâchez-vous facilement? Vous impatientez-vous facilement? Vous ennuyez-vous facilement? Vous énervez-vous facilement? Et votre meilleur(e) ami(e) (votre femme / mari / mère / père etc.), se fâche-t-il / elle facilement? etc.

14. Comment vous portez-vous aujourd'hui?

H. *Describe a typical day in your life. Use as many pronominal (reflexive) verbs from this lesson as possible. Begin with:* «**Je me réveille . . . .**» *End with:* «**Je me couche . . . .**»

I. *Répondez à ces questions au passé composé:*

1. À quelle heure vous êtes-vous couché(e) hier soir?

2. À quelle heure est-ce que vous vous êtes réveillé(e) ce matin?

3. À quelle heure vous êtes-vous levé(e) ce matin?

4. Est-ce que vous vous êtes bien amusé(e) récemment? Où? Avec qui?

5. Est-ce que vous vous êtes promené(e) hier soir? aujourd'hui? Où? Avec qui?

6. Vous êtes-vous disputé(e) récemment avec quelqu'un? Avec qui?

7. Vous êtes-vous brossé les dents aujourd'hui?

J. *Qu'est-ce que vous avez fait le week-end dernier? Utilisez au moins dix verbes pronominaux au passé composé:*

Par exemple: **Je me suis douché(e). Je me suis brossé les dents. Je me suis reposé(e)** etc.

EXPANSION: Chez le dentiste, Chez l'opticien, À la pharmacie

1. **Puis-je avoir un rendez-vous avec le docteur Dupont demain?**	*Can I have an appointment with Doctor Dupont tomorrow?*
2. **J'ai perdu un plombage / mes verres de contact.**	*I've lost a filling / my contact lenses.*
3. **J'ai cassé mon dentier / mon bridge. Pouvez-vous me le réparer?**	*I've broken my dentures / my bridge. Can you repair it (them) for me?*
4. **J'ai cassé mes lunettes / mes lunettes de soleil. Pouvez-vous me les réparer?**	*I've broken my eyeglasses / my sunglasses. Can you fix them for me?*
5. **Cette dent est très sensible au chaud / au froid / aux choses sucrées.**	*This tooth is very sensitive to heat / cold / sweets.*
6. **J'ai fait plomber une dent cariée.**	*I had a decayed tooth filled.*
7. **J'ai fait arracher une dent de sagesse.**	*I had a wisdom tooth pulled.*
8. **J'ai fait détartrer mes dents.**	*I had my teeth cleaned.*
9. **J'ai fait refaire un plombage.**	*I had a filling replaced.*
10. **Je suis myope / presbyte / astigmate.**	*I'm near-sighted / far-sighted / astigmatic.*
11. **(À la pharmacie) J'ai besoin de quelque chose contre le rhume des foins / le mal de mer / le mal de l'air / les coups de soleil / la constipation / le mal de cœur / la migraine.**	*(At the pharmacy) I need something, for hay-fever / sea sickness / air sickness / sunburn / constipation / nausea / headache.*

Exercice

Répondez par des phrases complètes aux questions suivantes:

1. Vous avez très mal aux dents. Vous voulez consulter votre dentiste. Vous téléphonez chez lui (ou chez elle) et vous dites: _____?
2. Vous avez cassé vos lunettes de soleil. Vous dites à l'opticien: _____?
3. Êtes-vous allé(e) récemment chez le dentiste? Pourquoi? Chez l'opticien? Pourquoi?
4. Portez-vous des lunettes? des verres de contact? Depuis combien de temps? Qui dans la classe porte des lunettes? des verres de contact?
5. Êtes-vous myope? presbyte? astigmate?
6. Vous avez très mal à la tête. Vous allez à la pharmacie et vous dites au pharmacien: _____
7. Vous êtes allergique au foin. Vous allez à la pharmacie et vous dites: _____
8. Avez-vous des dents de sagesse? Combien? En avez-vous fait arracher? Combien? Quand?
9. Avez-vous déjà perdu un plombage? Quand? Où?
10. Est-ce que vos dents sont sensibles au chaud? au froid? aux choses sucrées?
11. Racontez votre dernière visite chez le dentiste. Qu'a-t-il / elle dit? Qu'avez-vous répondu? Que vous a-t-il / elle fait? etc.

PRONONCIATION

1.   Sound (Phonetic Symbol): [ø]

SPELLING: **eu, œu, eû**

ENGLISH SOUND RESEMBLED: Vowel sound in words *put, sir, good*

PRONUNCIATION: Round and protrude lips tensely. Do not let the sound glide as in English. Make it short and abrupt. It might help first saying the French sound [e] (see Chapter 7), then rounding and protruding the lips while still trying to say [e].

EXAMPLES FROM THIS CHAPTER: **deuxième   eux**
                              deux   un peu
                              bleu   yeux

2.   Sound (Phonetic Symbol): [œ]

SPELLING: **eu, œu, œ (+il), eu (+il), ue (+il)**

ENGLISH SOUND RESEMBLED: Vowel sound in words *putt* or *cup*.

PRONUNCIATION: Open mouth wider than for [ø] sound. Do not let the sound glide as in English. Keep it short and abrupt. It might help first saying the French sound [ɛ] (see Chapter 7), then rounding and protruding the lips, while still trying to say [ɛ].

EXAMPLES FROM THIS CHAPTER: **douleur   mal de cœur**
                              peur   œil
                              docteur   (also: feuille, fauteuil)

NOTES:

1. The spelling **eu** is pronounced [ø] when it is the final sound of a syllable, as in **peu, deux, courageux, deuxième,** or when it is followed by the consonant sounds [d], [t], [z], [ʒ], [k], as in **courageuse.**

2. The spelling **eu** is pronounced [œ] when it occurs in a syllable ending in a consonant sound other than [d], [t], [z], [ʒ], [k]. Examples: **docteur, heure, acteur.**

3. The spelling **œu** is pronounced [œ] when followed by a pronounced consonant, (as in

œuf [œf], **hors-d'œuvre** [ɔrdœvr], **bœuf** [bœf]). It is pronounced [ø] when it is the final sound of a syllable (as in **des œufs** [ø]).

IMPROVISATION

Complétez ce dialogue. Employez le vocabulaire et les structures de la leçon:

LE DENTISTE: Asseyez-vous dans le fauteuil, je vous prie. Alors, qu'est-ce qui ne va pas?
VOUS: _____
LE DENTISTE: _____
VOUS: _____
LE DENTISTE: _____
VOUS: _____
LE DENTISTE: _____
VOUS: Aïe!!! _____

PROJET

Prepare your own dental history: dental visits, cavities filled, teeth pulled, X-rays, etc. Utilize the vocabulary and structures of the **Dialogue** and **Expansion** sections of this lesson.

ACTIVITÉ

Everyone will have an eye examination in class. Begin by asking your partner some pertinent questions. See the **Expansion** and **Exercices** sections of this chapter for vocabulary to use, such as: **Portez-vous des lunettes? des verres de contact? Êtes-vous myope? presbyte? astigmate?** Then test your partner's vision. Using the blackboard or a sheet of paper, make a simple eye chart **(un tableau),** with rows of letters or numbers of different sizes. Ask:

> **Regardez ce tableau.**
> **Pouvez-vous lire la première ligne?**
> **Lisez la deuxième ligne.**
> **C'est un E ou un F? etc.**

LE CHEVALIER DU GUET

Qu'est-ce qui passe i - ci si tard, Com - pa - gnons de la Mar - jo - lai - ne? Qu'est-ce qui passe i - ci si tard, Gai, gai, des - sus le quai?_____

2. C'est le chevalier du guet
   Compagnons de la Marjolaine,
   C'est le chevalier du guet,
   Gai, gai, dessus le quai.

3. Que demande le chevalier?
   Compagnons, etc.

4. Une fille à marier,
   Compagnons, etc.

ADJECTIVES: HOROSCOPE SIGNS

Sous quel signe astrologique êtes-vous né(e)?
—Je suis né(e) sous le signe _____ .

du bélier	*Aries*	de la balance	*Libra*
du taureau	*Taurus*	du scorpion	*Scorpio*
des gémeaux	*Gemini*	du sagittaire	*Sagittarius*
du cancer	*Cancer, Moonchild*	du capricorne	*Capricorn*
du lion	*Leo*	du verseau	*Aquarius*
de la vierge	*Virgo*	des poissons	*Pisces*

LES GÉMEAUX   21 MAI—21 JUIN

changeant(e)	*changeable*	imaginatif / imaginative	*imaginative*
enthousiaste	*enthusiastic*	ingénieux / ingénieuse	*ingenious*
habile	*skillful, clever*	intelligent(e)	*intelligent*

CANCER   22 JUIN — 22 JUILLET

complexe	*complex*	sentimental(e)	*sentimental*
imaginatif / imaginative	*imaginative*	timide	*timid*
sensible	*sensitive*		

LION   23 JUILLET — 22 AOÛT

ambitieux / ambitieuse	*ambitious*	fier / fière	*proud*
énergique	*energetic*	généreux / généreuse	*generous*
extraverti(e)	*extroverted*	optimiste	*optimistic*

VIERGE   23 AOÛT — 23 SEPTEMBRE

économe	*economical*	pratique	*practical*
intellectual / intellectuelle	*intellectual*	travailleur / travailleuse	*hardworking*
méthodique	*methodical*		

BALANCE   24 SEPTEMBRE — 22 OCTOBRE

affectueux / affectueuse	*affectionate*	bien équilibré(e)	*well-balanced, well-adjusted*
charmant(e)	*charming*	logique	*logical*
diplomate	*diplomatic*	raisonnable	*reasonable*

SCORPION   23 OCTOBRE — 21 NOVEMBRE

courageux / courageuse	*courageous*	loyal(e)	*loyal*
énergique	*energetic*	passionné(e)	*passionate*
indépendant(e)	*independent*		

SAGITTAIRE   22 NOVEMBRE — 21 DÉCEMBRE

amical(e)	*friendly*	philosophe	*philosophical*
impulsif / impulsive	*impulsive*	sociable	*sociable*
optimiste	*optimistic*	sportif / sportive	*athletic*

CAPRICORNE   22 DÉCEMBRE — 20 JANVIER

actif / active	*active*	persévérant(e)	*persevering*
ambitieux / ambitieuse	*ambitious*	pratique	*practical*
économe	*economical*		

VERSEAU   21 JANVIER — 19 FÉVRIER

humanitaire	*humanitarian*	intelligent(e)	*intelligent*
idéaliste	*idealistic*	libéral(e)	*liberal*

POISSONS   20 FÉVRIER — 20 MARS

doux / douce	*gentle, kind*	patient(e)	*patient*
généreux / généreuse	*generous*	romantique	*romantic*
mélancolique	*melancholy*	sage	*wise*

BÉLIER   21 MARS—19 AVRIL

ambitieux / ambitieuse	*ambitious*	enthousiaste	*enthusiastic*
courageux / courageuse	*courageous*	optimiste	*optimistic*
énergique	*energetic*	sincère	*sincere*

TAUREAU   20 AVRIL—20 MAI

affectueux / affectueuse	*affectionate*	persévérant(e)	*persevering*
généreux / généreuse	*generous*	pratique	*practical*
patient(e)	*patient*		

SPRINGBOARDS FOR CONVERSATION

1. Sous quel signe astrologique êtes-vous né(e)?
   Je suis né(e) sous le signe _____.
2. Quelles sont vos qualités selon votre signe du zodiaque? Êtes-vous d'accord?
   Je suis _____.
3. Quels sont les traits de caractère de votre mère? de votre père? de votre sœur? de votre frère? de votre mari / femme / meilleur(e) ami(e)? etc.
   Il / Elle est _____.
4. Sous quel signe est né votre père? votre frère? Sous quel signe est née votre mère? votre sœur? etc. Sa personnalité correspond-elle à son signe?
   Il / Elle est né(e) sous le signe _____.
   Oui / Non. Il / Elle est _____.
5. Quels sont les traits de caractère de Monsieur / Madame / Mademoiselle . . . ? de votre voisin(e) de gauche / de droite? Devinez sous quel signe il / elle est né(e).
   Il / Elle est _____.
   Je crois qu'il / elle est né(e) sous le signe _____.
6. Sous quel signe est né(e) Monsieur / Madame / Mademoiselle . . . ?
   Il / Elle est né(e) sous le signe _____.
7. Devinez sous quel signe est né votre professeur.
   Il / Elle est né(e) sous le signe _____. Car il / elle est _____.
8. Votre personnalité correspond-elle à votre signe?
   Oui, je suis _____.
   Non, je ne suis pas _____. Je suis plutôt _____.
9. Consultez-vous votre horoscope dans le journal? Tous les jours? Parfois? Jamais? Souvent?

PROJETS

1. What are the horoscope (astrological) signs of your three favorite people? (Relatives, friends, celebrities, etc.) What are their personality traits according to their signs? Do you agree? Do they? List and discuss.
2. Using the vocabulary of this lesson, make captions for photos of people. Use magazines, newspapers or photographs you have on hand. For example: **Il est énergique. Elle est sociable. Il est dynamique,** etc.

ACTIVITÉ

Have a fortune telling session in class. Everyone has a partner. One partner, endowed with special mystical powers, tells the fortune of the other. Then the roles are reversed. For example: **Je regarde dans ma boule de cristal . . . Sous quel signe êtes-vous né(e? . . . Ah, oui . . . Vous êtes né(e) sous le signe de la vierge . . . Vous êtes économe . . . Alors, vous serez riche . . . Vous êtes travailleur / travailleuse . . . Alors, vous serez célèbre et heureux / heureuse,** etc.

THE FAMILY

Combien êtes-vous dans votre famille?
—Dans ma famille, nous sommes _____ .

1. **un**	4. **quatre**	7. **sept**
2. **deux**	5. **cinq**	8. **huit**
3. **trois**	6. **six**	9. **neuf**

—Voyons. Il y a _____ .

mon mari	*my husband*
ma femme	*my wife*
moi	*I (me)*

PARENTS

ma mère / maman	*my mother / mom*
mon père / papa	*my father / dad*
mon parrain	*my godfather*
ma marraine	*my godmother*
mon beau-père	*my father-in-law / stepfather*
ma belle-mère	*my mother-in-law / stepmother*

mes beaux-parents   my parents-in-law
mes parents   *my parents / relatives*

CHILDREN

mon enfant   *my child*
mes enfants   *my children*
ma fille   *my daughter*
mon fils   *my son*
mon beau-fils   *my stepson / son-in-law*
ma belle-fille *my stepdaughter / daughter-in-law*
ma bru   *my daughter-in-law*
mon gendre   *my son-in-law*
mon filleul   *my godson*
ma filleule   *my goddaughter*

SISTERS AND BROTHERS

ma sœur (aînée, cadette)   *my sister (older, younger)*
mon frère (aîné, cadet)   *my brother (older, younger)*
mon frère jumeau   *my twin brother*
ma sœur jumelle   *my twin sister*
ma belle-sœur   *my sister-in-law*
mon beau-frère   *my brother-in-law*
ma demi-sœur   *my half-sister, stepsister*
mon demi-frère   *my half-brother, stepbrother*

GRANDPARENTS AND GRANDCHILDREN

mes arrière-grands-parents   *my great grandparents*
mon arrière-grand-père   *my great grandfather*
mon arrière-grand-mère   *my great grandmother*
mes grands-parents   *my grandparents*
mon grand-père (maternel / paternel)   *my grandfather* (maternal / paternal)
ma grand-mère (maternelle / paternelle)   *my grandmother* (maternal / paternal)
mes petits-enfants   *my grandchildren*
mon petit-fils   *my grandson*
ma petite-fille   *my granddaughter*
mes arrière-petits-enfants   *my great grand-children*

AUNTS, UNCLES, ETC.

ma tante   *my aunt*
mon oncle   *my uncle*
mon cousin   *my cousin (m.)*
ma cousine   *my cousin (f.)*

mon cousin germain	*my first cousin*
mon neveu	*my nephew*
ma nièce	*my niece*

OTHERS

mon chat / ma chatte	*my cat*
mon cheval	*my horse*
mon chien / ma chienne	*my dog*
mon lapin	*my rabbit*
ma perruche	*my parakeet*
ma plante	*my plant*
mon poisson rouge	*my goldfish*
mon serin	*my canary*
ma tortue	*my turtle*

—**Je suis** _____.

le benjamin / la benjamine (de la famille)	*the youngest (in the family)*
célibataire	*single*
divorcé(e)	*divorced*
marié(e)	*married*
veuf / veuve	*widowed*
fils / fille unique	*an only child*

SPRINGBOARDS FOR CONVERSATION

1. Combien êtes-vous dans votre famille?
   Dans ma famille, nous sommes _____. Il y a _____.
2. Combien de cousins / de sœurs / de frères / d'enfants avez-vous?
   J'ai _____ cousins / sœurs / frères / enfants.
   Je n'ai pas de cousins. Je n'ai pas de sœurs, etc.
3. Comment s'appelle votre frère? votre père? votre oncle? etc.
   Il s'appelle _____.
4. Comment s'appelle votre tante? votre mère? votre sœur? etc.
   Elle s'appelle _____.
5. À qui ressemblez-vous?
   À ma / mon _____.
6. Est-ce que votre famille est grande ou petite?
   Elle est _____.
7. Combien de personnes y a-t-il dans la famille du professeur? de Monsieur . . . ? de
   Madame . . . ? de Mademoiselle . . . ? etc.

8. Êtes-vous marié(e) / célibataire / fils unique / fille unique, etc.?
   Oui, je suis _____ .
   Non, je ne suis pas _____ .

9. Avez-vous un chien? un chat? un cheval? une perruche? etc.
   Oui. J'ai un / une _____ .
   Non. Je n'ai pas de _____ .

10. Qui dans la classe a un chien? un chat? une perruche? etc.

PROJET

Make a family tree (**un arbre généalogique**). Indicate each person's name and his or her relationship to you. Be thorough. Include aunts, uncles, in-laws, etc. Photographs may be attached. For example: **Ma tante s'appelle Henriette. Mon oncle s'appelle Marc,** etc.

On fixe un rendez-vous

Making a Date

Proverbe: Quand le chat n'y est pas, les souris dansent.

Proverb: When the cat's away, the mice will play. (*Literally:* When the cat isn't there, the mice dance.)

«Aimeriez-vous aller dans un cabaret ce soir?»

DIALOGUE

VOTRE AMI(E): Aimeriez-vous aller **au cinéma** ce soir?	YOUR FRIEND: Would you like to go *to the movies* tonight?

au cinéma auto (*Au Canada:* au ciné-parc) dans une boîte de nuit dans un cabaret dans une discothèque au concert au théâtre danser déjeuner / dîner au restaurant voir une exposition au musée	to the drive-in movies to a night club to a cabaret to a discotheque to a concert to the theater dancing have lunch / dinner in a restaurant see an exhibit at the museum

VOUS: **Avec plaisir.**	YOU: *I'd love to.* (*Literally:* With pleasure.)

(Bien) volontiers. Ce serait avec joie. Cela me ferait grand plaisir. C'est une bonne idée. Oui, je veux bien. Je vous remercie, mais je ne suis pas libre.	Gladly. *Literally:* It would be with joy. *Literally:* That would please me greatly. That's a good idea. Yes, I'd like to. Thanks, but I'm not free.

VOTRE AMI(E): Voyons . . . Qu'est-ce qu'on joue? Aimez-vous **les westerns?**	YOUR FRIEND: Let's see. . . . What's playing? Do you like *westerns?*

les actualités
les comédies musicales
les dessins animés
les documentaires
les films d'aventures
les films étrangers (doublés, sous-titrés,
   en version originale)
les films d'amour
les films d'épouvante, les films d'horreur
les films policiers
les vieux films muets
	newsreels
	musical comedy
	cartoons
	documentaries
	adventure films
	foreign films (dubbed, sub-titled,
	   original version)
	love stories
	horror films
	detective films
	old silent movies

VOUS: Franchement, je n'aime pas tellement les westerns. VOTRE AMI(E): Vous savez, nous pouvons toujours **écouter de la musique.**	YOU: Frankly, I don't like westerns all that much. YOUR FRIEND: You know, we can always *listen to music.*

jouer aux cartes écouter la radio regarder la télévision regarder un film / un match à la télé causer jouer aux échecs jouer aux dames	play cards listen to the radio watch television watch a film / a (sports) game on (the) T.V. chat play chess play checkers

Aimez-vous **la musique classique?**   Do you like *classical music?*

le jazz la musique pop la musique disco	jazz pop music disco music

VOUS: Oui, beaucoup.

VOTRE AMI(E). Alors, je viendrai vous chercher vers sept heures.

VOUS: D'accord. Merci beaucoup. À plus tard.

YOU: Yes, a lot.

YOUR FRIEND: Then, I'll come get you around seven o'clock.

YOU: Fine. Thanks a lot. See you later.

EXERCICES D'APPLICATION

*1. Dites que vous aimeriez aller au cinéma ce soir . . . que vous aimeriez aller au théâtre ce soir . . . que cela vous ferait grand plaisir . . . que cela vous ferait grand plaisir d'aller au concert . . . que vous n'aimez pas tellement les westerns . . . que vous n'aimez pas beaucoup les films policiers . . . que vous aimez beaucoup les films étrangers . . . que vous aimez regarder la télévision . . . que vous aimez écouter de la musique . . . que vous aimez la musique classique.

2. Put the preceding **Dialogue** into the less formal, **tu** form of address. Start with «**Ça te plairait d'aller au cinéma ce soir?** . . . » or, «**Veux-tu aller au cinéma ce soir?**» or, «**J'aimerais aller au cinéma ce soir, et toi?**»

VERBES IRRÉGULIERS: sortir, partir

sortir	*to go out, to leave*	
Le présent:	**je sors**	**nous sortons**
	tu sors	**vous sortez**
	il / elle sort	**ils / elles sortent**
Le participe passé: **sorti(e)** (conjugué avec **être**)		
La base du futur et du conditionnel: **sortir-**		

---

partir:	*to depart, to leave*	

Le présent:	**je pars**	**nous partons**
	tu pars	**vous partez**
	il / elle part	**ils / elles partent**

Le participe passé: **parti(e)** (conjugué avec **être**)
La base du futur et du conditionnel: **partir-**

STRUCTURES

1. **Sortir, quitter, partir, laisser** *(to leave)*

   a. **sortir:** *to leave, to go out, to go out* (on a date); **sortir de:** *to go out of, to get out of*

   Pourquoi **est-elle sortie de** la classe?
   Why did she leave (go out of) the class?

   À quelle heure **sortez-vous du** bureau?
   What time do you get out of the office?

   Aimeriez-vous **sortir** avec moi ce soir?
   Would you like to go out with me tonight?

   Sortir is conjugated with **avoir** when it is used transitively (that is, with a direct object), to mean *to take out:*

   Avez-vous sorti la voiture?
   Have you taken out the car?

   b. **quitter:** *to leave* (to go away from a person or place). This verb always takes a direct object.

   À quelle heure **avez-vous quitté** la maison?
   What time did you leave the house?

   Ne me quittez pas!
   Don't leave me!

   c. **partir:** *to leave* (to depart); **partir pour:** *to leave for*

   Je vais **partir** demain.
   I'm going to leave tomorrow.

   Il est parti pour le Canada hier soir.
   He left for Canada last night.

d. laisser: *to leave behind*

> **J'ai laissé** mon livre à la maison.
> *I left my book at home.*

2.   L'Imparfait

a. Formation

The **imparfait** of all regular and irregular verbs (*except* **être**) is formed by dropping the letters **-ons** from the **nous** form of the present tense and adding the appropriate endings: **-ais, -ais, -ait, -ions, -iez, -aient** (the same endings as those used for the conditional tense):

INFINITIF	LE PRÉSENT →	LA BASE DE L'IMPARFAIT
aimer	nous aim**ons** →	**aim-**
finir	nous finiss**ons** →	**finiss-**
attendre	nous attend**ons** →	**attend-**
avoir	nous av**ons** →	**av-**
prendre	nous pren**ons** →	**pren-**

IMPARFAIT		
VERBES EN -er	**VERBES EN -ir**	**VERBES EN -re**
aimer	finir	attendre
j'aim**ais**	je finiss**ais**	j'attend**ais**
tu aim**ais**	tu finiss**ais**	tu attend**ais**
il / elle aim**ait**	il / elle finiss**ait**	il / elle attend**ait**
nous aim**ions**	nous finiss**ions**	nous attend**ions**
vous aim**iez**	vous finiss**iez**	vous attend**iez**
il / elles aim**aient**	ils / elles finiss**aient**	ils / elle attend**aient**

être
j'étais
tu étais
il / elle était
nous étions
vous étiez
ils / elles étaient

b. Uses

The **imparfait** usually means *was* _____*ing* or *used to* _____ (*I was going, we were talking, I used to like,* etc.).

1. To express an action that was going on in the past at the time when another action took place:

   J'allais au cinéma quand je l'ai rencontré.
   I was going to the movies when I met him.

   Il faisait beau lorsque j'ai quitté la maison.
   It was nice weather when I left home.

2. To express repeated or habitual actions in the past.

   J'allais au cinéma chaque samedi.
   I used to go to the movies every Saturday.

   Je regardais le télévision beaucoup.
   I used to watch / I watched (habitual action, **l'imparfait**) *television a lot.*

   But:

   J'ai regardé la télévision hier soir.
   I watched (not habitual action, **le passé composé**) *television last night.*

3. With the verbs **avoir** and **être** in sentences which relate descriptions, age, or time:

   Descriptions:

J'avais soif.	*I was thirsty.*
J'étais malade.	*I was sick.*
Il était très content.	*He was very happy.*
Il y avait beaucoup de monde.	*There were a lot of people.*
J'avais de l'argent.	*I had some money.*
Il avait l'air fatigué.	*He looked tired.*

Age:

Il avait vingt ans.	*He was twenty years old.*
Il était jeune.	*He was young.*

Time:

Il était trois heures.	*It was 3 o'clock.*
C'était en avril.	*It was in April.*

Avoir and **être** are used in the **passé composé** to indicate what has happened in the past. For example:

J'ai eu un accident.	*I had an accident.*
J'ai été en France.	*I've been to France.*

4. With verbs expressing attitudes, feelings, or beliefs. The following verbs and expressions tend to be used in the **imparfait** rather than in the **passé composé:**

croire	*to believe, to think*	**Je croyais** que vous étiez au cinéma. *I thought that you were at the movies.*
penser	*to think*	**Je pensais** que vous étiez en France. *I thought that you were in France.*
espérer	*to hope*	**J'espérais** vous voir à l'exposition. *I was hoping to see you at the exhibit.*
vouloir	*to wish, to want*	**Je voulais** aller au cinéma. *I wanted to go to the movies.*
pouvoir	*to be able, can*	**Je ne pouvais pas** aller au théâtre. *I wasn't able to (I couldn't) go to the theater.*
savoir	*to know*	**Je ne savais pas!** *I didn't know!*
avoir peur	*to be afraid*	**J'avais peur** de sortir. *I was afraid to go out.*
avoir envie	*to feel like*	**J'avais envie** de voir un bon film. *I felt like seeing a good film.*
avoir l'intention de	*to intend*	**J'avais l'intention** d'étudier un peu. *I was intending / I intended to study a little*

These verbs and expressions are used, however, in the **passé composé** to relate what has happened in the past. For example:

> **J'ai eu peur.**   *I became frightened.*

3.   Si + l'imparfait, le conditionnel

a. When the main clause of a sentence is in the **conditionnel** (would), the **si** or *if* clause must be in the **imparfait.** (See Chapter 6 to review the formation of the conditional tense.):

> **Si j'étais libre, nous pourrions aller au cinéma.**
> *If I were free, we could go to the movies.*
>
> **Si je savais bien jouer aux cartes, je jouerais avec vous.**
> *If I really knew how to play cards, I would play with you.*
>
> **Je le ferais si je pouvais.**
> *I would do it if I could.*

b. Si + l'imparfait may also mean: *How about . . . ?*

> **Si nous allions au cinéma ce soir?**
> *How about going to the movies tonight?*

EXERCICES DE SYNTHÈSE

A.* *Employez la forme correcte du verbe* **sortir** *au présent:*

1. Je _____ ce soir.
2. Avec qui _____ -vous ce soir?
3. Pourquoi est-ce qu'elle _____ de la classe?
4. À quelle heure _____ -tu?
5. Nous _____ avec des amis.
6. Il _____ de son bureau à huit heures.

B.* *Mettez les phrases de l'Exercice A au passé composé. Puis traduisez:*

C. *Répondez aux questions suivantes par des phrases complètes:*

1. Sortez-vous souvent? Avec qui? avec des amis? avec votre femme / mari? Où allez-vous? au cinéma? au théâtre? au restaurant? au bar? à la discothèque?
2. Sortez-vous le week-end prochain? Avec qui? Où irez-vous?
3. À quelle heure avez-vous quitté votre maison / appartement / chambre ce matin?

4. Votre professeur est-il / elle parti(e) pour la France la semaine dernière? Va-t-il / elle en France cet été?

5. Êtes-vous sorti(e) hier soir? samedi dernier? Avec qui? Où êtes-vous allé(e)?

6. Avec qui aimeriez-vous sortir ce soir?

D.   *Répondez à ces questions basées sur le dialogue:*

1. Préférez-vous le cinéma ou le théâtre?

2. Allez-vous souvent au cinéma? deux fois par semaine? chaque dimanche? rarement? de temps en temps? Avec qui?

3. Aimez-vous les westerns? les films d'épouvante? les films policiers? Beaucoup?

4. Préférez-vous les films étrangers doublés, sous-titrés, ou en version originale?

5. Êtes-vous allé(e) récemment au cinéma? Quel film avez-vous vu? Était-il bon? intéressant? Le recommandez-vous? Avez-vous déjà vu un film français? Lequel? Était-il sous-titré? doublé?

6. Aimez-vous écouter de la musique? seul(e)? avec des amis? dans votre chambre? pendant que vous étudiez? pendant que vous cuisinez? Aimez-vous la musique classique?

7. Regardez-vous la télévision? souvent? de temps en temps? beaucoup? Qu'est-ce que vous regardez?

8. Aimez-vous jouer aux cartes? jouer aux échecs? jouer aux dames?

9. Écoutez-vous la radio? souvent? de temps en temps? rarement? Quels postes préférez-vous? *WCCC-FM? WCDE-AM?* etc.

10. Qu'avez-vous fait hier soir? Avez-vous joué aux cartes? Avez-vous regardé la télévision? Avez-vous écouté de la musique? Êtes-vous allé(e) au cinéma? au théâtre? dans une boîte de nuit?

11. Qu'est-ce que vous allez faire ce soir? jouer aux cartes? regarder la télévision? écouter de la musique? aller au cinéma? etc.

12. Êtes-vous déjà allé(e) au cinéma auto? Où? Quand? Avec qui? Quel film avez-vous vu?

13. Êtes-vous déjà allé(e) au théâtre? Où? Avec qui? Quand?

14. Quel est votre acteur préféré? Quelle est votre actrice préférée?

15. Êtes-vous allé(e) au concert récemment?

16. Avez-vous des billets de théâtre? de concert? etc.

E.*   *Transformez. Employez l'imparfait:*

EXEMPLE: Je regardais la télévision. (Elle)
Elle regardait la télévision.

1. Je regardais un vieux film à la télévision. (Il, Elle, Nous).
2. J'allais au cinéma. (Tu, Nous, Vous)
3. Je jouais aux cartes. (Tu, Il, On)

4. J'aimais beaucoup les westerns. (Il, Elle, Ils, Elles)
5. Je parlais. (Il, Elle, Ils, Elles)

F. *Répondez selon l'indication:*

EXEMPLE: Que faisiez-vous hier soir à dix heures? **(regarder la télévision)**
Hier soir à dix heures, **je regardais la télévision.**

jouer aux cartes, regarder un film à la télévision, écouter la radio, écouter de la musique, jouer aux échecs, jouer aux dames, causer, être au cinéma, être au théâtre, être dans une boîte de nuit, danser, dîner avec des amis, dormir, parler au téléphone

G. *Répondez avec l'imparfait:*

Quand vous étiez jeune. . . .

1. quel était votre acteur préféré? quelle était votre actrice préférée?
2. quel était votre chanteur préféré? quelle était votre chanteuse préférée?
3. aviez-vous beaucoup d'amis?
4. comment s'appelait votre meilleur(e) ami(e)?
5. où habitiez-vous?
6. avec qui sortiez-vous?
7. quels programmes regardiez-vous à la télévision?
8. alliez-vous souvent au cinéma?
9. vouliez-vous être professeur?
10. aviez-vous une collection de disques?
11. étiez-vous timide?
12. de quoi aviez-vous peur? du noir? de vos professeurs?
13. croyiez-vous au Père Noël?
14. preniez-vous des leçons de piano? de guitare?
15. aimiez-vous étudier?
16. travailliez-vous?

H.* *Imaginez que vous êtes à la maison. Vous regardez la télévision. Tout d'un coup, vous entendez un bruit étrange. Vous racontez cet événement à un(e) ami(e). Mettez les phrases au passé en remplaçant le présent par le passé composé ou par l'imparfait, selon le cas:*

Hier soir. . . .

1. Je regarde la télévision.
2. Il est neuf heures.
3. Je suis seul(e).
4. Le programme n'est pas très intéressant.

5. J'entends un bruit étrange.
6. Je vais à la porte.
7. Je vois un homme.
8. Il est jeune.
9. Il a à peu près *(about)* vingt ans.
10. Il a une moustache.
11. Il a l'air bizarre.
12. Je ferme la porte.
13. J'ai peur.
14. Je téléphone à la police.
15. L'homme part.
16. La police arrive.
17. Je n'ai plus peur.

I.   *An exercise using: si + l'imparfait, conditionnel. Ask other class members what they would do if you were to give them a kick:* **Que feriez-vous si je vous donnais un coup de pied?** *Possible responses include:*

Si vous me donniez un coup de pied. . . .

> **je hurlerais** *(yell)*
> **je pleurerais** *(cry)*
> **je crierais «Aïe!»** *(yell ''Ouch!'')*
> **je me fâcherais** *(get angry)*
> **je vous le rendrais** *(kick you back)*
> **je vous donnerais un coup de poing** *(punch you)*
> **je le dirais à ma mère** *(tell my mother on you)*
> **je vous dirais que vous êtes méchant(e)** *(call you mean)*
> **je vous donnerais une claque / une gifle** *(slap you)*
> **je vous accuserais de brutalité** *(accuse you of brutality)*
> **je vous demanderais pourquoi** *(ask you why)*
> **je serais stupéfait(e)** *(be stunned)*
> **je vous mordrais** *(bite you)*
> **je téléphonerais à la police** *(call the police)*

Now ask them what they would do if you were to give them a kiss instead: **Si je vous donnais un baiser, que feriez-vous?** *Possible responses, in addition to those given above, include:*

Si vous me donniez un baiser. . . .

> **je vous le rendrais** *(kiss you back)*
> **je rougirais** *(blush)*
> **je sourirais** *(smile)*

j'en serais très touché(e) *(be very touched)*
je serais content(e) *(be happy)*

For additional practice, review what your classmates have said, using the third person form **(il, elle).**

J.   *Ask another class member any questions you can think of related to going out. For example:* **Êtes-vous sorti(e) hier soir? Allez-vous souvent au cinéma? Aimez-vous les westerns?**, *or even* **Aimeriez-vous sortir avec moi ce soir?**

EXPANSION

TÉLÉVISION

1. **Aimez-vous la publicité à la télévision?**
2. **Quels programmes (quelles émissions) regardez-vous? les actualités? les matchs de baseball? les variétés? les feuilletons (les mélodrames)? les émissions enfantines? les dessins animés? les jeux télévisés? les émissions instructives?**
3. **Combien de chaînes y a-t-il chez vous?**
4. **Allumez (Ouvrez) / Coupez (Fermez) la télévision.**

Do you like the commercials on television?
What shows do you watch? the news? baseball games? variety shows? soap operas? children's shows? cartoons? game shows? educational T.V.?

How many channels do you get?
Turn on / Shut off the television.

THÉÂTRE, CINÉMA

1. **Où se trouve le bureau de location? le vestiaire?**
2. **Y a-t-il des places pour ce soir? Est-ce complet?**
3. **Je voudrais une place à l'orchestre / au balcon. C'est combien?**
4. **À quelle heure commence (se termine) la pièce / le film?**
5. **L'ouvreur / L'ouvreuse: Votre billet, s'il vous plaît. Par ici, s'il vous plaît.**
6. **Puis-je avoir un programme, s'il vous plaît?**
7. **Bravo! Encore!**
8. **Pouvez-vous m'indiquer un bon film?**

Where's the ticket office? the coat room?

Are there any seats left for tonight? Is it full (sold out)?
I would like a seat in the orchestra / balcony. How much is it?
What time does the play / film start (end)?

Usher / Usherette: Your ticket, please. This way, please.
Can I have a program, please?

Hurrah! Encore!
Can you recommend a good film?

9. **Est-ce que le film est en noir et blanc ou en couleur?**   *Is the film in black and white or in color?*

10. **Quelle vedette préférez-vous?**   *Who is your favorite movie star?*

Exercices

   A. *Répondez à ces questions:*

   1. Quels programmes regardez-vous à la télévision?
   2. Quel est votre programme préféré?
   3. Regardez-vous les actualités? Toujours? Parfois?
   4. Aimez-vous la publicité à la télévision?
   5. Combien de chaînes y a-t-il chez vous?
   6. Regardez-vous les émissions de sports à la télévision?
   7. Préférez-vous des places à l'orchestre ou au balcon? Pourquoi?

   B. *Que dites vous. . . .*

   1. quand vous cherchez le bureau de location?
   2. quand vous voulez acheter un programme?
   3. au bureau de location pour savoir s'il y a encore des places?
   4. pour savoir l'heure du film?
   5. pour savoir si le film est en noir et blanc ou en couleur?

PRONONCIATION

1. **Sound (Phonetic Symbol): [a]**

   SPELLING: **a, à**

   ENGLISH SOUND RESEMBLED: Half way between the vowel sounds of *cat* and *cot*.

   PRONUNCIATION: This sound is often referred to as *front a*, since it is produced towards the front of the mouth. Do not let the sound glide as in English. Keep it short and abrupt.

   EXAMPLES FROM THIS CHAPTER: **la**   **jazz**
                                 aller   **d'accord**
                                 ami   **Bravo!**
                                 cela   **chat**

NOTE:

The spellings **oi, oî, oy** indicate the vowel sound [a]. Examples from this lesson: **boîte** [bwat], **v**o**y**ons [vwajɔ̃], **j**oie [ʒwa], **s**oir [swar].

2. **Sound (Phonetic Symbol): [ɑ]**

SPELLING:	**â, ât, as, a (+ ille), ah** (only in **Ah!**)
ENGLISH SOUND RESEMBLED:	Vowel sound in words *car* and *hot*.
PRONUNCIATION:	Since this sound [ɑ] is produced farther back in the mouth than the vowel sound [a], it is often referred to as *back a*. Do not prolong the sound.
EXAMPLES FROM THIS CHAPTER:	**thé**â**tre, p**a**s, je p**a**sserai.**

NOTE:

Although we have distinguished here between the vowel sounds [a] and [ɑ], there is a growing tendency in present-day French to ignore this distinction. An intermediary vowel sound is frequently employed for both cases.

IMPROVISATION

Vous invitez un(e) ami(e) à passer la soirée avec vous. Vous pourrez ou sortir ou rester chez vous. Demandez à votre ami(e) ses préférences.

Vous: _____
Votre Ami(e): _____
Vous: _____
Votre Ami(e): _____
Vous: _____
Votre Ami(e): _____
Vous: _____
Votre Ami(e): _____

PROJETS

1. On the opposite page is a typical television schedule. Read the program listings. Check off those broadcasts which you feel you might be interested in watching.
2. What have you done socially during the last month? Make a personal diary of movies, plays, concerts, etc. you have attended: where and when they were held, your companion(s) for the evening, where you went afterwards, and so forth.

ACTIVITÉ

Using the vocabulary of this lesson: make a date to go to the theater with a classmate, buy tickets from a student ticket seller, and be seated by a student usher. (*N.B.* In France, it is customary to tip the usher.) Plays seen can be skits performed by class members, based on **Improvisations** sections of the preceding chapters.

MARDI  22 AOÛT

12.30 QUOI DE NEUF ?
Présentation de Patrick Lecocq

12.45 A 2 PREMIÈRE ÉDITION

13.25 TOM ET JERRY
Ⓙ
Dessin animé

13.35 LES ARPENTS VERTS
Série américaine
UN CADEAU MAGNIFIQUE

Oliver Wendell Douglas	Eddie Albert
Lisa	Eva Gabor
M. Haney	Pat Buttram
La mère d'Oliver	Eleonor Audley
Eb	Tommy Lester

Pour l'anniversaire d'Oliver, Lisa a acheté un magnifique tracteur.

14.00 AUJOURD'HUI MADAME
HISTOIRE DE L'AMOUR
ET DE LA SEXUALITÉ
Une émission de Valérie Manuel
Présentation de Valérie Manuel
et Jacques Garat
Réalisation de Jean Roques
Neuvième émission

COMMENT,
DANS CETTE FIN DU XXᵉ SIÈCLE,
SONT·VÉCUS
L'AMOUR ET LA SEXUALITÉ

Avec **Marie-Françoise Hans** et **Gilles Lapouge**, coauteurs de « Les Femmes, la Pornographie et l'Erotisme » (Le Seuil), **Alain Finkielkraut**, écrivain; le docteur **Jacques Waynberg**, sexologue, **Judith Belladonna**, psychanalyste, **Régine Deforges**, éditeur et écrivain.

Diffusé en avril 1978

15.00 DROLES DE DAMES
Série américaine
MEURTRE A L'HOPITAL
Scénario d'Edward J. Lakso
Réalisation de Bob Kelljan

Jaclyn Smith, Kate Jackson, Farah Fawcett-Majors.

Sabrina	Kate Jackson
Jill	Farrah Fawcett-Majors
Kelly	Jaclyn Smith
Bosley	David Doyle

Diffusé en janvier 1978

Un mystérieux personnage terrorise les infirmières de nuit d'un grand hôpital. M. Charlie demande à son équipe de choc d'élucider cette affaire. Jill et Kelly s'introduisent dans l'hôpital, se faisant passer pour des élèves infirmières et Sabrina pour une journaliste...

15.50 SPORTS
En direct de Versailles
HOCKEY SUR GAZON
COUPE DU MONDE JUNIORS
ALLEMAGNE-PAKISTAN
Commentaires d'Alain Teulère
Réalisation de Gérard Van der Gucht

Le hockey sur gazon, sport méconnu, connaît un renouveau en France. Depuis plusieurs saisons, ses résultats montrent qu'il progresse au niveau mondial. Ainsi, chez les juniors, la France s'est classée quatrième de la Coupe d'Europe (remportée par les Pays-Bas). Il est donc logique de trouver en France, à Versailles, l'organisation de la première Coupe du monde juniors (22 août au 2 septembre). La télévision s'est intéressée à cet événement — chose impensable, il y a peu — et nous pourrons suivre les principales rencontres de ce championnat.

En direct de Saint-Gervais
PATINAGE ARTISTIQUE
GRAND PRIX DE SAINT-GERVAIS
**Commentaires de Léon Zitrone
et Jean Marquet**
Réalisation de Jean-René Vivet
Voir la présentation page 21

18.00 RÉCRÉ A2
Ⓙ
LES QUAT'Z'AMIS
WATTO WATTOO
L'Alimentation
LES CONTES JAPONAIS
Dessin animé
La Puissance du vent et du soleil.

18.30 C'EST LA VIE
LETTRES OUVERTES A L'AN 2000
RECETTES A HISTOIRES
LA BOURGOGNE

**18.55 DES CHIFFRES
ET DES LETTRES**

19.20 Actualités régionales

**19.45 LES TROIS CAMÉRAS
DE L'ÉTÉ**
Avec **Jean Ferrat,
Eddy Mitchell, Michel Fugain,
Claudia Barry**

20.00 JOURNAL

J'AI DU BON TABAC

J'ai du bon ta - bac dans ma ta - ba -

tiè - re. J'ai du bon ta - bac, tu n'en au - ras pas.

J'en   ai   du   fin   et   du   bien   râ - pé,
Mais   ce   n'est   pas   pour   ton   vi - lain   nez.

10

PASTIMES, SPORTS, HOBBIES, ENTERTAINMENT

Qu'est-ce que vous aimez faire?
—**J'aime** _____ .

aller à la pêche / pêcher	*go fishing*
aller à l'opéra	*go to the opera*
aller au ballet	*go to the ballet*
aller au cinéma	*go to the movies*
aller au concert	*go to a concert*
aller aux courses	*go to the races*
aller au musée	*go to a museum*
aller au théâtre	*go to the theater*
aller voir des amis	*go see friends*
assister à ma classe de français	*go to my French class*
assister à un match de football / de baseball	*go to a football game / a baseball game*
bavarder avec des amis	*chat with friends*

bricoler	*putter around / do odd jobs*
causer	*chat*
chanter	*sing*
chantonner / fredonner	*hum*
conduire ma voiture (à toute vitesse)	*drive my car (fast)*
coudre / faire de la couture	*sew*
courir	*run*
danser (dans une boîte de nuit)	*dance (in a night club)*
dépenser de l'argent	*spend money*
dessiner	*draw*
dîner au restaurant	*eat out*
dormir	*sleep*
écouter des disques	*listen to records*
écouter de la musique	*listen to music*
écouter la radio	*listen to the radio*
écrire des lettres	*write letters*
étudier le français	*study French*
être en plein air	*be outdoors*
faire des achats	*go shopping*
faire du bateau	*go boating*
faire de la bicyclette / du vélo	*go biking*
faire de la broderie	*embroider*
faire du camping	*go camping*
faire du cheval	*go horseback riding*
faire des courses	*run errands*
faire du crochet	*crochet*
faire la cuisine / cuisiner	*cook*
faire des exercices	*do exercises*
fair du footing, du jogging	*run / jog*
faire du lèche-vitrines	*go window shopping*
faire de la moto	*ride a motorcycle*
faire des mots-croisés	*do crossword puzzles*
faire de la musique	*make music*
faire un pique-nique	*go on a picnic*
faire des projets	*make plans*
faire de longues promenades à pied	*hike*
faire une promenade	*go for a walk*
faire des rêveries	*daydream*
fair du ski	*ski*
faire du ski de fond / de randonnée	*cross country ski*
faire du ski nautique	*water ski*
faire un somme / la sieste	*nap*
faire du sport	*play / do sports*
faire un tour en auto / en voiture	*go for a ride in a car*
faire des vers	*write poetry*

faire de la voile	*go sailing*
fumer des cigarettes / des cigares / une pipe	*smoke cigarettes / cigars / a pipe*
jouer au base-ball	*play baseball*
jouer au billard	*play billiards / pool*
jouer aux boules	*bowl*
jouer au bridge	*play bridge*
jouer aux cartes	*play cards*
jouer aux dames	*play checkers*
jouer aux échecs	*play chess*
jouer au football (américain)	*play football*
jouer au golf	*play golf*
jouer de la guitare	*play guitar*
jouer au jacquet	*play backgammon*
jouer du piano	*play piano*
jouer au ping-pong	*play ping-pong*
jouer au tennis	*play tennis*
jouer avec mon chien / avec mes enfants / avec mon enfant / avec mes petits-enfants	*play with my dog / children / child / grandchildren*
lire le journal / des revues / des romans / des vers	*read the newspaper / magazines / novels / poetry*
manger	*eat*
nager	*swim*
organiser / donner une soirée / une réception	*give a party*
parler (au téléphone)	*talk (on the phone)*
partir en week-end	*go away for the weekend*
passer une soirée avec de bons amis	*spend an evening with good friends*
prendre un bain / une douche	*take a bath / shower*
prendre un bain de soleil	*sunbathe*
prendre des photos	*take pictures*
prendre un verre avec un(e) ami(e)	*have a drink with a friend*
patiner	*skate*
recevoir des amis (à déjeuner, à dîner)	*have friends over (for lunch, for dinner)*
regarder la télévision	*watch television*
restaurer les meubles anciens	*refinish old furniture*
sculpter	*sculpt*
sortir avec un(e) ami(e) / avec mon mari / ma femme	*go out with a friend / with my husband / wife*
jardiner / travailler dans le jardin	*garden*
tricoter	*knit*
voyager	*travel*

SPRINGBOARDS FOR CONVERSATION

1. Qu'est-ce que vous aimez faire? Quand? (le soir, l'après-midi, le matin, pendant la semaine, le week-end, pendant les vacances, avant de vous coucher, avant le dîner, après de dîner, etc.) Toujours? Régulièrement? Souvent? Parfois? De temps en temps? Rarement?

2. Qu'est-ce que le professeur aime faire? Madame . . . ? Monsieur . . . ? Mademoiselle . . . ? Votre voisin(e) de gauche /de droite? etc.
   Il / Elle aime _____ .

3. Qui dans la classe aime écouter de la musique? jouer au golf? etc. Qui d'autre?

4. Qu'est-ce que vous avez fait hier soir? Ce matin? la semaine passée? etc.

5. Qui dans la classe sait jouer de la guitare? du piano? etc.

6. Qu'est-ce que vous n'aimez pas faire? Pourquoi?
   Je n'aime pas _____ .

7. Qu'est-ce que vous aimez faire seul(e)? Avec un(e) ami(e)? En groupe?
   J'aime _____ .

8. Qu'aimez-vous faire lorsqu'il fait beau? lorsqu'il pleut?
   J'aime _____ .

9. Lorsque vous vous sentez un peu déprimé(e) ou triste, que faites-vous pour vous distraire?
   J'aime _____ .

10. Qu'aimeriez-vous apprendre à faire? Qu'avez-vous appris à faire récemment?
    J'aimerais apprendre à _____ .
    J'ai appris à _____ .

11. Qu'aimeriez-vous faire après cette classe? Avec qui?
    J'aimerais _____ .

12. Qu'est-ce que vous allez faire aujourd'hui? cet après-midi? ce soir? cette semaine?
    Je vais _____ .

13. Que faites-vous d'habitude le weekend? le samedi soir? chaque jour? en hiver? en été?

14. Quand êtes-vous heureux / heureuse?
    Je suis heureux / heureuse lorsque je _____ .

15. Avez-vous déjà pris des leçons de tennis? de piano? etc. Quand?

16. Faites-vous du sport? souvent? de temps en temps? chaque jour?
    Je fais du /de la _____ .
    Je joue au _____ .

17. Quels sports pratique le professeur? Monsieur . . . ? Madame . . . ? Mademoiselle . . . ? votre voisin(e) de gauche /de droite? etc.
    Il / Elle fait du /de la _____ .
    Il/ Elle joue au _____ .

18. Avez-vous déjà fait du bateau? du camping? Avez-vous déjà joué au golf? au jacquet? etc. Quand? Où? Avec qui?

19. Qu'est-ce que vous aimiez *(used to like)* faire quand vous étiez jeune?
    J'aimais _____ .
20. Qu'avez-vous cessé de faire *(stopped doing)?* Pourquoi?
    J'ai cessé de _____ .

PROJETS

1. Make a list of all the activities from this lesson which you have done in the past two weeks.
2. Make another list of all those activities which you did on your last vacation.
3. Using illustrations clipped from magazines, caption each with the activity depicted.

ACTIVITÉ

Everyone has a partner. One partner acts out a pastime, sport, hobby or form of entertainment selected from the list given in this **Entracte,** while the other tries to guess which one it is. Then roles are reversed. Alternative: One class member at a time acts out a chosen pastime, sport, or hobby while the whole class guesses. For example: **Vous nagez! Vous faites du ski! Vous faites du cheval!** etc.

Chapitre

11

Au téléphone	On the Telephone

Proverbe: Il n'est pire sourd que celui qui ne veut entendre.	Proverb: No one is deafer than he who refuses to listen.

DIALOGUE
EXERCICES D'APPLICATION
VERBE IRRÉGULIER: **recevoir**
STRUCTURES:
1. Interrogative Pronouns
2. Disjunctive or Intensive Pronouns
EXERCICES DE SYNTHÈSE
EXPANSION: **Au téléphone**
PRONONCIATION: [p], [t], [k]
IMPROVISATION
PROJET
ACTIVITÉ
CHANSON: **Il court, il court, le furet**

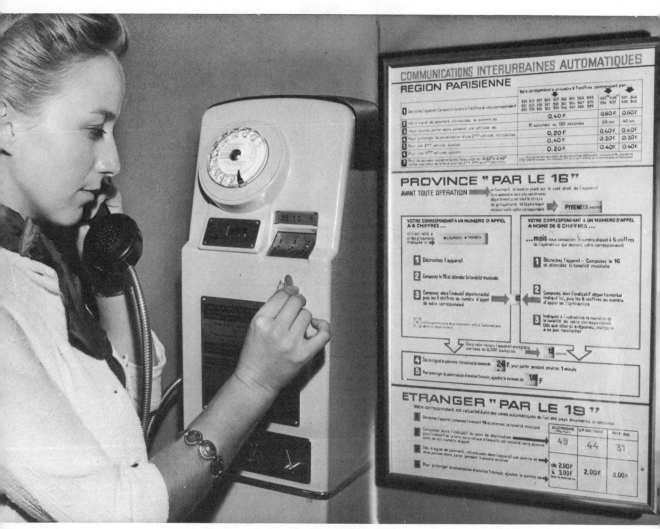

«Ca sonne. On ne répond pas.»

DIALOGUE

Le / La Standardiste: Renseignements, j'écoute.

Vous: Pourriez-vous me donner le numéro de Monsieur X, 20, rue Manin à Paris? Je ne trouve pas son numéro dans l'annuaire.

Le / La Standardiste: C'est le 765.43.21. (Sept cent soixante-cinq / quarante-trois / vingt et un.)

Un / Une Secrétaire: Allô. Le bureau de Monsieur X, Ici Madame / Mademoiselle / Monsieur _____, le / la secrétaire de Monsieur X.[1]

Vous: Bonjour, Madame / Mademoiselle / Monsieur, Je voudrais parler à Monsieur X, s'il vous plaît.

Le / La Secrétaire: Ne quittez pas, je vous prie. Je vais voir s'il est là. C'est de la part de qui?

Vous: De _____.
(votre nom)

Le / La Secrétaire: Monsieur X est **sorti pour le moment.**

OPERATOR: Directory assistance. May I help you? (*Literally:* I'm listening.)

YOU: Operator, could you give me the phone number for Mister X, 20 Manin Street in Paris? I can't find his number in the phone book.

OPERATOR: It's 765-4321. (*Note that in French the number is given as follows: seven hundred sixty-five / forty-three / twenty-one.*)

SECRETARY: Hello, Mister X's office, Mrs. / Miss / Mr. _____ speaking. Mister X's secretary.[1]

YOU: Hello. I would like to speak with Mister X, please.

SECRETARY: Hold on, please. I'll see if he is in. Who is calling please?

YOU: _____.
(your name)

SECRETARY: Mister X is *out for the moment.*

---

en réunion
absent
en vacances
au téléphone
occupé
parti déjeuner

in conference / in a meeting
out
on vacation
on the phone
busy
out to lunch

Vous: Quand sera-t-il de retour?

Le / La Secrétaire: **Je ne sais pas exactement.**

YOU: When will he be back?

SECRETARY: *I don't know exactly.*

Dans un instant.
Dans quelques minutes.
Dans une heure.
Avant cinq heures.
Vers six heures.
Pas avant sept heures.
Demain.

In a moment.
In a few minutes.
In an hour.
Before five o'clock.
Around six o'clock.
Not before seven o'clock.
Tomorrow.

---

1. A switchboard operator might answer by identifying the name of the company or business: «**Société Laroque, bonjour.**» Or you, the caller, might begin by verifying: «**Allô, L'Hôtel Pierre?**» or «**Allô, le 765.43.21?**»

Puis-je prendre un message?	Can I take a message?
Vous: Oui, s'il vous plaît. Veuillez lui dire que j'ai appelé.	You: Yes, please, Please tell him (that) I called.
Le / La Secrétaire: Certainement. Au revoir, Monsieur / Madame / Mademoiselle.	Secretary: Certainly. Good-by.

EXERCICES D'APPLICATION

*1. Dites à la standardiste que vous voulez le numéro de téléphone de votre professeur . . . que vous ne trouvez pas son numéro dans l'annuaire . . . que vous voulez le 765.43.21 à Paris.

2. Qu'est-ce que vous répondez quand on vous dit: «C'est de la part de qui?» . . . «Monsieur X est sorti pour le moment» . . . «Puis-je prendre un message?» . . . «Quel est votre numéro de téléphone?»

3. Vous êtes le / la secrétaire de Madame X. Donnez quatre raisons pour lesquelles Madame X ne peut pas recevoir le client qui téléphone.

VERBE IRRÉGULIER: recevoir

recevoir	*to receive*		
Le présent:	**je reçois**	**nous recevons**	
	tu reçois	**vous recevez**	
	il / elle reçoit	**ils / elles reçoivent**	
Le participe passé: **reçu**			
La base du futur et du conditionnel: **recevr-**			

recevoir un appel, recevoir un coup de téléphone = *to receive a phone call*

Hier soir **j'ai reçu** trois appels.
Last night I received three calls.

recevoir des amis = *to have friends over, to entertain friends*

J'aime **recevoir** des amis pendant le week-end.
I like to have friends over on weekends.

recevoir quelqu'un = *to see someone* (in business)

Il peut vous **recevoir** le 8 à 9 heures.
He can see you on the 8th at 9 o'clock.

STRUCTURES

1.   Interrogative Pronouns

Interrogative pronouns ask questions.

a. To designate persons

qui? *who? whom?* (either subject or object):

Qui est-ce?	*Who* (subject) *is it?*
Qui est ce monsieur?	*Who* (subject) *is that man?*
Qui avez-vous appelé?	*Whom* (object) *did you call?*
À **qui** avez-vous parlé?	*To whom* (object of the preposition **à**) *did you speak?*
À **qui** pensez-vous?	*Whom are you thinking about?* (**penser à quelqu'un, à quelque chose,** *to think of / about someone, something*)

«C'est de la part de **qui?**»

À **qui** is also used to denote ownership:

À **qui** est ce livre?	*Whose book is this / that?*

b. To designate things and animals

qu'est-ce qui? *what?* (subject only):

Qu'est-ce qui est dans le sac?	*What is in the bag?*
Qu'est-ce qui se passe?	*What's going on?*
Qu'est-ce qui est arrivé?	*What happened?*

que? *what?* (object only):

Que voulez-vous dire?	*What do you mean?*

que becomes **qu'** before a vowel:

Qu'avez-vous dit?	*What did you say?*

qu'est-ce que (**qu'est-ce qu'** before a vowel) may be used to indicate *what?* as object instead of **que.** note that there is no inversion of the verb in this case:

Qu'est-ce que vous avez dit = **Qu'**avez-vous dit?
Qu'est-ce qu'il fait? = **Que** fait-il?

Qu'est-ce que is used in the construction **Qu'est-ce qu'il y a?** to mean *What is wrong?* or *What is (there) . . . ?:*

Qu'est-ce qu'il y a dans le sac?	*What is (there) in the bag?*

quoi? *what?* (after prepositions):

De quoi parlez-vous?	*What are you talking about?*
De quoi avez-vous besoin?	*What do you need?*
De quoi s'agit-il?	*What is it about?*
À quoi bon?	*What's the use?*

c. To ask for a description or definition

qu'est-ce que c'est que . . . ? *What is . . . ?:*

Qu'est-ce que c'est qu'un annuaire?	*What is an "annuaire"?*
Qu'est-ce que c'est que cela?	*What's that?*

NOTE: **Qu'est-ce que c'est?** means *What is it?*

2. Disjunctive or Intensive Pronouns

These pronouns are called disjunctive because they are separated or "disjoined" from the verb:

moi	**nous**
toi	**vous**
lui	**eux**
elle	**elles**

a. After **c'est** and **ce sont:**

Qui est-ce? C'est **toi?**
Who is it? Is it you?

b. For emphasis:

Moi, je vais téléphoner.
I'm going to phone.

c. In comparisons:

Il est plus grand que **toi.**
He is taller than you.

d. In simple statements without verbs:

Qui téléphone? **Toi** ou **moi?**
Who is phoning? You or I?

e. With the expression **être à** to express ownership:

> À qui est-ce? —**C'est à moi.**
> *Whose is it? —It's mine.*

f. In compound subjects or objects:

> Mon mari et **moi** aimerions vous revoir.
> *My husband and I would like to see you again.*

g. After prepositions:

avec **elle**	*with her*
chez **lui**	*at his place*
de **moi**	*of / about me*

Here are common prepositions:

à cause de	*because of*
à côté de	*next to*
après	*after*
au lieu de	*instead of*
autour de	*around*
avant	*before*
contre	*against*
d'après	*according to*
de la part de	*on behalf of, on the part of, from*
derrière	*behind*
devant	*in front of*
en dépit de	*in spite of*
entre	*between*
en face de	*opposite, facing*
grâce à	*thanks to*
loin de	*far from*
malgré	*in spite of*
parmi	*among*
pour	*for*
près de	*near*
sans	*without*
sauf	*except*
selon	*according to*
sous	*under*
sur	*on*
vers	*towards*

The addition of **-même(s)** to a disjunctive pronoun further emphasizes the subject and corresponds to the English *myself, yourself,* etc.:

Je vais le faire **moi-même.**
I'm going to do it myself.

«Je voudrais parler à Monsieur / Madame *X*, s'il vous plaît.»
—**Lui-même / Elle-même.**
—*This is he / she speaking.*

EXERCICES DE SYNTHÈSE

A. *Répondez à ces questions:*

1. Téléphonez-vous souvent? À qui?
2. À qui avez-vous téléphoné aujourd'hui? Avez-vous téléphoné de votre chambre? de votre bureau? d'une cabine téléphonique?
3. Qui vous a téléphoné aujourd'hui? hier soir?
4. Combien de coups de téléphone avez-vous reçus hier? pendant le week-end?
5. Aimez-vous parler au téléphone? Avec qui? Quand? Avec qui n'aimez-vous pas parler?

B.* *Formez des questions. Remplacez le sujet en italique par* **qui** *ou* **qu'est-ce qui:**

EXEMPLES: *L'annuaire* est sur la table.   *Pierre* est sorti.
           Qu'est-ce qui est sur la table?   Qui est sorti?

1. *Jean* a téléphoné hier soir.
2. *Il* est à Paris.
3. *C'*est impossible!
4. *Monsieur La France* est sorti pour le moment.
5. *Il* a reçu un coup de téléphone.
6. *Le téléphone* est par là.
7. *L'annuaire* n'est pas là.
8. *Son numéro* n'est pas dans l'annuaire.
9. *Jeanne* voudrait téléphoner à Montréal.
10. *Il* a rappelé.
11. *Pierre* est à l'appareil.
12. *Henriette* a téléphoné aux renseignements.

C.* *Formez des questions. Remplacez l'objet en italique par* **qui** *ou* **que** *(qu' devant une voyelle):*

EXEMPLES: J'ai vu *son bureau*.   J'ai vu *Marie*.
            Qu'avez-vous vu?   Qui avez-vous vu?

1. J'ai rencontré *Monsieur X*.   5. J'ai *son numéro de téléphone*.
2. J'ai reçu *une lettre*.   6. Je cherche *la secrétaire*.
3. J'ai dit *bonjour* à la secrétaire. 7. J'aime *mon professeur*.
4. J'ai pris *un message*.   8. J'ai rappelé *le monsieur*.

D.*   *Employez* **qui** *ou* **quoi** *après la préposition en italique pour poser des questions:*

EXEMPLE: J'ai téléphoné *à* mon ami.
           À qui?

1. Votre numéro n'est pas *dans* l'annuaire.
2. Pourriez-vous me donner le numéro *de* Monsieur *X?*
3. Je vais téléphoner *à* Henriette.
4. L'annuaire est *sur* la table.
5. Je voudrais parler *avec* Georges.
6. C'est de la part *de* Mademoiselle Vincent.

E.   *Formez des questions avec* **À qui?** *Suivez le modéle:*

MODÈLE: Ce livre est à moi.
          À qui est ce livre?

1. Ce stylo est à la secrétaire.   4. Ces stylos sont à la standardiste.
2. Ces livres sont à moi.   5. La voiture est à moi.
3. Ce bureau est à Monsieur *X*.

F.*   *Transformez selon le modèle. Puis traduisez:*

MODÈLE: Que recevez-vous?
          Qu'est-ce que vous recevez?

1. Que mangez-vous?   3. Que faites-vous?   5. Que regardez-vous?
2. Que dites-vous?   4. Que prenez-vous?   6. Que voyez-vous?

MODÈLE: Qu'avez-vous reçu?
          Qu'est-ce que vous avez reçu?

1. Qu'avez-vous mangé?   3. Qu'avez-vous fait?   5. Qu'avez-vous vu?
2. Qu'avez-vous dit?   4. Qu'avez-vous pris?

MODÈLE: Qu'a-t-il reçu?
                Qu'est-ce qu'il a reçu?

1. Qu'a-t-il mangé?	3. Qu'a-t-il fait?	5. Qu'a-t-il vu?
2. Qu'a-t-il dit?	4. Qu'a-t-il pris?	

G.*   *Remplacez les mots en italique par la forme correcte du pronom disjonctif:*

EXEMPLE: À qui est-ce? C'est à *Pierre*.
                  C'est à lui.

1. Je vais chez *Robert*.
2. C'est *Marie* qui a téléphoné?
3. Il est plus grand que *son père*.
4. Selon *le secrétaire* Monsieur Alpert est sorti pour le moment.
5. Qui est à la porte? C'est *Jean*?
6. Allez-vous à Paris avec *vos amis*?
7. Il est devant *Madame La France et Mademoiselle Vincent*.
8. Je vais voyager avec *mes enfants*.
9. Il est assis entre *Monsieur et Madame Smith*.
10. C'est *Antoine* qui a pris le message.
11. C'est *Pierre*, n'est-ce pas?
12. Ce sont *Marc et Jacques*, n'est-ce pas?
13. Il a rendez-vous avec *Henriette*.
14. Je vais au cinéma sans *François*.

EXPANSION: Au téléphone

1. **Où se trouve la cabine téléphonique, s'il vous plaît?**	*Where is the phone booth, please?*
2. **Le téléphone est en dérangement.**	*The telephone is out of order.*
3. **Décrochez / Raccrochez.**	*Pick up the receiver. / Hang up the receiver.*
4. **Ça sonne. On ne répond pas.**	*It's ringing. There's no answer.*
5. **La ligne est occupée. / Ça sonne occupé.**	*The line is busy. / It's busy.*
6. **Excusez-moi. Je me suis trompé(e) de numéro.**	*Excuse me. I dialed the wrong number.*
7. **Vous avez le mauvais numéro. Quel numéro avez-vous appelé?**	*You have the wrong number. What number did you call?*
8. **La communication est mauvaise. J'entends très mal. Parlez plus fort, s'il vous plaît.**	*It's a bad connection. I can't hear (you) very well. Please speak louder.*
9. **On nous a coupés.**	*We've been cut off.*

10. **On vous demande au téléphone.**	*You have a call.*
11. **Je vous le / la passe.**	*I'll put him / her on.*
12. **Puis-je lui laisser un message?**	*May I leave him / her a message?*
13. **Quel est votre indicatif de zone?**	*What's your area code?*
14. **Veuillez lui demander de me rappeler.**	*Please ask him / her to call me back.*
15. **C'est urgent!**	*It's urgent!*
16. **Merci d'avoir téléphoné. / Merci de votre appel.**	*Thank you for calling.*

17. **Qui est à l'appareil? C'est _____. Ici**
    (votre nom)
    _____. Mon nom est _____.
    (votre nom)

    Who's calling? It's _____. It's _____. My
    (your name)   (your name)
    name is _____.

18. **Je voudrais téléphoner avec préavis / en P.C.V.** (In Canada: **Je voudrais placer un appel de personne à personne / à frais virés,** ou **à frais renversés.**)

    I would like to make a person-to-person call / collect call.

19. **Je voudrais faire un appel interurbain.**

    I'd like to make a long-distance call.

Exercices

A.   *Que dites-vous quand:*

1. Vous voulez téléphoner en P.C.V.: _____
2. Le téléphone sonne. Vous décrochez et on demande votre ami: _____
3. Vous êtes au restaurant. Vous voulez téléphoner à votre ami. Vous cherchez la cabine téléphonique: _____
4. Le téléphone sonne. Vous décrochez et vous entendez, «Allô, Charles?» Mais ce n'est pas votre nom: _____
5. Vous n'entendez pas bien parce que la communication est mauvaise: _____
6. Vous voulez téléphoner à votre ami dans une autre ville. Vous n'avez pas d'argent, mais vous croyez que votre ami acceptera de payer la communication: _____
7. Vous téléphonez à votre ami Georges. Il habite seul. On répond. Vous dites, «Allô, Georges?» Mais ce n'est pas Georges: _____
8. Vous téléphonez et que l'on vous demande, «Qui est à l'appareil?»: _____
9. Vous voulez remercier un ami de vous avoir téléphoné: _____
10. Vous voulez parler au docteur et que c'est très urgent: _____

B.   *Répondez aux questions suivantes.*

1. Combien de fois laissez-vous sonner quand vous téléphonez à quelqu'un?
2. Avez-vous téléphoné en P.C.V. ou avec préavis cette semaine? À qui? Quand?
3. Avez-vous déjà reçu un appel obscène? Qu'avez-vous fait? raccroché? téléphoné à la police? changé de numéro?

4. Votre numéro est-il inscrit dans l'annuaire ou est-ce un numéro privé?
5. Faites-vous beaucoup d'appels interurbains? Quand? le soir après cinq heures?
   la nuit? pendant le week-end? À qui?
6. Quel est votre indicatif de zone?

PRONONCIATION

Sounds:

[p]	SPELLINGS:	**p**
[t]		**t, th**
[k]		**qu, q, c** (followed by **a, o, u**),
		c (+ consonant), **k, que,**
		c (at end of word)

PRONUNCIATION:

In English, there are two pronunciations of these consonants:

1. With an explosion of air (as in: p̲ie, t̲ie, k̲ey)
2. Without an explosion of air (as in: sp̲y, st̲y, sk̲i)

To distinguish between the two, hold your hand in front of your mouth as you say the following:

p̲ie — sp̲y
t̲ie — st̲y
k̲ey — sk̲i

In French, the [p] [t] [k] sounds are always made without the additional puff of air.

EXAMPLES FROM THIS CHAPTER:

[p]	[t]	[k]
P . . . Pierre	**T . . .** Thérèse	**qu**estion
Paris	**t**éléphone	**qu**atre
possible	**t**rois	**qu**i
pour	**t**reize	**qu**e
	toi	**qu**oi
		comme
		coup
		cabine
		se**c**rétaire
		ave**c**

IMPROVISATION

Préparez un monologue. Racontez à un(e) ami(e) tout ce que vous avez fait pour lui téléphoner. Essayez d'employer le vocabulaire et les expressions de la leçon. Par exemple: «Votre numéro n'est pas dans l'annuaire. Alors, j'ai téléphoné aux renseignements. La standardiste m'a donné votre numéro. J'ai composé le numéro. Une dame a répondu: 'Allô, allô. . . . Qui est à l'appareil? . . . .» etc.

PROJET

Later on today or perhaps this evening, you might find a telephone message waiting for you. Fill out the form below with the sort of message you might expect.

MESSAGE TÉLÉPHONIQUE. ☐ VISITE . . . . ☐	DATE et HEURE:
De:	Pour:
ADRESSE:	Rappelez correspondant . . . . . ☐
	Correspondant rappellera . . . . ☐
	Suite à votre appel . . . . ☐
	Demande rendez-vous . . . .
TÉLÉPHONE: POSTE:	Reçu par:
OBJET:	
Peut être rappelé le . . . entre . . . h et . . . h au numéro ci-dessus ou à	

ACTIVITÉ

Répertoire Adresses. Using the vocabulary and structures of this lesson, ask your class-mates for their addresses **(Quelle est votre adresse?),** for their phone numbers **(Quel est votre numéro de téléphone?),** and for the correct spelling of their names **(Quelle est l'orthographe exacte de votre nom?).** Enter this information on your **Répertoire Adresses.**

RÉPERTOIRE ADRESSES		
NOMS	ADRESSES	NUMÉROS DE TÉLÉPHONE

IL COURT, IL COURT, LE FURET*

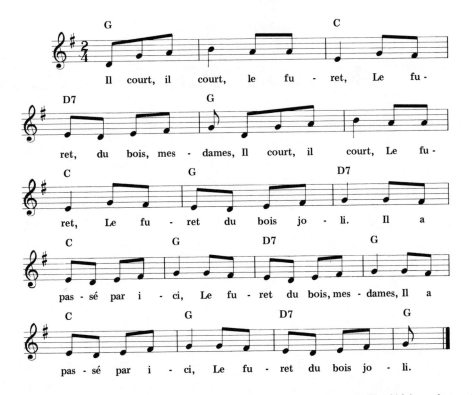

*French children sing this song while standing in a circle, secretly passing from hand to hand a ring which is on a long cord tied together at the ends to form a loop. When the song ends, the person in the center tries to guess where the ring is.

CLOTHING, COLORS, MATERIALS

Qu'est-ce que vous portez aujourd'hui?
—Je porte _____ .

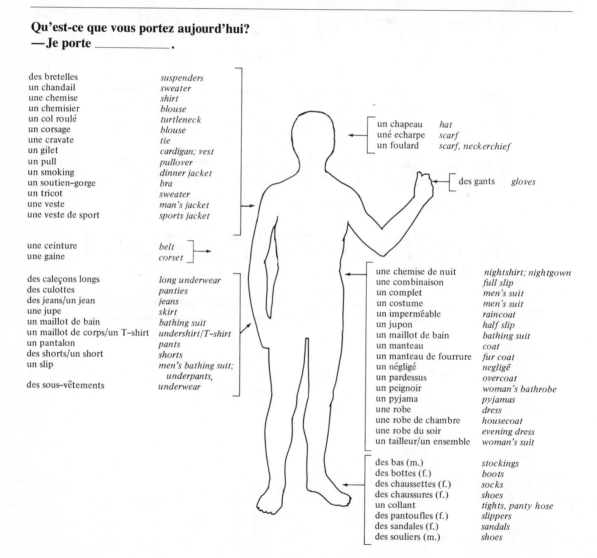

des bretelles	*suspenders*
un chandail	*sweater*
une chemise	*shirt*
un chemisier	*blouse*
un col roulé	*turtleneck*
un corsage	*blouse*
une cravate	*tie*
un gilet	*cardigan; vest*
un pull	*pullover*
un smoking	*dinner jacket*
un soutien–gorge	*bra*
un tricot	*sweater*
une veste	*man's jacket*
une veste de sport	*sports jacket*

une ceinture	*belt*
une gaine	*corset*

des caleçons longs	*long underwear*
des culottes	*panties*
des jeans/un jean	*jeans*
une jupe	*skirt*
un maillot de bain	*bathing suit*
un maillot de corps/un T–shirt	*undershirt/T–shirt*
un pantalon	*pants*
des shorts/un short	*shorts*
un slip	*men's bathing suit; underpants,*
des sous–vêtements	*underwear*

un chapeau	*hat*
uné echarpe	*scarf*
un foulard	*scarf, neckerchief*

des gants	*gloves*

une chemise de nuit	*nightshirt; nightgown*
une combinaison	*full slip*
un complet	*men's suit*
un costume	*men's suit*
un imperméable	*raincoat*
un jupon	*half slip*
un maillot de bain	*bathing suit*
un manteau	*coat*
un manteau de fourrure	*fur coat*
un négligé	*negligé*
un pardessus	*overcoat*
un peignoir	*woman's bathrobe*
un pyjama	*pyjamas*
une robe	*dress*
une robe de chambre	*housecoat*
une robe du soir	*evening dress*
un tailleur/un ensemble	*woman's suit*

des bas (m.)	*stockings*
des bottes (f.)	*boots*
des chaussettes (f.)	*socks*
des chaussures (f.)	*shoes*
un collant	*tights, panty hose*
des pantoufles (f.)	*slippers*
des sandales (f.)	*sandals*
des souliers (m.)	*shoes*

Accessoires (*Accessories*)

une alliance	*wedding ring*
une bague (de fiançailles)	*(engagement) ring*
des bijoux	*jewelry*
des boutons de manchette *(m.)*	*cufflinks*
des boucles d'oreilles *(f.)*	*earrings*
un bracelet	*bracelet*
une broche	*brooch*
une chevalière	*signet ring*
un collier / une rivière (de diamants, d'émeraudes, de perles, de rubis)	*necklace (diamond, emerald, pearl, ruby)*
des lunettes (de soleil)	*(sun) glasses*
une montre	*watch*
un mouchoir	*handkerchief*
un pendentif sur une chaîne	*pendant on a chain*
des verres de contact	*contact lenses*

Couleurs (*Colors*)

beige	*beige*
blanc (blanche)	*white*
bleu(e)	*blue*
brun(e)	*brown*
gris(e)	*grey*
jaune	*yellow*
lie de vin	*maroon, burgundy*
marron *(invariable adjective)*	*chestnut*
noir(e)	*black*
orange	*orange*
pourpre	*purple*
rose	*pink*
rouge	*red*
turquoise	*turquoise*
vert(e)	*green*
violet(te)	*violet*
à rayures	*striped*
écossais(e)	*plaid*
à carreaux	*checked*

NOTE: Color adjectives agree with the noun they describe: **une jupe blanche, elle est verte, ils sont bruns.**

MATIÈRES ET TISSUS (*MATERIALS, FABRICS, ETC.*)

argent	*silver*
bois	*wood*
bronze	*bronze*
cristal taillé	*cut crystal*
cuir	*leather*
cuir verni	*patent leather*
cuivre	*copper*
étain	*tin*
jade	*jade*
laiton	*brass*
métal	*metal*
opale	*opal*
or	*gold*
plastique	*plastic*
platine	*platinum*
verre	*glass*
coton	*cotton*
caoutchouc	*rubber*
daim	*suede*
dacron	*dacron*
dentelle	*lace*
feutre	*felt*
flanelle	*flannel*
laine	*wool*
nylon	*nylon*
orlon	*orlon*
rayonne	*rayon*
satin	*satin*
soie	*silk*
taffetas	*taffeta*
toile	*canvas, calico, linen*
velours	*velvet*
velours côtelé	*corduroy*

NOTE: **en coton** = *made of cotton*
      en or = *made of gold*
      un collier en or = *a gold necklace*
      une jupe en laine = *a wool(en) skirt*

AUTRES TERMES DESCRIPTIFS (*OTHER DESCRIPTIVE TERMS*)

à la mode	*stylish, fashionable*
bon marché (*invariable adjective*)	*inexpensive*
cher (chère)	*expensive*
chic (*invariable adjective*)	*stylish*
chiffonné(e)	*wrinkled, rumpled*
confortable	*comfortable*
déchiré(e)	*ripped, torn*
démodé(e)	*out of style*
infroissable	*permanent-press, crease-resistant*
en lambeaux / en loques	*ragged, tattered, torn*
lavable	*washable*
neuf (neuve)	*new*
propre	*clean*
sale	*dirty*
taché(e)	*spotted, stained*
troué(e)	*torn, full of holes*
usé(e)	*worn-out*
vieux (vieille)	*old*

SPRINGBOARDS FOR CONVERSATION

1. Qu'est-ce que vous portez aujourd'hui?
   Je porte _____ .
2. Que porte le professeur? Monsieur . . . ? Madame . . . ? Mademoiselle . . . ? etc.
   Il / Elle porte _____ .
3. Est-ce que les boucles d'oreilles de Madame / Mademoiselle . . . sont en plastique?
   en or? en argent? etc.
   Oui, elles sont en _____ .
   Non, elles sont en _____ .
4. En quel tissu est votre _____ ? en coton? en laine? etc.
   Il / Elle est en _____ .
5. De quelle couleur est la chemise, le pantalon, etc., de Monsieur . . . ? Et la jupe, la
   robe, le tailleur, etc., de Madame / Mademoiselle . . . ? etc.

Il / Elle est _____ .

De quelle couleur sont les chaussures, les chaussettes, les gants, etc., de Monsieur / Madame / Mademoiselle . . . ? etc.

Ils / Elles sont _____ .

6. Qui dans la classe porte un chandail? une ceinture? des lunettes? un maillot de bain? etc.

   Qui d'autre? Personne? Tout le monde?

7. Que portez-vous à la maison?

   Je porte _____ .

8. Lorsque vous partez en vacances, qu'emportez-vous comme vêtements?

   J'emporte _____ .

9. Quels vêtements avez-vous mis hier?

10. Vous habillez-vous *(Do you dress)* chaque jour différemment?

11. D'habitude que mettez-vous en hiver? en été? pour aller à la plage *(beach)?* à une soirée? en classe? au travail? etc.

12. Qu'avez-vous mis au linge sale *(into the dirty laundry)* cette semaine?

13. Avez-vous un smoking? un manteau de fourrure? des pantoufles vertes? une chemise jaune? etc.

    Oui, j'ai un / une / des _____ .

    Non, je n'ai pas de _____ .

14. Quel est le dernier vêtement que vous mettez le matin? Quel est le premier vêtement que vous enlevez le soir?

15. Quels vêtements avez-vous achetés récemment?

16. Quels vêtements avez-vous raccommodés *(mended)* ou avez-vous fait raccommoder récemment? Lesquels de vos vêtements ont besoin d'être raccommodés?

17. De quoi avez-vous besoin? d'une ceinture? d'un pull? de chaussures? de lunettes de soleil? etc.

PROJETS

1. List and describe your entire wardrobe. Be as thorough as possible.
2. Fill out the form on the opposite page. Which of your clothes *really* need to be cleaned?
3. You have to go away this week on an unexpected quick trip. What will you take with you? (You will have to decide first where you are going and what sort of trip it will be. Be realistic. For example, an unexpected business trip to California or New York, a college weekend near-by, a family gathering, etc.)
4. Using pictures of people taken from magazines, newspapers, or actual photographs you may have, describe the clothing items worn. Include accouterments such as wristwatches, eyeglasses, earrings, etc. Specify colors and materials whenever possible.

Blanchissage, Nettoyage et Repassage

HOTEL BAKOUA MARTINIQUE

NOM _____

CHAMBRE   No _____ DATE _____ HEURES _____

(Ayez l'obligeance de remplir cette liste avec précision afin que l'on puisse prendre le linge en charge)

A RENDRE

DANS LA JOURNÉE (50% majoration)	POUR DEMAIN	PAS PRESSÉ
☐	☐	☐

RECOMMANDATIONS SPÉCIALES   : _____

BLANCHISSAGE MESSIEURS

NOMBRE	CONTRÔLE		FRS	US	TOTAL
		CHEMISE ORDINAIRE			
		AUTRES CHEMISES			
		CHEMISETTE			
		CHAUSSETTES			
		MAILLOT DE CORPS			
		MOUCHOIR			
		PANTALON			
		PYJAMA			
		SHORT			
		SLIP			
		. . . .			

DAMES

NOMBRE	CONTRÔLE		FRS	US	TOTAL
		BLOUSES			
		CHEMISE DE NUIT			
		COMBINAISON			
		CULOTTE			
		MOUCHOIR			
		PEIGNOIR			
		ROBE			
		SHORT			
		PANTALON			
		JUPE			
		. . . .			

NETTOYAGES A SEC MESSIEURS   72 HEURES MINIMUM

NOMBRE	CONTRÔLE		FRS	US	TOTAL
		COMPLET			
		VESTON			
		PANTALON			
		PARDESSUS			
		VESTE			
		CHANDAIL			
		CRAVATE			
		CHEMISES			
		. . . .			
		. . . .			

DAMES

NOMBRE	CONTRÔLE		FRS	US	TOTAL
		ROBE			
		JUPE			
		CORSAGE			
		MANTEAU			
		. . . .			

L'HÔTEL NE SE REND PAS RESPONSABLE DES OBJETS DE VALEUR LAISSÉS DANS LES VÊTEMENTS.

ACTIVITÉS

1. Here is a variation on the memory game "I Packed My Grandmother's Bag." This game may be played in groups of two, three or more players or with the entire class. Using the vocabulary of this lesson, the first player pretends he or she is packing a suitcase and names an item of apparel to be included. For example: **Je fais ma valise et j'y mets un manteau.** The second player must remember that item, name it, and then add to it another item of his or her own selection. For example: **Je fais ma valise et j'y mets: un manteau et un pantalon.** The next player (either a third player or the first player over again) must recapitulate, in order, the items that have already been named, and then add to this list a third item of his or her own choosing. For example: **Je fais ma valise et j'y mets un manteau, un pantalon et un bracelet.** The game continues in this fashion, with each player recapitulating the entire list and then adding his or her own new selection to it. When a player forgets or incorrectly names an item, he or she drops out of the game. The game continues until only one person is left, who is then declared the winner.

2. A color is named. For example: **Bleu.** Everyone in class wearing something of that particular color must stand up. In order to sit down again, students must correctly use the vocabulary of this lesson to name the garment they are wearing of that color. For example: «**Je porte un pantalon bleu**». «**Ma chemise est bleue**». «**Mes chaussettes sont bleues**», etc.

Appartement à louer	Renting an Apartment
Proverbe: Petit à petit, l'oiseau fait son nid.	Proverb: Rome wasn't built in a day. (*Literally:* Little by little, the bird builds his nest.)

«Je voudrais louer une petite maison au bord de la mer.»

DIALOGUE

(À l'agence immobilière)

VOUS: Je voudrais louer
un appartement. Il me faut un quatre-pièces.

un studio
une maison de banlieue
une maison de campagne
une maison individuelle
une petite maison au bord de la mer
une villa / un pavillon
un château
une ferme
un hôtel particulier

L'AGENT: Très bien, Monsieur / Madame. J'ai un appartement à louer dans un nouvel immeuble. L'appartement se trouve au **troisième étage.**[1] Il n'est pas luxueux mais il

sous-sol
rez-de-chaussée
quatrième étage
cinquième étage
sixième étage

est **agréable.**

charmant
climatisé
confortable
ensoleillé
habitable
joli
moderne
spacieux
tranquille / calme

(At the rental agency)

YOU: I would like to rent an
apartment. I need a four-room apartment.

studio apartment
house in the suburbs
country house
single-family dwelling
little house by the sea
villa, cottage
chateau, manor, pavillion
farm
town house

THE RENTAL AGENT: Very well. I have an apartment for rent in a new building. The apartment is *on the fourth floor* (literally: third

in the basement
on the ground floor
on the fifth (*literally:* fourth) floor
on the sixth (*literally:* fifth) floor
on the seventh (*literally:* sixth) floor

floor).[1] It is not luxurious but it is *pleasant*.

charming
air-conditioned
comfortable
sunny
livable
pretty
modern
spacious
peaceful

1. In Europe, the American "first floor" or "ground floor" is called **le rez-de-chaussée.** The American "second floor" is called **le premier étage,** etc.

Vous: Est-il meublé?

L'Agent: Oui, il y a tout ce qu'il faut.

Vous: Combien de chambres y a-t-il?[1]

L'Agent: Il y en a deux.

Vous: Et comment est
la cuisine?

la chambre d'amis
la salle de séjour (le séjour)
la salle à manger
la salle de bains / la salle d'eau
la salle de jeux
le salon
le cabinet de travail

L'Agent: Elle est grande et claire.

Vous: Quand est-ce que l'appartement sera libre?

L'Agent: À partir de **demain.**

lundi
mardi
mercredi
jeudi
vendredi
samedi
dimanche

Vous: Quel est le loyer?

L'Agent: Sept cents francs par mois.

Vous: Cela me paraît raisonnable. J'aimerais visiter l'appartement.

You: Is it furnished?

Agent: Yes, there's everything you need.

You: How many bedrooms are there?[1]

Agent: There are two.

You: And what is the *kitchen* like?

guest room
living room
dining room
bathroom
game / recreation room
parlor
study

Agent: It's large and bright.

You: When will the apartment be free?

Agent: Starting *tomorrow*.

Monday
Tuesday
Wednesday
Thursday
Friday
Saturday
Sunday

You: What is the rent?

Agent: Seven hundred francs a month.

You: That seems reasonable (to me). I'd like to see the apartment.

---

1. **Une chambre** is a bedroom. **Une pièce** is any room in a house or apartment. **Une salle** is used with certain fixed expressions, such as **salle de séjour** and **salle de bains.** In France, by the way, the toilet is often separate from the bathroom and is referred to as **les W.C.**

EXERCICES D'APPLICATION

*1. Dites que vous voulez louer un appartement . . . que vous préférez un nouvel immeuble . . . que vous préférez un immeuble moderne . . . qu'il vous faut un quatre-pièces . . . que vous voulez habiter au rez-de-chaussée . . . que le loyer vous paraît raisonnable . . . que vous aimeriez visiter l'appartement.

*2. Demandez à quel étage se trouve l'appartement . . . s'il est climatisé . . . s'il est moderne . . . s'il est meublé . . . combien de chambres il y a . . . comment est la salle à manger . . . si la salle à manger est grande . . . quand l'appartement sera libre . . . quel est le loyer.

3. Comment est la salle de classe? Est-elle agréable? climatisée? confortable? ensoleillée? jolie? moderne? spacieuse? tranquille? luxueuse? claire? grande? petite?

VERBE IRRÉGULIER: vivre

vivre *to live*	
Le présent:	**je vis** **nous vivons**
	tu vis **vous vivez**
	il / elle vit **ils / elles vivent**
Le participe passé: **vécu**	
La base de futur et du conditionnel: **vivr-**	

a. The verb **vivre** means *to live* in the sense of "to spend one's time," "to exist":

  J'ai vécu deux ans en France.

  être vivant means *to be living, to be alive:*

  Sont-ils encore **vivants?** Are they still alive?

b. The verb **habiter** means *to live* in the sense of "to reside" and is followed by the place of residence—apartment, building, city, country, continent:

  Où habitez-vous?
  —**J'habite** un petit appartement.
  —**J'habite (à)** Paris.

STRUCTURES

1.   Present Participle

a. The present participle of regular and irregular verbs is formed by substituting the ending **-ant** for the **-ons** of the **nous** form of the present indicative:

> donner (nous donnons) → donn**ant**
> finir (nous finissons) → finiss**ant**
> vendre (nous vendons) → vend**ant**

Only the following verbs have irregular present participles:

> avoir **(ayant)**   être **(étant)**   savoir **(sachant)**

b. The ending **-ant** is equivalent to **-ing** in English; **parlant** means *speaking, talking:*

> J'ai vu la dame **parlant** avec le propriétaire.
> *I saw the lady speaking with the owner.*

Present participles do not agree with the noun or pronoun they modify.

NOTE: Do *not* use the present participle in French as an equivalent for the English progressive tenses:

> **Je parle** (le présent).   *I am speaking.*
> **Je parlais** (l'imparfait).   *I was speaking.*

c. The preposition **en** with the present participle denotes that the same person is performing two actions simultaneously; **en** may be equivalent to *while, where, upon, through, by:*

> **En** entrant, vous trouverez la salle de bains sur votre gauche.
> *Upon entering, you will find the bathroom on your left.*
> *When (you are) entering, ...*

> **En** partant à deux heures, vous serez chez vous avant quatre heures.
> *By leaving at two o'clock, you will be home before four o'clock.*

> **En** dînant il regarde la télévision.
> *While having dinner, he watches television.*
> *While he has dinner, ...*

2.   Infinitives after Prepositions

a. An infinitive is used in French after prepositions other than **en:**

avant de	**Avant de** louer un appartement, il faut le visiter. *Before renting an apartment, you must visit it.*
sans	Il est parti **sans** dire au revoir. *He left without saying good-by.*
au lieu de	**Au lieu de** louer, achetez. *Instead of renting, buy.*
passer son temps à	**Je passe mon temps à** travailler. *I spend my time working.*

b. The French equivalent of the English *after* + present participle or *after having* + past participle is **après** + **être / avoir** + **le participe passé:**

Après avoir fini, il est parti.
After finishing (after having finished), he left.

Après être partie, elle a téléphoné.
After leaving (after having left), she telephoned.

3.   Relative Pronouns: ce qui, ce que

a. Ce qui *(what)* and **tout ce qui** *(all that, everything)* are the subjects of clauses, relating back to something already mentioned:

Dites-moi **ce qui** vous intéresse.
Tell me what interests you.

Tout ce qui est dans l'appartement est nouveau.
Everything in the apartment is new.

b. Ce que *(what)* and **tout ce que** *(all that, everything)* are objects of clauses:

Dites-moi **ce que** vous voulez.
Tell me what you want.

«Il y a **tout ce qu'**il faut.»

EXERCICES DE SYNTHÈSE

A.   *Répondez à ces questions:*

1. Vivez-vous seul(e)? Avec votre famille? Avec un(e) ami(e)?
2. Avez-vous toujours vécu dans la même ville? Dans quelles villes avez-vous vécu? à Paris? à Montréal?

3. Avez-vous vécu en France? au Canada? à l'étranger?

4. Vos grands-parents sont-ils encore vivants?

5. Où habitez-vous? Dans un appartement? À quel étage? Dans une maison? Dans une résidence universitaire? Dans une ville? Dans un petit village? À la campagne? Dans la banlieue?

B.   *Répondez:*

1. Avez-vous déjà loué un appartement? Dans quelle ville? à Paris? à Québec? Quand? il y a deux ans? il y a dix ans? Dans un grand immeuble? À quel étage? Combien de pièces y avait-il? Décrivez l'appartement. Était-il grand? moderne? etc.

2. Avez-vous déjà loué une maison? un château? une ferme? Dans quelle ville? La maison était-elle meublée?

3. Votre maison est-elle grande? Est-elle nouvelle? Votre appartement est-il grand? Assez grand?

4. Combien de pièces y a-t-il chez vous? Quelles sont ces pièces? Nommez-les.

5. Combien de chambres à coucher y a-t-il chez vous? Combien de salles de bains?

6. À quel étage est votre chambre?

7. Comment est votre chambre? grande? petite? claire? sombre? ensoleillée? spacieuse? tranquille? bruyante *(noisy)?*

8. Dans quelles pièces de votre maison / appartement passez-vous le plus de temps?

9. Comment est la cuisine chez vous? Est-elle moderne? spacieuse? grande? petite?

10. Comment est la salle de séjour chez vous? Est-elle confortable? climatisée? moderne? tranquille?

11. Louez-vous l'appartement ou la maison où vous vivez? Le loyer est-il raisonnable? élevé? bas?

C.*   *Faites une phrase avec les éléments donnés en employant un participe présent avec* **en.** *Ensuite, traduisez:*

EXEMPLE: J'ai vu mon ami. (visiter l'appartement)
           En visitant l'appartement j'ai vu mon ami.

1. Je regarde la télévision. (dîner)

2. J'ai regardé la télévision. (attendre)

3. Il est tombé. (entrer dans l'immeuble)

4. Je l'ai vu. (visiter l'appartement)

5. J'ai parlé avec le propriétaire. (payer le loyer)

6. Vous trouverez la salle de bains sur votre gauche. (entrer)
7. Je pense toujours à vous. (regarder les photos)

D.   *Complétez chaque phrase en employant un infinitif. Puis traduisez la phrase:*

1. Le professeur passe son temps à _____ .
2. Moi, je passe mon temps à _____ , à _____ et à _____ .
3. Avant de / d' _____ , j'aime regarder la télévision.
4. Au lieu de / d' _____ , je regarde la télévision.
5. Ce matin j'ai quitté la maison sans _____ .

E.*   *Transformez selon le modèle:*

MODÈLE: J'ai vu l'appartement et puis je l'ai loué.
          Après avoir vu l'appartement, je l'ai loué.

1. J'ai fini le travail et puis je suis parti(e).
2. J'ai visité l'appartement et puis je l'ai loué.
3. J'ai payé le loyer et puis je suis parti(e).
4. J'ai vu mes amis et puis je suis rentré(e).
5. Je suis parti(e) et puis je vous ai téléphoné.
6. Je suis allé(e) à l'agence immobilière et puis je vous ai téléphoné.

F.   *Répondez aux questions suivantes. Employez les prépositions en italique:*

1. Aimez-vous prendre vos repas *en* regardant la télévision?
2. Écoutez-vous de la musique *en* étudiant?
3. Êtes-vous tombé(e) récemment? Quand? *En* marchant dans la rue? *En* entrant dans la salle de classe?
4. Chantez-vous *en* travaillant?
5. *Avant de* vous coucher, que faites-vous?
6. *Après* avoir étudié, qu'est-ce que vous aimez faire?
7. *En* entrant dans la salle de classe, avez-vous dit bonjour au professeur?

G.   *Employez* **ce qui** *ou* **ce que** *dans les phrases suivantes. Ensuite, traduisez:*

1. Je ne sais pas _____ vous voulez faire.
2. Je ne sais pas _____ vous amuse.
3. Je ne comprends pas _____ vous dites.
4. Je ne comprends pas _____ vous voulez.
5. Je ne sais pas _____ vous intéresse.
6. Dites-moi tout _____ vous en pensez.
7. Faites _____ est amusant.
8. Faites _____ je fais.

H.* *Employez* **ce que / ce qu'** *dans la réponse. Ensuite, traduisez:*

EXEMPLE: Qu'est-ce qu'il veut?
                  Je ne sais pas ce qu'il veut.

1. Qu'est-ce qu'il dit?
2. Qu'est-ce qu'il prend?
3. Qu'est-ce qu'elle ouvre?
4. Qu'est-ce que vous allez faire?
5. Qu'est-ce que l'agent a dit?
6. Qu'est-ce qu'il a demandé?
7. Qu'est-ce qu'elle fait?
8. Qu'est-ce qu'il aime faire?
9. Qu'est-ce qu'il regarde?
10. Qu'est-ce que vous allez acheter?

EXPANSION: Décrivez votre maison / appartement

1. **Y a-t-il . . . ? (Devant? Derrière? D'un côté? Des deux côtés?)**
   Is there / are there . . . ? (In front? In back? On one side? On both sides?

des arbres dans la propriété	*trees on the property*
des arbustes	*bushes / shrubs*
une barrière	*fence*
une cour de derrière	*backyard*
un court de tennis	*tennis court*
des (parterres de) fleurs	*(beds of) flowers*
une haie	*hedge*
un jardin	*garden*
un mur	*wall*
une pelouse	*lawn*
une piscine	*swimming pool*
un portail	*gate*
un potager	*vegetable garden*
des poubelles	*garbage cans*
un sentier	*path*
une sortie de voiture	*driveway*
un trottoir	*sidewalk*
une véranda	*veranda / porch*

2. **De quelle couleur est votre maison? et votre chambre? Est-elle . . . ?**
   What color is your house? and your (bed)room? Is it . . . ?

beige	*beige*	**noire**	*black*
blanche	*white*	**orange**	*orange*
bleue	*blue*	**pourpre**	*purple*
brune	*brown*	**rose**	*red*
grise	*gray*	**verte**	*green*
jaune	*yellow*	**violette**	*violet*

3. **Votre maison est-elle en . . . ?**
   Is your house made of . . . ?

pierre	*rock / stone*	**béton**	*concrete*
brique	*brick*	**aluminum**	*aluminum*
bois	*wood*		

4. **Combien de . . . y a-t-il chez vous?**
   How many . . . are there at your place?

placards	*closets / cupboards*	**étages**	*floors / stories*
cheminées	*fireplaces*	**fenêtres**	*windows*
couloirs	*hallways*	**portes**	*doors*
escaliers	*stairways*		

5. **Y a-t-il . . . ?**
   Is there / are there . . . ?

un grenier	*an attic*
un balcon	*a balcony*
de la moquette partout	*carpeting throughout*
un sous-sol	*a basement*
une terrasse	*a terrace*
des volets	*shutters*

6. **Quelles sont les dimensions de votre chambre?**
   What are the dimensions of your (bed)room?

   (Elle fait _____ mètres / pieds sur _____.)
   (It measures _____ meters / feet by _____ meters / feet.)

7. **Aimeriez-vous déménager? Pourquoi?**
   Would you like to move? Why?

   Exercices

   A.   *Répondez aux questions posées ci-dessus* (above) *par des phrases complètes.*

   B.   *En employant le vocabulaire et les structures de cette leçon, décrivez. . . .*

   1. . . . la maison où vous vivez. Comment est-elle différente des autres maisons du quartier? Qu'est-ce qui vous plaît le plus? la propriété? l'intérieur? les arbres?
   2. . . . la maison de vos rêves.
   3. . . . la maison ou l'immeuble de vos parents. De vos grands-parents. De vos enfants. De votre meilleur(e) ami(e).

4. . . . le bâtiment (*building*) où vous êtes en ce moment.
5. . . . votre maison natale.
6. . . . toutes les maisons / tous les appartements où vous avez vécu.
7. . . . le bâtiment où a lieu votre cours de français.
8. . . . la maison la plus intéressante que vous ayez jamais vue.
9. . . . votre résidence universitaire . . . votre maison de campagne . . . le bâtiment où vous travaillez.
10. . . . les maisons ou les bâtiments que vous voyez en regardant par la fenêtre.

PRONONCIATION

Sound (Phonetic Symbol): [j]

SPELLING:	**i** (followed by a pronounced vowel), **y** (followed by a pronounced vowel)
ENGLISH SOUND RESEMBLED:	Initial sound in word *you*
PRONUNCIATION:	This semi-vowel (or semi-consonant) is pronounced more tensely, forcefully, and rapidly than in English.
EXAMPLES FROM THIS CHAPTER:	immobil**iè**re mons**ie**ur v**io**let
	p**iè**ce tro**i**s**iè**me p**ie**rre
	stud**io** il **y** a p**ie**d
	b**ie**n **y** a-t-il lo**y**er

NOTE: The sound [j] may also be spelled **ill** or **il.** Examples from this chapter: **pavillon, ensoleillé, portail, travail.** Exceptions: **mille, ville, tranquille** are pronounced [mil], [vil], [trãkil].

IMPROVISATION

Préparez un dialogue. Employez le vocabulaire et les structures de la leçon:

Vous comptez habiter en France pendant un an. Vous vous adressez donc à une agence immobilière. Expliquez à l'employé(e) de cette agence exactement ce qu'il vous faut. Posez beaucoup de questions.

Vous: _____
L'Agent: _____
Vous: _____

L'Agent: _____
Vous: _____
L'Agent: _____
Vous: _____

PROJETS

1. Draw a floor plan of your house or apartment. Label all the rooms. Include cupboards, closets, doors, windows, halls, balconies, etc. When possible, include the approximate measurements of each room. See the **Dialogue** and **Expansion** sections of this lesson for the necessary vocabulary. If you have a photograph of your house or apartment (inside or outside), you may wish to attach it to the floor plan.
2. In today's newspaper find a house or apartment for sale or for rent that you think you would like. Describe it using vocabulary from the **Dialogue** and **Expansion** sections of this lesson.

ACTIVITÉ

Using the **Dialogue** and **Expansion** sections of this lesson, try to sell or rent the classroom to your classmates. Walk around the room with your prospective clients, convincing them of the merits of your property. For example: **Cette salle de classe est très moderne et spacieuse. Voici les placards, ils sont grands, n'est-ce pas?** etc.

CADET ROUSSELLE

ROOMS, HOUSEHOLD OBJECTS

Avez-vous un éléphant dans votre salle de bains?
—Non, mais j'ai un / une / des _____ dans ma _____.

LA CUISINE (KITCHEN)

un aspirateur	*vacuum cleaner*
une bassine	*dishpan*
une batterie de cuisine (une série de casseroles, une poêle, etc.)	*kitchen utensils (a set of pots, a frying pan, etc.)*
un batteur électrique	*electric mixer*
une cafetière	*coffee pot*
un chauffe-eau	*water heater*
un commutateur	*light switch*
un bar	*counter*
un congélateur	*freezer*
une cuisinière (à gaz / électrique)	*stove (gas / electric)*
un égouttoir	*dish rack*
des éponges (*f.*)	*sponges*
un escabeau	*stool, stepladder*

245

un évier	*(kitchen) sink*
un four	*oven*
des gadgets *(m.)*	*gadgets*
un grille-pain	*toaster*
un grille-viande	*broiler*
un lave-vaisselle	*dishwasher*
des livres de cuisine	*cookbooks*
une machine à laver	*washing machine*
un mixer	*mixer, blender*
un ouvre-boîtes électrique	*electric can opener*
une pendule	*clock*
des placards *(m.)*	*cupboards*
des plateaux *(m.)*	*trays*
une poignée	*potholder*
une poubelle	*garbage pail*
un réchaud	*hot plate*
un réfrigérateur / un ''frigo''	*refrigerator*
les robinets *(m.)*	*faucets*
un séchoir	*dryer*
un tabouret	*stool; footstool*
le téléphone	*telephone*
une théière	*teapot*
des tiroirs *(m.)*	*drawers*
un torchon	*dishtowel*
de la vaisselle	*dishes*

LA SALLE DE SÉJOUR (LIVING ROOM)

des abat-jour *(m.)*	*lampshades*
des bibelots *(m.)*	*knickknacks*
une bibliothèque	*bookcase*
un canapé	*sofa, couch*
un canapé-lit	*sofa bed*
un cendrier	*ashtray*
une chaise	*chair*
une cheminée	*fireplace*
un climatiseur	*air conditioner*
des coussins *(m.)*	*cushions*
un divan	*couch, divan*
des étagères *(f.)* / des rayons *(m.)*	*shelves*
un fauteuil	*armchair*
des lampes *(f.)*	*lamps*
un magnétophone	*tape recorder*
une moquette	*carpet*
des objets d'art *(m.)*	*works of art*
du papier peint	*wallpaper*

une pendule	*clock*
un piano	*piano*
des plantes *(f.)*	*plants*
un radiateur	*radiator*
une radio / un poste de radio	*radio*
des rideaux *(m.)* (aux fenêtres)	*curtains (on the windows)*
une stéréo	*stereo*
une table (basse)	*(coffee) table*
des tableaux *(m.)* (aux murs)	*paintings (on the walls)*
un tapis	*rug*
un téléviseur / un poste de télévision	*television*
des tentures *(f.)*	*drapes*
un tourne-disque / un électrophone	*record player*
des vases *(m.)*	*vases*
un ventilateur	*fan*

LA SALLE DE BAINS (BATHROOM)

une armoire à pharmacie	*medicine chest / cabinet*
une baignoire	*bathtub*
une douche	*shower*
un lavabo	*(bathroom) sink*
un miroir / une glace	*mirror*
un pèse-personne	*bathroom scale*
un porte-serviettes	*towel rack*
une prise de courant	*electric outlet*
une serviette de bain	*bath towel*
un tapis de bain	*bathmat*

LA CHAMBRE À COUCHER (BEDROOM)

une armoire	*wardrobe*
un bureau	*desk*
un cendrier	*ashtray*
une commode	*bureau, chest of drawers*
une corbeille à papier	*wastebasket*
des couvertures *(f.)*	*covers, blankets*
un couvre-lit / un dessus-de-lit	*bedspread*
des draps *(m.)*	*sheets*
un édredon	*quilt*
une lampe de chevet	*bedside lamp*
un lit (des lits jumeaux)	*bed (twin beds)*
des livres *(m.)*	*books*
une machine à écrire	*typewriter*
des oreillers *(m.)*	*pillows*
un ours en peluche	*teddy bear*
des photos *(f.)*	*photos*

une radio / un poste de radio	*radio*
une radio réveil	*radio alarm, clock radio*
un réveil	*alarm clock*
une table de nuit	*night table*

LA SALLE À MANGER (DINING ROOM)

l'argenterie	*silverware*
des assiettes *(f.)*	*plates, dishes*
des assiettes creuses *(f.)*	*bowls*
un bahut	*sideboard, cupboard, hutch*
des bougies *(f.)*	*candles*
un buffet	*buffet, cabinet*
des couteaux *(m.)*	*knives*
des couvertes *(m.)*	*place settings (spoons, forks, knives)*
des cuillères *(f.)*	*spoons*
des fourchettes *(f.)*	*forks*
un lustre	*chandelier*
une nappe	*tablecloth*
une table	*table*
des tasses *(f.)*	*cups*
des verres *(m.)*	*glasses*

SPRINGBOARDS FOR CONVERSATION

1. Avez-vous un éléphant dans votre salle de bains?
   Non, mais j'ai un / une / des _____ dans ma _____.
2. Quelles sont les pièces de votre maison ou de votre appartement? Nommez-les.
3. Décrivez votre chambre à coucher, votre cuisine, votre salle de séjour, etc.
   Dans ma chambre à coucher (ma cuisine, ma salle de séjour) il y a _____.
4. Qu'est-ce qu'il y a dans la salle de séjour de Monsieur . . . ? de Madame . . . ?
   de Mademoiselle . . . ? etc.
5. Imaginez la maison ou l'appartement du professeur. Combien de pièces y a-t-il?
   Qu'y a-t-il dans chaque pièce?
6. Quels sont les meubles *(furniture)* de votre salle à manger? de votre chambre? etc.
7. Quels meubles aimeriez-vous acheter? Pour quelle pièce?
8. Quels appareils ménagers *(household appliances)* vous sont indispensables?
9. Dans quelles pièces de votre maison / appartement passez-vous le plus de temps?

PROJETS

1. Make a floor plan of your house or apartment. Label each room. Label all the furniture, etc.
2. Make a floor plan of the house or apartment you would like to live in. Label all the rooms and their contents.
3. Make labels such as: **le lit, la table, le réfrigérateur,** etc. Attach them to the respective items in your house, apartment or dormitory room.

ACTIVITÉ

Ask the person next to you to describe a room in his or her house or apartment (or his or her dormitory room). As it is being described, try to sketch the room. Indicate the various pieces of furniture, the windows, the doors, etc. The following phrases are useful for this activity: **Il y a une table ici, juste devant la fenêtre. Il y a un divan ici, entre les deux fauteuils,** etc. When need be, the describer should point to the sketch in progress and indicate: **Il y a une table ici. Le lit se trouve ici. Et voici la porte,** etc.

dans le coin	*in the corner*
au centre / au milieu	*in the center*
(juste) devant le / la . . .	*(right) in front of the . . .*
au fond du / de la . . .	*at the far end of the . . .*
à côté du / de la . . .	*next to the . . .*
sur le / la . . .	*on the . . .*
à gauche (droite) du / de la . . .	*to the left (right) of the . . .*
au-dessus du / de la . . .	*above the . . . / over the . . .*
au-dessous du / de la . . .	*under(neath) the . . .*
entre . . .	*between . . .*
près du / de la . . .	*near the . . .*
derrière le / la . . .	*behind the . . .*

13

Sur la route   On the Road

Proverbe: Qui veut voyager loin, ménage sa monture.

Proverb: He who wishes to travel far takes care of his steed.

DIALOGUE
EXERCICE D'APPLICATION
VERBE IRRÉGULIER: **conduire**
STRUCTURES:
1. Compound Tenses
2. Special Uses of Verb Tenses
EXERCICES DE SYNTHÈSE
EXPANSION:
En auto, au garage, sur la route, location de voitures
Une leçon de conduite
PRONONCIATION: [w], [y]
IMPROVISATION
PROJETS
ACTIVITÉ
CHANSON: **Maman, les p'tits bateaux**

«Quel embouteillage! La circulation est insupportable.»

DIALOGUE

(*À la station-service*)	(*At the Service Station*)
LE / LA GARAGISTE: Bonjour, Monsieur / Madame. Ordinaire ou super?	THE GARAGE MECHANIC: Hello. Regular or high-test?
VOUS: Super, s'il vous plaît.	YOU: High-test, please.
LE / LA GARAGISTE: Combien?	GARAGE MECHANIC: How much?
VOUS: Je suis en panne sèche. **Faites le plein.**	YOU: I've run out of gas. *Fill 'er up.*

Donnez-moi vingt litres de super. Donnez-moi pour quarante francs d'essence ordinaire. Donnez-moi vingt litres d'essence sans plomb / vingt litres de gas-oil (Canada: diesel)	Give me 20 liters of high-test. Give me 40 francs worth of regular. Give me 20 liters of unleaded / diesel fuel.

LE / LA GARAGISTE: Y a-t-il autre chose?	GARAGE MECHANIC: Is there anything else?
VOUS: Pourriez-vous **vérifier la pression des pneus,** s'il vous plaît?	YOU: Could you *check the air in my tires,* please?

vérifier l'huile / l'antigel / les bougies changer le filtre changer ce pneu crevé faire le graissage faire la vidange gonfler les pneus	check the oil / antifreeze / spark plugs change the filter change this flat tire do a lubrication job change the oil inflate the tires

LE / LA GARAGISTE: Certainement, Monsieur / Madame. Et je vais **vérifier que tout va bien.**	GARAGE MECHANIC: Certainly. And I'll *check to see that everything's fine.*

mettre de l'eau dans le radiateur nettoyer le pare-brise recharger la batterie régler le carburateur / les freins / la direction remplacer les essuie-glaces réparer la fuite	put some water in the radiator clean the windshield recharge the battery adjust the carburator / brakes / steering replace the windshield wipers fix the leak

VOUS: Merci. Combien vous dois-je?	YOU: Thank you. How much do I owe you?

EXERCICE D'APPLICATION*

Dites bonjour au garagiste. Dites-lui que vous êtes en panne sèche . . . que vous voulez du super. Dites-lui de faire le plein . . . de vous donner dix litres de super . . . de vous donner pour quarante francs d'essence ordinaire. . . . de vérifier l'huile . . . de remplacer les essuie-glaces . . . de mettre de l'eau dans le radiateur . . . de régler les freins.

VERBE IRRÉGULIER: conduire

conduire	to drive	
Le présent:	**je conduis**	**nous conduisons**
	tu conduis	**vous conduisez**
	il / elle conduit	**ils / elles conduisent**
Le participe passé: **conduit**		
La base du futur et du conditionnel: **conduir-**		

STRUCTURES

1.   Compound Tenses

Compound tenses are composed of the auxiliary verb **avoir** or **être** and the past participle.

a. Le passé composé

parler	**arriver**	**se lever**
spoke /	*arrived /*	*got up /*
have spoken /	*have arrived /*	*have gotten up /*
did speak	*did arrive*	*did get up*
j'ai parlé	je suis arrivé(e)	je me suis levé(e)
tu as parlé	tu es arrivé(e)	tu t'es levé(e)
il a parlé	il est arrivé	il s'est levé
elle a parlé	elle est arrivée	elle s'est levée
nous avons parlé	nous sommes arrivé(e)s	nous nous sommes levé(e)s
vous avez parlé	vous êtes arrivé(e)(s)	vous vous êtes levé(e)(s)
ils ont parlé	ils sont arrivés	ils se sont levés
elles ont parlé	elles sont arrivées	elles se sont levées

b. Le plus-que-parfait is composed of the imperfect tense of either **avoir** or **être** and the past participle of the verb being conjugated:

parler *had spoken*	arriver *had arrived*	se lever *had gotten up*
j'avais parlé	j'étais arrivé(e)	je m'étais levé(e)
tu avais parlé	tu étais arrivé(e)	tu t'étais levé(e)
il avait parlé	il était arrivé	il s'était levé
elle avait parlé	elle était arrivée	elle s'était levée
nous avions parlé	nous étions arrivé(e)s	nous nous étions levé(e)s
vous aviez parlé	vous étiez arrivé(e)(s)	vous vous étiez levé(e)(s)
ils avaient parlé	ils étaient arrivés	ils s'étaient levés
elles avaient parlé	elles étaient arrivées	elles s'étaient levées

c. **Le futur antérieur** is composed of the future tense of either **avoir** or **être** and the past participle of the verb being conjugated:

parler *will have spoken*	arriver *will have arrived*	se lever *will have gotten up*
j'aurai parlé	je serai arrivé(e)	je me serai levé(e)
tu auras parlé	tu seras arrivé(e)	tu te seras levé(e)
il aura parlé	il sera arrivé	il se sera levé
elle aura parlé	elle sera arrivée	elle se sera levée
nous aurons parlé	nous serons arrivé(e)s	nous nous serons levé(e)s
vous aurez parlé	vous serez arrivé(e)(s)	vous vous serez levé(e)(s)
ils auront parlé	ils seront arrivés	ils se seront levés
elles auront parlé	elles seront arrivées	elles se seront levées

d. **Le conditionnel passé** is composed of the conditional tense of either **avoir** or **être** and the past participle of the verb being conjugated:

parler *would have spoken*	arriver *would have arrived*	se lever *would have gotten up*
j'aurais parlé	je serais arrivé(e)	je me serais levé(e)
tu aurais parlé	tu serais arrivé(e)	tu te serais levé(e)
il aurait parlé	il serait arrivé	il se serait levé
elle aurait parlé	elle serait arrivée	elle se serait levée
nous aurions parlé	nous serions arrivé(e)s	nous nous serions levé(e)s
vous auriez parlé	vous seriez arrivé(e)(s)	vous vous seriez levé(e)(s)
ils auraient parlé	ils seraient arrivés	ils se seraient levés
elles auraient parlé	elles seraient arrivées	elles se seraient levées

2.   Special Uses of Verb Tenses

a. Verbs in clauses introduced by **quand** or **lorsque** *(when)* and **aussitôt que** or **dès que** *(as soon as)* are in the future tense when they express a future action. The present tense is used in English:

> **Dès que le garagiste arrivera, il vous dira ce qui ne va pas.**
> *As soon as the garage mechanic arrives, he will tell you what's wrong.*

b. **Le futur antérieur** is used with **quand, lorsque, aussitôt que,** and **dès que** when referring to a future action that precedes the future action of the main clause. In English the past tense is used:

> **Je vous téléphonerai quand j'aurai fini mon travail.**
> *I'll call you when I have finished my work.*

> **Je lui donnerai l'argent dès qu'il aura vérifié l'huile.**
> *I'll give him the money as soon as he has checked the oil.*

c. When the main clause is in the **conditionnel passé**, the if clause is in the **plus-que-parfait.** English uses a similar construction:

> **Si tu m'avais téléphoné, je t'aurais tout dit.**
> *If you had phoned me, I would have told you everything.*

> **Si vous étiez resté, il ne serait jamais parti.**
> *If you had stayed, he would never have left.*

EXERCICES DE SYNTHÈSE

A.*   *Mettez les phrases suivantes au futur antérieur. Ensuite, traduisez la phrase:*

EXEMPLE: Elle part. (avant lundi)
            Elle sera partie avant lundi.

1. Le garagiste répare la voiture. (avant cinq heures)
2. Je termine. (avant ce soir)
3. Ils partent. (avant votre arrivée)
4. Nous faisons le travail. (avant demain)
5. Vous achetez une nouvelle voiture. (avant la fin du mois)

B.*   *Transformez. Commencez par:* **Si j'avais eu assez de temps . . .**

EXEMPLE: Pourquoi n'avez-vous pas téléphoné au garagiste?
            Si j'avais eu assez de temps, j'aurais téléphoné au garagiste.

1. Pourquoi n'êtes-vous pas allé(e) au garage?
2. Pourquoi n'avez-vous pas regardé la voiture?
3. Pourquoi n'avez-vous pas réparé la transmission?
4. Pourquoi ne m'avez-vous pas téléphoné?
5. Pourquoi n'avez-vous pas vérifié l'huile?
6. Pourquoi n'avez-vous pas conduit plus lentement?
7. Pourquoi n'avez-vous pas traduit les phrases?
8. Pourquoi n'êtes-vous pas arrivé(e) plus tôt?
9. Pourquoi n'avez-vous pas terminé votre travail?
10. Pourquoi ne m'avez-vous pas tout dit?

C. *Répondez à ces questions en employant le plus-que-parfait et le conditionnel passé.*

Qu'est-ce que vous auriez fait si . . .

1. vous aviez été en panne sèche ce matin?
2. vous aviez eu un pneu crevé ce matin?
3. vous vous étiez levé(e) de très bonne heure ce matin?
4. le professeur de français n'était pas venu en classe aujourd'hui?
5. on vous avait donné un million de dollars ce matin?
6. vous n'étiez pas venu(e) en classe aujourd'hui?
7. vous n'aviez pas été fatigué(e) hier soir?
8. vous aviez eu beaucoup d'argent la semaine dernière?

D. *An exercise on* **si** + *le plus-que-parfait, le conditionnel passé. Ask other class members what they would have done if you had given them a kick at the beginning of class:* **Qu'est-ce que vous auriez fait si je vous avais donné un coup de pied au début du cours?** *Some possible responses include:*

Si vous m'aviez donné un coup de pied, . . .

j'aurais hurlé *(yelled)*
j'aurais pleuré *(cried)*
j'aurais crié «Aïe!» *(yelled "Ouch!")*
je me serais fâché(e) *(been angry)*
je vous l'aurais rendu *(kicked you back)*
je vous aurais donné un coup de poing *(punched you)*
je l'aurais dit à ma mère *(told my mother on you)*
je vous aurais donné une claque / une gifle *(slapped you)*
je vous aurais accusé(e) de brutalité *(accused you of brutality)*
je vous aurais demandé pourquoi *(asked you why)*
j'aurais été stupéfait(e) *(been stunned)*
je vous aurais mordu(e) *(bitten you)*
j'aurais téléphoné à la police *(called the police)*

Now ask them what they would have done if you had given them a kiss instead: **Si je vous avais donné un baiser, qu'est-ce que vous auriez fait?** *Some possible responses, in addition to those given above, include:* **Si vous m'aviez donné un baiser, . . .**

> **je vous l'aurais rendu** *(kissed you back)*
> **j'aurais rougi** *(blushed)*
> **j'aurais souri** *(smiled)*
> **j'en aurais été très touché(e).** *(been very touched)*
> **j'aurais été content(e)** *(been happy)*

For additional practice, review what your classmates have said, using the third person from **(il, elle).**

EXPANSION: En auto, Au garage, Sur la route, Location de voitures

1. **Possédez-vous une voiture? Est-elle neuve? une bicyclette (un vélo)? une moto (une motocyclette)? un vélomoteur? Est-il neuf? une motoneige? Quelle marque?**

   Do you own a car? Is it new? a bicycle? a motorcycle? a motorbike? Is it new? a snowmobile? What make?

2. **Je cherche la route de Québec. Pourriez-vous m'indiquer la route de Québec?**

   I'm looking for the road to Quebec. Could you tell me how to get to Quebec?

3. **Où est le garage le plus proche?**

   Where's the nearest garage?

4. **J'ai besoin d'essence.**

   I need gasoline.

5. **Le pneu avant a éclaté.**

   The front tire blew out.

6. **Qu'est-ce qui ne va pas? Pouvez-vous faire la réparation?**

   What's wrong? Can you fix it?

7. **Dans le coffre il y a un cric / une clef anglaise / un tournevis / des pinces / une roue de secours / des outils / une couverture.**

   In the trunk of the car there is a jack / wrench / screw driver / pliers / spare tire / tools / blanket.

8. **Dans la boîte à gants (Canada: le compartiment à gants), il y a les papiers / mon permis de conduire / une lampe de poche / des Kleenex / une carte routière / des clés / un stylo / un crayon / des pièces de monnaie / des allumettes / une trousse de première urgence.**

   In the glove compartment, there are the papers / my driver's license / a flashlight / some tissues / a road map / some keys / a pen / a pencil / some change / some matches / a first aid kit.

9. **Je voudrais louer une voiture. Quel est le tarif par jour?**

   I would like to rent a car. What's the charge per day?

10. **Est-ce que le kilométrage est compris?**

    Is the mileage included?

11. **La route est glissante. Il y a beaucoup de virages.**

    The road is slippery. There are a lot of curves.

12. **Quel embouteillage! La circulation est insupportable.**	*What a traffic jam! The traffic is unbearable.*
13. **Il y a eu un accident.**	*There's been an accident.*
14. **Puis-je avoir votre nom, votre adresse, le nom de votre compagnie d'assurance, et le numéro d'immatriculation de votre voiture?**	*Can I have your name, your address, the name of your insurance company, and the registration number of your car?*
15. **Quel est le numéro de votre plaque minéralogique?**	*What is your license plate number?*
16. **J'ai fait de l'auto-stop.**	*I hitch-hiked.*
17. **L'agent de police m'a dressé une contravention.**	*The police officer gave me a ticket.*

Exercice

Répondez aux questions suivantes:

1. Possédez-vous une voiture? Quelle marque? Est-elle neuve? Possédez-vous une bicyclette? une moto? un vélomoteur?
2. Savez-vous conduire? Aimez-vous conduire? Avez-vous peur de conduire quand il y a beaucoup de circulation? D'habitude roulez-vous lentement? à grande vitesse?
3. Avez-vous déjà fait de l'auto-stop? Où? Quand? Avec qui?
4. Avez-vous un permis de conduire international?
5. Qu'est-ce qu'il y a dans le coffre de votre voiture? dans la boîte à gants?
6. Quelles questions posez-vous quand vous louez une voiture?
7. Avez-vous souvent des contraventions?
8. Avez-vous déjà eu un accident? Quand? À qui la faute?
9. Quel est le numéro de votre plaque minéralogique?

EXPANSION: Une leçon de conduite

1. **Montez dans la voiture.**	*Get into the car.*
2. **Fermez la portière.**	*Shut the car door.*
3. **Mettez votre ceinture de sécurité.**	*Put on your seat belt.*
4. **Tournez la clé de contact. / Mettez le contact.**	*Turn on the ignition.*
5. **Démarrez.**	*Start it up.*
6. **Embrayez.**	*Throw in the clutch.*
7. **Changez de vitesse.**	*Shift gears.*
8. **Passez en première / en deuxième / en troisième / en quatrième / au point mort.**	*Shift into first / second / third / fourth / neutral.*

9. **Débrayez.**	*Release the clutch.*
10. **Appuyez sur l'accélérateur.**	*Step on the accelerator.*
11. **Ne calez pas.**	*Don't stall.*
12. **Avancez.**	*Go forward.*
13. **Faites une marche-arrière. Doucement!**	*Back it up. Slowly!*
14. **Attention! C'est une route à deux sens / à sens unique.**	*Be careful! It's a two-way road / one-way road.*
15. **Attention au piéton / au chien / aux enfants!**	*Watch out for the pedestrian / dog / children!*
16. **Allumez vos phares / vos feux de position.**	*Turn on your headlights / parking lights.*
17. **Ralentissez!**	*Slow down!*
18. **Restez à droite.**	*Stay to the right.*
20. **Ne brûlez pas le feu rouge!**	*Don't go through the red light!*
20. **Ne roulez pas si vite!**	*Don't go so fast!*
21. **Ne dérapez pas!**	*Don't skid!*
22. **Ne klaxonnez pas.**	*Don't blow the horn.*
23. **Vous avez la priorité.**	*You have the right of way.*
24. **Accélérez!**	*Speed (it) up.*
25. **Tournez (le volant)! À gauche! À droite!**	*Turn (the steering wheel)! Left! Right!*
26. **Doublez! / Dépassez!**	*Pass!*
27. **Regardez dans le rétroviseur!**	*Look into the rearview mirror!*
28. **Mettez le clignotant de droite / de gauche.**	*Put on the right / left blinker (turn indicator).*
29. **Changez de voie / Changez de couloir.**	*Change lanes.*
30. **Passez sur la voie de gauche. Elle est libre.**	*Get into the left lane. It's clear.*
31. **Revenez sur la voie de droite.**	*Get back into the right lane.*
32. **Ne dépassez pas la vitesse limite.**	*Don't speed.*
33. **Freinez. Vite!**	*Put on the brakes! Quickly!*
34. **Ne rentrez pas dans la voiture de devant.**	*Don't hit the car in front (of you).*
35. **Arrêtez (la voiture) ici.**	*Stop (the car) here.*
36. **Coupez le contact.**	*Turn off the ignition.*
37. **Vous êtes un danger public!**	*You are a public menace!*

PRONONCIATION

1.   Sound (Phonetic Symbol): [w]

SPELLING:	**ou** (followed by a vowel), **oi, oî, oy**
ENGLISH SOUND RESEMBLED:	Initial sound in word *wet*
PRONUNCIATION:	This semivowel (or semiconsonant) sound resembles

the French vowel sound [u] (see Chapter 3). It is pronounced more tensely and briefly, however. It is
always combined in French with a following vowel
sound.

EXAMPLES FROM THIS CHAPTER: loin   noyer   pourquoi
                             dois   droit   soir
                             voiture   droite
                             besoin   voie
                             boîte   couloir
                             louer (Note: pronounced as one syllable)

2. Sound (Phonetic Symbol): [ɥ]

SPELLING: u (followed by a vowel)

PRONUNCIATION: The semivowel (or semiconsonant) sound [ɥ] resem-
                                 bles the French vowel sound [y] (see Chapter 4). The
                                 lips are protruded slightly further than for the [y]
                                 sound. Also, [ɥ] is said more rapidly and tensely than
                                 the related vowel sound [y]. [ɥ] is always combined
                                 in French with a following vowel. Do not confuse this
                                 sound with the English sound [w].

EXAMPLES FROM THIS CHAPTER: huile   je suis
                             fuite   puis-je
                             essuie-glaces traduire
                             conduire   aujourd'hui
                             appuyez

IMPROVISATION

*En employant le vocabulaire et les expressions tirés de toute la leçon, préparez des con-
versations humoristiques, sérieuses, ou ridicules sur les situations suivantes:*

1. Un agent de police vous dresse une contravention. Il / elle vous explique pourquoi.
   Vous n'êtes pas d'accord.
2. Vous êtes confortablement installé(e) sur le siège arrière de la voiture de votre
   ami(e). Quels conseils lui donnez-vous pendant qu'il / elle conduit?
3. Vous êtes en panne. Expliquez au mecanicien / à la mécanicienne ce qui ne va pas.
   Comprend-il / elle ce que vous dites?
4. Vous louez une voiture.

PROJETS

1. Fill out this **Memento** for your own car or for your family's car.

MEMENTO DE L'AUTOMOBILISTE

Permis de conduire

  Numéro:_____

  Délivré le:_____

  Par:_____

Immatriculation

  Lieu d'immatriculation:_____

  Numéro d'immatriculation:_____

  Marque:_____

  Année:_____

  Type:_____

  Numéro de série:_____

  Numéro du moteur:_____

  Date de délivrance:_____

Assurance

  Police Numéro:_____

  Compagnie:_____

  Adresse:_____

  Agent:_____

  Téléphone:_____

Club Automobile

  Adresse:_____

  Téléphone:_____

Garage

  Nom:_____

  Adresse:_____

  Téléphone:_____

  Nom du mécanicien:_____

---

2. List everything you have had done to your car this year. For example: **J'ai fait réparer les freins, gonfler les pneus,** etc.

3. Clip illustrations of cars, both interiors and exteriors, from advertisements in magazines. Using the vocabulary of the **Dialogue** and **Expansion** sections of this chapter, label the parts shown.

ACTIVITÉ

Teach a classmate how to drive. Sit next to each other, as if you were in a car together. See **Expansion: «Une leçon de conduite»** for appropriate vocabulary and structures.

MAMAN, LES P'TITS BATEAUX

Ma - man, les p'tits ba - teaux qui vont sur

l'eau ont - ils des jambes? Mais oui, mon gros bê -

ta s'ils n'en a - vaient pas, ils ne marche-raient pas!

SIGNS

Où avez-vous vu . . . ?
—J'ai vu _____ .

Ici.	Au supermarché.	Au bureau de poste.
À l'université.	Au cinéma.	À la banque.
À l'école.	Dans le métro.	Dans le train.
Chez moi.	Sur une porte.	À la gare.
Sur la route.	Dans le parc.	À la plage.
Au restaurant.	Au théâtre.	À la station-service.
Dans un grand magasin.	À la télévision.	Dans la rue.

Accès aux quais	*This way to the train platforms*	Chaud (C)	*Hot water faucet*
		Complet	*Full*
À louer	*For rent*	Dames	*Ladies*
Ascenseurs	*Elevators*	Danger	*Danger*
Attention	*Attention*	Défense de cracher	*No spitting*
Attention, Chien méchant	*Beware of the dog*	Défense de dépasser / doubler	*No passing*
À vendre	*For sale*	Défense d'entrer	*Keep out*
Avertissement	*Warning*	Défense de fumer	*No smoking*
Avis	*Notice*	Défense de stationner	*No parking*
Baignade interdite	*No swimming*		
Billets	*Tickets*	École	*School*
Caisse	*Cashier*	Entrée	*Entrance*

264

Entrée interdite	*No entrance*	Piétons	*Pedestrians*
Entrée gratuite	*Free entrance, no charge*	Plage privée	*Private beach*
		Poste aérienne	*Airmail*
Entrée libre	*Free entrance, no obligation to buy*	Poussez	*Push*
Entrez	*Enter*	Prière de ne pas déranger	*Please do not disturb*
Escalier de secours	*Fire escape*	Prière de ne pas stationner	*Please do not park*
Escalier roulant	*Escalator*		
Escalier mécanique	*Escalator*	Prière de ne pas toucher	*Please do not touch*
Fermé(e) le dimanche	*Closed Sundays*	Privé(e)	*Private*
Froid (F)	*Cold water*	Propriété privée	*Private property*
Frappez	*Knock*	Renseignements	*Information*
Fumeur(s)	*Smoking allowed*	Réservé	*Reserved*
Hôpital	*Hospital*	Sens interdit	*No entry*
Il est dangereux de se pencher	*It's dangerous to lean out*	Sens unique	*One way*
. . . interdit	*. . . forbidden*	Silence (Hôpital)	*Silence / Quiet (Hospital Zone)*
Interdiction de camper	*No camping*	Soldes	*Sale*
		Sonnez	*Ring*
Interdiction de stationner	*No parking*	Sortie	*Exit*
		Sortie de voiture	*Driveway (do not block)*
Libre	*Free, not in use*		
Locations	*Ticket office*	Stationnement interdit	*No parking*
Messieurs	*Gentlemen*		
Occupé	*Occupied*	Stop	*Stop*
Ouvert(e)	*Open*	Tirez	*Pull*
Passage interdit	*No entrance*	Toilettes	*Toilets, washrooms*
Péage	*Tolls*	Travaux	*Road repairs*
Pêche interdite	*No fishing*	Vestiaire	*Cloakroom, checkroom*

SPRINGBOARDS FOR CONVERSATION

1. Où avez-vous vu . . . ? Quand?
   J'ai vu _____.
2. Qu'est-ce qu'on voit dans le métro? à l'université? au restaurant? etc.
   On voit _____.
3. Où voit-on «Baignade Interdite»? «Complet»? «Stop»? etc.
   On le voit _____.
4. Que faites-vous en voyant «Silence»? «Défense de fumer»? «Stop»? etc.

5. Qu'est-ce qu'il ne faut pas faire quand on voit «Défense d'entrer»? «Défense de stationner«? «Prière de ne pas toucher»? etc.
6. Donnez le contraire de: Froid   Sortie
   Entrée   Occupé
   Dames   Poussez, etc.
   Fermé

PROJETS

1. Make a sign for each of the following locations: your bedroom door, your notebook, your car, the classroom door, the instructor's desk, the hallway outside the classroom, your back, in front of your house or apartment building, the street in front of your classroom building, etc.
2. Go through a magazine and clip photos of places, street scenes, buildings, etc. Caption each with a sign that would seem appropriate. For example: **Hôpital, Silence, Chien Méchant, Propriété Privée, École, Stop!**

Chapitre
14

À la poste	At the Post Office

Proverbe: Pas de nouvelles, bonnes nouvelles.	Proverb: No news is good news.

DIALOGUE
EXERCICES D'APPLICATION
VERBES IRRÉGULIERS: **envoyer, écrire**
STRUCTURES:
1. Formation of Adverbs
2. Position of Adverbs
3. Comparison of Adverbs
EXERCICES DE SYNTHÈSE
EXPANSION:
À la poste
Quel courrier avez-vous reçu cette semaine?
PRONONCIATION: [ʃ]
IMPROVISATION
PROJETS
ACTIVITÉ
CHANSON: **Au clair de la lune**

«Où se trouve la boîte au lettres?»

DIALOGUE

Vous: Où se trouve le bureau de poste[1] le plus proche, s'il vous plaît?

Un(e) Passant(e): Le voilà, juste devant vous.

Vous: Ah . . . Merci, Monsieur / Madame.

You: Where is the nearest post office[1], please?

A Passer-by: There it is, right in front of you.

You: Ah . . . Thank you.

Vous: Je voudrais envoyer cette carte postale par avion en Amérique. . . . Et combien faut-il pour envoyer **cette lettre?**

You: I would like to send this postcard airmail to America . . . And how much does it cost (*literally:* does it need) to send *this letter?*

ce gros paquet
ce colis
ce journal
ces deux lettres

this large package
this parcel
this newspaper
these two letters

Le Postier / La Postière: Je vais la / le / les peser. . . . C'est tout?

Vous: Je voudrais aussi **des timbres,** s'il vous plaît. . . .

The Postal Clerk: I'll weigh it / them . . . . Is that all?

You: I would also like *some stamps,* please. . . .

quatre timbres à un franc
des timbres de collection
un aérogramme
envoyer un télégramme
envoyer un mandat international
envoyer cette lettre en recommandé

four one-franc stamps
collectors' stamps
an air letter
to send a telegram
to send an international money order
to send this letter (by) registered mail

Alors, combien vous dois-je en tout?

Le Postier / La Postière: Ça fait vingt francs, Monsieur / Madame.

Vous: Voilà . . . Où se trouve le guichet de la poste restante, s'il vous plaît?

Le Postier / La Postière: C'est par là. À l'autre bout. Guichet numéro huit.

Vous: Merci.

So, how much do I owe you altogether?

Postal Clerk: (It comes to) twenty francs.

You: Here (it is / they are). . . . Where is the general delivery window / counter please?

Postal Clerk: It's over there. At the other end. Window / counter number eight.

You: Thank you.

---

1. The post office is often referred to as the **P.T.T. (Postes, télégraphes et téléphones)** or simply as **la poste.**

Vous: Avez-vous du courrier pour _____. (votre nom)	You: Do you have any mail for _____? (your name)
Le Postier / La Postière: Votre passeport, s'il vous plaît.	Postal Clerk: Your passport, please.
Vous: Le voici.	You: Here it is.
Le Postier / La Postière: Merci, Monsieur / Madame. Un instant, s'il vous plaît. Voilà. . .	Postal Clerk: Thank you. One moment, please. Here it is. . . .

EXERCICES D'APPLICATION*

1. Demandez où se trouve le bureau de poste le plus proche . . . combien il faut pour envoyer une lettre par avion en Amérique . . . combien vous devez en tout . . . où se trouve le guichet de la poste restante . . . s'il y a du courrier pour vous.
2. Dites que vous voulez envoyer cette carte postale par avion en Amérique . . . que vous voulez des timbres . . . que vous voulez quatre timbres à un franc . . . que vous voulez envoyer un télégramme . . . que vous voulez un aérogramme.

VERBES IRRÉGULIERS: envoyer, écrire

envoyer *to send*	
Le présent: **j'envoie** **nous envoyons**	
tu envoies **vous envoyez**	
il / elle envoie **ils / elles envoient**	
Le participe passé: **envoyé**	
La base du futur et du conditionnel: **enverr-**	

«Je voudrais **envoyer** cette carte postale par avion en Amérique.»
«Et combien faut-il pour **envoyer** cette lettre?»

écrire *to write*	
Le présent: **j'écris** **nous écrivons**	
tu écris **vous écrivez**	
il / elle écrit **ils / elles écrivent**	
Le participe passé: **écrit**	
La base du futur et du conditionnel: **écrir-**	

Comment est-ce que **cela s'écrit?**   *How is that written (spelled)?*

Like **écrire: décrire**   *to describe*

STRUCTURES

1.   Formation of Adverbs

a. Some adverbs are formed by adding **-ment** to the masculine singular of adjectives ending in a vowel:

absolu	**absolument**	*absolutely*
autre	**autrement**	*otherwise*
facile	**facilement**	*easily*
probable	**probablement**	*probably*
rapide	**rapidement**	*rapidly*
vrai	**vraiment**	*truly*
probable	**probablement**	*probably*
rapide	**rapidement**	*rapidly*
vrai	**vraiment**	*truly*

b. Some adverbs are formed by adding **-ment** to the feminine singular of adjectives whose masculine singulars do *not* end in a vowel:

actif, active	**activement**	*actively*
franc, franche	**franchement**	*frankly*
heureux, heureuse	**heureusement**	*fortunately*
lent, lente	**lentement**	*slowly*
naturel, naturelle	**naturellement**	*naturally, of course*
premier, première	**premièrement**	*firstly, first of all*
seul, seule	**seulement**	*only*
sûr, sûre	**sûrement**	*surely*

Note these irregularities:

brièvement	*briefly*
gentiment	*kindly, nicely*

With certain adverbs, the final **e** of the feminine adjective becomes **é** and is therefore pronounced:

aveugle	**aveuglément**	*blindly*
confus, confuse	**confusément**	*in a confused fashion*
énorme	**énormément**	*enormously*
précis, précise	**précisément**	*precisely, exactly*
profond, profonde	**profondément**	*profoundly, deeply*

c. Some adverbs are formed by replacing the final **-ant** or **-ent** of the adjective with **-amment** and **-emment**:

constant	**constamment**	*constantly*
différent	**différemment**	*differently*
évident	**évidemment**	*evidently*
fréquent	**fréquemment**	*frequently*
indépendant	**indépendamment**	*independently*
intelligent	**intelligemment**	*intelligently*
prudent	**prudemment**	*carefully*
récent	**récemment**	*recently*

d. Certain masculine adjectives are used as adverbs in fixed phrases:

Parlez plus bas.	*Speak more quietly.*
Ça sent bon / mauvais.	*That smells good / bad.*
Il travaille dur.	*He works hard.*
Ça coûte cher.	*That's expensive. That costs a lot.*

e. Here are some common adverbs that are not directly derived from adjectives in the fashion described above:

à présent	*now*	**hier**	*yesterday*
actuellement	*now*	**ici**	*here*
ailleurs	*elsewhere*	**jamais**	*ever; never*
assez	*enough*	**là**	*there*
aujourd'hui	*today*	**là-bas**	*over there*
aussi	*also*	**longtemps**	*for a long time*
autrefois	*formerly*	**mal**	*badly*
beaucoup	*very much, a lot*	**même**	*even*
bien	*well*	**parfois**	*sometimes*
bientôt	*soon*	**partout**	*everywhere*
bref	*in short*	**peut-être**	*perhaps*
d'abord	*at first*	**plutôt**	*rather*
de bonne heure	*early*	**presque**	*almost*
déjà	*already*	**puis**	*then*
demain	*tomorrow*	**quelquefois**	*sometimes*
de temps en temps	*from time to time*	**si**	*so*
encore	*still, again*	**souvent**	*often*
enfin	*at last, finally*	**surtout**	*above all, especially*
ensemble	*together*	**tant**	*so much, so many*
ensuite	*then*	**tard**	*late*
exprès	*on purpose*	**tellement**	*so much*
fort	*very*	**tôt**	*early*

toujours	*always*	vite	*quickly*
tout de suite	*immediately*	volontiers	*gladly, willingly*
trop	*too much, too many*		

2. Position of Adverbs

a. Many adverbs may be placed in different positions within the sentence. For example, the adverb **enfin** *(at last)* usually comes between the helping verb and the past participle: **Il est enfin parti.** It may be placed first in the sentence for emphasis: **Enfin il est parti!**

In conversation, adverbs may stand alone as answers:

Naturellement!   Moi, jamais!   Oui, probablement.

b. In simple French tenses (le présent, l'imparfait, le futur and le conditionnel), an adverb never comes between the subject and the verb. It usually follows the verb: **Il m'écrit toujours de longues lettres.** Note that in English, *always* would be placed between the subject and the verb: *He always writes me long letters.*

c. In compound tenses the following adverbs may come at the beginning of a sentence or after the past participle but never between the helping verb and the past participle:

  1. long adverbs like **facilement, franchement, rapidement,** etc.
  2. certain adverbs of time answering the question "when": **hier, aujourd'hui, demain, tôt, tard.**
  3. adverbs of place: **ailleurs, ici, là, là-bas.**
  4. adverbial phrases like **tout de suite, de temps en temps, en ce moment, de bonne heure.**

> **Votre lettre est arrivée tard.**
> *Your letter arrived late.*
> **Je lui ai envoyé un télégramme tout de suite après.**
> *I sent him a telegram immediately afterwards.*
> **Hier je lui ai envoyé deux lettres.**
> *Yesterday I sent him two letters.*

d. In compound tenses the following adverbs come between the helping verb and the past participle:

  1. short adverbs like **mal, bien, même, vite, surtout,** etc.
  2. the adverbs of time **bientôt, déjà, encore, enfin, jamais, longtemps, souvent,** and **toujours.**
  3. adverbs of quantity: **assez, beaucoup, peu, tant, trop.**
  4. the adverbs **certainement, particulièrement, peut-être, probablement, sûrement, tellement, vraiment.**

J'ai bien dormi.   Je n'ai pas bien dormi.
I slept well.   I did not sleep well.

Il m'a souvent écrit.   J'ai déjà beaucoup lu.
He often wrote to me.   I have already read a lot.

e. With a conjugated verb and an infinitive, the adverb generally precedes the infinitive:

Je voudrais aussi envoyer une lettre par avion.
I would also like to send a letter airmail.
Je vais beaucoup écrire.
I'm going to write a lot.

f. The adverb modifying another adjective or adverb always precedes:

Ces timbres sont très jolis.   *These stamps are very pretty.*
La lettre est arrivée trop tard.   *The letter arrived too late.*

3.   Comparison of Adverbs

a. plus... que   *more . . . than*
moins... que *less . . . than; not as . . . as*
aussi... que   *as . . . as* (with positive verbs)
si... que   *as . . . as* (with negative verbs)

Je lis plus vite que les autres étudiants.
I read faster than the other students (do).
Il m'écrit moins souvent qu'elle.
He writes to me less often than she (does).
Je parle aussi vite que vous.
I speak as fast as you (do).

b. Quantitative comparisons with nouns require **de:**

more: **J'ai envoyé plus de cartes postales que vous.**
less: **J'ai moins d'argent que vous.**
fewer: **J'ai reçu moins de lettres que vous.**
as many: **Avez-vous reçu autant de lettres que moi?**
as much: **J'ai autant d'argent que vous.**

c. Before numerals, *than* is expressed by **de:**

Ça va coûter plus de 100 francs.
That's going to cost more than 100 francs.

d. The superlative is formed by placing **le** before the comparative form:

Je parle le plus franchement de tous.
I speak the most frankly of all (of anybody).

e. Certain adverbs have irregular comparative and superlative forms:

bien / mieux / le mieux   *well / better / best*
beaucoup / plus / le plus   *much, a lot / more / the most*
peu / moins / le moins   *little / less / the least*

Je parle bien.   **Il parle mieux.**   **Elle parle le mieux de tous.**
I speak well.   *He speaks better.*   *She speaks the best of all.*

EXERCICES DE SYNTHÈSE

A.*   *Remplacez les mots en italique. Faites les changements nécessaires:*

EXEMPLE: *J'*ai envoyé une carte postale au professeur. (Elle)
              Elle a envoyé une carte postale au professeur.

1. *Elle* écrit souvent. (Nous, Vous, Ils)
2. *J'*envoie toujours des cartes postales. (Tu, Il, On)
3. Qu'est-ce qu'*il* écrit? (tu, elle, vous)
4. *Vous* avez écrit une lettre, n'est-ce pas? (Tu, Il, Elle)
5. *Elle* nous a décrit la maison. (Il, On, Vous)
6. Avez-*vous* envoyé la lettre? (tu, ils, elles)

B.   *Répondez à ces questions par des phrases complètes:*

1. Aimez-vous écrire?
2. Écrivez-vous souvent à vos amis? des lettres? des cartes postales? aussi souvent que possible? rarement? de temps en temps?
3. À qui écrivez-vous souvent? À qui n'écrivez-vous jamais? À qui écrivez-vous une fois par an?
4. Écrivez-vous à votre sénateur? au Président? au maire de votre ville? à votre acteur préféré? au Père Noël? à vos parents? Souvent? Parfois? De temps en temps? Rarement?
5. Écrivez-vous lisiblement?
6. Écrivez-vous avec la main droite ou avec la main gauche?
7. Avez-vous écrit une lettre aujourd'hui? hier soir? cette semaine? A qui?
8. Avez-vous déjà écrit un roman? des poèmes?
9. À qui avez-vous écrit récemment? Qui vous a écrit récemment?
10. Envoyez-vous des cartes postales lorsque vous êtes en vacances? À qui?

C.* *Donnez les adverbes dérivés des adjectifs suivants. Puis traduisez:*

> EXEMPLE: heureux
>   heureusement (*fortunately*)

autre	énorme	sérieux	évident
calme	premier	bref	lent
agréable	dangereux	franc	constant
seul	malheureux	naturel	fréquent

D.* *Donnez le contraire:*

> EXEMPLE: bien → mal

rapidement	vite	facilement	tard
peu	probablement	souvent	beaucoup
mal	ici	hier	bien
rarement	heureusement	toujours	séparément

E.   *Répondez à chaque question par une phrase complète. Employez les adverbes suivants:* **hier, récemment, ce matin, aujourd'hui, maintenant, trop, constamment, probablement, malheureusement, peut-être, ne . . . jamais, souvent, de temps en temps** *ou* **toujours:**

1. Quand êtes-vous arrivé(e)?
2. Fumez-vous?
3. Allez-vous à la poste?
4. Écrivez-vous à vos amis? à vos parents?
5. Téléphonez-vous à vos amis? à vos parents?
6. Avez-vous mangé?
7. Avez-vous parlé avec le professeur?
8. Parlez-vous au téléphone?

F.* *Placez l'adverbe en parenthèses dans la phrase. Ensuite, traduisez:*

> EXEMPLES: J'ai dormi hier soir. (bien)   La lettre est arrivée. (hier)
>   J'ai bien dormi hier soir.   La lettre est arrivée hier.

1. Votre lettre est arrivée. (aujourd'hui)
2. Je n'ai pas écrit. (assez)
3. J'ai parlé. (franchement)
4. J'ai téléphoné. (de bonne heure)
5. La lettre est arrivée. (tard)
6. Il m'a donné les timbres. (déjà)
7. Il m'en a parlé. (beaucoup)
8. Il en a parlé. (constamment)
9. J'ai compris. (mal)
10. J'ai compris. (enfin)
11. Tu as reçu ma lettre! (certainement)
12. J'ai compris le système. (vite)
13. Le télégramme est arrivé. (tôt)

G. *Faites des comparaisons en employant* **plus de, moins de** *et* **autant de:**

EXEMPLE: J'ai acheté cinq timbres. Elle en a acheté dix.
J'ai acheté moins de timbres qu'elle.
Elle a acheté plus de timbres que moi.

1. J'ai écrit deux lettres. Elle en a écrit quatre.
2. J'ai envoyé deux cartes postales. Elle en a envoyé cinq.
3. J'ai acheté cinq aérogrammes. Elle en a acheté cinq aussi.
4. J'ai lu quatre livres. Elle en a lu deux.

EXPANSION: À la poste

1. **Où puis-je poster cette lettre?**	*Where can I mail this letter?*
2. **Où se trouve la boîte aux lettres?**	*Where is the mail box?*
3. **Voulez-vous bien faire suivre mon courrier?**	*Please forward my mail.*
4. **Puis-je avoir une formule de télégramme?** **Quel est le tarif par mot? C'est urgent.**	*May I have a telegram form?* *How much does it cost per word? It's urgent.*
5. **Veuillez remplir cette formule pour la douane.**	*Please fill out this form for customs.*
6. **Signez ici, s'il vous plaît.**	*Sign here, please.*
7. **Attention! C'est fragile!**	*Careful! It's fragile!*

Exercice

Complétez ou répondez, selon le cas:

1. Vous envoyez quelque chose de très fragile. Vous dites au postier: _____
2. Vous quittez la France. Vous voulez faire suivre votre courrier. Vous dites: _____
3. Vous voulez envoyer un télégramme en Amérique. Vous demandez: _____
4. Vous voulez poster une lettre. Vous demandez: _____
5. Y a-t-il une boîte aux lettres près de chez vous? Un bureau de poste?

EXPANSION: Quel courrier avez-vous reçu cette semaine?
What mail have you received this week?

J'ai reçu. . . .

1. **une annonce (un faire-part) de mariage / de naissance**	*wedding / birth announcement*
2. **un cadeau**	*present*

3. une carte postale	postcard
4. une carte de vœux	greeting card
5. un catalogue	catalogue
6. un chèque / de l'argent	check / money
7. un colis	package
8. des imprimés	printed matter
9. une invitation	invitation
10. un journal	newspaper
11. une lettre	letter
12. un magazine	magazine
13. des notes	bills
14. un paquet	package
15. de la publicité	advertisements

Exercice

Répondez à ces questions:

1. Quel courrier avez-vous reçu cette semaine? De qui?
2. Qu'aimez-vous recevoir? des invitations? de l'argent? des magazines?
3. Que n'aimez-vous pas recevoir? des notes? des imprimés?
4. Quel courrier avez-vous envoyé cette semaine? une carte de vœux? une carte postale? une invitation? À qui?

PRONONCIATION

Sound (Phonetic Symbol): [ʃ]

SPELLING:	**ch, sch, sh**
ENGLISH SOUND RESEMBLED:	Initial sound in word *shall*
PRONUNCIATION:	Avoid adding a [t] sound before it, as in the English words *cheese* or *French*.

EXAMPLES FROM THIS CHAPTER:

proche	**cher**
guichet	**chèque**
franche	**échantillon**

NOTE: The spelling **ch** is pronounced [k] in some words of Greek origin, such as: **écho, orchestre, psychologie, archéologie, psychiatre.**

IMPROVISATION

Vous avez des lettres, des paquets, et beaucoup de cartes postales à envoyer à vos amis. Vous entrez dans le bureau de poste. Préparez un dialogue:

Vous: _____
Le Postier / La Postière: _____
Vous: _____
Le Postier / La Postière: _____
Vous: _____
Le Postier / La Postière: _____
Vous: _____
Le Postier / La Postière: _____

PROJETS

1. Write and address a postcard to a classmate. (An index card will do.) Here are some ideas:

le _____
(la date)

Timbre

Cher ami/Chère amie,

Mon cher Marc/Ma chère Henriette,

Cher Marc/Chère Henriette,

Vacances merveilleuses, pense à toi/vous.

Avec toi/vous par la pensée.

Tu me manques. / Vous me manquez.

Je m'amuse bien ici.

Il fait un temps splendide.

Je t'aime éperdument.

Juste quelques lignes pour te/vous dire que . . .

C
A
R
T
E
|
P
O
S
T
A
L
E

_____
(nom du destinataire)

_____
(salle de classe, numéro)

_____
(ville, état, code postal)

À bientôt de tes/vos bonnes nouvelles,
Bien amicalement à toi/vous,
Affectueusement,
Amitiés,
Je t'embrasse très fort,
Grosses bises,

_____
(Signature)

2. Using this form, write a telegram message to a classmate.

ACTIVITÉ

Write and address postcards, letters or telegrams to your classmates. Buy stamps from a
student postal worker. Then, mail these items at an appropriately designated area. Pick
up your own mail from another student postal worker. Use as many phrases and structures from the **Dialogue** and **Expansion** sections of this lesson as possible.

AU CLAIR DE LA LUNE

Au clair de la lu - ne, Mon a - mi Pier - rot,

Prê - te - moi ta plu - me, Pour é - crire un mot.

Ma chan - delle est mor - te, Je n'ai plus de feu.

Ou - vre - moi ta por - te, Pour l'a - mour de Dieu.

2. Au clair de la lune,
   Pierrot répondit:
   «Je n'ai pas de plume,
   Je suis dans mon lit.
   Va chez la voisine,
   Je crois qu'elle y est;
   Car dans sa cuisine,
   On bat le briquet.»

3. Au clair de la lune,
   L'aimable Lubin
   Frappe chez la brune
   Elle répond soudain:
   Qui frappe de la sorte?
   Il dit à son tour:
   Ouvrez votre porte
   Pour le Dieu d'amour!

14

PERSONAL POSSESSIONS

Qu'avez-vous dans vos poches / dans votre sac à main . . . ?
— J'ai _____ .

des affaires personnelles	*personal belongings*
un agenda	*engagement book / calendar*
des allumettes	*matches*
un appareil photo	*camera*
de l'argent	*money*
de l'aspirine	*aspirin*
une attache / un trombone	*paper clip*
un billet (d'avion, de train, de théâtre, etc.)	*ticket (plane, train, theater, etc.)*
un bloc	*pad of paper*
une boîte à pilules	*pill box*
un bon de réduction	*coupon*
des bonbons	*candy*
des boucles d'oreilles	*earrings*
un bout de papier / un petit morceau de papier (sur lequel j'ai noté . . .)	*scrap of paper (on which I've written . . .)*
un bouton	*button*

un briquet	*cigarette lighter*
une brosse	*brush*
une brosse à dents	*toothbrush*
un calendrier	*calendar*
une calculatrice de poche	*pocket calculator*
une capuche en plastique pour la pluie	*plastic rain hat*
un petit carnet	*little notebook*
un carnet d'adresses	*address book*
un livret de caisse d'épargne	*bankbook (savings)*
un carnet de chèques / un chéquier	*checkbook*
une carte de crédit	*credit card*
une carte d'identité	*I.D. card*
une carte de lecteur	*library card*
une carte de membre (d'un club, d'une société)	*membership card*
une carte postale	*postcard*
une carte de rendez-vous (avec le docteur, le dentiste)	*appointment card (doctor, dentist)*
une carte de visite / ma carte	*(my) card / calling card*
un chapelet	*rosary*
un chèque	*check*
des chèques de voyage	*traveler's checks*
du chewing-gum	*chewing gum*
un cigare	*cigar*
des cigarettes	*cigarettes*
des ciseaux (à ongles)	*(nail) scissors*
des clés	*keys*
une contravention / un papillon	*parking ticket*
un couteau de poche / un canif	*pocket knife*
un crayon	*pencil*
un cure-dents	*toothpick*
des devoirs	*homework*
un dictionnaire anglais-français	*dictionary (English-French)*
une écharpe	*scarf*
un élastique	*rubber band*
une enveloppe	*envelope*
une épingle (à cheveux)	*(hair) pin*
une épingle de sûreté	*safety pin*
un étui à lunettes	*glasses case*
une feuille de papier	*sheet of paper*
de la ficelle	*string*
des gants	*gloves*
une glace / un miroir	*mirror*
un horaire de poche	*timetable (bus, train, etc.)*
un journal	*newspaper*

des Kleenex / des mouchoirs en papier / des mouchoirs à jeter	*Kleenex / tissues*
une lettre (de) . . .	*letter (from)* . . .
une lime à ongles	*nail file*
une liste d'achats à faire	*shopping list*
un livre	*book*
des lunettes (de soleil)	*(sun) glasses*
un magazine / une revue	*magazine*
une trousse de maquillage	*make-up kit / cosmetics bag*
des produits de beauté	*make-up / cosmetics*
un médicament / des médicaments	*medecine*
des mots-croisés	*crossword puzzles*
un nécessaire de couture	*sewing kit*
une ordonnance	*prescription*
un ouvre-boîtes	*can opener*
un ouvre-bouteilles	*bottle opener*
un pansement adhésif	*Bandaid*
du papier à lettres	*stationery*
un paquet de cacahuètes / de biscottes, etc.	*package of peanuts / crackers, etc.*
un parapluie pliant	*folding umbrella*
du parfum	*perfume*
un passeport	*passport*
des pastilles contre la toux	*cough drops*
des pastilles pour la gorge	*throat lozenges*
un peigne	*comb*
un permis de conduire	*driver's license*
des pilules	*pills*
une pipe	*pipe*
un porte-bonheur	*good-luck charm*
un porte-cartes	*credit card holder*
un portefeuille	*wallet*
un porte-monnaie	*change purse*
un petit poste de radio / un transistor	*small radio / transistor*
un pulvérisateur	*atomizer (perfume, mouthspray, etc.)*
de la poussière	*dust*
un reçu	*receipt*
un rince-doigts	*Wash & Dry*
un sac en plastique	*plastic bag*
du savon	*soap*
du scotch	*scotch tape*
une serviette hygiénique	*sanitary napkin*
un sifflet	*whistle*
un stylo	*pen*
un souvenir	*souvenir*
une tablette de chocolat	*chocolate bar*
un Tampax	*Tampax*

des timbres / un carnet de timbres	*stamps / book of stamps*
un tire-bouchon	*cork screw*
un trou	*hole*
des verres de contact	*contact lenses*

SPRINGBOARDS FOR CONVERSATION

1. Qu'avez-vous dan vos poches / dans votre sac à main / dans votre serviette *(brief case)* / dans votre porte-documents *(attache case)* / dans votre fourre-tout *(carry-all, tote bag)*, etc.? C'est tout? Quoi d'autre?
   J'ai _____ .

2. Qui dans la classe a un peigne? une brosse? de l'argent? un porte-clés? etc. Qui d'autre?
   Moi, j'ai _____ .
   Il / Elle a _____ .
   Je n'ai pas de _____ .

3. Qu'est-ce que Monsieur / Madame / Mademoiselle . . . a dans ses poches / dans son sac à main, etc.?

4. Votre peigne est-il neuf? Et votre stylo? Et votre portefeuille? etc.
   Votre brosse est-elle neuve? Et votre boîte à pilules? etc.
   Oui, il / elle est neuf (neuve).
   Non, il / elle est vieux (vieille).

5. Avez-vous un porte-bonheur? Le portez-vous toujours sur vous? Despuis quand?

6. Quels objets de cette liste avez-vous aujourd'hui? Comptez-les. Soyez exact(e).
   Dix-huit? Vingt-cinq? Trente? Plus de quarante?
   J'en ai _____ . (EXEMPLE: J'en ai trois. J'en ai dix, etc.)

7. Combien de cigarettes avez-vous? Combien de cartes de crédit? Combien de Kleenex? Combien de stylos? etc.
   J'en ai. . . .

8. Quelles choses devez-vous absolument porter sur vous? Des Kleenex? De l'argent? Votre porte-bonheur? Vos lunettes? etc.

9. De quelles choses pouvez-vous vous passer assez facilement? D'élastiques? De cigarettes? D'enveloppes? De lunettes de soleil? De chewing-gum? etc. (NOTE: **se passer (de)** = *to do without*, and is followed simply by **de** or **d'** before the noun.)
   Je peux me passer de / d' _____ .

10. Que portez-vous sur vous tous les jours? Quels sont les objets que vous portez rarement? Que portez-vous uniquement aujourd'hui?

11. Quels objets de cette liste se trouvent dans les tiroirs de votre bureau *(in the drawers of your desk)?*

PROJET

Go through your handbag, your pockets (*all* of them), your wallet, your briefcase, your bookbag, etc. Make a list of everything you find.

ACTIVITÉS

1. Everyone goes through all the items in his or her pockets, handbags, wallets, briefcases, bookbags, etc. The student who produces the greatest number of items from this lesson is declared the winner.
2. Have a quick competition. «**Qui dans la classe a une peigne? une brosse? un porte-clés? etc.**» The first student to produce the requested item wins.
3. Here is a variation on the word game "I Packed My Grandmother's Bag." This game may be played in groups of two, three or more players, or with the entire class. The first player says «**Dans le sac de grand-maman, il y a. . . .**», naming an item from this lesson. The second player must remember that item, name it, and then add to it with his or her own selection. The next player (either a third player or the first player over again), must recapitulate, in order, the items that have been already named, and then add to this list a third item of his or her own choosing. The game continues in this fashion, with each player recapitulating the entire list and then adding his or her own new selection to it. When a player forgets or incorrectly names an item, he drops out of the game. The game continues until only one person is left, who is declared the winner.
4. The class is divided into two teams. Each team reviews the list of items given above. The team that produces the greatest number of items from this list wins.

Chapitre
15

En Voyage	Traveling

<table>
<tr><td>Proverbe: Pierre qui roule n'amasse pas mousse.</td><td>Proverb: A rolling stone gathers no moss.</td></tr>
</table>

DIALOGUE

EXERCICES D'APPLICATION

VERBE IRRÉGULIER: **mettre**

STRUCTURES:

1. Geographical Place Names
2. **y** and **en** Used to Replace Prepositional Phrases
3. Expressions of Time: ahead of time, on time, in time, early, late

EXERCICES DE SYNTHÈSE

EXPANSION:

En autobus, En métro, En taxi

À la gare, En train

À l'aéroport, En avion

PRONONCIATION: [ʒ], [g]

IMPROVISATIONS

PROJET

ACTIVITÉ

CHANSON: **Il était un petit navire**

«Je pense y aller en avion.»

DIALOGUE

(*À l'agence de voyages*)	(*At the travel agency*)

VOUS: J'ai très envie de voir **Marseille.** Je pense

YOU: I really want to see *Marseilles*. I'm think-

l'Amérique	America
le Canada	Canada
les États-Unis	the United States
l'Europe	Europe
la France	France

y aller **en avion.** Pourriez-vous me donner les

ing of going (there) by *plane*. Could you tell

en auto	car
en autobus	bus, city bus
en (auto)car	coach, interurban bus, limousine
en bateau / par bateau	boat
à bicyclette / à vélo	bicycle
à cheval	horse
en hélicoptère	helicopter
en métro	subway
à moto	motorcycle
à pied	foot
en taxi	taxi
par le train	train
à vélomoteur	motorbike
en voiture	car, auto

heures de départ, s'il vous plaît?

me the departure times, please?

L'AGENT: Certainement. Asseyez-vous. Quand pensez-vous partir?

THE TRAVEL AGENT: Certainly. Sit down. When were you thinking of leaving?

VOUS: Ça dépend. Combien de temps faut-il pour y aller?

YOU: That depends. How long does it take to get there?

L'AGENT: Environ trois heures. **Le lundi** il y a

AGENT: About three hours. *Mondays* there's a

Le mardi	Tuesdays
Le mercredi	Wednesdays
Le jeudi	Thursdays
Le vendredi	Fridays
Le samedi	Saturdays
Le dimanche	Sundays

un vol direct le matin à dix heures.

direct flight at ten o'clock in the morning.

VOUS: Faut-il réserver une place longtemps à l'avance?

L'AGENT: Oui. C'est toujours préférable.

VOUS: Quels sont les prix, s'il vous plaît?

L'AGENT: L'aller simple touriste fait cent francs. En première classe, cent cinquante francs.

VOUS: Alors, je voudrais un aller retour en première classe.

L'AGENT: Un instant, je vais vérifier. . . . Je peux vous confirmer une place sur le vol numéro huit de dimanche prochain. Les autres vols sont complets.

VOUS: Très bien. Merci. Mais dites-moi, comment puis-je me rendre à l'aéroport (à l'aérogare)?

L'AGENT: Il y a un car entre la ville et l'aéroport. Et n'oubliez pas. Il faut y arriver une heure à l'avance.

VOUS: Où dois-je **faire peser mes bagages?**

prendre mon billet
faire enregistrer mes bagages
confirmer ma réservation
confirmer mon départ

L'AGENT: Au comptoir de la ligne aérienne.

VOUS: Où est **la salle d'attente?**

le bureau des objets trouvés
la consigne
le guichet N° 3
la place N° 32
la porte N° 2
la sortie

L'AGENT: Vous pouvez toujours demander au bureau de renseignements. Bon voyage!

YOU: Do you have to reserve a seat way ahead of time?

AGENT: Yes. It's always better (to do so).

YOU: What are the rates, please?

AGENT: One-way tourist class costs 100 francs. First class (costs) 150 francs.

YOU: Okay, I would like a round-trip ticket, first class.

AGENT: One moment, I'll check . . . . I can confirm a space for you next Sunday on flight number eight. The other flights are full.

YOU: Fine. Thank you. But tell me, how can I get to the airport (air terminal)?

AGENT: There is a bus between the city and the airport. And don't forget. You have to arrive there an hour ahead of time.

YOU: Where should I *have my luggage weighed?*

get my ticket
have my luggage checked in
confirm my reservation
confirm my departure

AGENT: At the airline counter.

YOU: Where is the *waiting room?*

lost and found office
checkroom / baggage room
ticket window N° 3
place / seat N° 32
gate N° 2
exit

AGENT: You can always ask at the information booth. (Have a) good trip!

EXERCICES D'APPLICATION

*1. Dites que vous avez très envie de voir Paris . . . que vous pensez y aller en avion
. . . que vous pensez partir lundi prochain . . . que vous voulez une place en première classe . . . Demandez les heures de départ . . . combien de temps il faut pour
y aller . . . s'il y a un vol direct . . . s'il faut réserver une place longtemps à l'avance
. . . les prix . . . comment vous pouvez vous rendre à l'aéroport . . . où vous devez
faire peser vos bagages . . . où est la salle d'attente . . . où est le bureau des objets
trouvés.

2. Vous êtes agent de voyage. Répondez aux questions suivantes posées par votre
client:
Je pense aller à Québec en avion. Pourriez-vous me donner les heures de départ? . . .
Combien de temps faut-il pour y aller? . . . Et les prix, s'il vous plaît? . . . Faut-il
réserver une place? . . . Comment puis-je me rendre à l'aéroport? . . . Où dois-je
faire enregistrer mes bagages? . . . Où est la consigne?

VERBE IRRÉGULIER: mettre

mettre	*to put, to place, to put on; to take* (time)	
Le présent:	**je mets**	**nous mettons**
	tu mets	**vous mettez**
	il / elle met	**ils / elles mettent**
Le participe passé: **mis**		
La base du futur et du conditionnel: **mettr-**		

Je ne sais pas où **j'ai mis** les billets.
I don't know where I put the tickets.

Qu'est-ce que **je mets** ce soir?
What should I wear tonight?

Combien de temps **mettez-vous** pour aller au bureau?
How long does it take you to get to the office?

À cause de la pluie **j'ai mis** plus de temps que d'habitude.
Because of the rain I took longer than usual.

Combien de temps **met** un télégramme pour Washington?
How long does it take for a telegram to reach Washington?

STRUCTURES

1. **Geographical Place Names**

   a. With cities and some islands **à** means *to* or *in,* **de** means *from.*

Bruxelles	*Brussels*	**Montréal**	*Montreal*
Genève	*Geneva*	**New-York**	*New York*
Haïti	*Haiti*	**Paris**	*Paris*
Londres	*London*	**Québec**	*Quebec City*

   b. With countries beginning with a vowel, feminine countries, and continents, **en** means *to* or *in,* **de** means *from.*

Afrique	*Africa*	**Europe**	*Europe*
Allemagne	*Germany*	**France**	*France*
Amérique	*America*	**Grèce**	*Greece*
Angleterre	*England*	**Italie**	*Italy*
Asie	*Asia*	**Russie**	*Russia*
Belgique	*Belgium*	**Suisse**	*Switzerland*
Espagne	*Spain*		

   Je vais **en** France.
   Elle est **de** Belgique.

   c. With masculine countries, **au** means *to* or *in,* **du** means *from.*

Brésil	*Brazil*	**Mexique**	*Mexico*
Canada	*Canada*	**Portugal**	*Portugal*
Japon	*Japan*		

   Je pense aller **au** Mexique.
   Il vient **du** Canada.

   d. With plural geographical names, **aux** means *to* or *in,* **des** means *from.*

   États-Unis *United States*

   J'habite **aux** États-Unis.

   e. With U.S. states, **dans l'état de** means *to* or *in.*

   Elle habite **dans l'état de** Connecticut.

   f. With Canadian provinces, **dans le / la** means *to* or *in.*

   g. The definite article **le, la, l', les** is used before continents, countries, provinces, mountains and rivers, but not before cities (unless the article is part of the name of the city as in **le Havre, la Havane, la Nouvelle-Orléans**):

«J'ai très envie de voir Marseille / l'Amérique / le Canada / les États-Unis / l'Europe / la France.»

2. y and en Used to Replace Prepositional Phrases

y replaces prepositional phrases, except those beginning with **de,** which are replaced by **en.**

a. Meanings of **y:** *there, to that place, to there, in there, on it, to it, in,* etc.:

Allez-vous à l'aéroport? —Oui, j'**y** vais.
Are you going to the airport? —Yes, I'm going (there).

Comment puis-je **y** aller?
How can I get there?

Est-ce que la voiture est au garage? —Oui, elle **y** est.
Is the car in the garage? —Yes, it is (there, in there, in).

b. Meanings of **en:** *from there, from that place* (for the partitive use of **en,** see Chapitre 4, Structure 4):

Ils arrivent de France. Ils **en** arrivent.
They're arriving from France. They're arriving from there.

Je viens de chez elle. J'**en** viens.
I'm coming from her house. I'm coming from there.

c. **y** and **en** precede the conjugated verb except in positive commands:

Allez-**y!**   *Go to it! / Go there!*

d. When there is a conjugated verb and an infinitive, **y** and **en** come immediately before the infinitive:

«Je pense **y** aller en avion.»
«Combien de temps faut-il pour **y** aller?»
«Il faut **y** arriver une heure à l'avance.»

3. Expressions of Time: ahead of time, on time, in time, early, late

«Faut-il réserver une place longtemps **à l'avance?**»
«Il faut y arriver une heure **à l'avance.**»

Je suis toujours **à l'heure.**
I'm always on time.
Les avions sont toujours **à l'heure.**
The planes are always on time.

J'espère qu'ils arriveront **à temps.**
I hope they will arrive in time.

Je suis **en avance / en retard (de cinq minutes).**
I'm (five minutes) early / late.
L'avion est **en avance / en retard (de cinq minutes).**
The plane is (five minutes) early / late.

NOTE: **En avance / en retard** are used following the verbs **être** and **arriver.**

L'avion a **de l'avance / du retard.**
The plane is early / late.

L'avion a deux heures **d'avance / de retard.**
The plane is two hours early / late.

Je préfère partir **de bonne heure** (= **tôt**) / **tard.**
I prefer to leave early / late.

Il est **tôt / tard.**
It's early / late.

Il se fait **tard.**
It's getting late.

Il y a **un retard de** deux heures.
There's a two-hour delay.

Ma montre **avance / retarde de cinq minutes.**
My watch is five minutes fast / slow.

Avancez / retardez votre montre.
Put (set) your watch ahead / back.

EXERCICES DE SYNTHÈSE

A.   *Répondez à ces questions:*

1. Où aimeriez-vous aller?
   (J'aimerais bien aller à / en / au / aux. . . . .)
2. Où allez-vous cette année? cet été?
3. Où êtes-vous allé(e) l'année dernière?
4. Où pensez-vous aller?
5. Où aimeriez-vous passer vos vacances? Où comptez-vous passer vos prochaines vacances?

B. *Répondez:*

1. Où habitez-vous?[1] Dans quel pays? dans quelle province? dans quel état? dans quelle ville?
2. Où habite le professeur? votre mère / père? votre meilleur(e) ami(e)? Monsieur . . . ? Madame . . . ? Mademoiselle . . . ? etc.
3. Où habitent vos parents? vos grands-parents? Monsieur et Madame . . . ?
4. Où aimeriez-vous habiter?
5. Dans quel pays avez-vous habité? Dans quelles villes? Pendant combien de temps? Quand?

C. *Répondez:*

1. D'où venez-vous? d'Amérique? de France? du Japon? des États-Unis? de Montréal? de l'état de Pennsylvanie? etc.
2. Où êtes-vous né(e)?
3. Où est né votre père? Où est née votre mère?
4. Où est né votre grand-père maternel? votre grand-père paternel? Où est née votre grand-mère maternelle? votre grand-mère paternelle?

D. *Répondez:*

1. Quels pays aimeriez-vous visiter? le Canada? la France? etc.
2. Quels pays avez-vous visités?
3. Quelles villes aimeriez-vous visiter? Paris? Québec? etc.
4. Quelles villes avez-vous visitées?
5. Avez-vous fait un voyage pendant ces dernières années? Où êtes-vous allé(e)? Quand?

E.* *Remplacez les mots en italique pay* **y** *ou* **en.** *Ensuite, traduisez la phrase:*

EXEMPLES: Je pars *pour la France* le 5 juin.
              J'y pars le 5 juin.

              Il vient *d'Italie.*
              Il en vient.

1. Il va *à Paris* cette semaine.
2. Je pense aller *à Marseille* en avion.
3. Je viens *de chez lui.*
4. Elle arrive *de France.*
5. Allez *en ville.*

---

1. With **habiter** the preposition is optional: **J'habite (à) Paris.**

  6. J'ai mis la voiture *au garage.*
  7. Vous allez *au Canada,* n'est-ce pas?
  8. Je suis descendu(e) *de l'autobus* trop tard.
  9. Nous allons *en ville* ce soir.
 10. Comment puis-je me rendre *à l'aéroport?*
 11. Je vais *à la consigne.*
 12. Oui, il faut aller *à Paris.*
 13. Il est sorti *de la gare* très vite.
 14. Est-ce que vous allez au bureau *des objets trouvés?*
 15. Je vais *dans la salle d'attente.*

F.*   *Donnez le contraire des mots en italique. Puis traduisez:*

  1. L'avion a *du retard.*   6. Je préfère partir *de bonne heure.*
  2. Le train a cinq minutes *d'avance.*   7. Je suis *en avance* de cinq minutes.
  3. Ma montre *retarde* de cinq minutes.   8. Ma montre *avance* de trois minutes.
  4. Il est arrivé *en retard.*   9. *Avancez* votre montre.
  5. Il est *tôt.*

G.   *Répondez à ces questions:*

  1. Quelle heure est-il? Est-ce que votre montre avance ou retarde? De combien?
  2. Êtes-vous arrivé(e) en classe en avance? en retard? De combien? êtes-vous arrivé(e)
     à l'heure?
  3. Préférez-vous vous lever de bonne heure ou tard le matin?
  4. Ce matin vous êtes-vous levé(e) tôt ou tard?
  5. Hier soir vous êtes-vous couché(e) tôt ou tard?

H.   *Répondez aux questions suivantes:*

  1. Comment allez-vous au supermarché? au travail? à vos cours?
  2. Avez-vous déjà voyagé en avion? Quand? Où êtes-vous allé(e)? Comment êtes-vous
     allé(e) à l'aéroport? en taxi?
  3. Aimez-vous voyager en avion?
  4. En avion voyagez-vous en première classe ou en classe touriste? Pourquoi?
  5. Avez-vous déjà voyagé par le train? Quand? Où êtes-vous allé(e)? Comment êtes-
     vous allé(e) à la gare? Avez-vous pris l'autobus? le métro? un taxi? Est-ce qu'on vous
     a conduit(e) à la gare?
  6. Avez-vous déjà voyagé en bateau? fait une croisière? Où? Quand?
  7. Comment voyagez-vous le plus souvent? Pourquoi? Est-ce plus pratique? plus
     économique? plus rapide? etc.
  8. Combien de temps faudrait-il pour aller de chez vous à Paris? à Québec? à Tahiti?
     Six heures par air? deux heures par train? cinq heures par route?

EXPANSION: En autobus, En métro, En taxi

1. **Où se trouve l'arrêt d'autobus / la station de taxis / la station de métro?**
   Where is the bus stop / taxi stand / subway station?
2. **Un carnet première / seconde, s'il vous plaît.**
   A book of tickets, please, first class / second class. (subway, bus)
3. **S'il vous plaît, Monsieur / Madame, quel autobus faut-il prendre pour aller Avenue Carnot? Le dix?**
   What bus do I take to get to Avenue Carnot, please? Number 10?
4. **Je voudrais descendre à la rue Manin.**
   I would like to get off at rue Manin (Manin Street).
5. **Taxi! Êtes-vous libre?**
   Taxi! Are you free!
6. **À la gare, s'il vous plaît. Je suis pressé(e).**
   To the train station, please. I'm in a hurry.

Exercice

1. Vous cherchez la station de métro. Vous demandez: _____
2. Vous devez aller Avenue Carnot. Vous ne savez pas quel autobus il faut prendre. Vous demandez: _____
3. Votre train part à cinq heures. Il est cinq heures moins dix. Vous dites au chauffeur de taxi: _____
4. Il vous faut des billets de seconde. Vous préférez acheter un carnet parce que vous prenez le métro tous les jours. Au guichet vous demandez: _____
5. Vous allez rue Manin. Vous expliquez au conducteur que vous voulez descendre à la rue Manin: _____
6. Vous voyez passer un taxi. Vous levez le bras et vous criez: _____

EXPANSION: À la gare, En train

1. **Où se trouve le bureau de location de la gare / le compartiment non-fumeurs / le quai N° 1 / la voie N° 5 / le wagon-bar / le wagon-lit / le wagon-restaurant?**
   Where is the train station ticket office / no-smoking compartment / train platform N° 1 / track N° 5 / club car / sleeping car / restaurant car?
2. **Un aller simple / un aller retour première classe / deuxième classe pour le train de sept heures pour Québec, s'il vous plaît.**
   A one-way ticket / round-trip ticket first class / second class for the seven o'clock train to Québec, please.
3. **Je voudrais louer une couchette.**
   I'd like to reserve a berth.
4. **À quelle heure part le prochain train pour Paris?**
   What time does the next train for Paris leave?
   (Often the twenty-four hour clock is used. *One p.m.* = **treize heures.** *10 p.m.* = **vingt-deux heures,** etc.)

5. **C'est bien le train pour Paris?**	*This is the train for Paris, isn't it?*
6. **En voiture! Vos billets, s'il vous plaît.**	*All aboard! (Your) Tickets, please.*
7. **Pardon, est-ce que cette place est libre?**	*Excuse me, is this seat free?*

Exercice

1. Vous arrivez à la gare et vous cherchez le bureau de location. Vous demandez: _____
2. Vous prenez un train de nuit. Vous voulez louer une couchette. Vous allez au bureau de location de la gare et vous dites: _____
3. Vous allez à Paris. Vous ne savez pas à quelle heure partent les trains. En arrivant à la gare vous demandez: ___•___
4. Vous voulez un billet aller et retour en première pour le train de six heures. Vous dites: _____
5. Vous montez dans le train, mais vous pensez que ce n'est peut-être pas le train pour Paris. Vous demandez: _____
6. Vous trouvez une place dans le train, mais elle n'est peut-être pas libre. Vous demandez: _____

EXPANSION: À l'aéroport, En avion

1. **Pardon, Monsieur / Madame, l'avion pour Paris, s'il vous plaît?**	*Excuse me, please, (where can I find) the plane to Paris?*
2. **Le départ / l'arrivée du vol dix est retardé(e) de trois heures.**	*The departure / arrival of flight ten has been delayed for three hours.*
3. **Je voudrais un siège-fenêtre.**	*I would like a window seat.*
4. **Je voudrais annuler ma réservation.**	*I'd like to cancel my reservation.*
5. **Je suis sujet (sujette) au mal de l'air.**	*I'm subject to air sickness. (I get airsick.)*
6. **Je vais à l'étranger en voyage d'affaires / d'agrément.**	*I'm going abroad on business / for pleasure.*

Exercice

1. Êtes-vous sujet (sujette) au mal de l'air?
2. Allez-vous souvent à l'étranger en voyage d'affaires?
3. Vous voulez annuler votre réservation. Vous dites: _____
4. Vous cherchez l'avion pour Paris. Vous demandez: _____

PRONONCIATION

1. Sound (Phonetic Symbol): [ʒ]

SPELLING: **j, g** (followed by **i, e, y**)

ENGLISH SOUND RESEMBLED: Middle consonant sound in the words *pleasure* and *treasure*.

PRONUNCIATION: Do not add a [d] sound before the [ʒ] sound, as in the English words *age* or *jump*.

EXAMPLES FROM THIS CHAPTER:
en voyage	objets
agence de voyages	toujours
agent	bon voyage
jeudi	Genève
je	Belgique

2. Sound (Phonetic Symbol): [g]

SPELLING: **g** (followed by **a, o, u**), **g** (followed by **r**)

ENGLISH SOUND RESEMBLED: Initial sound in English word *get*.

EXAMPLES FROM THIS CHAPTER:
aérogare	gardez
guichet	Portugal
Grèce	grand-mère
gare	

NOTES:
1. **Second** is pronounced [səgɔ̃].
2. The spelling **e + x + vowel** is pronounced [gz].
   Examples from this chapter: **exercice, par exemple.**

IMPROVISATIONS

1. Vous attendez un(e) ami(e) à la gare, mais il (elle) n'arrive pas. Vous allez au bureau de renseignements. Informez-vous au sujet du train, s'il a du retard, à quelle heure il arrive, etc.
2. Vous vous adressez à une agence de voyages à Paris. Vous avez envie de voir toute la France. Vous posez des questions à l'agent. Il vous demande vos préférences. Vous établissez un itinéraire.

PROJET

Compile a listing of all the cities, countries, and continents you have visited or have lived in during your lifetime. Give years and approximate lengths of stay whenever possible. You may wish to include photos, postcards, magazine pictures, etc. of the places mentioned.

ACTIVITÉ

Transform the classroom into an airport. Go to the **comptoir de la ligne aérienne** and purchase a ticket from the student ticket agent who will ask you the appropriate questions in order to fill out your ticket. (**Votre nom, s'il vous plaît? Où allez-vous? Quand partirezvous? À quelle heure? Quelle classe—économique ou première? Fumeur ou nonfumeur?** etc.)

BILLET
AIR FRANCE

Nom de voyageur:_____

À destination de:_____

Date:_____

Départ:_____ heures

Prix:_____ francs

Air France Vol Numéro:_____

Classe ☐ touriste/économique/seconde   ☐ première

☐ Fumeurs   ☐ Non–fumeurs

☐ Aller simple   ☐ Aller–retour

IL ÉTAIT UN PETIT NAVIRE

Il é - tait un pe - tit na - vi - re, Il é - tait
un pe - tit na - vi - re, Qui n'a - vait ja, ja,
ja, mais na - vi - gué, Qui n'a - vait ja, ja,
ja, mais na - vi - gué, o - hé, o - hé!

2. Il entreprit un long voyage (bis)
   Sur la Mer Mé, Mé, Méditerranée (bis)

3. Au bout de cinq à six semaines (bis)
   Les vivres vin, vin, vinrent à manquer (bis)

4. On tira à la courte paille (bis)
   Pour savoir qui, qui, qui serait mangé (bis)

5. Le sort tomba sur le plus jeune (bis)
   Le mousse qui s'est, s'est, s'est mis à pleurer. (bis)

6. Ô sainte Vierge, ô ma patronne (bis)
   Empêchez-les, les, les de me manger! (bis)

7. Au même instant un grand miracle (bis)
   Pour l'enfant fut, fut, fut réalisé (bis)

8. Des p'tits poissons dans le navire (bis)
   Sautèrent bien, bien, bientôt par milliers. (bis)

9. On les prit, on les mit à frire (bis)
   Et le p'tit mous, mous, mousse fut sauvé. (bis)

10. Si cette histoire vous amuse (bis)
    Nous allons la, la, la recommencer. (bis)

Entracte
15

NATIONALITIES

De quelle origine êtes-vous?
—Je suis d'origine _____ .

In the lists below the feminine form of the adjective is given first, followed by the masculine form. The feminine form is used in the answer because the word **origine** is feminine. Nationalities used as adjectives do not begin with capital letters, unlike English.

AMÉRICAINE, AMÉRICAIN (*AMERICAN*)

canadienne, canadien	*Canadian*	guyannaise,	*from French,*
mexicaine, mexicain	*Mexican*	guyannais	*British, Dutch*
américaine, américain	*American*		*Guiana*
	(U.S.)	paraguayenne,	*Paraguayan*
argentine, argentin	*Argentinian*	paraguayen	
bolivienne, bolivien	*Bolivian*	péruvienne, péruvien	*Peruvian*
brésilienne, brésilien	*Brazilian*	vénézuélienne,	*Venezuelan*
chilienne, chilien	*Chilean*	vénézuélien	
colombienne, colombien	*Colombian*		

EUROPÉENNE, EUROPÉEN (*EUROPEAN*)

allemande, allemand	*German*	autrichienne, autrichien	*Austrian*
anglaise, anglais	*English*	belge	*Belgian*

302

danoise, danois	*Danish*	norvégienne, norvégien	*Norwegian*
écossaise, écossais	*Scottish*	polonaise, polonais	*Polish*
espagnole, espagnol	*Spanish*	portugaise, portugais	*Portuguese*
finlandaise, finlandais	*Finnish*	roumaine, roumain	*Rumanian*
française, français	*French*	russe	*Russian*
grecque, grec	*Greek*	suédoise, suédois	*Swedish*
hollandaise, hollandais	*Dutch*	suisse	*Swiss*
hongroise, hongrois	*Hungarian*	tchèque	*Czechoslovakian*
irlandaise, irlandais	*Irish*	yougoslave	*Yugoslavian*
italienne, italien	*Italian*		

AFRICAINE, AFRICAIN *(AFRICAN)*

algérienne, algérien	*Algerian*	nigérienne, nigérien	*Nigerian*
égyptienne, égyptien	*Egyptian*	sénégalaise, sénégalais	*Senegalese*
marocaine, marocain	*Moroccan*	tunisienne, tunisien	*Tunisian*

ASIATIQUE *(ASIAN)*

chinoise, chinois	*Chinese*	pakistanaise, pakistanais	*Pakistani*
indienne, indien	*Indian*		
indonésienne, indonésien	*Indonesian*	philippine, philippin	*Philippine*
iranienne, iranien	*Iranian*	turque, turc	*Turkish*
israélienne, israélien	*Israeli*	vietnamienne, vietnamien	*Vietnamese*
japonaise, japonais	*Japanese*		

(OTHER)

australienne, australien	*Australian*	martiniquaise, martiniquais	*from Martinique*
cubaine, cubain	*Cuban*		
quadeloupéenne, guadeloupéen	*from Guadeloupe*	néo-zélandaise, néo-zélandais	*from New Zealand*
haïtienne, haïtien	*Haitian*	porto-ricaine, porto-ricain	*Puerto Rican*
jamaïquaine, jamaïquain	*Jamaican*		

SPRINGBOARDS FOR CONVERSATION

1. De quelle origine êtes-vous? Du côté maternel *(On your mother's side)?* Du côté paternel *(father's side)?*
Je suis d'origine _____.
2. De quelle origine est le professeur? Monsieur . . . ? Madame . . . ? Mademoiselle . . . ? votre mari / votre femme? votre mère? votre père? votre grand-mère maternelle? votre grand-père maternel? votre grand-mère paternelle? votre grand-père paternel? votre meilleur(e) ami(e)? etc.
Il / Elle est d'origine _____.

3. Qui dans la classe est d'origine _____?
   Le professeur / Monsieur . . . Madame . . . Mademoiselle . . . est d'origine _____.
4. Connaissez-vous quelqu'un d'origine _____? Qui?
   Mon ami / mon mari (ma femme) / mon professeur / Monsieur . . . etc. est d'origine

   _____.
5. Quelle est votre nationalité? américain(e)? canadien(ne)? etc.
   Je suis _____.

PROJETS

1. Think of your neighbors, your close friends, your relatives, the people you deal with every day (such as merchants, lawyers, doctors, dentists, etc.) Make a list. For each person indicate a national origin.
2. Go through a current news magazine, clipping photos of people from around the world. Using the vocabulary of this lesson, caption each with a national origin. For example: **Il est chinois, elle est africaine,** etc.

Chapitre
16

En vacances	On Vacation

Proverbe: Après la pluie le beau temps.   Proverb: After the rain, fair weather (comes).

«Voulez-vous faire un pique-nique?»

DIALOGUE

(En vacances)	*(On Vacation)*
Un(e) Ami(e): Où allez-vous passer **vos vacances?**	A Friend: Where are you going to spend your *vacation?*

les vacances d'été les vacances de Noël les vacances de Pâques le week-end	summer vacation Christmas vacation Easter vacation weekend

Vous: Je vais **faire un voyage.**	You: I'm going *to take a trip.*

passer mes vacances chez des amis rester ici à la campagne à la montagne au bord de la mer à la plage dans une station de ski à l'étranger en Europe en Floride à New-York, etc.[1]	to spend my vacation with friends to stay here to the country to the mountains to the ocean / by the sea to the beach to a ski resort abroad to Europe to Forida to New York, etc.

Votre Ami(e): Qu'est-ce que vous allez faire pendant les vacances? Vous: Je vais **me reposer.**[2]	Your Friend: What are you going to do during vacation? You: I'm going to *rest* (take it easy).

me détendre dormir le plus possible travailler faire du ski faire du camping jouer au tennis voir des amis	relax sleep as much as possible work ski / go skiing camp / go camping play tennis see friends

Votre Ami(e): Quand comptez-vous partir?	Your Friend: When do you plan to leave?

---

1. For additional places and place names, see *Entracte 17: Places* and *Chapter 15, Structures* 1, *Geographical Place Names.*
2. For additional activities see *Entracte 10: Pastimes, Hobbies, Sports, Entertainment.*

VOUS: **Aujourd'hui.**

> Cet après-midi.
> Ce soir.
> Demain.
> Demain matin de bonne heure.
> Demain après-midi.

VOTRE AMI(E): Au revoir. Passez
de bonnes vacances!

> un bon week-end
> un bon séjour

VOUS: Merci. Vous aussi!

(À la plage / À la piscine / Au bord de la mer)

VOUS: Il fait vraiment chaud aujourd'hui!
VOTRE AMI(E): Avez-vous envie de vous
baigner? Vous savez nager, n'est-ce pas?
VOUS: Oui, comme un poisson. Comment est
l'eau?
VOTRE AMI(E): **Froide!**

> Bonne.
> Rafraîchissante.

VOUS: Je crois que je vais
m'allonger sur la plage.

> prendre un bain de soleil
> faire du ski nautique
> faire de la pêche sous-marine
> faire du bateau
> me faire bronzer

VOTRE AMI(E): Amusez-vous bien, mais
attention aux coups de soleil!

YOU: *Today*.

> This afternoon.
> This evening / Tonight.
> Tomorrow.
> Early tomorrow morning.
> Tomorrow afternoon.

YOUR FRIEND: Good-by. Have a
good vacation!

> good weekend
> good stay

YOU: Thank you. You, too!

(At the Beach / At the Swimming Pool / By the Sea)

YOU: It's really hot today!
YOUR FRIEND: Do you want to go swimming?
You know how to swim, don't you?
YOU: Yes, like a fish. How's the water?

YOUR FRIEND: *Cold!*

> Nice. (Good.)
> Refreshing.

YOU: I think I'll *lie down on the beach*. (*Literally:* I think that I am going to. . . .)

> take a sunbath / sunbathe
> go water skiing
> go scuba diving
> go boating
> get a suntan

YOUR FRIEND: Have fun, but
watch out for sunburn!

Attention! La mer est très agitée.
Attention! Il y a de grosses vagues.
Attention! Il y a des courants dangereux.
Attention! La mer monte / descend.
Attention! Le soleil / le sable est chaud.

Watch out! (Be careful!) The sea is rough.
Watch out! There are big waves.
Watch out! There are dangerous currents.
Watch out! The tide is coming in / going out.
Watch out! The sun / the sand is hot.

VOUS: On se retrouve ici pour le déjeuner?
VOTRE AMI(E): Entendu! À tout à l'heure.

YOU: We'll meet (back) here for lunch?
YOUR FRIEND: Fine. (*Literally:* Understood.)
See you later.

(Aux sports d'hiver / Dans une station de ski)

(Winter Sports / At a Ski Resort)

VOTRE AMI(E): Savez-vous skier?
VOUS: Pas très bien. . . . Et franchement j'ai
peur de **me casser une jambe.**

YOUR FRIEND: Do you know how to ski?
YOU: Not very well. . . . And frankly, I'm
afraid of *breaking a leg.*

me fracturer un bras
me fouler une cheville

fracturing an arm
twisting / spraining an ankle

VOTRE AMI(E): Mais les pistes (les pentes) sont
formidables!

YOUR FRIEND: But the trails (the slopes) are
terrific!

faciles
difficiles
moyennes
bien balisées
en excellent état

easy
difficult, hard
of average difficulty
well-marked
in excellent condition

VOUS: Et la neige?
VOTRE AMI(E): Elle est **poudreuse.**

YOU: And the snow?
YOUR FRIEND: It's *powdery.*

gelée
un peu molle
damée

frozen
a little soft
packed hard

Prenons le remonte-pente!
VOUS: D'accord. Je vous retrouve ici dans cinq
minutes. Je vais d'abord louer
des skis.

Let's take the ski lift.
YOU: O.K. I'll meet you back here in five minutes. First I'm going to rent (some) *skis.*

| des chaussures de ski
des bâtons | ski boots
ski poles |

(À la campagne / En camping)

(In the Country / On a Camping Trip)

VOUS: Peut-on camper ici?

YOU: Can we camp here?

VOTRE AMI(E): Je pense que oui. C'est un terrain de camping autorisé. Je vais sortir
les provisions du coffre.

YOUR FRIEND: I think so. It's an authorized
campground. I'm going to take the
food supplies out of the (car) trunk.

| le matériel de camping
la tente
les sacs de couchage
les sacs à dos
la glacière
le panier | camping equipment
tent
sleeping bags
backpacks / knapsacks
ice chest / cooler
picnic basket |

VOUS: Ce n'est pas mal ici. Il y a même
de l'eau potable.

YOU: It's not bad here. There's even
drinking water.

| du bois pour faire du feu
des douches
l'électricité
des toilettes
un lac
un fleuve
une rivière
très peu d'insectes | firewood
showers
electricity
toilets
a lake
a river
a stream, a river
very few insects |

VOTRE AMI(E): Voulez-vous
aller à la pêche?

YOUR FRIEND: Do you want to
go fishing?

| faire un pique-nique
vous promener dans la forêt
courir dans les champs | have a picnic
go for a walk in the forest
run in the fields |

VOUS: Demain peut-être. Pour l'instant je vais
m'amuser à **cueillir des fleurs.**

YOU: Tomorrow, perhaps. For the
moment I'm going to have fun
picking flowers.

écouter chanter les oiseaux
regarder le ciel / les étoiles / les
   nuages
respirer l'air pur
m'étendre dans l'herbe
	listening to the birds sing
	looking at the sky / stars /
	   clouds
	breathing the clean air
	lying down in the grass

VOTRE AMI(E): Je suis sûr(e) que nous allons passer des vacances formidables.

YOUR FRIEND: I'm sure we're going to have a great vacation.

EXERCICES D'APPLICATION

*1. Dites que vous allez passer vos vacances chez des amis . . . que vous allez passer le weekend à la campagne . . . que vous allez passer vos vacances au bord de la mer. . . . que vous allez vous reposer pendant les vacances . . . que vous avez l'intention de faire du ski . . . que vous comptez travailler . . . que vous aimeriez voir des amis . . . que vous comptez partir ce soir . . . que vous avez envie de vous baigner . . . que vous savez nager comme un poisson . . . que vous préférez faire du ski nautique . . . que vous ne savez pas skier . . . que vous avez peur de vous casser une jambe . . . que vous allez louer des skis . . . que vous allez sortir le matériel de camping du coffre . . . que vous aimeriez faire un pique-nique . . . que vous allez vous amuser à cueillir des fleurs.

2. Put all the above **Dialogue** into the more familiar **tu** form of address.

VERBE IRRÉGULIER: courir

courir *to run*	
Le présent: **je cours**	**nous courons**
tu cours	**vous courez**
il / elle court	**ils / elles courent**
Le participe passé: **couru**	
La base du futur et du conditionnel: **courr-**	

«Voulez-vous **courir** dans les champs?»

STRUCTURES

1.   Third-Person Pronouns, Indefinite Pronouns and Expressions

    a. The third-person singular pronouns **il** and **elle** used as subjects of the verb **être** are equivalent to *it* when there is a specific antecedent:

> «Comment est l'eau?»
> «—(**Elle** est) bonne / froide / rafraîchissante.»

> «Et la neige?»
> «—**Elle** est poudreuse / gelée / un peu molle / damée.»

    b. The pronoun **on** designates unspecified persons: someone, somebody. It can mean *one, you, we, they*. **On** is always the subject of a verb in the third-person singular.

> «**On** se retrouve ici pour le déjeuner?»
> «Peut-**on** camper ici?»

    c. les personnes = *people, persons, individuals* (a determined number)

> Il y avait plus de deux cents **personnes** sur la plage.
> *There were more than two hundred people on the beach.*

> Plusieurs **personnes** ont dit la même chose.
> *Several people (have) said the same thing.*

An equivalent of **il y a beaucoup de personnes** is **il y a beaucoup de monde:**

> **Il y a beaucoup de monde** sur la plage.

    d. les gens = *people* (in general, an undetermined number)

> **Les gens** sont gentils partout.
> *People are nice everywhere.*

> Où vont tous **ces gens?**
> *Where are all these people going?*

> **les jeunes gens** = *young people, young men*

2.   Complementary Infinitives

    a. The following verbs commonly used in conversational French take no preposition when followed by an infinitive:

adorer	to adore	falloir	to be necessary
aimer	to like, to love	oser	to dare
aimer mieux	to prefer	penser	to intend, to think (of)
aller	to go	pouvoir	to be able, can
compter	to intend, to plan	préférer	to prefer
désirer	to desire, to wish	savoir	to know how (to)
détester	to detest, to hate	sembler	to seem
devoir	to have (to)	vouloir	to wish, to want
espérer	to hope		

«Où **allez-vous** passer les vacances?» (**aller**)

«Quand **comptez-vous** partir?» (**compter**)

«Je **vais** me reposer . . .» (**aller**)

«**Savez-vous** skier?» (**savoir**)

«**Peut-on** camper ici?» (**pouvoir**)

«**Voulez-vous** aller à la pêche?» (**vouloir**)

b. The following verbs commonly used in conversational French take the preposition **à** when followed by an infinitive:

aider à	to help	être habitué à	to be accustomed
s'amuser à	to enjoy, to have fun	s'habituer à	to get used to
apprendre à	to learn	hésiter à	to hesitate
avoir tendance à	to tend	s'intéresser à	to be interested in
commencer à	to begin	inviter à	to invite
continuer à	to continue	se préparer à	to prepare, to get ready
être décidé à	to be determined	réussir à	to succeed in
encourager à	to encourage	tarder à	to delay in
forcer à	to force		

«Pour l'instant je vais **m'amuser à** cueillir des fleurs.» (**s'amuser à**)

J'apprends à faire du ski. (**apprendre à**)
I'm learning (how) to ski.

Je me prépare à partir en vacances. (**se préparer à**)
I'm getting ready to go on vacation.

c. The following verbs commonly used in conversational French take the proposition **de** when followed by an infinitive:

accepter de	to accept	avoir envie de	to feel like
accuser de	to accuse	avoir l'intention de	to intend
s'arrêter de	to stop	avoir peur de	to be afraid
avoir l'air de	to seem	cesser de	to stop
avoir besoin de	to need	choisir de	to choose

décider de	*to decide*	**s'excuser de**	*to excuse, to be sorry*
décourager de	*to discourage*	**finir de**	*to finish*
se dépêcher de	*to hurry*	**oublier de**	*to forget*
empêcher de	*to prevent*	**persuader de**	*to persuade*
envisager de	*to envisage, to intend*	**refuser de**	*to refuse*
essayer de	*to try*	**regretter de**	*to regret*
être en train de	*to be in the process of*	**remercier de**	*to thank*

«**Avez-vous envie de** vous baigner?» (**avoir envie de**)
«**J'ai peur de** me casser une jambe.» (**avoir peur de**)

d. The following verbs commonly used in conversational French take the preposition **de** when followed by an infinitive. The noun or pronoun objects of these verbs are indirect. Remember that the indirect object pronouns are: **me, te, lui, nous, vous, leur:**

commander		*to order*	
conseiller		*to advise*	
défendre		*to forbid*	
demander	+ **à quelqu'un de faire**	*to ask*	+ *someone to do something*
dire	**quelque chose**	*to tell*	
ordonner		*to order*	
permettre		*to permit*	
promettre		*to promise*	

Le docteur a conseillé à Pierre de se reposer.
The doctor advised Pierre to rest.

Je lui ai dit de rester ici.
I told him / her to stay here.

EXERCICES DE SYNTHÈSE

A. *Répondez aux questions suivantes:*

1. Aimez-vous courir? nager? faire du ski nautique? aller à la pêche? faire du camping? jouer au tennis? aller à l'étranger? rester à la maison pendant les vacances? partir en vacances?

2. Où allez-vous passer vos prochaines vacances? les vacances de Noël? le week-end? Où avez-vous passé vos vacances d'été l'année dernière?

3. Qu'est-ce que vous allez faire pendant les vacances d'été? les vacances de Noël? Qu'est-ce que vous avez fait pendant vos vacances d'été l'année dernière? pendant les vacances de Noël? le jour de Noël?

4. Partez-vous en vacances bientôt? Quand comptez-vous partir? Où allez-vous? Avec qui?

5. Êtes-vous parti(e) en vacances récemment? Où êtes-vous allé(e)? Quand? Avec qui?

6. Savez-vous nager? Préférez-vous vous baigner dans une piscine ou à la plage? Nagez-vous bien? comme un poisson? Avez-vous peur de l'eau?

7. Qu'est-ce que vous avez envie de faire en ce moment? de partir en vacances? de jouer au tennis? de faire du ski?

8. Savez-vous skier? Faites-vous souvent du ski? de temps en temps? Où? Avez-vous des skis?

9. Qu'aimeriez-vous apprendre à faire? à nager? à skier? à pêcher?

10. Aimez-vous la montagne et les sports d'hiver? la plage et les sports nautiques?

B. *Répondez aux questions suivantes:*

1. Avez-vous déjà suivi des cours dans une école de ski? Avez-vous appris à bien skier?

2. Combien de semaines de vacances avez-vous cette année? Avez-vous déjà pris vos vacances?

3. Avez-vous une maison de vacances? Où? Au bord de la mer? À la montagne? À la campagne? Aimeriez-vous avoir une maison de vacances? Où?

4. Avez-vous déjà fait du ski? du camping?

5. Vous êtes-vous déjà cassé une jambe? un bras? Vous êtes-vous déjà foulé une cheville? Quand? Comment? en courant? en faisant du ski? en faisant du camping?

6. Avez-vous un sac de couchage?

7. Avez-vous fait un pique-nique récemment? Où? Avec qui?

C.* *Répondez à chaque question en vous servant de **il est** ou **elle est** et de l'élément donné entre parenthèses. Ensuite, traduisez la phrase:*

EXEMPLE: Comment est la pláge? (jolie)
Elle est jolie.

1. Comment est l'eau? (froide)
2. La plage vous plaît-elle? (trop petite)
3. Où avez-vous mis le sac de couchage? (dans le coffre)
4. Comment trouvez-vous le bateau? (beau)
5. Que pensez-vous de la piscine? (petite)
6. Comment est la neige? (poudreuse)
7. Aimez-vous la piscine? (jolie)
8. Que pensez-vous de ce terrain de camping? (énorme)
9. Comment est la plage? (belle)
10. Que pensez-vous de la tente? (très grande)

D. *Complétez avec **gens** ou **personnes**:*

1. Il y a des _____ qui sont toujours en vacances.
2. Il y a des avions qui transportent trois cent cinquante _____.

3. J'aime les _____ qui font du camping.
4. Plusieurs _____ m'ont dit la même chose.
5. Il y a beaucoup de _____ dans la piscine.
6. Les _____ sont parfois bizarres!
7. Beaucoup de _____ se posent cette question.

E.* *Substituez les mots indiqués entre parenthèses. Puis traduisez:*

EXEMPLE: J'ai décidé de partir en vacances (refusé)
                 J'ai refusé de partir en vacances.

1. J'ai *envie* de me baigner (l'intention / peur / besoin)
2. *Aimeriez*-vous partir en vacances? (Pensez, Comptez, Espérez, Voulez)
3. *Savez*-vous faire du ski? (Pensez, Osez, Voulez, Pouvez)
4. Il m'a *demandé* de le faire (défendu, dit, permis, conseillé)
5. J'ai *continué* à nager. (commencé, appris, hésité)
6. J'ai *cessé* de fumer. (décidé, refusé, fini, essayé)
7. Il a *oublié* d'apporter ses skis. (refusé, décidé, essayé, choisi)

F.   *Remplacez les tirets par* **à, de,** *ou* **d'.** *Ensuite traduisez:*

1. Pourriez-vous m'aider _____ le faire?
2. J'aimerais vous inviter _____ dîner.
3. A-t-il cessé _____ fumer?
4. Avez-vous envie _____ vous baigner?
5. Je vais m'amuser _____ cueillir des fleurs.
6. Qu'avez-vous décidé _____ faire?
7. Avez-vous essayé _____ trouver un autre hôtel?
8. Je suis en train _____ préparer ma valise.
9. Ne tardez pas _____ le faire.
10. Je suis décidé(e) _____ le faire.
11. Je m'excuse _____ être en retard.
12. Je vous conseille _____ vous reposer.
13. Le docteur m'a dit _____ me reposer.
14. Il m'a demandé _____ le faire.
15. J'ai oublié _____ le faire.
16. Il a refusé _____ me voir.
17. Permettez-moi _____ vous présenter mon ami.
18. J'ai besoin _____ partir en vacances.
19. J'ai peur _____ me casser une jambe.
20. Je me prépare _____ partir pour la France.

EXPANSION: Qu'emportez-vous lorsque vous partez en vacances?[1]

un appareil photo	*camera*
de l'argent / des chèques de voyage	*money / travelers' checks*
de l'aspirine	*aspirin*
ma bicyclette	*my bicycle*
des billets	*tickets*
une brosse à dents	*toothbrush*
mon carnet d'adresses	*my address book*
des cartes de crédit	*credit cards*
des cartes à jouer	*playing cards*
de la crème anti-solaire	*sun-tan lotion*
du dentifrice	*toothpaste*
du déodorant	*deodorant*
des Kleenex	*Kleenex (tissues)*
une lampe de poche	*flashlight*
des lunettes de soleil	*sunglasses*
un maillot de bain	*bathing suit*
une montre	*watch*
des objets de toilette	*toilet articles*
mon oreiller	*my pillow*
un peigne	*comb*
des pellicules	*film*
mon permis de conduire	*my driver's license*
un rasoir (électrique)	*(electric) razor*
un réveil	*alarm clock*
un séchoir	*hair dryer*
un transistor	*transistor radio*
des valises	*suitcases*
des vêtements	*clothing*

Exercice

Répondez à ces questions:

1. Qu'emportez-vous lorsque vous partez en vacances?
2. Qu'oubliez-vous souvent (toujours) de mettre dans votre valise?
3. Que mettez-vous toujours dans votre valise?
4. Qu'est-ce que vous êtes toujours obligé(e) d'acheter lorsque vous êtes en vacances? des pellicules? du dentifrice? etc.

1. For additional travel items, see *Entracte 11: Clothing* and *Entracte 14: Personal Possessions.*

5. Parmi les objets que vous emportez, de quoi vous servez-vous très souvent? De quoi vous servez-vous très peu? de votre brosse à dents? de votre appareil photo? etc.
6. Emportez-vous le même matériel et les mêmes vêtements si vous allez en vacances dans un pays chaud ou dans un pays froid? si vous descendez à l'hôtel ou si vous campez? si vous voyagez en avion ou en auto? etc.

PRONONCIATION

Sound (Phonetic Symbol): [ɲ]

SPELLING:	**gn**
ENGLISH SOUND RESEMBLED:	Medial sound in words *onion* and *canyon*
PRONUNCIATION:	Tenser and briefer than in English.
EXAMPLES FROM THIS CHAPTER:	campa**gn**e, monta**gn**e, bai**gn**er, si**gn**ez.

IMPROVISATIONS

1. Vous êtes à la plage. Vous n'avez pas envie de lire. Voilà un homme (ou une femme) qui a l'air assez sympathique. Vous commencez à lui parler. «Il fait vraiment beau aujourd'hui, n'est-ce pas? . . . Comment est l'eau? . . .» Préparez un dialogue.
2. Vous passez un week-end à la campagne avec des amis. Vos amis vous demandent ce que vous voulez faire, ce qui vous ferait plaisir. Imaginez la conversation. Expliquez vos préférences.
3. C'est la première fois que vous passez vos vacances dan une station de ski. Vous entrez dans la salle à manger. Tout le monde y parle français. Vous vous mettez à table. Vous dites: «Bonjour. Je m'appelle. . . . Depuis quand êtes-vous ici? . . .» Préparez un dialogue.

PROJET

How have you spent your vacations for the past five years? Where did you go? With whom? For how long? What did you do? Prepare a brief summary. You may wish to include some photos or other souvenirs (such as postcards, ski lift tickets, menus, hotel bills, etc.), as illustrations.

ACTIVITÉ

Fill out the passport form given below for a classmate. Obtain the necessary information by asking:

1. Comment vous appelez-vous? Quelle est l'orthographe exacte de votre prénom? de votre nom de famille? . . . Pardon?
2. Quand êtes-vous né(e)?
3. Où êtes-vous né(e)?
4. Quelle est votre nationalité?
5. De quelle couleur sont vos yeux? (bleus? bruns? gris? marron? verts? noirs?)
6. De quelle couleur sont vos cheveux? (blancs? blonds? bruns? châtains? gris? noirs? roux?)
7. Où habitez-vous? Quelle est votre adresse?
8. Quelle est la date aujourd'hui? C'est le . . . , 19 . . . Ce passeport expire donc le . . . , 19 . . . (dans cinq ans).

```
┌─────────────────────┬─────────────────────────┐
│                     │         PASSEPORT       │
│    ┌─────────┐      │                         │
│    │         │      │  Nom: _____   │
│    │         │      │  Sexe: _____   │
│    │         │      │  Date de naissance: ___ │
│    └─────────┘      │  Lieu de naissance: ___ │
│       Photo         │  Nationalité: _____ │
│                     │  Yeux: _____   │
│                     │  Cheveux: _____  │
│  Numéro du passeport: ___  Adresse du titulaire: __ │
│  Signature du titulaire:   Date de délivrance: ___  │
│                     │  Date d'expiration: _____│
│  _____  │                         │
└─────────────────────┴─────────────────────────┘
```

To assign a passport number, ask for a telephone number or a social security number, etc. («**Quel est votre numéro de téléphone?** . . .»)

To secure a signature, say: «**Signez ici, s'il vous plaît.**»

In the space marked **Photo,** sketch their face!

À LA CLAIRE FONTAINE

À la clai - re fon - tai - ne, M'en all - ant
pro - me - ner, J'ai trou - vé l'eau si bel - le,
Que je m'y suis bai - gné. Il y a long -
temps que je t'ai - me, Ja - mais je ne t'oub - lie - rai.

2. Chante, rossignol, chante
   Toi qui as le cœur gai
   Tu as le cœur à rire
   Moi je l'ai à pleurer!

WEATHER

Quel temps fait-il aujourd'hui?

LE TEMPS (WEATHER)

Il fait beau.	*It's nice (weather) out.*
Il fait (très) chaud.	*It's (very) hot.*
Il fait frais.	*It's chilly, cool.*
Il fait (très) froid.	*It's (very) cold.*
Il fait gris.	*It's gray and cloudy.*
Il fait humide.	*It's humid.*
Il fait mauvais.	*It's bad weather.*
Le temps est nuageux. / Le ciel est nuageux.	*It's cloudy. There are clouds.*
Il fait un temps couvert. / Le temps se couvre.	*It's cloudy (totally covered with clouds) / It's getting cloudy.*
Il fait de l'orage.	*It's stormy / storming.*
Il fait du soleil / Le soleil brille.	*It's sunny. / The sun is shining.*
Il fait du vent.	*It's windy.*
Il grêle.	*It's hailing.*
Il grésille.	*It's sleeting.*
Il neige.	*It's snowing.*

Il pleut (légèrement).	*It's raining (lightly).*
Il pleut à seaux / à torrents / à verse.	*It's pouring.*
Il va pleuvoir.	*It's going to rain.*
Il tonne.	*It's thundering.*
Il y a des éclairs.	*There's lightning.*

Vous dites:

Quel beau / mauvais temps!	*What beautiful / bad weather!*
Quelle belle journée!	*What a beautiful day!*
Il fait un temps affreux!	*The weather is awful!*
Quelle chaleur / Quel froid aujourd'hui!	*How hot / cold it is today!*
Il fait bien chaud / froid pour la saison.	*It's really hot / cold for this time of year.*

SPRINGBOARDS FOR CONVERSATION

1. Quel temps fait-il aujourd'hui?
2. Que dites-vous quand il grésille? quand il fait beau? quand il pleut à torrents? quand il fait chaud? etc.
3. Quel temps fait-il en hiver? en été? au printemps? en automne?
4. Quel temps a-t-il fait hier? avant-hier? la semaine passée? A-t-il fait beau? A-t-il plu? A-t-il neigé? etc.
5. Quel temps fera-t-il demain?
6. Fait-il chaud pour la saison? Fait-il froid pour la saison? Fait-il plus chaud (froid) que l'année passée?
7. Fait-il beau maintenant? Pleut-il? Neige-t-il? etc.
8. Avez-vous peur *(Are you afraid)* quand il tonne? quand il y a des éclairs? quand il grêle? etc.
9. Quelle température fait-il dehors? dans la salle de classe? chez vous?
   —**Il fait _____ degrés.**

C	F
40°	104°
30	85
20	68
10	50
0	32
−10	14
−20	−4

PROJETS

1. Write a letter to a friend or relative. Discuss the weather at great length. (What the weather has been this past week, what it is doing now, what they are predicting it will be, etc.)
2. Keep track of the weather for one week. Note changes, weather predictions, temperatures, etc.
3. Clip illustrations of outdoor scenes from magazines. Caption each with the weather condition depicted. For example: **Il neige. Le soleil brille. Il fait beau,** etc.

À la banque

At the Bank

Proverbe: L'argent ne fait pas le bonheur.

Proverb: Money doesn't buy happiness.
(*Literally:* Money doesn't make happiness.)

«Donnez-moi un billet de cent, sept de cinquante, quatre de dix et de la monnaie, s'il vous plaît.»

326

VOUS: Je voudrais me faire payer ce chèque de voyage. Voici mon passeport.

YOU: I would like to cash this traveler's check. Here is my passport.

LE CAISSIER / LA CAISSIÈRE: Votre adresse à Paris, s'il vous plaît?

TELLER: Your address in Paris, please?

VOUS: L'Hôtel Carnot, avenue Carnot. Pouvez-vous me changer cent dollars?

YOU: Hotel Carnot, Avenue Carnot. Can I cash one hundred dollars' worth?

LE CAISSIER / LA CAISSIÈRE: Certainement.

TELLER: Certainly.

VOUS: Quel est le cours du change aujourd'hui?

YOU: What is the rate of exchange today?

LE CAISSIER / LA CAISSIÈRE: Il est à cinq francs. Ça vous fait donc cinq cents francs. Les voulez-vous en petites coupures?

TELLER: It's five francs (for a dollar). That gives you five hundred francs. Do you want it in small bills?

VOUS: Donnez-moi un billet de cent, sept de cinquante, quatre de dix, et de la monnaie, s'il vous plaît.

YOU: Give me a one hundred-franc bill, seven fifties, four tens, and some small change please.

LE CAISSIER / LA CAISSIÈRE: Très bien. Signez ici, s'il vous plaît. . . Voilà. Merci, Monsieur / Madame.

TELLER: Very well. Sign here, please . . . Here it is. Thank you.

EXERCICE D'APPLICATION

Complétez:

VOUS: Bonjour, Monsieur / Madame. Je voudrais me faire payer ce chèque de voyage.
LE CAISSIER / LA CAISSIÈRE: Votre passeport, s'il vous plaît.
VOUS: _____
LE CAISSIER / LA CAISSIÈRE: _____
VOUS: _____
LE CAISSIER / LA CAISSIÈRE: _____

VERBE IRRÉGULIER: lire

lire	*to read*

Le présent:	je lis	nous lisons
	tu lis	vous lisez
	il / elle lit	ils / elles lisent

Le participe passé: **lu**
La base du futur et du conditionnel: **lir-**

STRUCTURES

1.   Subjunctive Mood: Formation

The subjunctive is used to express possibility, feelings and emotions. It usually occurs in dependent clauses introduced by **que.** The most commonly used subjunctive tenses are **le présent** and **le passé.** There is no future or conditional subjunctive; the present subjunctive is used to indicate present or future actions. The perfect subjunctive is used to indicate actions that have occurred before the action of the main verb.

a. Formation of the present subjunctive:

To form the present subjunctive of regular verbs and some irregular verbs, drop the letters **-ent** from the third-person plural present indicative and add to this base the present subjunctive endings: **-e, -es, -e, -ions, -iez, -ent:**

VERBES EN **-er**		VERBES EN **-ir**	
parler		**finir**	
je parle	nous parl**ions**	je finisse	nous finiss**ions**
tu parles	vous parl**iez**	tu finisses	vous finiss**iez**
il / elle parle	ils / elles parl**ent**	il / elle finisse	ils / elles finiss**ent**

VERBES EN **-re**	
répondre	
je réponde	nous répond**ions**
tu répondes	vous répond**iez**
il / elle réponde	ils / elles répond**ent**

Some verbs have irregular subjunctive forms. These must be learned individually. The subjunctive endings, however, remain the same:

aller	avoir	boire	croire
to go	*to have*	*to drink*	*to believe*
j'aille	j'aie	je boive	je croie
tu ailles	tu aies	tu boives	tu croies
il aille	il ait	il boive	il croie
nous allions	nous ayons	nous buvions	nous croyions
vous alliez	vous ayez	vous buviez	vous croyiez
ils aillent	ils aient	ils boivent	ils croient

être	faire	pouvoir	prendre
to be	*to make, to do*	*to be able*	*to take*
je sois	je fasse	je puisse	je prenne
tu sois	tu fasses	tu puisses	tu prennes
il soit	il fasse	il puisse	il prenne
nous soyons	nous fassions	nous puissions	nous prenions
vous soyez	vous fassiez	vous puissiez	vous preniez
ils soient	ils fassent	ils puissent	ils prennent

savoir	venir	voir	vouloir
to know	*to come*	*to see*	*to want*
je sache	je vienne	je voie	je veuille
tu saches	tu viennes	tu voies	tu veuilles
il sache	il vienne	il voie	il veuille
nous sachions	nous venions	nous voyions	nous voulions
vous sachiez	vous veniez	vous voyiez	vous vouliez
ils sachent	ils viennent	ils voient	ils veuillent

b. Formation of the past subjunctive:

The past subjunctive is made up of the present subjunctive of **avoir** or **être** and the past participle of the main verb. Remember that verbs of coming and going and reflexive verbs are conjugated with **être** as the helping verb:

VERBES EN **-er**	VERBES EN **-ir**	VERBES EN **-re**
parler	**guérir**	**répondre**
j'aie parlé	j'aie guéri	j'aie répondu
tu aies parlé	tu aies guéri	tu aies répondu
il ait parlé	il ait guéri	il ait répondu
elle ait parlé	elle ait guéri	elle ait répondu
nous ayons parlé	nous ayons guéri	nous ayons répondu
vous ayez parlé	vous ayez guéri	vous ayez répondu
ils aient parlé	ils aient guéri	ils aient répondu
elles aient parlé	elles aient guéri	elles aient répondu

VERBS OF COMING AND GOING	REFLEXIVE VERBS
aller	**se coucher**
je sois allé(e)	je me sois couché(e)
tu sois allé(e)	tu te sois couché(e)
il soit allé	il se soit couché
elle soit allée	elle se soit couchée
nous soyons allé(e)s	nous nous soyons couché(e)s
vous soyez allé(e)(s)	vous vous soyez couché(e)(s)
ils soient allés	ils se soient couchés
elles soient allées	elles se soient couchées

2.   Subjunctive Mood: Uses

a. After impersonal expressions of necessity, doubt, emotional reaction, and possibility., the subjunctive is used in the subordinate clause and is introduced by **que:**

il est absurde	*it is absurd, it is ridiculous*	**c'est dommage**	*it is too bad, it is a shame*
il est bien	*it is good*	**il est douteux**	*it is doubtful*
il convient	*it is suitable, it is appropriate*	**il est drôle**	*it is funny*
		il est essentiel	*it is essential*
il est curieux	*it is strange*	**il est étonnant**	*it is surprising*

il faut	*it is necessary*	**il est urgent**	*it is urgent*
il est important	*it is important*	**il vaut mieux**	*it is better*
il est impossible	*it is impossible*	**il est vexant**	*it is annoying*
il est nécessaire	*it is necessary*	**il n'est pas certain**	*it is not sure*
il est normal	*it is normal*	**il n'est pas clair**	*it is not clear*
il est possible	*it is possible*	**il n'est pas évident**	*it is not evident*
il est regrettable	*it is unfortunate*	**il n'est pas probable**	*it is not probable*
il semble	*it seems*	**il n'est pas sûr**	*it is not sure*
il se peut	*it is possible*	**il n'est pas vrai**	*it is not true*
il est temps	*it is time*		

Il est possible que je sois en retard.
It is possible that I'll be late. / I may be late.
Il faut que j'y aille.
I must go.
C'est dommage qu'il soit déjà parti.
It's too bad that he's left already.

NOTE that the indicative mood is used after the following expressions of certainty and probability:

il est certain	*it is sure*
il est clair	*it is clear*
il est évident	*it is evident*
il est probable	*it is probable*
il est sûr	*it is sure*
il est vrai	*it is true*
il me semble	*it seems to me*
il n'y a aucun doute	*there is no doubt*

Il est vrai que je me sens un peu fatigué.
It is true that I feel a little tired.

With the expression **il faut,** the indirect object pronoun (**me, te, lui, nous, vous, leur**) and an infinitive may be used instead of the subjunctive:

Il te faut aller à la banque. = Il faut que tu ailles à la banque.
You must go to the bank.

Il leur a fallu partir. = Il a fallu qu'ils partent.
They had to leave.

Certain of the impersonal expressions listed above, which normally require the subjunctive, may be followed by an infinitive to convey a general meaning, when no subject is indicated:

Il est absurde de . . .	
Il est bien de . . .	
Il est essentiel de . . .	
Il faut . . .	
Il est important de . . .	
Il est impossible de . . .	**. . . partir**
Il est nécessaire de . . .	
Il est normal de . . .	
Il est possible de . . .	
Il est temps de . . .	
Il vaut mieux . . .	

b. The subjunctive is used in clauses introduced by **que** after verbs which express a wish, an order, a doubt, or an emotional reaction. Whenever the subject of the main clause is different from the subject of the subordinate clause, the subjunctive is used. When the subject of the main verb is the same as that of the subordinate verb, the infinitive, sometimes preceded by **de** or **à,** is used instead of the subjunctive:

aimer	*to like, to love*	**être surpris (de)**	
aimer mieux	*to prefer*	**être étonné (de)**	*to be surprised*
attendre que	*to wait until*	**être fâché (de)**	*to be angry, to*
s'attendre à ce que	*to expect*		*be sorry*
avoir peur (de)	*to be afraid*	**être fier (de)**	*to be proud*
défendre	*to forbid*	**être désolé (de)**	*to be sorry*
désirer	*to wish, to desire*	**être ravi (de)**	*to be delighted*
détester	*to hate, to detest*	**être triste (de)**	*to be sad*
douter (de)	*to doubt*	**ordonner**	*to order*
empêcher	*to prevent*	**permettre**	*to permit*
s'étonner (de)	*to be surprised*	**préférer**	*to prefer*
être content (de),		**regretter (de)**	*to be sorry*
être heureux (de)	*to be happy*	**souhaiter**	*to wish*
être mécontent (de),		**suggérer**	*to suggest*
être malheureux (de)	*to be unhappy*	**tenir à ce que**	*to insist*
être d'accord	*to agree*	**vouloir**	*to wish, to want*

Je regrette qu'il soit en retard.
I'm sorry that he's late.

But: **Je regrette d'être en retard.**
I'm sorry that I'm late. / I'm sorry to be late.

J'aime mieux qu'il vienne chez moi.
I prefer that he come to my house.

But: **J'aime mieux aller chez lui.**
I prefer to go to his house.

Il veut que je parte.
He wants me to leave.

But: **Il veut partir.**
He wants to leave.

The following verbs, often used with the subjunctive, may also be used with infinitives (**qqn = quelqu'un; qqch = quelque chose**):

défendre à qqn de faire qqch   **proposer à qqn de faire qqch**
ordonner à qqn de faire qqch   **suggérer à qqn de faire qqch**
permettre à qqn de faire qqch   **empêcher qqn de faire qqch**

Le docteur a ordonné à mon père de se reposer. =
Le docteur a ordonné que mon père se repose.
The doctor ordered my father to rest.

c. The subjunctive is used after certain conjunctions:

afin que, pour que	*in order that, so that*
à moins que (ne)	*unless*
avant que (ne)	*before*
bien que, quoique	*although*
jusqu'à ce que	*until*
malgré que	*in spite of the fact that*
de peur que (ne), de crainte que (ne)	*for fear that*
pourvu que, à condition que	*provided that*
sans que	*without*
supposé que	*supposing that*

J'irai **pourvu que vous m'accompagniez.**
I will go provided that you accompany me.
Il va au cinéma **bien qu'il soit** très fatigué.
He's going to the movies, although he's very tired.

ne is often used, even in conversation, in subjunctive clauses introduced by **avoir peur, de peur que, de crainte que, avant que,** and **à moins que.** It does not make the clause negative. The sentence would still be correct without **ne:**

Partez **avant qu'il (ne) soit trop tard.**
Leave before it's too late.

The following conjunctions do not take the subjunctive:

après que	*after*	**puisque**	*since, as long as*
comme	*as, since*	**quand**	*when*
lorsque	*when*	**si**	*if, whether*
parce que	*because*	**tandis que**	*while*
pendant que	*while*		

> **Puisque je n'ai pas** d'argent, je vais à la banque.
> *Since I don't have any money, I'm going to the bank.*

EXERCICES DE SYNTHÈSE

A.   *Répondez à ces questions par des phrases complètes:*

1. Aimez-vous lire? Lisez-vous beaucoup? souvent? fréquemment? de temps en temps? constamment? jamais?
2. Que lisez-vous en ce moment? un roman? des poèmes? un roman policier?
3. Quels journaux lisez-vous? Quels magazines?
4. Avez-vous lu le journal de ce matin?
5. Que lirez-vous ce soir?
6. Lisez-vous rapidement ou lentement?

B.   *Mettez les verbes entre parenthèses au présent du subjonctif. Ensuite, traduisez la phrase:*

1. Je doute qu'elle _____ venir. (pouvoir)
2. Il est possible que vous _____ la grippe. (avoir)
3. Il veut que je lui _____. (téléphoner)
4. Il vaut mieux que j'_____ à la banque. (aller)
5. C'est vraiment dommage que vous _____ malade. (être)
6. Il faut que vous le _____. (faire)
7. Il est normal qu'il _____ cela. (dire)
8. Il a suggéré que je _____ l'autobus. (prendre)
9. Il défend que je _____. (voyage)
10. Elle tient à ce que je _____ tout. (savoir)

C.*   *Commencez chaque phrase par l'expression entre parenthèses. Employez le présent du subjonctif. Ensuite, traduisez:*

EXEMPLE: Elle a mal à la tête. (Il est possible que)
Il est possible qu'elle ait mal à la tête.

1. Il est malade. (C'est dommage qu')
2. Vous allez chez vos parents. (Il faut que)
3. Vous êtes en avance. (Il se peut que)
4. Nous ne pouvons pas venir. (Je regrette que)
5. Vous restez à la maison. (Il vaut mieux que)
6. Je pars. (Mon ami veut que)
7. Je parle français. (Elle est contente que)
8. Vous lisez le livre. (Je suggère que)
9. Ce n'est pas grave. (Il est heureux que)
10. Vous revenez dans quelques jours. (Il voudrait que)

D.* *Faites suivre la proposition entre parenthèses par la phrase qui la précède. Employez le passé du subjonctif. Puis, traduisez:*

EXEMPLE: Je ne suis pas parti . . . (Il est heureux que)
                 Il est heureux que je ne sois pas parti.

1. Elle n'est pas allée chez son ami. (C'est dommage que)
2. Le professeur n'a pas beaucoup parlé aujourd'hui. (Je suis content(e) que)
3. Il est déjà parti. (Je doute qu')
4. Vous lui avez parlé. (Il est bon que)
5. Vous n'avez pas pris de vacances. (Je m'étonne que)
6. Elle est déjà partie. (Il se peut qu')
7. Ils n'ont pas répondu. (Il est possible qu')
8. Il n'a pas téléphoné. (Je suis étonné(e) qu')
9. Il n'a rien dit. (Il est vexant qu')
10. Je ne suis pas parti(e). (Mes amis sont heureux que)

E.* *Remplacez l'infinitif en ajoutant le sujet indiqué entre parenthèses. Traduisez:*

EXEMPLE: Il est temps d'y aller. (vous)
                 Il est temps que vous y alliez.

1. J'aimerais aller chez le docteur. (vous)
2. Je préfère le faire tout de suite. (il)
3. Il vaut mieux dormir. (elles)
4. Mon professeur veut partir. (nous)
5. Je voudrais le voir. (vous)
6. Que voulez-vous faire? (je)

F. *Complétez en employant soit le subjonctif soit l'indicatif du verbe entre parenthèses:*

1. Je vous accompagnerai pourvu que vous ne _____ pas trop. (parler)
2. Nous resterons à moins que vous ne _____ trop fatigué. (être)
3. Avant que vous ne _____, téléphonez chez lui. (partir)
4. Téléphonez-lui pendant que je _____ le dîner. (préparer)

5. Nous partirons à condition que vous _____ avec nous. (venir)
6. Bien qu'il ne le _____ pas, il va le faire. (dire)
7. Je vous en parlerai si vous _____ . (vouloir)
8. De peur que vous n'_____ avant nous, nous partons tout de suite. (arriver)
9. Je vais lui répondre parce qu'il m'_____ toujours. (écrire)
10. Quand il _____ , il est content. (voyager)

EXPANSION: À la banque

1. **Où se trouve la banque la plus proche / le bureau de change le plus proche?**	*Where's the nearest bank / currency exchange office?*
2. **Je voudrais ouvrir un compte bancaire.**	*I'd like to open a bank account.*
3. **Avez-vous une pièce d'identité?**	*Do you have some identification?*
4. **Passez à la caisse, s'il vous plaît.**	*Go to the cashier's window, please.*
5. **J'ai besoin d'argent liquide.**	*I need some cash.*
6. **Je n'ai pas de monnaie. Avez-vous une pièce d'un franc?**	*I don't have any change. Do you have a one-franc piece?*
7. **Je voudrais toucher un chèque.**	*I'd like to cash a check.*
8. **Pourriez-vous me changer un billet de cent francs?**	*Could you give me change for a hundred-franc bill?*
9. **Haut les mains! Au voleur!**	*Stick 'em up! Stop thief!*

Exercices

1. Vous avez besoin d'une pièce d'un franc mais vous n'avez pas de monnaie. Vous dites à votre ami: _____
2. Vous cherchez la banque. Vous demandez: _____
3. Quand on vous dit d'aller chercher votre argent à la caisse, on dit tout simplement: _____
4. Vous voulez qu'on vous change un billet de cent francs. Vous dites: _____
5. Vous voulez toucher un chèque. Vous dites au caissier: _____

PRONONCIATION

1.   Sound (Phonetic Symbol): [z]

SPELLING: **s** (between two vowels), **z**

ENGLISH SOUND RESEMBLED: Initial sound in word *zebra*

| PRONUNCIATION: | Sound is pronounced with more force and tension than in English. |

EXAMPLES FROM THIS CHAPTER:
nous lisons   désolé(e)
vous lisez   proposer
ils lisent   besoin
le présent

2. Sound (Phonetic Symbol): [s]

SPELLING: **s, ss, sc** (followed by **i, e, y**), **c** (followed by **i, e, y**), **ç**

ENGLISH SOUND RESEMBLED: Final sound in word *hiss*

EXAMPLES FROM THIS CHAPTER:
voici   cent
passeport   cinq
caissier   ça
adresse   sept

NOTES:

1. The spelling **-tion** in French is pronounced [sjɔ̃]. Examples from this chapter: **application, improvisation.**

2. **ç** (**c** with a cedilla) only appears before **a, o,** and **u.** It is always pronounced [s].

Contrast the voiceless consonant [s] with the voiced consonant [z], using the following words and expressions:

[s]	[z]
dessert	désert
baisser	baiser
poisson	poison
ils sont	ils ont

IMPROVISATION

Imaginez une scène où vous essayez de vous faire payer un chèque de voyage. On vous pose beaucoup de questions. Vous répondez aux questions et vous expliquez comment vous voulez votre argent:

Vous: _____
Le Caissier / La Caissière: _____

Vous: _____
Le Caissier / La Caissière: _____
Vous: _____
Le Caissier / La Caissière: _____
Vous: _____

PROJET

Look through your wallet, change purse, handbag, pockets, etc. Pile all your financial resources in front of you. Count it out. Make a list. For example: **J'ai deux billets de cinq** *dollars* **et un de dix. J'ai trois pièces de cinq** *cents,* etc.

ACTIVITÉS

1. Fill out this sample check. Now go to **La Banque** (a designated area in the classroom) to have your check cashed by a student teller. (Play money can be used for these purposes.) Ask for appropriate denominations.

```
┌─────────────────────────────────────────────────────────────────────────────┐
│ No. 5311238                 Banque Île–de–France              BIF_____  ( 1 )│
│                                                                               │
│                                                                               │
│ Payez contre ce chèque la somme de_____   │
│                                        Somme en toutes lettres                │
│                                                                               │
│ _____ │
│                                                                               │
│ à l'ordre de _____ │
│                        Chèque NON ENDOSSABLE sauf au profit d'une banque,     │
│                        d'une caisse d'épargne ou d'un établissement assimilé. │
│                                                                               │
│                                            _____ le _____ 19_____ │
│  ┌── Payable à ──┐                              lieu de création               │
│  Paris, Bureau Central                                                         │
│  6, Rue des Moines                                                            │
│  Tél.: 370.21.68                                                              │
│  └────────────────┘                                                           │
└─────────────────────────────────────────────────────────────────────────────┘
```

2. Using the vocabulary from the **Dialogue** and **Expansion** sections of this lesson, stage a bank hold-up. The robber should make it very clear to the teller what he / she wants. (Play money may again be used for this exercise.)
3. Take out a bill and ask classmates for change: **«Pourriez-vous me changer un billet de. . . .** *dollars?***»** **«Oui, voilà un billet de. . . , deux de. . . , et quatre pièces de vingt-cinq** *cents.***»** **«Non, je suis désolé(e). . . .»** etc.

LA MARSEILLAISE

Entracte

17

PLACES

Où êtes-vous allé(e) cette semaine?
—Je suis allé(e) _____ .

à l'aéroport	*airport*
à l'agence de voyages	*travel agency*
chez l'antiquaire	*antique dealer's*
à la banque	*bank*
à la bibliothèque	*library*
à la blanchisserie	*laundry*
à la boucherie	*butcher's*
à la boulangerie-pâtisserie	*bakery*
au bureau	*office*
au bureau de tabac	*tobacconist's*
à la campagne	*country*
au cinéma	*movies*
à la charcuterie	*delicatessen*
au cirque	*circus*
chez le coiffeur	*barber's, hairdresser's*
au commissariat de police	*police station* (in cities)
au concert	*concert*

340

chez le cordonnier	*shoemaker's, cobbler's*
aux courses	*races*
chez le dentiste	*dentist's*
chez le docteur	*doctor's*
à l'école	*school*
à l'église	*church*
à la gendarmerie	*police station* (rural)
au grand magasin	*department store*
à l'hôpital	*hospital*
à la laverie automatique (en libre service)	*laundromat*
à la librairie	*bookstore*
au magasin de chaussures	*shoe store*
à la Mairie	*Town Hall*
au bord de la mer / à la mer	*seashore, the sea*
à la montagne	*mountains*
au musée	*museum*
à l'opéra	*opera*
à la papeterie	*stationery store*
au parc	*park*
chez mes parents / ma sœur / mon frère / mes grands-parents / mon fils / ma fille / mon cousin / mon ami(e), etc.	*my parents' / my sister's / my brother's / my grandparents' / my son's / my daughter's / my cousin's / my friend's, etc.*
à la pharmacie	*pharmacy*
à la piscine	*swimming pool*
à la plage	*beach*
à la poste	*post office*
à la préfecture de police	*police headquarters*
à la quincaillerie	*hardware store*
au restaurant	*restaurant*
au salon de beauté	*beauty parlor*
à la station-service	*service station*
à la synagogue	*temple*
au supermarché	*supermarket*
à la teinturerie	*dry-cleaner's*
au théâtre	*theater*
au travail	*work*
à l'université	*university*
à l'usine	*factory*
en ville	*town*
[Je suis resté(e)] chez moi / à la maison	[I stayed] *home*

SPRINGBOARDS FOR CONVERSATION

1. Où êtes-vous allé(e) cette semaine? Pourquoi? Avec qui? Qu'est-ce que vous y avez fait? Y allez-vous souvent? de temps en temps? rarement?
   Je suis allé(e) _____.
2. Où êtes-vous allé(e) la semaine passée? le week-end passé? Avec qui? Qu'est-ce que vous y avez fait?
   Je suis allé(e) _____.
3. Où allez-vous ce week-end? Avec qui?
   Je vais _____.
4. D'habitude où allez-vous le week-end? Qu'est-ce que vous y faites?
   Je vais _____.
5. Où aimeriez-vous aller ce week-end? Avec qui? Pourquoi?
   J'aimerais aller _____.
6. Où allez-vous tous les jours? Pourquoi?
   Je vais _____.
7. Où devez-vous *(do you have to)* aller cette semaine? Aujourd'hui? Pourquoi?
   Je dois aller _____.
8. Où passez-vous beaucoup de temps?
9. Qui dans la classe est allé chez le coiffeur? à la bibliothèque? à la pharmacie? etc.
10. Où Monsieur. . . . . est-il allé cette semaine? Et Madame. . . , où est-elle allée? Et Mademoiselle . . . ? Et le professeur . . . ? Et votre mari (femme)? etc.
11. Y a-t-il des absents aujourd'hui? Où est Monsieur / Madame / Mademoiselle . . . ? Au cinéma? Au lit? Chez ses parents? etc.
    Il / Elle est probablement _____.
    Il / Elle est peut-être *(perhaps)* _____.
12. Y a-t-il un parc près d'ici? près de chez vous? une pharmacie? un restaurant? une église? etc.
    Oui, il y a un / une _____ près d'ici / près de chez moi.
    Non, il n'y a pas de _____ près d'ici / près de chez moi.
13. Travaillez-vous *(Do you work)?* Où? dans une banque? dans un grand magasin? dans un hôpital? etc.
    Je travaille _____.
14. Où aimeriez-vous travailler? Pourquoi?
    J'aimerais travailler _____.
15. Aimeriez-vous être propriétaire *(owner)* d'un restaurant? d'une station-service? d'un théâtre? etc. Pourquoi?

PROJETS

1. **Mon Agenda.** Where do you have to go this week? Make a list including dates and, whenever possible, times. You may choose to extend this project to cover a whole month, in which case use engagement calendar format.
2. Where have you gone this past week? Be comprehensive. Include dates. You may again choose to extend this project to cover a whole month, in which case use engagement calendar format.
3. What would you tell a visitor to your town to do during his or her stay there? What places to visit? Which sights to see? and so on. For example: **Le musée, le zoo,** etc.
4. Draw a touristic map of your town, neighborhood or region indicating monuments, buildings, sights, restaurants, etc.

ACTIVITÉ

A selected student acts out an activity that would occur at a place chosen from the above list, while the rest of the class tries to guess just where this activity is taking place: **À la piscine? Au supermarché? Chez le dentiste?** etc. The person who guesses correctly acts out the next "place," and so on.

Chapitre 18

Échange de cadeaux

Exchanging Gifts

Proverbe: Il y a plus de bonheur à donner qu'à recevoir.

Proverb: 'Tis more blessed to give than to receive. (*Literally:* There is more happiness in giving than in receiving.)

DIALOGUE
EXERCICE D'APPLICATION
VERBES IRRÉGULIERS: **devoir, falloir, offrir**
STRUCTURES:
Past-Participle Agreement
EXERCICES DE SYNTHÈSE
EXPANSION: **Fêtes et vœux**
PRONONCIATION: [ə]
IMPROVISATION
PROJET
ACTIVITÉ
CHANSON: **Il pleut, il pleut, bergère**

«Bon Anniversaire!»

DIALOGUE

VOUS *(offrant un cadeau):*
Bon Anniversaire!

> Bonne Année
> Bonne Fête[1]
> Bonne et heureuse retraite
> Bon Voyage
> Joyeux Noël
> Joyeuses Pâques
> Félicitations

J'espère que cela vous fera plaisir.

VOTRE AMI(E): **C'est très gentil à vous.**

> C'est très gentil de votre part.
> Vous êtes très gentil(le).
> Vous êtes trop aimable.
> Vraiment, je suis confus(e).
> Mais, il ne fallait pas!
>
> Vous n'auriez pas dû!

VOUS: C'est peu de chose . . . un tout petit rien. Ouvrez-le! Regardez!

VOTRE AMI(E): Oh! C'est vraiment **magnifique!**

> adorable
> exquis
> joli
> mignon
> splendide

YOU *(offering a gift): Happy Birthday!*

> Happy New Year
> Happy Saint's Day
> Happy Retirement
> (Have a) good trip
> Merry Christmas
> Happy Easter
> Congratulations

I hope that you like this.

YOUR FRIEND:
How nice! (Literally: That's very nice of you.)

> It's very nice of you.
> You are very kind.
> You are too kind.
> Truly, I'm overwhelmed!
> But, you shouldn't have. (*Literally:* It was not necessary.)
> You shouldn't have (done it)!

YOU: It's nothing. (*Literally:* It's only a little thing . . . a very little something.) Open it! See what it is! (*Literally:* Look!)

YOUR FRIEND: Oh! It's really *magnificent!*

> adorable
> exquisite
> pretty
> cute
> splendid, great

---

1. For a listing of Saint's Days (Name Days), see *Entracte 3: Dates.*

C'est tout à fait ce qu'il me fallait. | *It's just what I needed.*

C'est précisément ce que je voulais.
C'est justement ce que je voulais m'acheter.
Qu'est-ce que c'est?

It's precisely what I wanted.
It's just what I wanted to buy myself.
What is it?

Merci mille fois! | Thanks so much! (*Literally:* Thanks a thousand times!)

(On échange des baisers.) | *(Exchange of kisses.)*

EXERCICE D'APPLICATION

*1. *Que dites-vous . . .*

1. pour souhaiter à quelqu'un un bon anniversaire? un bon voyage? une bonne année? un Joyeux Noël? etc.
2. pour féliciter quelqu'un?
3. quand vous offrez un cadeau?
4. en acceptant le cadeau que l'on vous offre?
5. quand vous voulez que votre ami(e) ouvre le cadeau que vous venez de lui offrir?
6. en ouvrant le cadeau?

2. *Put the preceding dialogue into the more familiar* **tu** *form of address.*

VERBES IRRÉGULIERS: devoir, falloir, offrir

devoir	*to have to, to owe*	
Le présent:	**je dois**	**nous devons**
	tu dois	**vous devez**
	il / elle doit	**ils / elles doivent**
Le participe passé: **dû**		
La base du futur et du conditionnel: **devr-**		

a. The verb **devoir** means *to owe:*

Combien vous **dois-je?** *How much do I owe you?*

b. When **devoir** is followed by an infinitive, it may have various English equivalents, depending both on tense and context:

Au présent:

(must / have to)
Je dois me lever de très bonne heure demain matin.
I must / have to get up very early tomorrow morning.

(must / probably)
Où est Pierre? **Il doit** être malade.
Where is Pierre? He must be (is probably) sick.

(supposed to / expected to)
Je dois partir la semaine prochaine.
I am supposed to (expected to) leave next week.
I must (have to) leave next week.

Au passé composé:

(had to)
J'ai dû partir de bonne heure.
I had to leave early.

(must have)
J'ai dû recevoir une invitation.
I must have received an invitation.

À l'imparfait:

(was supposed to)
Je devais le faire.
I was supposed to do it.

Au futur:

(will have to)
Vous devrez lui dire si vous acceptez ou non.
You will have to tell him / her if you accept or not.

Au conditionnel:

(should / ought to)
Je devrais aller le voir.
I should / ought to go see him.

Au conditionnel passé:

(should have / ought to have)
«**Vous n'auriez pas dû!**»

J'aurais dû les inviter.
I should have (ought to have) invited them.

c. The verb **devoir** can be used impersonally:

Il doit faire chaud dehors.   *It must be hot out.*
Il doit être tard.   *It must be late.*

---

falloir   *to be necessary*
Le présent: **il faut**
Le participe passé: **fallu**
Le futur: **il faudra**
L'imparfait: **il fallait**
Le conditionnel: **il faudrait**

«Mais **il ne fallait pas!**»

a. Falloir is an impersonal verb whose subject is always **il.** It can be used in any tense and translated in a variety of ways:

falloir + **infinitif:** *must / have to / to be necessary*

Il faut étudier.
It is necessary to study.
You / We / People must (have to) study.
One must (has to) study.

falloir + **nom:** *to need*

When used in this way, indirect object pronouns are needed:

Il me / te / lui / nous / vous / leur **faut** de l'argent.
I / you / he or *she / we / you / they need(s) some money.*

«C'est tout à fait ce qu'**il me fallait.**»

falloir + **période de temps:** *to take*

Combien de temps faut-il pour y aller? *How long does it take to get there?*

s'il le faut. = *If it is necessary. / If I have to. / If I must.*

b. falloir and **devoir** are sometimes interchangeable:

Il me faut étudier. = **Je dois** étudier.
I must study.

Uses of **falloir** + **que** + **le subjonctif** are presented in Chapter 17: **Structures (Le Subjonctif)**.

---

offrir *to offer*	

Le présent:	**j'offre**	**nous offrons**
	tu offres	**vous offrez**
	il / elle offre	**ils / elles offrent**

Le participe passé: **offert**
La base du futur et du conditionnel: **offrir-**

«(**Offrant** un cadeau): Bon Anniversaire!»

Il m'a offert un joli sac.   *He gave me (a gift of) a pretty handbag.*

Qu'**avez-vous offert** comme cadeau?   *What did you give as a gift?*

Past-Participle Agreement

1. Intransitive verbs of motion are conjugated with **être** in compound tenses, and the past participle agrees with the subject in gender and number; that is, with verbs of "coming and going" like **aller, venir** and **arriver,** add **e** to the past participle if the subject is feminine, **s** to the past participle if the subject is plural, **es** to the past participle if the subject is both feminine and plural.

	INFINITIVE	PAST PARTICIPLE
to go	**aller**	**allé**
to arrive	**arriver**	**arrivé**
to go down	**descendre** (when intransitive)	**descendu**
to become	**devenir**	**devenu**
to enter	**entrer**	**entré**
to go up	**monter** (when intransitive)	**monté**
to die	**mourir**	**mort**
to be born	**naître**	**né**
to leave	**partir**	**parti**
to pass (by), to stop off (at)	**passer**	**passé**
to go home	**rentrer** (when intransitive)	**rentré**
to stay	**rester**	**resté**
to return	**retourner**	**retourné**
to come back	**revenir**	**revenu**
to go out	**sortir**	**sorti**
to fall	**tomber**	**tombé**
to come	**venir**	**venu**

EXEMPLE:

je suis allé(e)	nous sommes allé(e)s
tu es allé(e)	vous êtes allé(e)(s)
il est allé	ils sont allés
elle est allée	elles sont allées

2. When a verb is conjugated with **avoir,** the past participle agrees in gender and number with a preceding direct object. Remember that direct object pronouns (**me, te, le, la, l',** **nous, vous, les**) are placed before the auxiliary or "helping" verb in compound tenses:

Elle a appelé. (No agreement, there is no preceding direct object.)
She called.

Elle a appelé ses amis. (No agreement. The direct object **ses amis** follows the past participle.)
She called her friends.

Elle les a appelés. (Agreement. The direct object **les** precedes the past participle.)
She called them.

J'ai vu la dame. (No agreement. The direct object **la dame** follows the past participle.)
I saw the lady.

Voilà la dame que j'ai vue. (Agreement. The direct object **que** which refers to **la dame** precedes the past participle.)
There's the lady (whom) I saw.

Quelle dame avez-vous vue? (Agreement. The direct object **Quelle dame** precedes the past participle.)
What lady did you see?

There is, however, no past participle agreement with preceding indirect object pronouns: **me, te, lui, nous, vous, leur.** The following verbs take **à** plus an indirect object:

qqn = quelqu'un   *s.o. = someone*
qqch = quelque chose   *s.th. = something*

commander à qqn de faire qqch	*to order s.o. to do s.th.*
conseiller à qqn de faire qqch	*to advise s.o. to do s.th.*
défendre à qqn de faire qqch	*to forbid s.o. to do s.th.*
demander à qqn de faire qqch	*to forbid s.o. to do s.th.*
désobéir à qqn	*to disobey s.o.*
dire qqch à qqn	*to tell s.o. s.th.*
donner qqch à qqn	*to give s.o. s.th.*
écrire à qqn	*to write s.o.*
enseigner qqch à qqn	*to teach s.th. to s.o.*
envoyer qqch à qqn	*to send s.o. s.th.*
faire mal à qqn	*to hurt s.o.*
obéir à qqn	*to obey s.o.*
offrir qqch à qqn	*to offer / give s.o. s.th.*
ordonner à qqn de faire qqch	*to order s.o. to do s.th.*
pardonner à qqn	*to pardon s.o.*
permettre à qqn de faire qqch	*to permit s.o. to do s.th.*
poser une question à qqn	*to ask s.o. a question*
promettre à qqn de faire qqch	*to promise s.o. to do s.th.*
raconter qqch à qqn	*to tell s.o. s.th.*
répondre à qqn	*to answer s.o.*
ressembler à qqn	*to resemble s.o.*
téléphoner à qqn	*to telephone s.o.*

J'ai offert un cadeau à mes parents. (No agreement. There is no preceding direct object.)
I gave my parents a gift.

Je leur ai offert un cadeau. (No agreement; **leur** is an indirect object.)
I gave them a gift.

3. Reflexive verbs are conjugated with **être** in the compound tenses. There is past-participle agreement with the preceding reflexive pronoun when it functions as a direct object.

> **Elle s'est lavée.** (Agreement; **se** functions as a direct object.)
> *She washed (herself).*

> **Elle s'est lavé les mains.** (No agreement; **se** functions as an indirect object; **les mains** is the direct object.)
> *She washed her hands.*

> **Ils se sont écrit.** (No agreement; **se** functions as an indirect object.)
> *They wrote (to) each other.*

4. Since the final letters **e** and **s** are not pronounced, in conversational French past participle agreement often goes unnoticed. For example, **allé, allée, allés,** and **allées** are all pronounced alike. Past participle agreement is apparent in spoken French, however, with verbs whose past participles end in consonants. In these cases the letter **e** which has been added to make the past participle agree with a preceding feminine direct object causes the final consonant to be pronounced. The following verbs commonly used in conversational French have past participles which end in the consonants **s** or **t** which become sounded when the letter **e** is added for past-participle agreement:

INFINITIVE	PAST PARTICIPLE	
apprendre	**appris**	*to learn*
asseoir	**assis**	*to sit*
comprendre	**compris**	*to understand*
couvrir	**couvert**	*to cover*
découvrir	**découvert**	*to discover*
dire	**dit**	*to say*
faire	**fait**	*to make, to do*
mettre	**mis**	*to put*
ouvrir	**ouvert**	*to open*
plaindre	**plaint**	*to pity*
se plaindre	**(se) plaint**	*to complain*
prendre	**pris**	*to take*
surprendre	**surpris**	*to surprise*
traduire	**traduit**	*to translate*

Où est le cadeau? Où l'avez-vous **mis?** (The final **s** of **mis** is not pronounced.)
Where is the gift? Where did you put it?

Où est la clé? Où l'avez-vous **mise?** (The s of **mise** is now pronounced because the letter **e** has been added for past-participle agreement.)
Where is the key? Where did you put it?

EXERCICES DE SYNTHÈSE

A.* *Transformez selon le modèle. Ensuite traduisez:*

MODÈLE: Je dois le faire tout de suite. (Elle)
          Elle doit le faire tout de suite.

1. Je dois le faire tout de suite. (Tu, Il, On, Nous, Vous, Ils)
2. Je ne devrais pas fumer. (Tu, Elle, Nous, Vous, Ils)

B.* *Transformez selon le modèle. Puis traduisez:*

MODÈLE: Je n'ai pas apporté mon manteau.
          J'aurais dû apporter mon manteau.

1. Je n'ai pas dit bonjour au professeur.
2. Je n'ai pas fumé.
3. Je n'ai pas téléphoné.
4. Je n'ai pas apporté mes gants.
5. Je ne suis pas parti(e) de bonne heure.
6. Je ne suis pas allé(e) chez elle.

C.   *Répondez à ces questions:*

1. À qui avez-vous offert un cadeau cette année? À votre mère? À votre père? À votre professeur? Qu'est-ce que vous avez offert comme cadeau? Des bonbons? Des chocolats? Des fleurs? À quelle occasion?
2. Qui vous a offert un cadeau récemment? À quelle occasion? Qu'est-ce qu'on vous a offert comme cadeau?
3. Qu'est-ce que vous avez reçu comme cadeaux de Noël l'année dernière? De qui? Quel cadeau vous a fait le plus plaisir? Qu'est-ce que vous aimeriez recevoir pour Noël cette année? Quels cadeaux avez-vous offerts? Que pensez-vous offrir à votre mère cette année? à votre père? à votre mari? à votre femme? à vos amis?
4. Quel est le dernier cadeau que vous avez offert à quelqu'un? À qui? À quelle occasion?

D. *Mettez les verbes entre parenthèses au passé composé. Employez l'auxiliaire **être**. Ensuite traduisez:*

1. Elle _____ aujourd'hui. (arriver)
2. Ils _____ ce matin. (partir)
3. Il _____ devant la maison. (tomber)
4. Je _____ dans la chambre. (entrer)
5. Nous _____ en France. (rester)
6. Est-ce qu'elle _____ dans sa chambre? (monter)
7. Ils _____ en Italie. (aller)
8. Est-ce que vous _____ hier soir? (sortir)
9. À quelle heure est-ce qu'ils _____? (rentrer)
10. Tu _____ en Amérique, n'est-ce pas? (naître)

E.* *Mettez les phrases suivantes au passe composé. Faites attention à l'accord du participe passé. Ensuite, traduisez:*

EXEMPLE: Nous allons à Paris.
Nous sommes allés à Paris.

1. Part-elle vers cinq heures?
2. Ils sortent avant six heures.
3. Elle tombe.
4. Ils restent ici.
5. Ma mère se lave.
6. À quelle heure est-ce qu'ils rentrent?
7. Elle se lave les mains.
8. À quelle heure arrivent-ils?
9. Elle va voir son ami.
10. Est-ce qu'elle sort avec Marc?

F. *Répondez aux questions suivantes par **oui** ou par **non** selon le cas. Remplacez la partie de la phrase en italique par un pronom. Faites l'accord nécessaire du participe passé:*

EXEMPLE: Avez-vous appelé *vos amis?*
Oui, je les ai appelés.
ou, Non, je ne les ai pas appelés.

1. Avez-vous téléphoné *à vos parents* cette semaine?
2. Avez-vous vu *vos amis* récemment?
3. Aujourd'hui, en classe, avez-vous posé une question *au professeur?*
4. Avez-vous appelé *votre amie* hier soir?
5. Avez-vous téléphoné *à votre amie* hier soir?
6. Avez-vous demandé *le numéro?*
7. Avez-vous offert un cadeau *au professeur* récemment?
8. Avez-vous parlé *à votre professeur de français* récemment?
9. Avez-vous appelé *vos parents* cette semaine?

G.* *Transformez les questions selon le modèle. Faites l'accord nécessaire du participe passé:*

MODÈLE: Qui a ouvert la porte?
          Qui l'a ouverte?

1. Qui a pris la clé?
2. Qui a ouvert la valise?
3. Qui a mis les valises là?
4. Qui a compris la leçon?

5. Qui a découvert l'Amérique *(f.)*?
6. Qui a appris la leçon?
7. Qui a traduit la phrase?

EXPANSION: Fêtes et Vœux

1. **Heureux (Bon / Joyeux) Anniversaire**	*Happy Birthday*
2. **Heureux Anniversaire de Mariage**	*Happy Wedding Anniversary*
3. **Bonne (Heureuse) Fête**	*Happy Saint's / Name Day*
4. **Bonne Fête des Mères / des Pères**	*Happy Mother's Day / Father's Day*
5. **Joyeux Noël**	*Merry Christmas*
6. **Bonne (Heureuse) Année**	*Happy New Year*
7. **Joyeuses Pâques**	*Happy Easter*
8. **Bonne Fête à la Saint-Valentin**	*Happy Saint Valentine's Day*
9. **Bon Voyage**	*(Have a) Good Trip. Bon Voyage*
10. **Vœux de prompt rétablissement**	*Get Well*
11. **Félicitations!**	*Congratulations!*
. . . pour la naissance de ce beau bébé	*. . . on your new baby*
. . . pour votre diplôme	*. . . on your graduation*
. . . pour votre promotion	*. . . on your promotion*
12. **Vœux (sincères) de Bonheur** (par exemple, à l'occasion de votre mariage . . .)	*Best Wishes (for example, on the occasion of your marriage)*
13. **Bonne (Heureuse) Retraite**	*Happy Retirement*
14. **Meilleurs Vœux**	*Best Wishes*
15. **Bonne Chance dans votre nouveau travail**	*Good luck in your new job*

Exercice

Using the preceding list for inspiration, wish everyone in the classroom: Happy Birthday, Happy Mother's Day, Have a Good Trip, Congratulations on your new baby / house / job, Get Well, etc. (Birthdays, Anniversary's, upcoming holidays, Saint's Days, etc. may be determined by using **Entracte** 3: **Dates.**) Some ways to begin are: **Je te (vous) souhaite un / une . . .** or, **Félicitations pour. . . .**

PRONONCIATION

Sound (Phonetic Symbol): [ə]

SPELLING: **e**

ENGLISH SOUND RESEMBLED: Vowel sound in word *p<u>u</u>sh*

PRONUNCIATION: The sound [ə] is pronounced similarly to the French vowel sound [ø] (see Chapter 9). It is often referred to as *Mute E* or *Unstable E,* since it may be pronounced or silent depending upon its position within a word or word group. Furthermore, a pronounced [ə] in slow speech is often silent in faster speech. (A similar dropping of sounds happens in English. Compare a slow, careful pronunciation of *good-by* with a speedy *g'by.*

EXAMPLES FROM THIS CHAPTER: J'espère que cela vous fera plaisir.
C'est très gentil de votre part.
Vraiment je suis confus.
C'est peu de chose . . . un tout petit rien.
C'est précisément ce que je voulais!
Qu'est-ce que c'est?
C'est vraiment adorable.
Merci mille fois.
Il ne fallait pas.
C'est justement ce que je voulais m'acheter.

Knowing just when to retain or drop the [ə] sound will come with practice. Here, however, are some general guidelines:

[ə] is pronounced in the following cases:

1. In the interrogative pronoun **que** (Que dit-il?)
2. In **le** after a positive command (Ouvrez-le!)
3. When preceded by two or more pronounced consonants and followed by one (ven*dre*di)
4. In proper names (**V**enise)

[ə] is silent in the following cases:

1. In final syllables (Bon Anniversair¢!). In everyday French, the final **le** and **re** are often dropped entirely, as in **tabl¢, quatr¢, livr¢,** etc.
2. When preceded and followed by single pronounced consonants (sam¢di, ach¢ter)
3. In certain fixed groups of monosyllables: **c¢ que, j¢ te, n¢ se, je n¢, je m¢, ne l¢.**

NOTES:

1. When [ə] occurs in successive syllables separated from each other by single pronounced consonants, every other [ə] is dropped. (Je l¢ sais. Je n¢ le sais pas.)
2. The correct pronunciation of the spelling **e** (with no accent marks on it) is determined as follows:

   a. The spelling **e** is pronounced [ə] when it ends a syllable (de-voir, je, pe-tit).
   b. The spelling **e** is pronounced [ɛ] (see Chapter 7) when it is followed by a consonant sound within the same syllable (e*ll*e, ve*r*t, annive*r*saire)
   c. The spelling **e** followed by a double consonant may be pronounced either [e] (see Chapter 7) or [ɛ] (see Chapter 7): de*ss*ert, me*ss*age, e*ff*ort. Exception: Before a double **r**, the letter **e** must be pronounced [ɛ] (ε*rr*eur, te*rr*eur).

IMPROVISATION

Complétez ce dialogue. Employez le vocabulaire et les structures de la leçon.

Vous (offrant un cadeau): Bon Anniversaire! _____
Votre Ami(e): _____
Vous: _____
Votre Ami(e): _____
Vous: _____
Votre Ami(e): _____

PROJET

Cartes de vœux. Using the expressions given in the **Expansion** section of this chapter, make several greeting cards for occasions that will soon take place. For example: a birthday card for your sister, a get-well card for an absent class member, a Christmas card for a friend, etc. Construction paper, crayons, colored pens and pencils, etc. can all be used effectively.

ACTIVITÉ

Exchanging gifts. Everyone brings a token (very inexpensive) gift to class for a classmate. Using the vocabulary and structures from the **Dialogue** and **Expansion** sections of this lesson, exchange gifts.

IL PLEUT, IL PLEUT, BERGÈRE

Il pleut, il pleut, ber - gè - re, Pres - se tes blancs mou - tons,

Allons sous ma chau - miè - re, Ber - gè - re, vi - te al -

lons.____ J'en - tends sur le feuil - la - ge.

L'eau qui tombe à grand - bruit.____ Voi - ci, voi - ci l'o -

ra - ge. Voi - là l'é - clair qui luit.____

Entracte
18

SCHOOL SUBJECTS

Quels sont vos cours préférés?
—J'aime beaucoup _____.

l'algèbre	*algebra*
l'allemand	*German*
l'anatomie	*anatomy*
l'anglais	*English*
l'anthropologie	*anthropology*
l'archéologie	*archeology*
l'art	*art*
les arts ménagers	*home economics*
l'astronomie	*astronomy*
les beaux-arts	*fine arts*
la biochimie	*biochemistry*
la biologie	*biology*
le calcul	*calculus*
la chimie	*chemistry*
le chinois	*Chinese*
le commerce	*commerce, business*
la composition anglaise	*English composition*
la comptabilité	*bookkeeping, accounting*

361

la dactylographie	*typing*
la danse	*dance*
le dessin	*design, drawing*
le droit	*law*
l'écologie	*ecology*
l'économie	*economics*
l'éducation / la pédagogie	*education*
l'éducation physique	*physical education*
l'espagnol	*Spanish*
le français	*French*
le génie	*engineering*
la géographie	*geography*
la géologie	*geology*
la géométrie	*geometry*
la gestion	*management, administration*
le gouvernement	*government*
la grammaire	*grammar*
le grec	*Greek*
l'hébreu	*Hebrew*
l'histoire	*history*
l'histoire d'art	*art history*
l'instruction civique	*social studies, citizen education*
l'italien	*Italian*
le japonais	*Japanese*
le journalisme	*journalism*
les langues	*languages*
le latin	*Latin*
les lettres / la littérature	*literature*
les mathématiques / les maths	*mathematics / math*
la médecine	*medicine*
la musique	*music*
l'océanographie	*oceanography*
l'orthographe	*spelling*
la peinture	*painting*
la philosophie	*philosophy*
la physique	*physics*
la psychologie	*psychology*
la religion	*religion*
le russe	*Russian*
les sciences	*science*
les sciences politiques	*political science*
la sculpture	*sculpture*

la sociologie	sociology
la sténographie	shorthand
les travaux manuels	industrial arts, "shop"
la trigonométrie	trigonometry
la zoologie	zoology

SPRINGBOARDS FOR CONVERSATION

1. Quels sont vos cours préférés? Pourquoi?
   J'aime beaucoup _____ .
2. Quels cours suivez-vous maintenant? Un cours de français? Un cours de chimie? etc.
   Je suis un cours de / d'_____ .
3. Quels cours aimeriez-vous suivre? Un cours de philosophie? Un cours de sociologie? etc. Pourquoi?
   J'aimerais suivre un cours de / d'_____ .
4. Qu'est-ce que vous avez étudié? L'italien? La biologie? La géographie? etc. Quand?
   J'ai étudié _____ .
5. Dans le temps *(in the past),* quels étaient vos cours préférés / vos matières *(subjects)* préférées? Pourquoi?
   J'aimais beaucoup _____ .
6. En quelle matière vous spécialisez-vous? / En quelle matière vous êtes-vous spécialisé(e)? en biologie? en mathématiques? etc.
   Je me spécialise en _____ . / Je me suis spécialisé(e) en _____ .

PROJET

Make a report card resembling a real one you may have received at some time. List subjects and enter grades. (Complete honesty is not necessary.)

Une Soirée

A Party

Proverbe: Plus on est de fous, plus on rit.

Proverb: The more, the merrier. (*Literally:* The more crazy people there are, the more one laughs.)

DIALOGUE
EXERCICE D'APPLICATION
VERBE IRRÉGULIER: **venir**
STRUCTURES:
Possessive Pronouns
EXERCICES DE SYNTHÈSE
EXPANSION:
Rencontres
Exclamations / Formules-réflexes
PRONONCIATION:
1. Intonation
2. Tension
IMPROVISATION
PROJET
ACTIVITÉ
CHANSON: **Chevaliers de la table ronde**

«M'accorderez-vous cette danse?»

DIALOGUE

(Accueil des invités)   *(Welcoming the guests)*

L'Hôte / L'Hôtesse: Entrez, entrez, je vous prie. Soyez le / la bienvenu(e). Puis-je prendre **votre manteau?** . . . .

THE HOST / HOSTESS: Come in, come in, please. Welcome. Can I take your *coat?*

vos bottes	boots
votre cape	cape
votre chapeau	hat
votre étole (de fourrure)	(fur) stole
votre foulard	scarf
votre gilet	sweater
votre imperméable	rain coat
votre parapluie	umbrella
votre serviette	briefcase
votre veste	jacket, sports coat

Vous: Merci.

You: Thank you.

L'Hôte / L'Hôtesse: Venez, je voudrais vous présenter à Monsieur / Madame / Mademoiselle _____.

Host / Hostess: Come (with me), I'd like to introduce you to _____.

Vous: Enchanté(e) (de faire votre connaissance). J'ai beaucoup entendu parler de vous.

You: Delighted (to know you). I've heard a lot about you.

L'Hôte / L'Hôtesse: Que puis-je vous offrir? Une bière? un whisky? des chips?

Host / Hostess: What can I offer you? A beer? Whisky? Potato chips?

Vous: **Un apéritif,** s'il vous plaît.

You: *A cocktail,* please . . .

des amuse-gueule	hors-d'œuvres, appetizers
des bonbons	candy
du café	coffee
du champagne	champagne
du cidre	cider
un cognac	cognac
un digestif	after-dinner drink
de l'eau minérale / gazeuse	mineral / sparkling water
un gin	gin
un jus de fruits	fruit juice
une limonade	lemonade
des noix	nuts
un Perrier	Perrier
un petit blanc sec	small glass of white wine
des petits fours	little cakes

un porto	port (wine)
un rhum	rum
du thé	tea
un verre de vin (blanc / rouge / rosé)	glass of wine (white / red / rosé)
un Xérès	Sherry

L'Hôte / L'Hôtesse *(trinquant):*
À votre santé!

Host / Hostess *(proposing a toast):*
To your health!

À vos amours	To your loves
À vos succès	To your successes

Vous: **À la vôtre!** . . .

You: *To yours!* . . .

Aux vôtres!	To yours *(plural)*

Ce vin est délicieux!

This wine is delicious.

C'est délicieux!	It's delicious.
C'est très rafraîchissant!	It's very refreshing!
Quel parfum!	What an aroma / taste!
Ces petits fours sont délicieux!	These little cakes are delicious!

L'Hôte / L'Hôtesse: Encore un peu?
Vous: **Bien volontiers.**

Host / Hostess: A little more?
You: *Gladly!*

Avec plaisir.	With pleasure.
Oui, s'il vous plaît.	Yes, please.
Non, merci.	No, thank you.
Un peu.	A little (bit).
Un doigt / une goutte / une larme.	Just a drop. (*Literally:* A finger / A drop / A tear.)

L'Hôte / L'Hôtesse *(renversant accidentellement le contenu de la bouteille sur vous):* Oh! Pardon. Comme je suis maladroit(e)!
Vous: Il n'y a pas de mal . . . Je vous en prie, ce n'est pas grave. . . .

Host / Hostess *(accidentally spilling the contents of the bottle on you):* Oh! Excuse me. How clumsy I am!
You: That's o.k. . . . really. (*Literally:* There's no harm . . . Really, it's not serious.)

(*Au salon*)

L'Hôte / L'Hôtesse: Je suis vraiment content(e) de vous revoir.

Vous: Moi de même. C'est vraiment charmant chez vous.

L'Hôte / L'Hôtesse: Merci beaucoup. Mais dites-moi, que faites-vous ces temps-ci?

Vous: **Pas grand-chose.**

> Rien de particulier.
> Rien de très intéressant.
> Je travaille dur comme toujours.
> Je suis très occupé(e) ces jours-ci.
> Toujours la même chose.
> Je voyage beaucoup depuis quelque temps.

L'Hôte / L'Hôtesse: Voulez-vous une cigarette?

Vous: Merci.[1] Je ne fume plus.

L'Hôte / L'Hôtesse: Vous avez très bonne mine. . . .

Vous: Je me sens en forme. Et de toute façon à quoi bon se plaindre?

(*Fin d'une agréable soirée*)

Vous: Déjà **dix heures** !?! Pas possible!

> huit heures
> huit heures et demie
> neuf heures
> onze heures
> minuit
> une heure

Que le temps passe vite!

L'Hôte / L'Hôtesse: Vous partez déjà?

(*In the living room*)

Host / Hostess: I'm really happy to see you again.

You: I am too. You have a lovely place here. (*Literally:* It's really charming at your place.)

Host / Hostess: Thanks so much. But tell me, what are you doing these days?

You: *Not much.*

> Nothing in particular.
> Nothing very interesting.
> I'm working hard, as always.
> I'm very busy these days.
> Always the same thing.
> I've been traveling a lot recently.

Host / Hostess: Do you want a cigarette?

You: (No), thank you.[1] I don't smoke any more.

Host / Hostess: You look very well. . . .

You: I feel fine. And in any case, what's the use of complaining?

(*The end of a pleasant evening*)

You: *Ten o'clock* already?!? (It's) not possible!

> eight o'clock
> eight thirty
> nine o'clock
> eleven o'clock
> midnight
> one o'clock

How time flies! (*Literally:* How time passes quickly!)

Host / Hostess: Are you leaving already?

---

1. Implication: "No. Thank you." The **non** is understood.

Vous: Hélas, oui. Je dois me lever de très bonne heure demain matin.

You: Alas, yes. I have to get up very early tomorrow morning.

L'Hôte / L'Hôtesse: Nous sommes désolés. Merci d'être venu(e)!

Host / Hostess: We're so sorry. Thanks for coming!

Vous: J'ai passé une soirée très agréable. Merci de m'avoir invité(e).

You: I had a very pleasant evening. Thanks for having invited me (Thanks for inviting me).

L'Hôte / L'Hôtesse: . . . Attention à la marche.

Host / Hostess: . . . Watch out for the step.

Vous: Au revoir. Bonsoir. Et merci encore.

You: Good-by. Good night. And thank you again.

L'Hôte / L'Hôtesse: Je vous en prie. . . .

Host / Hostess: You're welcome. . . .

EXERCICE D'APPLICATION*

Que dites-vous . . .

1. quand on frappe à la porte, vous ouvrez, et c'est un de vos invités.
2. quand vous voulez prendre le manteau de votre invité(e).
3. quand vous voulez présenter une personne à une autre.
4. lorsque vous faites la connaissance de quelqu'un.
5. quand vous voulez offrir quelque chose à boire ou à manger à vos invités.
6. quand vous buvez à la santé de quelqu'un.
7. pour offrir encore un peu à boire ou à manger.
8. quand le vin que vous buvez est délicieux.
9. quand vous renversez accidentellement quelque chose sur un invité.
10. quand on renverse accidentellement quelque chose sur vous.
11. quand on vous demande ce que vous faites ces temps-ci.
12. pour offrir une cigarette:
13. pour refuser la cigarette que l'on vous offre.
14. quand vous regardez votre montre et que vous voyez qu'il est déjà dix heures.
15. pour remercier un ami d'être venu chez vous.
16. quand vous avez passé une soirée très agréable chez des amis et que vous voulez les remercier.

VERBE IRRÉGULIER: venir

venir	*to come*

Le présent: **je viens**   **nous venons**
            tu viens   **vous venez**
            il / elle vient   **ils / elles viennent**
Le participe passé: **venu** (conjugué avec **être**)
La base du futur et du conditionnel: **viendr-**

«Merci d'**être venu(e)!**»

a. When the verb **venir** is used in the present tense and is followed by **de** plus an infinitive, the English equivalent is *(to have) just . . .*:

    Je viens de téléphoner.   *I (have) just telephoned.*
    Je viens de téléphoner. = Je téléphone à l'instant. = J'ai téléphoné il y a un instant *(a moment ago).*

b. **venir chercher** is equivalent to *to come for, to pick up*:

    Il est venu nous **chercher** en auto.
    He came for us. / He picked us up in his car.

    Je viendrai vous **chercher** à neuf heures.
    I will come (to) get you / pick you up at nine (o'clock).

c. **D'où venez-vous?** has several equivalents in English:

    D'où venez-vous? —Je viens de New-York.
    Where are you from? —I'm from New York.
    Where do you come from? —I come from New York.

    D'où venez-vous? —Je viens du cinéma.
    Where are you coming from? —I'm coming from the movies.
    Where have you been? —I've been to / at the movies.

STRUCTURES

Possessive Pronouns

a. Possessive pronouns are used in place of nouns modified by possessive adjectives. In French, both the possessive pronoun along with the definite article **(le, la, les)** which normally precedes it, assume the gender (masculine / feminine) and number (singular / plural) of the specified object possessed:

POSSESSIVE PRONOUNS		
SINGULAR		
MASCULINE	FEMININE	
(mon livre) **le mien**	(ma voiture) **la mienne**	(my book / car) *mine*
(ton livre) **le tien**	(ta voiture) **la tienne**	(your . . .) *yours*
(son livre) **le sien**	(sa voiture) **la sienne**	(his, her, its . . .) *his, hers, its*
(notre livre) **le nôtre**	(notre voiture) **la nôtre**	(our . . .) *ours*
(votre livre) **le vôtre**	(votre voiture) **la vôtre**	(your . . .) *yours*
(leur livre) **le leur**	(leur voiture) **la leur**	(their . . .) *theirs*

PLURAL		
MASCULINE AND FEMININE		
(mes livres / mes voitures)	**les miens / les miennes**	(my books / my cars) *mine*
(tes livres / tes voitures)	**les tiens / les tiennes**	(your . . .) *yours*
(ses livres / ses voitures)	**les siens / les siennes**	(his . . .) *his, hers, its*
(nos livres / nos voitures)	**les nôtres / les nôtres**	(our . . .) *ours*
(vos livres / vos voitures)	**les vôtres / les vôtres**	(your . . .) *yours*
(leurs livres / leurs voitures)	**les leurs / les leurs**	(their . . .) *theirs*

«À votre santé!» «**À la vôtre!**»
«À vos amours!» «**Aux vôtres!**»
«À vos succès!» «**Aux vôtres!**»

Votre manteau est noir. **Le mien** est gris. *Your coat is black. Mine is grey.*

b. The English expression *a . . . of mine* or *one of my . . .* is expressed in French by **un(e) de mes . . .:**

   C'est **un de mes** amis.   *He's a friend of mine / one of my friends.*
   C'est **un de nos** amis.   *He's a friend of ours / one of our friends.*

c. The expression **Serez-vous des nôtres?** means *Will you be joining us?:*

   Serez-vous des nôtres demain soir?

EXERCICES DE SYNTHÈSE

A.   *Donnez la forme correcte du verbe* **venir** *au present:*

1. D'où _____ -vous?
2. D'où _____ -elle?
3. Est-ce que tu _____ ?
4. Nous _____ de New-York.

5. _____ -vous cet après-midi?
6. Je _____ de Paris.
7. Il _____ aujourd'hui.
8. Ils _____ n'est-ce pas?

B.*   *Transformez selon le modèle:*

MODÈLE: J'arrive à l'instant.
          Je viens d'arriver.

1. Je termine le travail à l'instant.
2. Je me lève à l'instant.
3. Je mange à l'instant.
4. Il arrive à l'instant.

5. Il téléphone à l'instant.
6. Il fume à l'instant.
7. Nous rentrons à l'instant.
8. Vous arrivez à l'instant.

C.*   *Transformez selon le modèle:*

MODÈLE: J'ai fumé une cigarette il y a un instant.
          Je viens de fumer une cigarette.

1. J'ai pris son manteau il y a un instant.
2. J'ai offert du vin à Marie il y a un instant.
3. J'ai acheté un cadeau pour ma mère il y a un instant.
4. J'ai bu quelque chose il y a un instant.
5. J'ai téléphoné il y a un instant.
6. Il est arrivé il y a un instant.
7. Elle est rentrée il y a un instant.
8. Le train est arrivé il y a un instant.

D.   *Répondez à ces questions:*

1. De quelle ville venez-vous?
2. De quelle ville vient votre père? votre mère? votre femme / mari? votre meilleur(e) ami(e)?
3. Que venez-vous de faire? de regarder le professeur? de prendre des notes? de parler avec votre voisin(e)? de regarder votre montre? de mordiller *(bite on, nibble)* votre stylo / votre crayon? de regarder par la fenêtre? de lever la main? de fermer votre livre? de bâiller *(yawn)?*
4. Venez-vous (Allez-vous) en classe à pied? en voiture? en métro? en autobus?
5. Qu'est-ce que vous venez de dire? bonjour? au revoir? merci? rien?
6. D'où venez-vous? du cinéma? de votre chambre? de chez vous? d'un autre cours? du travail? du magasin? du restaurant? du parking?

E.*   *Donnez le pronom possessif qui remplace les mots suivants:*

EXEMPLE: mon frère *(m.)*
            le mien

1. mon chapeau *(m.)*
2. votre foulard *(m.)*
3. son imperméable *(m.)*
4. votre fourrure *(f.)*
5. mon sac *(m.)*
6. leur cadeau *(m.)*
7. mon café *(m.)*
8. notre maison *(f.)*
9. vos gants *(m.)*
10. mes bottes *(f.)*

F.*   *Donnez le pronom possessif qui remplace les mots en italique:*

EXEMPLE: mon frère et *votre frère*
            mon frère et le vôtre

1. ma sœur et *votre sœur*
2. mon imperméable et *votre imperméable*
3. mon foulard et *votre foulard*
4. mon sac et *votre sac*
5. mes gants et *vos gants*
6. ma maison et *votre maison*
7. mes bottes et *vos bottes*
8. mon cadeau et *votre cadeau*
9. mes parents et *vos parents*
10. mes amis et *vos amis*

G.   *Répondez. Employez* **un(e) de mes ami(e)s** *ou* **personne:**

EXEMPLE: Qui vous a dit bonjour aujourd'hui?
            Une de mes amis. *ou,*
            Une de mes amies. *ou,*
            Personne!

1. Qui vous a dit merci aujourd'hui?
2. Qui vous a offert quelque chose à boire cette semaine?
3. Qui vous a téléphoné récemment?

4. Qui vous a offert un cadeau récemment?
5. Qui vous a écrit cette semaine?
6. Qui est venu chez vous pendant le week-end?
7. Qui avez-vous vu hier?
8. Qui vous a dit que vous êtes adorable?
9. Qui vous a dit récemment que vous êtes très aimable?

EXPANSION: Rencontres

1. **Attendez-vous quelqu'un? Êtes-vous seul(e)?**
   Are you waiting for someone? Are you alone?
2. **M'accorderez-vous cette danse?**
   May I have this dance?
3. **Puis-je aller vous chercher quelque chose à boire?**
   Can I get you something to drink?
4. **Peut-on se revoir demain?**
   Can we see each other tomorrow?
5. **Si vous êtes libre, nous pourrions, peut-être, déjeuner ensemble.**
   If you're free, we could, perhaps, have lunch together.
6. **Voici ma carte avec le nom et l'adresse de ma société.**
   Here's my card with the name and address of my company.
7. **Quel est votre numéro de téléphone?**
   What's your phone number?
8. **Puis-je vous raccompagner?**
   Can I take you home?

Exercice

Que dites-vous . . .

1. si vous voulez entamer une conversation avec quelqu'un?
2. quand vous voulez danser avec quelqu'un?
3. quand vous voulez aller chercher quelque chose à boire pour quelqu'un?
4. si vous avez envie de revoir votre nouvel(le) ami(e) le lendemain?
5. si vous voulez déjeuner avec votre nouvel(le) ami(e)?
6. quand vous donnez votre carte à quelqu'un?
7. quand vous voulez savoir le numéro de téléphone de quelqu'un?

EXPANSION: Exclamations / Formules-réflexes

1. **Oui. C'est ça.**   *Yes. That's it. That's right.*
2. **Certainement!**   *Certainly! Of course!*
3. **D'accord / Entendu**   *O.K. Fine. I agree.*
4. **Oui, je crois. Oui, je pense.**   *Yes. I think so.*

5. **Bon!**	*Good! Fine! O.K. All right.*
6. **Bien sûr. Évidemment.**	*Of course. Evidently.*
7. **Bonne idée.**	*Good idea.*
8. **Pourquoi pas?**	*Why not?*
9. **Au contraire.**	*No. On the contrary.*
10. **Ah non!**	*No!*
11. **Hélas, non.**	*No, alas. Unfortunately not.*
12. **Au grand jamais!**	*Never!*
13. **Mais si!**	*But yes! (To contradict a preceding negative statement or question)*
14. **Ah oui?**	*Do you think so? Is that so?*
15. **Ça dépend.**	*It depends.*
16. **Vous trouvez?**	*Do you think so?*
17. **Et alors?**	*So what? And so? So what of it?*
18. **Formidable!**	*Great! Terrific!*
19. **Parfait!**	*Perfect! Great! (Can also be used sarcastically)*
20. **Bravo!**	*Hooray! Bravo!*
21. **Chic alors! Oh chic!**	*Great!*
22. **Oh là là.**	*Wow! My goodness! Tsk tsk. etc.*
23. **Quelle chance!**	*What good luck!*
24. **Ma foi!**	*My goodness! (My faith!)*
25. **Ma parole!**	*My word!*
26. **Sans blague!?**	*No kidding?!*
27. **Comment!!?**	*What?! How can that be?*
28. **Tenez!**	*Hey! Wow! (**Tiens** = familiar form)*
29. **Dites donc.**	*My goodness. You don't say. (**Dis donc** = familiar form)*
30. **Ah bon?**	*Oh really?*
31. **Quelle histoire!**	*What a story! What an ordeal!*
32. **Allez-y!**	*Go to it! Get going!*
33. **Un moment. Une petite seconde.**	*Hold on a moment.*
34. **Eh! Doucement!**	*Hey! Hold on there! Take it easy!*
35. **Zut alors!**	*Darn it!*
36. **Ça suffit!**	*That's enough. Cut it out!*
37. **Chut! Silence!**	*Shh! Be quiet!*
38. **Voyons!**	*Stop that! Come on now!*
39. **Attention!**	*Watch out!*

PRONONCIATION

1. Intonation

In French there are two basic types of intonation: "rising" and "falling."

a. In statements (declarative sentences) the voice rises in pitch at the end of every phrase or word group and falls at the end of the sentence. In American English, by contrast, the voice drops or remains on the same pitch after each portion of the sentence.

b. In questions which can be answered by *yes* or *no,* the voice begins on a fairly low note and rises until the end of the question, as in English.

c. In questions beginning with an interrogative pronoun (**qui, que,** etc.) or interrogative adverb (**pourquoi, où,** etc.), the voice falls at the end of the sentence.

2. Tension

In American English there is a tendency to have gliding vowels (diphthongs), prolonged consonants, mumbled final consonants and generally relaxed delivery. In French, on the other hand, the enunciation of vowels and consonants is short, clipped, distinct. Pronounced final consonants are articulated forcefully and distinctly. There is a general tension or tightness of articulation.

Listen carefully to the following sentences taken from this lesson. Imitate them, paying close attention to intonation and tension:

> Entrez, entrez, je vous prie.
> Puis-je prendre votre manteau?
> Voulez-vous une cigarette?
> Que puis-je vous offrir?
> C'est vraiment charmant chez vous.
> Que le temps passe vite!
> Je dois me lever de très bonne heure demain matin.
> J'ai passé une soirée très agréable.
> Merci de m'avoir invité(e).
> Au revoir!

IMPROVISATION

Vous êtes à une soirée. Vous remarquez un homme (ou une femme) qui a l'air sympathique. Vous commencez à lui parler. Vous dites, «**Bonsoir. Permettez-moi de me présenter. Je m'appelle. . . .** » Préparez un dialogue.

PROJET

Racontez votre dernière soirée:

Êtes-vous allé(e) récemment à une soirée? Chez qui? À quelle occasion? Avez-vous reçu une invitation? Qui vous a accompagné(e), ou y êtes-vous allé(e) seul(e)? À quelle heure êtes-vous arrivé(e)? Avez-vous offert un cadeau? Y avait-il beaucoup de monde? Y avait-il de la musique? Avez-vous dansé? Avec qui? Qu'est-ce qu'il y avait à boire? à manger? De qui avez-vous fait la connaissance? Avec qui avez-vous parlé? Avez-vous fumé? Y êtes-vous resté(e) longtemps? À quelle heure êtes-vous parti(e)? Avez-vous remercié vos hôtes en partant? Avez-vous passé une soirée agréable?

ACTIVITÉ

Have a party in class. Use the vocabulary and structures from the **Dialogue** and **Expansion** sections of this lesson.

CHEVALIERS DE LA TABLE RONDE

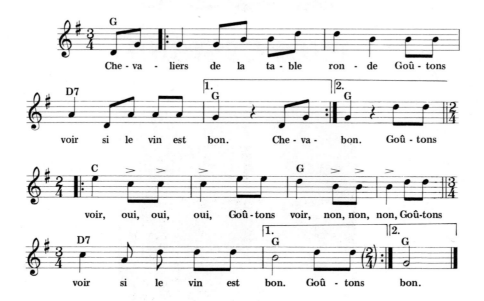

Che - va - liers de la ta - ble ron - de Goû - tons

voir si le vin est bon. Che - va - bon. Goû - tons

voir, oui, oui, oui, Goû - tons voir, non, non, non, Goû-tons

voir si le vin est bon. Goû - tons bon.

2. S'il est bon, s'il est agréable
J'en boirai jusqu'à mon plaisir. (bis)
J'en boirai, oui, oui, oui, (etc.)

Entracte
19A

PROFESSIONS

Êtes-vous astronaute?
—Non. Je ne suis pas astronaute. Je suis _____ .

In French, professions are treated like adjectives:

Je suis étudiant(e).   *I am a student.*

acteur / actrice	*actor / actress*
agent d'assurances	*insurance agent*
agent immobilier	*real estate agent*
agent de location	*rental agent*
agent de police	*police officer*
agent de voyages	*travel agent*
aide-serveur	*bus boy*
aide-soignante	*nurse's aid*
archéologue	*archeologist*
architecte	*architect*
artiste	*artist*
assistant(e) social(e)	*social worker*
avocat(e)	*lawyer*
babysitter	*babysitter*

380

banquier / banquière	*banker*
bibliothécaire	*librarian*
boucher / bouchère	*butcher*
boulanger / boulangère	*baker*
cadre	*executive, manager*
cadre moyen	*middle management person*
cadre supérieur	*top executive*
caissier / caissière (de banque, de supermarché)	*cashier (bank, supermarket)*
camionneur	*truckdriver*
chanteur / chanteuse	*singer*
chauffeur (de taxi)	*(taxi) driver*
chef	*head cook*
chef d'orchestre	*conductor, bandleader*
chef du personnel	*personnel director*
chimiste	*chemist*
chirurgien / chirurgienne	*surgeon*
coiffeur / coiffeuse	*hairdresser*
commerçant(e)	*tradesperson, merchant*
commis	*clerk*
commis voyageur	*traveling salesman*
comptable	*bookkeeper, accountant*
conducteur d'autobus	*bus driver*
contremaître / contremaîtresse	*foreman (in a factory)*
contrôleur / contrôleuse	*ticket collector*
cordonnier / cordonnière	*shoemaker*
courtier de bourse / agent de change	*stockbroker*
cuisinier / cuisinière	*cook*
cultivateur / cultivatrice	*farmer*
curé	*parish priest*
dactylo(graphe)	*typist*
danseur / danseuse	*dancer*
décorateur / décoratrice d'intérieurs	*interior decorator*
diplomate	*diplomat*
directeur / directrice	*manager*
directeur commercial / directrice commerciale	*sales manager*
docteur / doctoresse	*doctor*
ébéniste	*cabinetmaker*
éboueur	*street cleaner, garbage collector*
écrivain	*writer*
électricien / électricienne	*electrician*
employé(e) de bureau	*employee, office worker, clerical worker*
entrepreneur	*contractor*
entrepreneur de pompes funèbres	*mortician*
épicier / épicière	*grocer*
étudiant(e)	*student*

fabricant(e)	*manufacturer*
facteur / factrice	*letter carrier*
femme d'affaires	*businesswoman*
fonctionnaire	*civil servant, government worker*
garagiste	*garage owner*
garçon	*waiter*
gardienne d'enfants	*nanny*
garde de nuit	*night watchman*
gérant(e)	*manager*
grand industriel, chef d'industrie	*business executive*
homme d'affaires	*businessman*
hôtesse de l'air / steward	*flight attendant*
infirmier / infirmière	*nurse*
ingénieur	*engineer*
instituteur / institutrice	*schoolteacher*
interprète	*interpreter*
journaliste	*journalist*
juge	*judge*
livreur / livreuse	*delivery boy / girl (man / woman)*
maire / mairesse	*mayor*
maître nageur	*lifeguard*
maîtresse de maison / ménagère	*housewife*
marchand(e)	*merchant*
marchand(e) de chaussures, de voitures, de voitures d'occasion	*shoe, car, used car salesperson*
mécanicien / mécanicienne	*mechanic*
médecin	*medical doctor, physician*
menuisier, charpentier	*carpenter*
metteur en scène	*director*
mineur	*miner*
moniteur / monitrice de ski	*ski instructor*
moniteur / monitrice de colonie de vacances	*camp counselor*
musicien / musicienne	*musician*
notaire	*notary*
opticien / opticienne	*optician*
ouvreur / ouvreuse	*usher*
ouvrier / ouvrière	*worker*
pasteur	*minister*
patron / patronne	*boss*
P.-D.G. (Président-Directeur Général)	*Equivalent to Chairman of the Board of Directors, corporation president*
pêcheur / pêcheuse	*fisherman / woman*
pédiatre	*pediatrician*
peintre	*painter*
pharmacien / pharmacienne	*pharmacist*

photographe	photographer
physicien / physicienne	physicist
pilote	pilot
plombier	plumber
plongeur / plongeuse	dishwasher
poète / poétesse	poet
politicien / politicienne	politician
pompier / pompière	fireman / woman
pompiste	filling station attendant
porteur / porteuse	porter
postier / postière	postal worker
préposé(e) à la réception	receptionist
prêtre / prêtresse	priest
professeur (d'école secondaire, d'université)	(secondary school) teacher, (college) professor
programmeur / programmeuse	computer programmer
psychiatre	psychiatrist
psychologue	psychologist
rabbin	rabbi
rédacteur / rédactrice (en chef)	editor (in chief)
religieuse	nun
réparateur / réparatrice	repairman / woman
reporter	reporter
représentant(e)	company representative
sculpteur	sculptor
secrétaire	secretary
serrurier	locksmith
serveuse	waitress
soudeur / soudeuse	welder
speaker / speakerine (présentateur / présentatrice)	radio or T.V. announcer
sténo-dactylo	stenographer
technicien / technicienne	technician (e.g. laboratory)
téléphoniste, standardiste	(telephone) operator
traducteur / traductrice	translator
vendeur / vendeuse	salesperson
vétérinaire	veterinarian

Je suis en chômage / en grève / en retraite.	I am unemployed (out of work) / on strike / retired.
Je travaille comme volontaire / à mi-temps / à plein temps.	I work as a volunteer (I do volunteer work) / I work part-time / I work full-time.
Je ne travaille pas.	I don't work.
Je ne travaille plus.	I don't work any more.
On vient de me renvoyer	I was just fired.

SPRINGBOARDS FOR CONVERSATION

1. Êtes-vous astronaute?
   Non, mais je suis _____ .
2. Quel est votre profession? Quel est votre métier *(occupation)?* Quel genre de travail *(type of work)* faites-vous?
   Je suis _____ .
3. Travaillez-vous actuellement *(presently)?* à mi-temps? à plein temps? Êtes-vous en chômage? en retraite?
   Oui, je suis _____ .
   Je suis en retraite, mais dans le temps j'étais *(formerly I was a)* _____ .
4. Quel genre de travail fait Monsieur . . . ? Madame . . . ? Mademoiselle . . . ? votre mari (femme)? votre mère? votre père? votre meilleur(e) ami(e)? etc.
5. Quand vous étiez jeune, vouliez-vous être astronaute? professeur? chirurgien(ne)? etc. Pourquoi? Est-ce un métier bien rémunéré *(well paid)?* intéressant? etc.
   Quand j'étais jeune, je voulais être _____ .
6. Aimeriez-vous être dentiste? architecte? etc. Pourquoi?
   J'aimerais être _____ .
7. Quel genre de travail n'aimeriez-vous pas faire? Pourquoi? Est-ce monotone? ennuyeux *(boring)?* fatigant? etc.
   Je n'aimerais pas être _____ .
8. Avez-vous travaillé pendant les vacances? Qu'avez-vous fait? Où? Allez-vous travailler cet été? Que ferez-vous? Où?
9. Avez-vous déjà travaillé dans un hôpital? dans un restaurant? dans un magasin? dans une station-service? dans un supermarché? etc. Quand?

PROJETS

1. Think of all the people you know and their various occupations. Make a list. Be comprehensive.
2. Clip ten or so pictures from newspapers or magazines showing people performing various occupations. Caption each accordingly. For example: **Il est médecin. Elle est hôtesse de l'air,** etc.

ACTIVITÉ

Everyone has a partner. One partner acts out a profession selected from the above list, while the other tries to guess which one it is. Then the roles are reversed. Alternative: One class member at a time acts out a chosen profession while the whole class guesses. For example: **Vous êtes danseur / danseuse! Vous êtes dentiste! Vous êtes pilote! Vous êtes chanteur / chanteuse!** etc.

CHORES, OBLIGATIONS

Qu'avez-vous à faire?
—Je dois ⸺.

acheter un cadeau (pour . . .)	*but a gift (for . . .)*
aller à la banque, chez le médecin, chez le coiffeur, etc.	*go to the bank, doctor's, barbershop (beauty parlor), etc.*
aller en classe	*go to class*
aller au travail	*go to work*
aller chercher mes enfants à l'école, un ami à la gare, etc.	*go pick up my children at school, a friend at the station, etc.*
aller m'entraîner	*go practice (sports)*
assister à mon cours (de . . .)	*go to (my . . .) class*
cirer mes chaussures	*shine my shoes*
conduire les enfants à l'école, mon ami chez le docteur, etc.	*drive my children to school, my friend to the doctor's, etc.*
déblayer la neige	*shovel snow*
écrire un compte-rendu / un rapport	*write a report*
écrire un petit mot (à . . .)	*write a note (to . . .)*
envoyer une carte de vœux / un mot de remerciement (à . . .)	*send a greeting card / thank you note (to . . .)*

étudier	*study*
faire des courses	*run errands*
faire mes devoirs	*do homework*
faire ma gymnastique	*do (my) exercises*
faire la lessive	*do laundry*
faire le ménage / nettoyer la maison	*do housework / clean the house*
faire le plein d'essence	*fill up the car with gasoline*
faire mes provisions	*buy food, do marketing*
faire du raccommodage	*do some mending*
faire du repassage	*do some ironing*
faire la vaisselle	*do the dishes*
faire ma valise	*pack my suitcase*
faire un voyage d'affaires	*take a business trip*
faire réparer la voiture, le lave-vaisselle, la télévision, etc.	*have the car, dishwasher, television, etc. fixed.*
inviter la famille à déjeuner, à dîner	*invite the family over for lunch, dinner*
laver / cirer le parquet	*wash / wax the floor*
me laver la tête	*wash my hair*
passer l'aspirateur	*vacuum, run the vacuum*
passer chez le teinturier, à la banque, à la pharmacie, etc.	*stop by the cleaner's, the bank, the pharmacy, etc.*
passer la tondeuse	*mow the lawn*
payer le loyer, les impôts, etc.	*pay the rent, taxes, etc.*
prendre des billets (d'avion, de théâtre, de concert, etc.)	*pick up some (airplane, theater, concert, etc.) tickets*
prendre ma leçon de piano, etc.	*take my piano (etc.) lesson*
prendre un rendez-vous chez le docteur, le dentiste, le coiffeur	*make an appointment with the doctor, dentist, hairdresser*
préparer le dîner, les repas	*prepare dinner, meals*
préparer mes leçons	*prepare my lessons*
promener le chien	*walk the dog*
rendre visite à ma grand-mère, etc.	*visit my grandmother, etc.*
sortir la poubelle / vider les ordures	*take out the garbage*
taper un rapport	*type (up) a paper*
téléphoner (à . . .)	*telephone / call . . .*
(Je n'ai) rien (à faire).	*(I have) nothing (to do).*
(J'ai) beaucoup (à faire).	*(I have) a lot (to do).*

SPRINGBOARDS FOR CONVERSATION

1. Qu'avez-vous à faire cette semaine? C'est tout? C'est urgent?
   Je dois _____.

2. Qu'avez-vous à faire aujourd'hui? demain? le week-end prochain? la semaine prochaine?

3. Qu'avez-vous fait aujourd'hui avant de venir en classe? Avez-vous promené le chien? Avez-vous passé l'aspirateur? Avez-vous fait vos devoirs? Avez-vous étudié? Avez-vous écrit un petit mot à un ami? Êtes-vous allé(e) à la banque? etc.

4. Que devez-vous faire après cette classe?
   Je dois _____.

5. Que doit faire Monsieur. . . . cette semaine? Madame . . . ? Mademoiselle . . . ? le professeur . . . ? Aujourd'hui? Pendant le week-end?
   Il / Elle doit _____.

6. Quelles sont les corvées *(chores)* que vous devez accomplir chaque jour?
   Je dois _____.

7. Que détestez-vous faire? Que n'aimez-vous pas faire?
   Je déteste _____. Je n'aime pas _____.

8. Qu'est-ce que vous aimez faire?
   J'aime _____.

9. Qu'est-ce que vous auriez dû faire *(should you have done)* hier, et que vous n'avez pas fait?
   J'aurais dû *(I should have)* _____.

10. Avez-vous un agenda? Cette semaine qu'avez-vous inscrit sur votre agenda?

11. Combien de temps par jour passez-vous à étudier? à faire le ménage? etc.
    Je passe . . . minutes / heures par jour à _____.

12. Que remettez-vous volontiers au lendemain / à plus tard? *(What do you like to put off until later? What do you procrastinate about doing?)* étudier? (faire) la vaisselle? (faire) la lessive? etc.

13. Qu'est-ce qui vous met de mauvaise humeur? de bonne humeur? Promener le chien? Sortir la poubelle? Payer les impôts? etc.

14. Est-ce que ça vous ennuie *(bore, annoy)* de promener le chien? de faire le ménage? etc.
    Oui, ça m'ennuie de _____.
    Non, ça ne m'ennuie pas du tout de _____.

15. Que refusez-vous de faire?
    Je refuse de _____.

16. Que demandez-vous souvent à quelqu'un d'autre *(someone else)* de faire? De passer la tondeuse? De faire la vaisselle? De sortir la poubelle? etc.

PROJET

Mon agenda. What do you have to do this week? Make a complete listing. Indicate days and times whenever possible.

ACTIVITÉ

Everyone has a partner. One partner acts out a chore or obligation selected from the above list, while the other tries to guess which one it is. Then roles are reversed. Alternative: One class member at a time acts out a chosen chore or obligation while the whole class guesses. For example: **Vous déblayez la neige! Vous faites la lessive! Vous passez l'aspirateur! Vous promenez le chien!** etc.

Conjugaison des verbes

VERBES EN -er

INFINITIF:	**parler**
PARTICIPE PRÉSENT:	**parlant**
PARTICIPE PASSÉ:	**parlé**

INDICATIF

	PRÉSENT	IMPARFAIT	PASSÉ SIMPLE	FUTUR
je	parle	parlais	parlai	parlerai
tu	parles	parlais	parlas	parleras
il	parle	parlait	parla	parlera
nous	parlons	parlions	parlâmes	parlerons
vous	parlez	parliez	parlâtes	parlerez
ils	parlent	parlaient	parlèrent	parleront

	PASSÉ COMPOSÉ	PLUS-QUE-PARFAIT	FUTUR ANTÉRIEUR
j'	ai parlé	avais parlé	aurai parlé
tu	as parlé	avais parlé	auras parlé
il	a parlé	avait parlé	aura parlé
nous	avons parlé	avions parlé	aurons parlé
vous	avez parlé	aviez parlé	aurez parlé
ils	ont parlé	avaient parlé	auront parlé

CONDITIONNEL

	PRÉSENT	PASSÉ
je	parlerais	aurais parlé
tu	parlerais	aurais parlé
il	parlerait	aurait parlé
nous	parlerions	aurions parlé
vous	parleriez	auriez parlé
ils	parleraient	auraient parlé

IMPÉRATIF

parle
parlons
parlez

SUBJONCTIF

	PRÉSENT	PASSÉ	IMPARFAIT
que je	parle	aie parlé	parlasse
que tu	parles	aies parlé	parlasses
qu'il	parle	ait parlé	parlât
que nous	parlions	ayons parlé	parlassions
que vous	parliez	ayez parlé	parlassiez
qu'ils	parlent	aient parlé	parlassent

Spelling Changes in Certain -er Verbs

Verbs ending in **-cer** change **c** to **ç** before the vowels **a** and **o** in order to keep the soft **c** sound:

> commencer: nous **commençons**
> je **commençais**
> en **commençant,** etc.

Verbs ending in **-ger** add **e** after **g** before **a** and **o** in order to keep the soft **g** sound:

> manger: nous **mangeons**
> je **mangeais**
> en **mangeant,** etc.

Verbs ending in **e** + consonant + **er** change **e** to **è** before mute **e:**

> se promener: je me **promène**
> je me **promènerai**
> je me **promènerais,** etc.

The verbs **appeler** and **jeter** double the **l** or **t** before mute **e:** je m'**appelle,** etc.

Verbs ending in **é** + consonant + **er** change **é** to **è** before mute **e** only in the present tense of the indicative and of the subjunctive:

> préférer: je **préfère**
> tu **préfères**
> qu'ils **préfèrent,** etc.

Verbs ending in **-yer** change **y** to **i** before mute **e.** Verbs ending in **-ayer** may, however, keep the **y:**

> ennuyer: j'**ennuie**
> j'**ennuierai**
> j'**ennuierais,** etc.

VERBES EN -ir

INFINITIF:	**finir**
PARTICIPE PRÉSENT:	**finissant**
PARTICIPE PASSÉ:	**fini**

INDICATIF

	PRÉSENT	IMPARFAIT	PASSÉ SIMPLE	FUTUR
je	fin**is**	finiss**ais**	fin**is**	finir**ai**
tu	fin**is**	finiss**ais**	fin**is**	finir**as**
il	fin**it**	finiss**ait**	fin**it**	finir**a**
nous	finiss**ons**	finiss**ions**	fin**îmes**	finir**ons**
vous	finiss**ez**	finiss**iez**	fin**îtes**	finir**ez**
ils	finiss**ent**	finiss**aient**	fin**irent**	finir**ont**

	PASSÉ COMPOSÉ	PLUS-QUE-PARFAIT	FUTUR ANTÉRIEUR
j'	ai fini	avais fini	aurai fini
tu	as fini	avais fini	auras fini
il	a fini	avait fini	aura fini
nous	avons fini	avions fini	aurons fini
vous	avez fini	aviez fini	aurez fini
ils	ont fini	avaient fini	auront fini

CONDITIONNEL

	PRÉSENT	PASSÉ
je	finir**ais**	aurais fini
tu	finir**ais**	aurais fini
il	finir**ait**	aurait fini
nous	finir**ions**	aurions fini
vous	finir**iez**	auriez fini
ils	finir**aient**	auraient fini

IMPÉRATIF

fin**is**
fin**issons**
fin**issez**

SUBJONCTIF

	PRÉSENT	PASSÉ	IMPARFAIT
que je	finisse	aie fini	finisse
que tu	finisses	aies fini	finisses
qu'il	finisse	ait fini	finît
que nous	finissions	ayons fini	finissions
que vous	finissiez	ayez fini	finissiez
qu'ils	finissent	aient fini	finissent

VERBES EN -re

INFINITIF: **vendre**
PARTICIPE PRÉSENT: **vendant**
PARTICIPE PASSÉ: **vendu**

INDICATIF

	PRÉSENT	IMPARFAIT	PASSÉ SIMPLE	FUTUR
je	vends	vendais	vendis	vendrai
tu	vends	vendais	vendis	vendras
il	vend	vendait	vendit	vendra
nous	vendons	vendions	vendîmes	vendrons
vous	vendez	vendiez	vendîtes	vendrez
ils	vendent	vendaient	vendirent	vendront

	PASSÉ COMPOSÉ	PLUS-QUE-PARFAIT	FUTUR ANTÉRIEUR
j'	ai vendu	avais vendu	aurai vendu
tu	as vendu	avais vendu	auras vendu
il	a vendu	avait vendu	aura vendu
nous	avons vendu	avions vendu	aurons vendu
vous	avez vendu	aviez vendu	aurez vendu
ils	ont vendu	avaient vendu	auront vendu

CONDITIONNEL

	PRÉSENT	PASSÉ
je	vendrais	aurais vendu
tu	vendrais	aurais vendu
il	vendrait	aurait vendu
nous	vendrions	aurions vendu
vous	vendriez	auriez vendu
ils	vendraient	auraient vendu

IMPÉRATIF

vends
vend**ons**
vend**ez**

SUBJONCTIF

	PRÉSENT	PASSÉ	IMPARFAIT
que je	vend**e**	aie vendu	vend**isse**
que tu	vend**es**	aies vendu	vend**isses**
qu'il	vend**e**	ait vendu	vend**ît**
que nous	vend**ions**	ayons vendu	vend**issions**
que vous	vend**iez**	ayez vendu	vend**issiez**
qu'ils	vend**ent**	aient vendu	vend**issent**

VERBES IRRÉGULIERS

INFINITIF PARTICIPES		PRÉSENT	FUTUR	IMPARFAIT	PASSÉ SIMPLE
acquérir	j'	acquiers	acquerrai	acquérais	acquis
to acquire	tu	acquiers	acquerras	acquérais	acquis
	il	acquiert	acquerra	acquérait	acquit
acquérant	nous	acquérons	acquerrons	acquérions	acquîmes
acquis	vous	acquérez	acquerrez	acquériez	acquîtes
	ils	acquièrent	acquerront	acquéraient	acquirent
aller	je	vais	irai	allais	allai
to go	tu	vas	iras	allais	allas
	il	va	ira	allait	alla
allant	nous	allons	irons	allions	allâmes
allé	vous	allez	irez	alliez	allâtes
	ils	vont	iront	allaient	allèrent
assaillir	j'	assaille	assaillirai	assaillais	assaillis
to assault	tu	assailles	assailliras	assaillais	assaillis
to assail	il	assaille	assaillira	assaillait	assaillit
	nous	assaillons	assaillirons	assaillions	assaillîmes
assaillant	vous	assaillez	assaillirez	assailliez	assaillîtes
assailli	ils	assaillent	assailliront	assaillaient	assaillirent
asseoir	j'	assieds	assiérai	asseyais	assis
to seat	tu	assieds	assiéras	asseyais	assis
	il	assied	assiéra	asseyait	assit
asseyant	nous	asseyons	assiérons	asseyions	assîmes
assis	vous	asseyez	assiérez	asseyiez	assîtes
	ils	asseyent	assiéront	asseyaient	assirent
or					
assoyant	j'	assois	assoirai	assoyais	
	tu	assois	assoiras	assoyais	
	il	assoit	assoira	assoyait	
	nous	assoyons	assoirons	assoyions	
	vous	assoyez	assoirez	assoyiez	
	ils	assoient	assoiront	assoyaient	
avoir	j'	ai	aurai	avais	eus
to have	tu	as	auras	avais	eus
	il	a	aura	avait	eut
ayant	nous	avons	aurons	avions	eûmes
eu	vous	avez	aurez	aviez	eûtes
	ils	ont	auront	avaient	eurent

CONDITIONNEL	IMPÉRATIF	SUBJONCTIF	
		PRÉSENT	IMPARFAIT
acquerrais		acquière	acquisse
acquerrais	acquiers	acquières	acquisses
acquerrait		acquière	acquît
acquerrions	acquérons	acquérions	acquissions
acquerriez	acquérez	acquériez	acquissiez
acquerraient		acquièrent	acquissent
irais		aille	allasse
irais	va	ailles	allasses
irait		aille	allât
irions	allons	allions	allassions
iriez	allez	alliez	allassiez
iraient		aillent	allassent
assaillirais		assaille	assaillisse
assaillirais	assaille	assailles	assaillisses
assaillirait		assaille	assaillît
assaillirions	assaillons	assaillions	assaillissions
assailliriez	assaillez	assailliez	assaillissiez
assailliraient		assaillent	assaillissent
assiérais		asseye	assisse
assiérais	assieds	asseyes	assisses
assiérait		asseye	assît
assiérions	asseyons	asseyions	assissions
assiériez	asseyez	asseyiez	assissiez
assiéraient		asseyent	assissent
or			
assoirais		assoie	
assoirais	assois	assoies	
assoirait		assoie	
assoirions	assoyons	assoyions	
assoiriez	assoyez	assoyiez	
assoiraient		assoient	
aurais		aie	eusse
aurais	aie	aies	eusses
aurait		ait	eût
aurions	ayons	ayons	eussions
auriez	ayez	ayez	eussiez
auraient		aient	eussent

INFINITIF PARTICIPES		PRÉSENT	FUTUR	IMPARFAIT	PASSÉ SIMPLE
			INDICATIF		
battre	je	bats	battrai	battais	battis
to beat	tu	bats	battras	battais	battis
	il	bat	battra	battait	battit
battant	nous	battons	battrons	battions	battîmes
battu	vous	battez	battrez	battiez	battîtes
	ils	battent	battront	battaient	battirent
boire	je	bois	boirai	buvais	bus
to drink	tu	bois	boiras	buvais	bus
	il	boit	boira	buvait	but
buvant	nous	buvons	boirons	buvions	bûmes
bu	vous	buvez	boirez	buviez	bûtes
	ils	boivent	boiront	buvaient	burent
bouillir	je	bous	bouillirai	bouillais	bouillis
to boil	tu	bous	bouilliras	bouillais	bouillis
	il	bout	bouillira	bouillait	bouillit
bouillant	nous	bouillons	bouillirons	bouillions	bouillîmes
bouilli	vous	bouillez	bouillirez	bouilliez	bouillîtes
	ils	bouillent	bouilliront	bouillaient	bouillirent
conclure	je	conclus	conclurai	concluais	conclus
to conclude	tu	conclus	concluras	concluais	conclus
	il	conclut	conclura	concluait	conclut
concluant	nous	concluons	conclurons	concluions	conclûmes
conclu	vous	concluez	conclurez	concluiez	conclûtes
	ils	concluent	concluront	concluaient	conclurent
conduire	je	conduis	conduirai	conduisais	conduisis
to drive	tu	conduis	conduiras	conduisais	conduisis
to lead	il	conduit	conduira	conduisait	conduisit
to conduct	nous	conduisons	conduirons	conduisions	conduisîmes
conduisant	vous	conduisez	conduirez	conduisiez	conduisîtes
conduit	ils	conduisent	conduiront	conduisaient	conduisirent
connaître	je	connais	connaîtrai	connaissais	connus
to know	tu	connais	connaîtras	connaissais	connus
	il	connaît	connaîtra	connaissait	connut
connaissant	nous	connaissons	connaîtrons	connaissions	connûmes
connu	vous	connaissez	connaîtrez	connaissiez	connûtes
	ils	connaissent	connaîtront	connaissaient	connurent

CONDITIONNEL	IMPÉRATIF	SUBJONCTIF	
		PRÉSENT	IMPARFAIT
battrais		batte	battisse
battrais	bats	battes	battisses
battrait		batte	battît
battrions	battons	battions	battissions
battriez	battez	battiez	battissiez
battraient		battent	battissent
boirais		boive	busse
boirais	bois	boives	busses
boirait		boive	bût
boirions	buvons	buvions	bussions
boiriez	buvez	buviez	bussiez
boiraient		boivent	bussent
bouillirais		bouille	bouillisse
bouillirais	bous	bouilles	bouillisses
bouillirait		bouille	bouillît
bouillirions	bouillons	bouillions	bouillissions
bouilliriez	bouillez	bouilliez	bouillissiez
bouilliraient		bouillent	bouillissent
conclurais		conclue	conclusse
conclurais	conclus	conclues	conclusses
conclurait		conclue	conclût
conclurions	concluons	concluions	conclussions
concluriez	concluez	concluiez	conclussiez
concluraient		concluent	conclussent
conduirais		conduise	conduisisse
conduirais	conduis	conduises	conduisisses
conduirait		conduise	conduisît
conduirions	conduisons	conduisions	conduisissions
conduiriez	conduisez	conduisiez	conduisissiez
conduiraient		conduisent	conduisissent
connaîtrais		connaisse	connusse
connaîtrais	connais	connaisses	connusses
connaîtrait		connaisse	connût
connaîtrions	connaissons	connaissions	connussions
connaîtriez	connaissez	connaissiez	connussiez
connaîtraient		connaissent	connussent

INFINITIF / PARTICIPES		INDICATIF			
		PRÉSENT	FUTUR	IMPARFAIT	PASSÉ SIMPLE
coudre	je	couds	coudrai	cousais	cousis
to sew	tu	couds	coudras	cousais	cousis
	il	coud	coudra	cousait	cousit
cousant	nous	cousons	coudrons	cousions	cousîmes
cousu	vous	cousez	coudrez	cousiez	cousîtes
	ils	cousent	coudront	cousaient	cousirent
courir	je	cours	courrai	courais	courus
to run	tu	cours	courras	courais	courus
	il	court	courra	courait	courut
courant	nous	courons	courrons	courions	courûmes
couru	vous	courez	courrez	couriez	courûtes
	ils	courent	courront	couraient	coururent
craindre	je	crains	craindrai	craignais	craignis
to fear	tu	crains	craindras	craignais	craignis
	il	craint	craindra	craignait	craignit
craignant	nous	craignons	craindrons	craignions	craignîmes
craint	vous	craignez	craindez	craigniez	craignîtes
	ils	craignent	craindront	craignaient	craignirent
croire	je	crois	croirai	croyais	crus
to believe	tu	crois	croiras	croyais	crus
	il	croit	croira	croyait	crut
croyant	nous	croyons	croirons	croyions	crûmes
cru	vous	croyez	croirez	croyiez	crûtes
	ils	croient	croiront	croyaient	crurent
croître	je	croîs	croîtrai	croissais	crûs
to grow	tu	croîs	croîtras	croissais	crûs
	il	croît	croîtra	croissait	crût
croissant	nous	croissons	croîtrons	croissions	crûmes
crû	vous	croissez	croîtrez	croissiez	crûtes
	ils	croissent	croîtront	croissaient	crûrent
cueillir	je	cueille	cueillerai	cueillais	cueillis
to gather	tu	cueilles	cueilleras	cueillais	cueillis
to pick	il	cueille	cueillera	cueillait	cueillit
	nous	cueillons	cueillerons	cueillions	cueillîmes
cueillant	vous	cueillez	cueillerez	cueilliez	cueillîtes
cueilli	ils	cueillent	cueilleront	cueillaient	cueillirent

CONDITIONNEL	IMPÉRATIF	SUBJONCTIF	
		PRÉSENT	IMPARFAIT
coudrais		couse	cousisse
coudrais	couds	couses	cousisses
coudrait		couse	cousît
coudrions	cousons	cousions	cousissions
coudriez	cousez	cousiez	cousissiez
coudraient		cousent	cousissent
courrais		coure	courusse
courrais	cours	coures	courusses
courrait		coure	courût
courrions	courons	courions	courussions
courriez	courez	couriez	courussiez
courraient		courent	courussent
craindrais		craigne	craignisse
craindrais	crains	craignes	craignisses
craindrait		craigne	craignît
craindrions	craignons	craignions	craignissions
craindriez	craignez	craigniez	craignissiez
craindraient		craignent	craignissent
croirais		croie	crusse
croirais	crois	croies	crusses
croirait		croie	crût
croirions	croyons	croyions	crussions
croiriez	croyez	croyiez	crussiez
croiraient		croient	crussent
croîtrais		croisse	crûsse
croîtrais	croîs	croisses	crûsses
croîtrait		croisse	crût
croîtrions	croissons	croissions	crûssions
croîtriez	croissez	croissiez	crûssiez
croîtraient		croissent	crûssent
cueillerais		cueille	cueillisse
cueillerais	cueille	cueilles	cueillisses
cueillerait		cueille	cueillît
cueillerions	cueillons	cueillions	cueillissions
cueilleriez	cueillez	cueilliez	cueillissiez
cueilleraient		cueillent	cueillissent

| INFINITIF | | INDICATIF | | | |
PARTICIPES		PRÉSENT	FUTUR	IMPARFAIT	PASSÉ SIMPLE
devoir	je	dois	devrai	devais	dus
to owe, must	tu	dois	devras	devais	dus
	il	doit	devra	devait	dut
devant	nous	devons	devrons	devions	dûmes
dû, due	vous	devez	devrez	deviez	dûtes
	ils	doivent	devront	devaient	durent
dire	je	dis	dirai	disais	dis
to say	tu	dis	diras	disais	dis
	il	dit	dira	disait	dit
disant	nous	disons	dirons	disions	dîmes
dit	vous	dites	direz	disiez	dîtes
	ils	disent	diront	disaient	dirent
dormir	je	dors	dormirai	dormais	dormis
to sleep	tu	dors	dormiras	dormais	dormis
	il	dort	dormira	dormait	dormit
dormant	nous	dormons	dormirons	dormions	dormîmes
dormi	vous	dormez	dormirez	dormiez	dormîtes
	ils	dorment	dormiront	dormaient	dormirent
écrire	j'	écris	écrirai	écrivais	écrivis
to write	tu	écris	écriras	écrivais	écrivis
	il	écrit	écrira	écrivait	écrivit
écrivant	nous	écrivons	écrirons	écrivions	écrivîmes
écrit	vous	écrivez	écrirez	écriviez	écrivîtes
	ils	écrivent	écriront	écrivaient	écrivirent
envoyer	j'	envoie	enverrai	envoyais	envoyai
to send	tu	envoies	enverras	envoyais	envoyas
	il	envoie	enverra	envoyait	envoya
envoyant	nous	envoyons	enverrons	envoyions	envoyâmes
envoyé	vous	envoyez	enverrez	envoyiez	envoyâtes
	ils	envoient	enverront	envoyaient	envoyèrent
être	je	suis	serai	étais	fus
to be	tu	es	seras	étais	fus
	il	est	sera	était	fut
étant	nous	sommes	serons	étions	fûmes
été	vous	êtes	serez	étiez	fûtes
	ils	sont	seront	étaient	furent

CONDITIONNEL	IMPÉRATIF	SUBJONCTIF	
		PRÉSENT	IMPARFAIT
devrais		doive	dusse
devrais	dois	doives	dusses
devrait		doive	dût
devrions	devons	devions	dussions
devriez	devez	deviez	dussiez
devraient		doivent	dussent
dirais		dise	disse
dirais	dis	dises	disses
dirait		dise	dît
dirions	disons	disions	dissions
diriez	dites	disiez	dissiez
diraient		disent	dissent
dormirais		dorme	dormisse
dormirais	dors	dormes	dormisses
dormirait		dorme	dormît
dormirions	dormons	dormions	dormissions
dormiriez	dormez	dormiez	dormissiez
dormiraient		dorment	dormissent
écrirais		écrive	écrivisse
écrirais	écris	écrives	écrivisses
écrirait		écrive	écrivît
écririons	écrivons	écrivions	écrivissions
écririez	écrivez	écriviez	écrivissiez
écriraient		écrivent	écrivissent
enverrais		envoie	envoyasse
enverrais	envoie	envoies	envoyasses
enverrait		envoie	envoyât
enverrions	envoyons	envoyions	envoyassions
enverriez	envoyez	envoyiez	envoyassiez
enverraient		envoyent	envoyassent
serais		sois	fusse
serais	sois	sois	fusses
serait		soit	fût
serions	soyons	soyons	fussions
seriez	soyez	soyez	fussiez
seraient		soient	fussent

INFINITIF		INDICATIF			
PARTICIPES		PRÉSENT	FUTUR	IMPARFAIT	PASSÉ SIMPLE
faire	je	fais	ferai	faisais	fis
to do	tu	fais	feras	faisais	fis
to make	il	fait	fera	faisait	fit
	nous	faisons	ferons	faisions	fîmes
faisant	vous	faites	ferez	faisiez	fîtes
fait	ils	font	feront	faisaient	firent
falloir	il	faut	faudra	fallait	fallut
to be necessary, must					

No present participle
Past participle: fallu
This is an impersonal verb, conjugated in the third-person singular only.

fuir	je	fuis	fuirai	fuyais	fuis
to flee	tu	fuis	fuiras	fuyais	fuis
	il	fuit	fuira	fuyait	fuit
fuyant	nous	fuyons	fuirons	fuyions	fuîmes
fui	vous	fuyez	fuirez	fuyiez	fuîtes
	ils	fuient	fuiront	fuyaient	fuirent
haïr	je	hais	haïrai	haïssais	haïs
to hate	tu	hais	haïras	haïssais	haïs
	il	hait	haïra	haïssait	haït
haïssant	nous	haïssons	haïrons	haïssions	haïmes
haï	vous	haïssez	haïrez	haïssiez	haïtes
	ils	haïssent	haïront	haïssaient	haïrent
lire	je	lis	lirai	lisais	lus
to read	tu	lis	liras	lisais	lus
	il	lit	lira	lisait	lut
lisant	nous	lisons	lirons	lisions	lûmes
lu	vous	lisez	lirez	lisiez	lûtes
	ils	lisent	liront	lisaient	lurent
mettre	je	mets	mettrai	mettais	mis
to put	tu	mets	mettras	mettais	mis
	il	met	mettra	mettait	mit
mettant	nous	mettons	mettrons	mettions	mîmes
mis	vous	mettez	mettrez	mettiez	mîtes
	ils	mettent	mettront	mettaient	mirent

| CONDITIONNEL | IMPÉRATIF | SUBJONCTIF | |
		PRÉSENT	IMPARFAIT
ferais		fasse	fisse
ferais	fais	fasses	fisses
ferait		fasse	fît
ferions	faisons	fassions	fissions
feriez	faites	fassiez	fissiez
feraient		fassent	fissent
faudrait		faille	fallût
fuirais		fuie	fuisse
fuirais	fuis	fuies	fuisses
fuirait		fuie	fuît
fuirions	fuyons	fuyions	fuissions
fuiriez	fuyez	fuyiez	fuissiez
fuiraient		fuient	fuissent
haïrais		haïsse	haïsse
haïrais	hais	haïsses	haïsses
haïrait		haïsse	haît
haïrions	haïssons	haïssions	haïssions
haïriez	haïssez	haïssiez	haïssiez
haïraient		haïssent	haïssent
lirais		lise	lusse
lirais	lis	lises	lusses
lirait		lise	lût
lirions	lisons	lisions	lussions
liriez	lisez	lisiez	lussiez
liraient		lisent	lussent
mettrais		mette	misse
mettrais	mets	mettes	misses
mettrait		mette	mît
mettrions	mettons	mettions	missions
mettriez	mettez	mettiez	missiez
mettraient		mettent	missent

INFINITIF PARTICIPES		INDICATIF			
		PRÉSENT	FUTUR	IMPARFAIT	PASSÉ SIMPLE
moudre	je	mouds	moudrai	moulais	moulus
to grind	tu	mouds	moudras	moulais	moulus
	il	moud	moudra	moulait	moulut
moulant	nous	moulons	moudrons	moulions	moulûmes
moulu	vous	moulez	moudrez	mouliez	moulûtes
	ils	moulent	moudront	moulaient	moulurent
mourir	je	meurs	mourrai	mourais	mourus
to die	tu	meurs	mourras	mourais	mourus
	il	meurt	mourra	mourait	mourut
mourant	nous	mourons	mourrons	mourions	mourûmes
mort	vous	mourez	mourrez	mouriez	mourûtes
	ils	meurent	mourront	mouraient	moururent
mouvoir	je	meus	mouvrai	mouvais	mus
to move	tu	meus	mouvras	mouvais	mus
	il	meut	mouvra	mouvait	mut
mouvant	nous	mouvons	mouvrons	mouvions	mûmes
mû, mue	vous	mouvez	mouvrez	mouviez	mûtes
	ils	meuvent	mouvront	mouvaient	murent
naître	je	nais	naîtrai	naissais	naquis
to be born	tu	nais	naîtras	naissais	naquis
	il	naît	naîtra	naissait	naquit
naissant	nous	naissons	naîtrons	naissions	naquîmes
né	vous	naissez	naîtrez	naissiez	naquîtes
	ils	naissent	naîtront	naissaient	naquirent
ouvrir	j'	ouvre	ouvrirai	ouvrais	ouvris
to open	tu	ouvres	ouvriras	ouvrais	ouvris
	il	ouvre	ouvrira	ouvrait	ouvrit
ouvrant	nous	ouvrons	ouvrirons	ouvrions	ouvrîmes
ouvert	vous	ouvrez	ouvrirez	ouvriez	ouvrîtes
	ils	ouvrent	ouvriront	ouvraient	ouvrirent
partir	je	pars	partirai	partais	partis
to leave	tu	pars	partiras	partais	partis
to go away	il	part	partira	partait	partit
	nous	partons	partirons	partions	partîmes
partant	vous	partez	partirez	partiez	partîtes
parti	ils	partent	partiront	partaient	partirent

CONDITIONNEL	IMPÉRATIF	SUBJONCTIF	
		PRÉSENT	IMPARFAIT
moudrais		moule	moulusse
moudrais	mouds	moules	moulusses
moudrait		moule	moulût
moudrions	moulons	moulions	moulussions
moudriez	moulez	mouliez	moulussiez
moudraient		moulent	moulussent
mourrais		meure	mourusse
mourrais	meurs	meures	mourusses
mourrait		meure	mourût
mourrions	mourons	mourions	mourussions
mourriez	mourez	mouriez	mourussiez
mourraient		meurent	mourussent
mouvrais		meuve	musse
mouvrais	meus	meuves	musses
mouvrait		meuve	mût
mouvrions	mouvons	mouvions	mussions
mouvriez	mouvez	mouviez	mussiez
mouvraient		meuvent	mussent
naîtrais		naisse	naquisse
naîtrais	nais	naisses	naquisses
naîtrait		naisse	naquît
naîtrions	naissons	naissions	naquissions
naîtriez	naissez	naissiez	naquissiez
naîtraient		naissent	naquissent
ouvrirais		ouvre	ouvrisse
ouvrirais	ouvre	ouvres	ouvrisses
ouvrirait		ouvre	ouvrît
ouvririons	ouvrons	ouvrions	ouvrissions
ouvririez	ouvrez	ouvriez	ouvrissiez
ouvriraient		ouvrent	ouvrissent
partirais		parte	partisse
partirais	pars	partes	partisses
partirait		parte	partît
partirions	partons	partions	partissions
partiriez	partez	partiez	partissiez
partiraient		partent	partissent

| INFINITIF | | INDICATIF | | | |
PARTICIPES		PRÉSENT	FUTUR	IMPARFAIT	PASSÉ SIMPLE
peindre	je	peins	peindrai	peignais	peignis
to paint	tu	peins	peindras	peignais	peignis
	il	peint	peindra	peignait	peignit
peignant	nous	peignons	peindrons	peignions	peignîmes
peint	vous	peignez	peindrez	peigniez	peignîtes
	ils	peignent	peindront	peignaient	peignirent
plaire	je	plais	plairai	plaisais	plus
to please	tu	plais	plairas	plaisais	plus
	il	plaît	plaira	plaisait	plut
plaisant	nous	plaisons	plairons	plaisions	plûmes
plu	vous	plaisez	plairez	plaisiez	plûtes
	ils	plaisent	plairont	plaisaient	plurent
pleuvoir	il	pleut	pleuvra	pleuvait	plut
to rain					

pleuvant
plu
This is an impersonal verb, conjugated in the third-person singular only.

INFINITIF		PRÉSENT	FUTUR	IMPARFAIT	PASSÉ SIMPLE
pourvoir	je	pourvois	pourvoirai	pourvoyais	pourvus
to provide	tu	pourvois	pourvoiras	pourvoyais	pourvus
	il	pourvoit	pourvoira	pourvoyait	pourvut
pourvoyant	nous	pourvoyons	pourvoirons	pourvoyions	pourvûmes
pourvu	vous	pourvoyez	pourvoirez	pourvoyiez	pourvûtes
	ils	pourvoient	pourvoiront	pourvoyaient	pourvurent
pouvoir	je	peux, puis	pourrai	pouvais	pus
to be able	tu	peux	pourras	pouvais	pus
can	il	peut	pourra	pouvait	put
	nous	pouvons	pourrons	pouvions	pûmes
pouvant	vous	pouvez	pourrez	pouviez	pûtes
pu	ils	peuvent	pourront	pouvaient	purent
prendre	je	prends	prendrai	prenais	pris
to take	tu	prends	prendras	prenais	pris
	il	prend	prendra	prenait	prit
prenant	nous	prenons	prendrons	prenions	prîmes
pris	vous	prenez	prendrez	preniez	prîtes
	ils	prennent	prendront	prenaient	prirent

CONDITIONNEL	IMPÉRATIF	SUBJONCTIF	
		PRÉSENT	IMPARFAIT
peindrais		peigne	peignisse
peindrais	peins	peignes	peignisses
peindrait		peigne	peignisse
peindrions	peignons	peignions	peignissions
peindriez	peignez	peigniez	peignissiez
peindraient		peignent	peignissent
plairais		plaise	plusse
plairais	plais	plaises	plusses
plairait		plaise	plût
plairions	plaisons	plaisions	plussions
plairiez	plaisez	plaisiez	plussiez
plairaient		plaisent	plussent
pleuvrait		pleuve	plût
pourvoirais		pourvoie	pourvusse
pourvoirais	pourvois	pourvoies	pourvusses
pourvoirait		pourvoie	pourvût
pourvoirions	pourvoyons	pourvoyions	pourvussions
pourvoiriez	pourvoyez	pourvoyiez	pourvussiez
pourvoiraient		pourvoient	pourvussent
pourrais		puisse	pusse
pourrais		puisses	pusses
pourrait		puisse	pût
pourrions		puissions	pussions
pourriez		puissiez	pussiez
pourraient		puissent	pussent
prendrais		prenne	prisse
prendrais	prends	prennes	prisses
prendrait		prenne	prît
prendrions	prenons	prenions	prissions
prendriez	prenez	preniez	prissiez
prendraient		prennent	prissent

INFINITIF PARTICIPES		INDICATIF			
		PRÉSENT	FUTUR	IMPARFAIT	PASSÉ SIMPLE
recevoir	je	reçois	recevrai	recevais	reçus
to receive	tu	reçois	recevras	recevais	reçus
	il	reçoit	recevra	recevait	reçut
recevant	nous	recevons	recevrons	recevions	reçûmes
reçu	vous	recevez	recevrez	receviez	reçûtes
	ils	reçoivent	recevront	recevaient	reçurent
résoudre	je	résous	résoudrai	résolvais	résolus
to resolve	tu	résous	résoudras	résolvais	résolus
	il	résout	résoudra	résolvait	résolut
résolvant	nous	résolvons	résoudrons	résolvions	résolûmes
résolu	vous	résolvez	résoudrez	résolviez	résolûtes
	ils	résolvent	résoudront	résolvaient	résolurent
rire	je	ris	rirai	riais	ris
to laugh	tu	ris	riras	riais	ris
	il	rit	rira	riait	rit
riant	nous	rions	rirons	riions	rîmes
ri	vous	riez	rirez	riiez	rîtes
	ils	rient	riront	riaient	rirent
savoir	je	sais	saurai	savais	sus
to know	tu	sais	sauras	savais	sus
	il	sait	saura	savait	sut
sachant	nous	savons	saurons	savions	sûmes
su	vous	savez	saurez	saviez	sûtes
	ils	savent	sauront	savaient	surent
servir	je	sers	servirai	servais	servis
to serve	tu	sers	serviras	servais	servis
	il	sert	servira	servait	servit
servant	nous	servons	servirons	servions	servîmes
servi	vous	servez	servirez	serviez	servîtes
	ils	servent	serviront	servaient	servirent
suffire	je	suffis	suffirai	suffisais	suffis
to suffice	tu	suffis	suffiras	suffisais	suffis
	il	suffit	suffira	suffisait	suffit
suffisant	nous	suffisons	suffirons	suffisions	suffîmes
suffi	vous	suffisez	suffirez	suffisiez	suffîtes
	ils	suffisent	suffiront	suffisaient	suffirent

CONDITIONNEL	IMPÉRATIF	SUBJONCTIF	
		PRÉSENT	IMPARFAIT
recevrais		reçoive	reçusse
recevrais	reçois	reçoives	reçusses
recevrait		reçoive	reçût
recevrions	recevons	recevions	reçussions
recevriez	recevez	receviez	reçussiez
recevraient		reçoivent	reçussent
résoudrais		résolve	résolusse
résoudrais	résous	résolves	résolusses
résoudrait		résolve	résolût
résoudrions	résolvons	résolvions	résolussions
résoudriez	résolvez	résolviez	résolussiez
résoudraient		résolvent	résolussent
rirais		rie	risse
rirais	ris	ries	risses
rirait		rie	rît
ririons	rions	riions	rissions
ririez	riez	riiez	rissiez
riraient		rient	rissent
saurais		sache	susse
saurais	sache	saches	susses
saurait		sache	sût
saurions	sachons	sachions	sussions
sauriez	sachez	sachiez	sussiez
sauraient		sachent	sussent
servirais		serve	servisse
servirais	sers	serves	servisses
servirait		serve	servît
servirions	servons	servions	servissions
serviriez	servez	serviez	servissiez
serviraient		servent	servissent
suffirais		suffise	suffisse
suffirais	suffis	suffises	suffisses
suffirait		suffise	suffît
suffirions	suffisons	suffisions	suffissions
suffiriez	suffisez	suffisiez	suffissiez
suffiraient		suffisent	suffissent

INFINITIF PARTICIPES		PRÉSENT	FUTUR	IMPARFAIT	PASSÉ SIMPLE
suivre *to follow* suivant suivi	je tu il nous vous ils	suis suis suit suivons suivez suivent	suivrai suivras suivra suivrons suivrez suivront	suivais suivais suivait suivions suiviez suivaient	suivis suivis suivit suivîmes suivîtes suivirent
tenir *to hold* tenant tenu	je tu il nous vous ils	tiens tiens tient tenons tenez tiennent	tiendrai tiendras tiendra tiendrons tiendrez tiendront	tenais tenais tenait tenions teniez tenaient	tins tins tint tînmes tîntes tinrent
traire *to milk* trayant trait	je tu il nous vous ils	trais trais trait trayons trayez traient	trairai trairas traira trairons trairez trairont	trayais trayais trayait trayions trayiez trayaient	
vaincre *to conquer* *to vanquish* vainquant vaincu	je tu il nous vous ils	vaincs vaincs vainc vainquons vainquez vainquent	vaincrai vaincras vaincra vaincrons vaincrez vaincront	vainquais vainquais vainquait vainquions vainquiez vainquaient	vainquis vainquis vainquit vainquîmes vainquîtes vainquirent
valoir *to be worth* valant valu	je tu il nous vous ils	vaux vaux vaut valons valez valent	vaudrai vaudras vaudra vaudrons vaudrez vaudront	valais valais valait valions valiez valaient	valus valus valut valûmes valûtes valurent
venir *to come* venant venu	je tu il nous vous ils	viens viens vient venons venez viennent	viendrai viendras viendra viendrons viendrez viendront	venais venais venait venions veniez venaient	vins vins vint vînmes vîntes vinrent

CONDITIONNEL	IMPÉRATIF	SUBJONCTIF	
		PRÉSENT	IMPARFAIT
suivrais		suive	suivisse
suivrais	suis	suives	suivisses
suivrait		suive	suivît
suivrions	suivons	suivions	suivissions
suivriez	suivez	suiviez	suivissiez
suivraient		suivent	suivissent
tiendrais		tienne	tinsse
tiendrais	tiens	tiennes	tinsses
tiendrait		tienne	tînt
tiendrions	tenons	tenions	tinssions
tiendriez	tenez	teniez	tinssiez
tiendraient		tiennent	tinssent
trairais		traie	
trairais	trais	traies	
trairait		traie	
trairions	trayons	trayions	
trairiez	trayez	trayiez	
trairaient		traient	
vaincrais		vainque	vainquisse
vaincrais	vaincs	vainques	vainquisses
vaincrait		vainque	vainquît
vaincrions	vainquons	vainquions	vainquissions
vaincriez	vainquez	vainquiez	vainquissiez
vaincraient		vainquent	vainquissent
vaudrais		vaille	valusse
vaudrais	vaux	vailles	valusses
vaudrait		vaille	valût
vaudrions	valons	valions	valussions
vaudriez	valez	valiez	valussiez
vaudraient		vaillent	valussent
viendrais		vienne	vinsse
viendrais	viens	viennes	vinsses
viendrait		vienne	vînt
viendrions	venons	venions	vinssions
viendriez	venez	veniez	vinssiez
viendraient		viennent	vinssent

| INFINITIF | | INDICATIF | | | |
PARTICIPES		PRÉSENT	FUTUR	IMPARFAIT	PASSÉ SIMPLE
vêtir	je	vêts	vêtirai	vêtais	vêtis
to dress	tu	vêts	vêtiras	vêtais	vêtis
to clothe	il	vêt	vêtira	vêtait	vêtit
	nous	vêtons	vêtirons	vêtions	vêtîmes
vêtant	vous	vêtez	vêtirez	vêtiez	vêtîtes
vêtu	ils	vêtent	vêtiront	vêtaient	vêtirent
vivre	je	vis	vivrai	vivais	vécus
to live	tu	vis	vivras	vivais	vécus
	il	vit	vivra	vivait	vécut
vivant	nous	vivons	vivrons	vivions	vécûmes
vécu	vous	vivez	vivrez	viviez	vécûtes
	ils	vivent	vivront	vivaient	vécurent
voir	je	vois	verrai	voyais	vis
to see	tu	vois	verras	voyais	vis
	il	voit	verra	voyait	vit
voyant	nous	voyons	verrons	voyions	vîmes
vu	vous	voyez	verrez	voyiez	vîtes
	ils	voient	verront	voyaient	virent
vouloir	je	veux	voudrai	voulais	voulus
to want	tu	veux	voudras	voulais	voulus
to wish	il	veut	voudra	voulait	voulut
	nous	voulons	voudrons	voulions	voulûmes
voulant	vous	voulez	voudrez	vouliez	voulûtes
voulu	ils	veulent	voudront	voulaient	voulurent

CONDITIONNEL	IMPÉRATIF	SUBJONCTIF	
		PRÉSENT	IMPARFAIT
vêtirais		vête	vêtisse
vêtirais	vêts	vêtes	vêtisses
vêtirait		vête	vêtît
vêtirions	vêtons	vêtions	vêtissions
vêtiriez	vêtez	vêtiez	vêtissiez
vêtiraient		vêtent	vêtissent
vivrais		vive	vécusse
vivrais	vis	vives	vécusses
vivrait		vive	vécût
vivrions	vivons	vivions	vécussions
vivriez	vivez	viviez	vécussiez
vivraient		vivent	vécussent
verrais		voie	visse
verrais	vois	voies	visses
verrait		voie	vît
verrions	voyons	voyions	vissions
verriez	voyez	voyiez	vissiez
verraient		voient	vissent
voudrais		veuille	voulusse
voudrais	veux (veuille)	veuilles	voulusses
voudrait		veuille	voulût
voudrions	voulons (veuillons)	voulions	voulussions
voudriez	voulez (veuillez)	vouliez	voulussiez
voudraient		veuillent	voulussent

Vocabulaire

The vocabulary contains all terms included in the various exercises, improvisations, folksongs, and springboards for conversation (except for a number of the most obvious cognates). The most frequently occurring irregular verb forms, such as past participles, are listed separately and are cross-referenced. All expressions are fully cross-referenced; for example, **faire le ménage** is listed under both **faire** and **ménage.** Definitions are given only for the contexts in this book.

ABBREVIATIONS

adj.	adjective	*m.*	masculine
adv.	adverb	*n.*	noun
conj.	conjunction	*p.p.*	past participle
def. art.	definite article	*pl.*	plural
f.	feminine	*prep.*	preposition
independ.	independant	*pron.*	pronoun
inf.	infinitive	*rel.*	relative

à to; at; in; toward; by
abreuver to water; to soak
absent *m.* absentee
absolument absolutely
accidentellement accidentally
accompagner to accompany
accomplir to accomplish
accord *m.* agreement; **être d'accord** to agree
achat *m.* purchase
acheter to buy
acteur *m.* actor
actrice *f.* actress
actualités *f. pl.* news
addition *f.* check, bill
adjectif *m.* adjective
admirateur *m.* admirer
admiratrice *f.* admirer
adorer to love, adore
s'adresser (à) to address oneself (to), go (to); to apply
aérogramme *m.* air letter
aéroport *m.* airport
affreux *(f.* **affreuse***)* horrible, awful
âge *m.* age; **quel âge avez-vous?** how old are you?
agence *f.* agency; **agence de voyages** travel agency; **agence immobilière** rental agency, real estate agency
agenda *m.* engagement book
agent *m.* agent; policeman; **agent de police** policeman; **agent de voyage** travel agent
agréable pleasant
aider to help
aigu sharp; **accent aigu** acute accent
aimable kind; likeable
aimer to like; to love; **aimer mieux** to prefer; **où aimeriez-vous aller?** where would you like to go?
air *m.* air; look, appearance; **avoir l'air de** to seem (to; to be); **avoir l'air inquiet** to look worried; **être en plein air** to be out in the fresh air; **mal** *(m.)* **de l'air** airsickness
ajouter to add
alimentation *f.* nourishment
Allemagne *f.* Germany
aller to go; to be *(of health);* to fit; to suit; **s'en aller** to go away; **aller à la pêche** to go fishing; **aller chercher** to go get; to pick up; **billet** *(m.)* **aller retour** round-trip ticket; **comment allez-vous?** how are you? **comment vas-tu?** how

are you? **lui va très bien** suits him / her very well
allumette *f.* match
alors therefore, then
alouette *f.* lark
ami *m.* *(f.* **amie***)* friend
amicalement cordially
amitié *f.* friendship; **amitiés** sincerely, cordially *(complimentary close to a letter)*
amour *m.* love
amusant amusing, funny
s'amuser to have a good time
an *m.* year
anesthésie *f.* anesthetic
ange *m.* angel
animal *m.* *(pl.* **animaux***)* animal
année *f.* year; **dans quelques années** in a few years, a few years from now
anniversaire (de naissance) *m.* birthday; **anniversaire de mariage** wedding anniversary; **bon anniversaire** happy birthday
anonyme anonymous
antiquités *f. pl.* antiques; **magasin d'antiquités** antique store
août *m.* August
apercevoir to see, to catch sight of
apéritif *m.* before-dinner drink; cocktail
appareil *m.* receiver; **qui est à l'appareil?** who's speaking?
appareil photo *m.* camera
appartement *m.* apartment
appel *m.* call; **appel interurbain** long-distance call
appeler to call; **s'appeler** to be named; to be called
applaudir to applaud
apporter to bring
apprendre to learn
appris *(p.p.* of **apprendre***)*
appuyer to press
après after
après-midi *m.* or *f.* afternoon
arbre *m.* tree
argent *m.* money; silver; **argent de poche** pocket money
argenterie *f.* silverware
arpent *m.* acres
arracher to pull, extract
arrêt *m.* stop; **arrêt d'autobus** bus stop
s'arrêter to stop
arrivée *f.* arrival

arriver to arrive; to happen
artichaut *m.* artichoke
article *m.* article; **article partitif** partitive article
artistique artistic; **patinage artistique** figure skating
ascenseur *m.* elevator
Asie *f.* Asia
asperge *f.* asparagus; **des asperges** asparagus *(stalks and tips used as food)*
aspirateur *m.* vacuum cleaner
aspirine *f.* aspirin
s'asseoir *to sit down*
assez enough; somewhat, rather, fairly, sufficient(ly)
assis seated, sitting
assister (à) to attend
assurance *f.* insurance
astigmate astigmatic
astronaute *m.* astronaut
attendre to wait (for)
attente *f.* wait; **salle** *(f.)* **d'attente** waiting room
attention be careful, pay attention, watch out
atterrir to land
au *(prep. + def. art.)* at the, to the, on the
aujourd'hui today
aussi also, too; **aussi . . . que** as . . . as
autant (de) as many, as much
auteur *m.* author
auto *f.* automobile, car; **faire un tour en auto** to go for a drive
autobus *m.* bus, city bus
automne *m.* autumn, fall; **en automne** in the fall
autoportrait *m.* self-portrait, self-description; **faites votre autoportrait** give your self-description
autorisé approved
autoroute *f.* superhighway
autre another, other; **l'autre** the other (one); **quelque chose d'autre** something else; **qui d'autre?** who else?; **quoi d'autre?** what else
autrefois formerly; of old
aux *(prep. + pl. def. art.)* at the, to the
avance *f.* advance; **avoir de l'avance** to be early *(train, bus, plane)*
avancer to be fast; to put ahead; **ma montre avance** my watch is fast

avant *(adv., prep.)* before; **avant de** before; **avant que** before

avant-hier day before yesterday

avare miserly

avec with

Avignon city in southern France

avion *m.* airplane; **en avion** by plane; **par avion** airmail

avis *m.* opinion; notice; notification; **changer d'avis** to change one's mind

avoir to have; **avoir besoin de** to need; **avoir bonne mine** to look healthy; **avoir chaud** to feel hot; **avoir de l'avance** to be early *(train, bus, plane)*; **avoir du mal (à)** to have difficulty; **avoir du retard** to be late *(train, bus, plane)*; **avoir envie de** to want (to; some of); **avoir faim** to be hungry; **avoir froid** to feel cold; **avoir l'air** to seem; **avoir lieu** to take place, to be held; **avoir mal (à)** to hurt, to have an ache; **avoir mal au cœur** to be sick to the stomach, feel nauseated; **avoir mal aux dents** to have a toothache; **avoir peur** to be afraid; **avoir soif** to be thirsty; **t'auras (tu auras)** you will have

bagages *m. pl.* baggage, luggage

baignade *f.* bathing, swimming; **baignade interdite** no swimming

se baigner to bathe

bain *m.* bath; **maillot** *(m.)* **de bain** bathing suit; **salle** *(f.)* **de bains** bathroom

baiser *m.* kiss

baisser to lower, to put down

balcon *m.* balcony

banlieue *f.* suburbs

banque *f.* bank

bas *(f.* **basse)** low; **en bas** downstairs

bataillon *m.* battalion

bateau *m.* boat; **bateau à voiles** sailboat; **faire du bateau** to go boating

bâtiment *m.* building

bâton *m.* stick

battre to beat; **battre le briquet** to get the fire going

bazin *m.* *type of cloth*

beau *(f.* **belle)** beautiful, handsome; **faire beau** to be nice weather; **il fait beau** it is nice weather

beaucoup (de) much, a lot, a great deal, many

beauté *f.* beauty; **produits** *(m. pl.)* **de beauté** cosmetics; **salon** *(m.)* **de beauté** beauty parlor

bec *m.* beak, bill

bergère *f.* shepherdess

besoin *m.* need; **avoir besoin de** to need

bêta *(slang)* silly one

bête stupid

beurre *m.* butter; **beurre de cacahuètes** peanut butter

bibliothèque *f.* library

bicyclette *f.* bicycle; **faire de la bicyclette** to go bicycle riding

bien well, fine; really *(intensifier)*; **bien cuit** well done *(meat)*

bien que although

bientôt soon; **à bientôt** see you soon; **à bientôt de vos bonnes nouvelles** looking forward to hearing from you soon

bière *f.* beer

bifteck *m.* steak

billet *m.* ticket; bill; **billet aller retour** round-trip ticket; **billet de seconde** second-class ticket

bis again; repeat

bise *f.* kiss *(slang)*; **grosses bises** hugs and kisses *(complimentary close to a letter)*

blanc *(f.* **blanche)** white

blanchisserie *f.* laundry

bleu blue

blond blonde

boire to drink

bois *m.* wood; woods

boisson *f.* drink, beverage

boîte *f.* box; **boîte aux lettres** mailbox; **boîte de nuit** night club; **boîte à gants** glove compartment; **boîte à pilules** pill box

bon *(f.* **bonne)** good; **bon marché** inexpensive

bonbon *m.* (piece of) candy

bonjour hello

bord *m.* edge; **au bord de la mer** at the sea shore, to the ocean, by the sea

botte *f.* boot

bouche *f.* mouth

boucle *f.* buckle; **boucle d'oreille** earring

boule *f.* ball

boussole *f.* compass

bout *m.* end

bouteille *f.* bottle

bouton *m.* button

bras *m.* arm

bref *(f.* **brève)** short, brief

briller to shine

briquet *m.* lighter; **battre le briquet** to get the fire going

brosse *f.* brush; **brosse à dents** toothbrush

brosser to brush

bronzer to tan; **se faire bronzer au soleil** to get a suntan

bruit *m.* noise; **à grand bruit** noisily

brun brown, brunette

bruyant noisy

bureau *m.* office; **bureau de location** ticket office; **bureau des objets trouvés** lost and found; **bureau de poste** post office

ça that

cabine *f.* booth; **cabine téléphonique** phone booth

cacahuète *f.* peanut

cadeau *m.* gift, present

café *m.* coffee

caisse *f.* cash register

caissier *m.* teller

caissière *f.* teller

camarade *m., f.* comrade; **camarade de chambre** roommate

caméra *f.* (movie, television) camera

campagne *f.* country; **à la campagne** in the country

cantine *f.* cafeteria, restaurant

car for, because

carié decayed

carnet *m.* book of tickets *(subway, bus)*

carotte *f.* carrot

carré square

carte *f.* card; menu; map; **carte de crédit** credit card; **carte postale** postcard; **jouer aux cartes** to play cards; **carte de vœux** greeting card

cas *m.* case; **cas d'urgence** emergency; **selon le cas** accordingly

case *f.* square, pigeonhole, post office box

casse-croûte *m.* snack

casser to break

cathédrale *f.* cathedral

causer to chat

caviar *m.* caviar

ce (*adj., pron.*) this, that, it; **ce que** (*rel. pron.*) what, that which; **ce qui** (*rel. pron.*) what, that which; **ce sont** these are; **qui est-ce?** who is it?

ceinture *f.* belt; **ceinture de sécurité** seat belt

cela that

célèbre famous

célibataire single, unmarried

cendrier *m.* ashtray

cent hundred

ces these

cesser to stop

cet this, that

cette this, that

chacun *m.* (*f.* **chacune**) each (one)

chaîne *f.* channel (*television*)

chaise *f.* chair; **chaise longue** deck chair

chambre *f.* bed(room); **chambre à coucher** bedroom; **femme de chambre** chambermaid

champ *m.* field; **aux champs** to the fields

champignon *m.* mushroom

championnat *m.* championship

chandail *m.* sweater

chandelle *f.* candle

changer to change; to cash; to alter, modify, make a change

chanter to sing

chanteur *m.* (*f.* **chanteuse**) singer

chapeau *m.* hat

chaque each, every

charmant charming

chasse *f.* hunting; hunting season

chasseur *m.* bellboy

chat *m.* cat

châtain chestnut (*color*)

château *m.* castle, chateau, mansion

chaud hot; **avoir chaud** to feel hot; **faire chaud** to be warm (hot) weather

chauffeur *m.* driver

chaumière *f.* thatched cottage

chaussette *f.* sock

chaussure *f.* shoe; **magasin** (*m.*) **de chaussures** shoe store

chauve bald

chemin *m.* track, path, way

chemise *f.* shirt

chèque *m.* check; **chèque de voyage** *m.* travelers check; **toucher un chèque** to cash a check

cher (*f.* **chère**) expensive; dear; **coûter cher** to be expensive

chercher to look for, seek; **aller chercher** to go get, pick up

cheval *m.* horse; **faire du cheval** to go horseback riding

chevalier *m.* knight, cavalier

cheveux *m. pl.* hair; **avoir les cheveux bruns** to have brown hair; **se faire couper les cheveux** to have one's hair cut

cheville *f.* ankle

chevron *m.* rafter

chez at, to, in the home of; at, to, in the office of; at the place of; **chez le coiffeur** at, to the hairdresser's; **chez lui** to his home; at his place; **chez les Smith** at, to the Smith's; **chez vous** (at) your house

chien *m.* dog

chiffonné wrinkled, crumpled, rumpled

chiffre *m.* figure, number

chimie *f.* chemistry

chinois Chinese

chirurgien *m.* surgeon

chocolat *m.* chocolate; hot chocolate

choisir to choose, to select

chômage *m.* unemployment; **en chômage** unemployed

chose *f.* thing

chou *m.* cabbage

ci-dessus above

cigale *f.* cicada, grasshopper

cigare *m.* cigar

cigarette *f.* cigarette

cinéma *m.* movies

cinq five

cinquante fifty

cintre *m.* hanger

circonflexe circumflex

circulation *f.* traffic

cirque *m.* circus

citoyen *m.* citizen

clair (*adj.*) clear; light (*in color*); *n.m.* light, brightness; **clair de lune** moonlight

classe *f.* class; **classe de français** French class

classique classical

clé *f.* key

climatisé air-conditioned

climatiseur *m.* air conditioner

code *m.* code; **code de la route** traffic regulations; **code postale** zip code

cœur *m.* heart; **avoir le cœur gai** to be light-hearted, happy; **avoir mal au cœur** to be sick to the stomach

coffre *m.* trunk (*of car*)

se coiffer to do one's (own) hair

coiffeur *m.* barber, hairdresser

coiffure *f.* hairdo, hairstyle

Colas nickname for Nicolas

colis *m.* parcel

collègue *m., f.* colleague

combien (de) how much, how many; **combien de temps?** how long?; **depuis combien de temps?** for how long?; **de combien?** by how much?

commander to order

comme like, as; **comme dîner** for dinner; **comme déjeuner** for lunch; **comme petit déjeuner** for breakfast

commencer (à) to begin

comment how; **comment allez-vous?** how are you? **comment ça va?** how are things?; **comment est la plage?** describe the beach; **comment est le professeur?** describe the professor; **comment est la salle de séjour?** describe the living room; **comment trouvez-vous ce bateau?** what do you think of this boat? **comment vous appelez-vous?** what is your name?

commissariat *m.* **de police** police station (*urban*)

communication *f.* connection

commutateur *m.* switch

compagnie *f.* company

compagnon *m.* or *f.* comrade, partner

comparaison *f.* comparison

complet (*f.* **complète**) full; complete

compléter to complete

compliqué complicated

composer to dial (*phone*)

comprendre to understand

compris (*p.p.* of **comprendre**)

compte *m.* reckoning; account; **se rendre compte** to realize

compter to intend, to count (on)

compteur *m.* odometer; speedometer

comptoir *m.* counter

à condition que on (the) condition that

conditionnel *m.* conditional

conducteur *m.* conductor, driver

conduire to drive; **permis** *(m.)* **de conduire** driver's license

conduit *(p.p.* of **conduire)**

conduite *f.* driving

confortable comfortable

congélateur *m.* freezer

conjugaison *f.* conjugation; **conjugaison des verbes** verb conjugations

connaissance *f.* acquaintance; **faire la connaissance (de)** to meet, to make the acquaintance (of)

connaître to know

conseil *m.* advice

conseiller to advise

consigne *f.* checkroom, baggage room

constamment constantly

consulter to consult, look at

conte *m.* tale, story

content happy

continuer to continue

contraire *m.* opposite

contravention *f.* traffic ticket; **avoir une contravention** to get a traffic ticket; **dresser une contravention** to write out a ticket

contre against

convenable suitable, proper, appropriate

convenir to be suitable

corps *m.* body

correspondance *f.* connection, change, transfer

correspondant corresponding; *(m.)* caller *(telephone)*

correspondre to correspond

côté *m.* side; **à côté de** next to; **de quel côté** on which side; **du côté** on the side

cou *m.* neck

couchage *m.* bedding; **sac de couchage** sleeping bag

se coucher to go to bed

couchette *f.* berth

coude *m.* elbow

couleur *f.* color

coup *m.* blow, knock; **coup de téléphone** phone call; **tout d'un coup** all of a sudden; **coup de pied** kick

coupe *f.* cup competition

couper to cut; **couper le gazon** to cut the grass, mow the lawn; **se faire couper les cheveux** to have one's hair cut; **on nous a coupés** we've been cut off

cour *f.* courtyard, square

courageux *(f.* **courageuse)** courageous

courir to run

courrier *m.* mail; **faire suivre le courrier** to have the mail forwarded

cours *m.* course; **au cours de la semaine** during the week; **suivre un cours** to take a course

court short

cousin *m.* cousin

coûter to cost; **coûter cher** to be expensive; **coûter moins cher** to be less expensive

couverture *f.* cover, blanket, bedspread

crêpe *f.* thin pancake

crevé flat

crier to cry out; to shout

croire to believe

croiser to cross

croisière *f.* cruise; **faire une croisière** to take a cruise

cueillir to pick, to gather

cuisine *f.* kitchen; cooking; cuisine; **faire la cuisine** to cook

cuisiner to cook

cuisinière *f.* stove, range; **cuisinière électrique** electric stove

dame *f.* lady, woman; **jouer aux dames** to play checkers

dangereux *(f.* **dangereuse)** dangerous

dans in; within

danser to dance

davantage more

de of, about, from; any

déblayer to clear, to clear away

début *m.* beginning; **au début** at the beginning

déchiré torn

décidé determined

décider to decide

déclarer to declare *(customs)*

décolorer to bleach; to fade; **se faire décolorer les cheveux** to have one's hair dyed

découvert *(p.p.* of **découvrir)**

décrire to describe

décrocher to pick up the receiver

défendre to forbid

défense *f.* defense; **défense d'entrer** keep out; **défense de fumer** no smoking; **défense de stationner** no parking

degré *m.* degree

dehors outside

déjà already

déjeuner *m.* lunch; **petit déjeuner** breakfast; **comme déjeuner** for lunch; **comme petit déjeuner** for breakfast; **déjeuner** to have lunch

délicieux *(f.* **délicieuse)** delicious

délivrance *f.* delivery

demain tomorrow

demande *f.* request

demander to ask

démarrer to start

dent *f.* tooth; **avoir mal aux dents** to have a toothache

dentifrice *m.* toothpaste

départ *m.* departure; **heures de départ** departure times

dépasser to exceed

se dépêcher to hurry

dépenser to spend *(money)*

dépensier *(f.* **dépensière)** spendthrift

déprimé depressed

depuis for, since; **depuis quand?** since when? for how long?

dernier *(f.* **dernière)** last; **la dernière** the last (one)

des of the, from the; some

descendre to go down, descend; to get off; to bring down; to take down; **descendre à l'hôtel** to go to a hotel, to stay at a hotel

descendu *(p.p.* of **descendre)**

se déshabiller to get undressed

désirer to want, to desire; **vous désirez?** may I help you?

désobéir to disobey

désolé sorry

dessert *m.* dessert

dessin *m.* drawing, sketch; **dessin animé** animated cartoon

dessus above

destinataire *m., f.* addressee

détester to hate

dette *f.* debt

deux two; **tous deux** both (of us, of you, of them)

deuxième second

devant ahead; in front (of)

la f. (def. art). the; (pron.) her, it
là there
lac m. lake
laid ugly
laine f. wool
laisser to let; to leave
lait m. milk
lampe f. lamp
lapin m. rabbit
laquelle which (one)
large wide; loose
latin m. Latin
laurier m. laurel
lavabo m. sink
laver to wash; se laver la tête to wash one's hair
laverie automatique f. laundromat
lave-vaisselle m. dishwasher
le m. (def. art.) the; (pron.) him, it
leçon f. lesson
léger (f. légère) light (in weight)
légume m. vegetable
lent slow
lentement slowly
lequel which (one)
les pl. (def. art.) the; (pron.) them
lessive f. washing (of clothes); wash
letter f. letter; boîte aux lettres mailbox
leur (adj.) their; (pron.) to them
se lever to get up
librairie f. bookstore
libre not occupied, free, unoccupied
lieu m. place; au lieu de instead of; avoir lieu to take place, to be held; lieu de travail place of work
ligne f. line; ligne aérienne airline
limité limited
linge m. laundry
lire to read
lisible legible
lisiblement legibly
lit m. bed; lit pliant folding bed
livre m. book
loger to lodge
loin far
lolo m. (slang) milk
long (f. longue) long
longtemps a long time; for a long time
longuement at length
lorsque when
louer to rent; to reserve
lourd heavy (in weight)
loyer m. rent

lu (p.p. of lire)
lui he, him, to her, to him, for her, for him; lui-même himself; c'est à lui it's his
luire to glow, to shine
lumière f. light
lundi Monday
lune f. moon
lunettes f. pl. eyeglasses; lunettes de soleil sunglasses
luxueux (f. luxueuse) luxurious

ma my
madame f. Mrs., Madam
mademoiselle f. Miss
magasin m. store; grand magasin department store; magasin d'antiquités antique store; magasin de chaussures shoe store
maigrir to get thin
maillot m. bathing suit; jersey; maillot de bain bathing suit
main f. hand
maintenant now
maire m. mayor
mais but
maison f. house; maison de campagne country house; à la maison at home
maître m. master; maître nageur lifeguard
majuscule capital
mal bad; poorly
mal m. pain; harm; trouble; adv. badly; avoir du mal (à) to have difficulty (in); avoir mal (à) to hurt, to have an ache; avoir mal au cœur to feel sick to the stomach; avoir mal aux dents to have a toothache; avoir mal à la tête to have a headache; se faire mal to hurt oneself; mal de l'air airsickness; mal de mer seasickness
malade sick
maladie f. disease
maladroit clumsy
malheureux (f. malheureuse) unhappy
malheureusement unfortunately
malle f. trunk
maman f. mommy, mama
manche f. sleeve
mandat m. money order
manger to eat; salle (f.) à manger dining room
manquer to be missing, to be lack-

ing; il vous manque you are missing; tu me manques I miss you; vous me manquez I miss you
manteau m. coat
marché m. market; bon marché inexpensive; meilleur marché cheaper, less expensive
marcher to walk; to march; to work (inanimate objects)
mardi Tuesday
mari m. husband
marié married
se marier to get married
marque f. make, brand
marron chestnut (color)
Marseille seaport city on Mediterranean coast
masculin masculine
matelas m. mattress; matelas pneumatique air mattress
matériel m. equipment
matière f. material; school subject; en quelle matière vous spécialisez-vous? what's your major?
matin m. morning
matines f. pl. morning bells, matins
mauvais bad
me me, to me, for me
mécanicien m. mechanic
méconnu underestimated, misunderstood
médecin m. doctor
médicament m. medicine
se méfier to distrust
meilleur better; best
même very; same; quand même just the same; though
ménage m. household; family; faire le ménage to do the housework
menton m. chin
menu m. menu
mer f. sea; mal (m.) de mer seasickness
mercredi Wednesday
mère f. mother
merveilleux (f. merveilleuse) marvelous, wonderful
mes my
métier m. occupation
métro m. subway
mettre to put; to display; to take (time); to put on (clothes), to wear; mettre à to put in; se mettre à to begin to; se mettre à table to sit down at the table
meuble m. (piece of) furniture

deviner to guess
devoir to owe, to have to; devoirs m. pl. homework, assignments
Dieu m. God
différemment differently
difficile difficult
digestif m. after-dinner drink
dilemme m. dilemma
dimanche m. Sunday
din ding (bell sound)
dîner m. dinner; dîner to dine, to have dinner; comme dîner for dinner
dire to say, tell; sans rien dire without saying anything; vouloir dire to mean; dire de gros mots to curse
disque m. record
se disputer to quarrel
distraire to distract, to amuse, to cheer up
distribuer to deliver
dit (p.p. of dire)
divorcer to get a divorce
dix ten
dommage m. loss, hurt; c'est dommage it's too bad, it's a pity
don dong (bell sound)
donc therefore, then; thus; now; soyez sérieux donc! (often used for emphasis) do be serious!
donner to give; donner sur to look out onto; donner pour quarante francs to give forty francs worth
dormir to sleep
dos m. back
douanier m. customs agent
doublé dubbed
doubler to pass
doublure f. lining
douche f. shower
se doucher to shower
douleur f. pain
doute f. doubt; sans doute undoubtedly
douter to doubt
doux (f. douce) sweet, kind, gentle; soft
drap m. sheet
drapeau m. flag
dresser to write up, to draw up; dresser une contravention to write up a ticket
droit straight; right; à droite to or on the right, to your right; tout

droit straight ahead
drôle funny
du of the, from the; some
dû, (p.p. of devoir, f. due)
dur hard

eau f. water; eau minérale mineral water
échanger to exchange
échecs m. pl. chess; jouer aux échecs to play chess
éclair m. flash of lightning; éclairs lightning
école f. school
économe economical
économique economical
écouter to listen (to)
écrire to write
écrit (p.p. of écrire)
écrivain m. writer
église f. church
égorger to cut the throat of
électrique electric
élément m. element
éléphant m. elephant
élève m., f. student
élevé high
s'élever to come to (bills); à combien s'élève votre . . . ? how much does your . . . (bill) come to?
elle she, her; c'est à elle it's hers
elles they
emballer to wrap
embrasser to embrace; to kiss
émission f. show (television)
empêcher to prevent
emploi m. job
employé m. employee; clerk
employer to use, employ
emporter to bring
emprunter (à) to borrow (from)
en (prep.) in, to, by; upon, while, when; dressed in, wearing; (pron.) some, any, (some) of it, (some) of them; from there; en ce moment now, at this time
enceinte pregnant
encore again; still, yet
énergique energetic
s'énerver to get nervous; to be exasperated
enfant m. child; être bon enfant to be good-natured
enfin at last, finally

ennemi m. enemy
ennuyer to bore; s'ennuyer to get bored
énorme enormous
enregistrer to check in; faire enregistrer mes bagages to have my luggage checked in
enseigner to teach
ensemble together
ensoleillé sunny
ensuite then, next; afterwards
entamer to begin; to engage in, to start (a conversation)
entendre to hear; s'entendre avec to get along with
entier (f. entière) entire, whole
entre between, among
entrée f. entrance
entreprendre to undertake
entrer (dans) to enter; défense d'entrer keep out
envie f. envy; desire; avoir envie (de) to want (to; some of), to feel like
envoyer to send
épais (f. épaisse) thick
épeler to spell
éperdument madly, wildly
épinard m. spinach; des épinards spinach (leaves used as food)
épouvante f. fright; film d'épouvante horror film
équipe f. team
erreur f. error
escalier m. stairs, stairway
escargot m. snail
escarpin m. dancing shoe
espagnol Spanish; m. Spanish language
espérer to hope
essayer to try; to try on
essence f. gasoline
essuie-glace m. windshield wiper
et and
établir to establish, to set up
établissement m. establishment, place
étage m. floor, level; à quel étage? on what floor?
États-Unis m. pl. United States
été m. summer; en été in summer
été (p.p. of être)
étendard m. flag, banner
étendu stretched out
éternuer to sneeze

étiquette f. label
étonné surprised
s'étonner to be surprised
étrange strange
étranger foreign; à l'étranger abroad
être to be; être de retour to be back; être en panne to have a breakdown; être en plein air to be out in the fresh air; être en retard to be late; être en train de to be in the process of; être en vacances to be on vacation; être enrhumé to have a cold; il était there was
étroit narrow, tight
étude f. study; faire ses études secondaires to go to high school
étudiant m. student
étudier to study
eu (p.p. of avoir)
événement m. event
éventuellement eventually
exactement exactly
examen m. examination; examen écrit written exam
s'excuser to excuse, to be sorry
exemple m. example
expéditeur m. sender
expliquer to explain

se fâcher to get angry
facile easy
facilement easily
facteur m. mailman
facture f. bill
faim f. hunger; avoir faim to be hungry
faire to do; to make; faire beau to be nice weather; se faire bronzer au soleil to get a suntan; faire chaud to be warm (hot) weather; se faire couper les cheveux to have one's hair cut; se faire décolorer les cheveux to have one's hair dyed; faire de la bicyclette to go bicycle riding; faire de longues promenades à pied to go for long walks, to hike; faire de l'auto-stop to hitchhike; faire des progrès to make progress, to progress; faire dodo (slang) to go to sleep; faire du bateau to go boating; faire du camping to go camping; faire du cheval to go horseback riding; faire du gâteau to bake a cake;

faire du lèche-vitrines to window-shop; faire du ski to ski, go skiing; faire du sport to play sports; faire le plein to fill 'er up; faire une croisière to take a cruise; faire la vaisselle to wash the dishes; faire enregistrer mes bagages to have my luggage checked in; faire la connaissance (de) to meet, to make the acquaintance (of); faire la cuisine to cook; faire le ménage to do housework; faire le tour du monde to go around the world; se faire mal to hurt oneself; faire partie de to belong to; se faire payer to cash; faire peur (à) to frighten; faire plaisir (à) to please; les faire réparer to have them repaired; faire ses études secondaires to go to high school; faire suivre le courrier to have the mail forwarded; faire un pique-nique to picnic; faire un tour en auto to go for a drive; faire un voyage to take a trip, to travel; faire une piqûre to give an injection; faire une promenade to take a walk; il fait beau it is nice weather; que feriez-vous si . . . ? what would you do if . . . ?; quelle température fait-il? what's the temperature?
faire-part m. announcement
fait (p.p. of faire)
falloir to be necessary; to need; il faut it is necessary; it takes (of time); il me faut I need; il lui faut he needs / she needs; il nous faut we need; il leur faut they need
famille f. family; en famille with one's family, with your family
faner to wilt
fatigant tiring
fatigué tired
faute f. fault; à qui la faute? whose fault is (was) it?
fauteuil m. chair; armchair
faux (f. fausse) false, wrong
favori (f. favorite) favorite
féliciter to congratulate
femme f. woman; wife; femme de chambre chambermaid
fenêtre f. window
ferme f. farm
fermer to close
féroce ferocious

feu m. fire
feuillage m. leaves, foliage
fiancé engaged
se fiancer to get engaged
ficelle f. string
fiche f. form
fièvre f. fever
filet m. rack
fille f. girl; daughter; fille unique (an) only daughter; jeune fille girl; nom de jeune fille maiden name
film m. movie
fils m. son; fils unique (an) only son
fin adj. fine, thin; finely (ground)
fin f. end
finir (par) to end up (by), finish
flacon m. flask, small bottle
fleur f. flower
foin m. hay; rhume des foins hay fever
fois f. time; la première fois the first time
foncé dark
fonctionner to work, function
fontaine f. fountain
forêt f. forest
forme f. form
formule f. form; formule de télégramme telegram form
fort strong; je t'embrasse fort I send you a big hug (complimentary close to a letter); parler fort to speak loudly
foulard m. scarf
fouler to sprain
fourrure f. fur (coat)
français French; m. French language
fraise f. strawberry
franc (f. franche) frank
frapper to knock; frapper à la porte to knock on the door
frein m. brake
fréquemment frequently
frère m. brother
fripon (f. friponne) knavish, rascally
frire to fry
froid cold; avoir froid to feel cold
fromage m. cheese
fumer to smoke; défense de fumer no smoking
furet m. ferret
futur m. future; au futur in(to) the future

gagner to earn
gai happy; avoir le cœur gai to be happy
galerie (f.) d'art art gallery
gant m. glove
garage m. garage
garagiste m. garage mechanic
garçon m. boy; waiter
garder to watch over, tend; to keep
gare f. train station
gâteau m. cake
gauche left; à gauche to / on the left, to your left
gazon m. lawn; couper le gazon to cut the grass, mow the lawn
gencive f. gum (of the teeth)
généreux (f. généreuse) generous
genre m. type, kind
gens m. pl. people (in general, an undetermined number)
gentil (f. gentille) nice; kind; agreeable
gérant (f. gérante) hotel manager
geste m. gesture
glace f. ice; ice cream
gloire f. glory
gonfler to inflate
gorge f. throat
goûter to taste
grand big, large, tall; à grand bruit noisily; de grands yeux large eyes
grand-père m. grandfather
grave serious, grave
grêler to hail (weather)
grésiller to sleet
grippe f. influenza
gris grey
gros (f. grosse) big; fat; gros mots curse(s)
groupe m. group; en groupe with a group of people
guichet m. window (in post office, bank, box office); counter (in bank)
guitare f. guitar

habillé (de) dressed (in)
s'habiller to get dressed
habiter to live
d'habitude usually
s'habituer à to get used to
haricot m. bean; haricot vert m. string bean, green bean
haut high; en haut upstairs
herbe f. grass
hésiter to hesitate
heure f. hour; time (of day),

o'clock; heures de départ departure times; six heures du soir six o'clock in the evening; à quelle heure? when?, at what time?; de bonne heure early; quelle heure est-il? what time is it?; vers huit heures around eight o'clock; à l'heure on time
heureux (f. heureuse) happy
heureusement fortunately
hier yesterday; hier soir last night, yesterday evening
hirondelle f. swallow
histoire f. story
hiver m. winter; en hiver in winter; sports d'hiver winter sports
homme m. man
hôpital m. hospital
hors de off, outside of
hôte m. host
hôtesse de l'air stewardess, flight attendant
hôtel m. hotel
huile f. oil
huit eight
huitième eighth
humeur f. humor; qu'est-ce qui vous met en mauvaise humeur? what puts you into a bad mood?

ici here; près d'ici near here, nearby
idée f. idea
idiot idiotic
il he
ils they
il y a there is, there are; ago; il y a deux jours two days ago; il y en a plusieurs there are several of them; y a-t-il is there, are there
imaginer to imagine
immeuble m. building
immobilier (f. immobilière) real estate, property; agence (f.) immobilière rental agency, real estate agency
s'impatienter to get impatient
impensable unthinkable
imperméable m. raincoat
index m. index finger
indicatif m. indicative; indicatif de zone area code
indiquer to indicate
infinitif m. infinitive
infirmière f. nurse
s'informer to get information

inquiet (f. inquiète) worried; av...
l'air inquiet to look worried
inscrire to record; to register; write
s'installer to move in
instant m. moment, instant
interdit forbidden; baignade dite no swimming
intéressant interesting
s'intéresser à to be interested
intérêt m. interest
intérieur m. interior
interurbain interurban, long distance
inutile useless
invité m. guest
inviter to invite
italien (f. italienne) Itali...
Italian language
itinéraire m. itinerary

jacquet m. backgammon
jambe f. leg
jambon m. ham
jamais never; ever
jardin m. garden
jardinage m. gardening
jaune yellow
je I
jeton m. token
jeune young; jeune fi...
joli pretty
jouer to play; jouer...
play cards; jouer...
play chess; jouer...
play guitar
jouir de to enjoy
jour m. day; tous...
day, daily
journal m. newsp...
diary
journée f. day; t...
day (long)
joyeux (f. joyeu...
Noël Merry ...
jupe f. skirt
jus m. juice;
juice; jus de...
jusqu'à as fa...
until
jusque even...
juste exactly...
deux heur...
two o'cloc...

kilométrage...

deviner to guess

devoir to owe, to have to; **devoirs** *m. pl.* homework, assignments

Dieu *m.* God

différemment differently

difficile difficult

digestif *m.* after-dinner drink

dilemme *m.* dilemma

dimanche *m.* Sunday

din ding *(bell sound)*

dîner *m.* dinner; **dîner** to dine, to have dinner; **comme dîner** for dinner

dire to say, tell; **sans rien dire** without saying anything; **vouloir dire** to mean; **dire de gros mots** to curse

disque *m.* record

se disputer to quarrel

distraire to distract, to amuse, to cheer up

distribuer to deliver

dit *(p.p. of dire)*

divorcer to get a divorce

dix ten

dommage *m.* loss, hurt; **c'est dommage** it's too bad, it's a pity

don dong *(bell sound)*

donc therefore, then; thus; now; **soyez sérieux donc!** *(often used for emphasis)* do be serious!

donner to give; **donner sur** to look out onto; **donner pour quarante francs** to give forty francs worth

dormir to sleep

dos *m.* back

douanier *m.* customs agent

doublé dubbed

doubler to pass

doublure *f.* lining

douche *f.* shower

se doucher to shower

douleur *f.* pain

doute *f.* doubt; **sans doute** undoubtedly

douter to doubt

doux *(f. douce)* sweet, kind, gentle; soft

drap *m.* sheet

drapeau *m.* flag

dresser to write up, to draw up; **dresser une contravention** to write up a ticket

droit straight; right; **à droite** to *or* on the right, to your right; **tout**

droit straight ahead

drôle funny

du of the, from the; some

dû, *(p.p. of devoir, f. due)*

dur hard

eau *f.* water; **eau minérale** mineral water

échanger to exchange

échecs *m. pl.* chess; **jouer aux échecs** to play chess

éclair *m.* flash of lightning; **éclairs** lightning

école *f.* school

économe economical

économique economical

écouter to listen (to)

écrire to write

écrit *(p.p. of écrire)*

écrivain *m.* writer

église *f.* church

égorger to cut the throat of

électrique electric

élément *m.* element

éléphant *m.* elephant

élève *m., f.* student

élevé high

s'élever to come to *(bills)*; **à combien s'élève votre . . . ?** how much does your . . . *(bill)* come to?

elle she, her; **c'est à elle** it's hers

elles they

emballer to wrap

embrasser to embrace; to kiss

émission *f.* show *(television)*

empêcher to prevent

emploi *m.* job

employé *m.* employee; clerk

employer to use, employ

emporter to bring

emprunter (à) to borrow (from)

en *(prep.)* in, to, by; upon, while, when; dressed in, wearing; *(pron.)* some, any, (some) of it, (some) of them; from there; **en ce moment** now, at this time

enceinte pregnant

encore again; still, yet

énergique energetic

s'énerver to get nervous; to be exasperated

enfant *m.* child; **être bon enfant** to be good-natured

enfin at last, finally

ennemi *m.* enemy

ennuyer to bore; **s'ennuyer** to get bored

énorme enormous

enregistrer to check in; **faire enregistrer mes bagages** to have my luggage checked in

enseigner to teach

ensemble together

ensoleillé sunny

ensuite then, next; afterwards

entamer to begin; to engage in, to start *(a conversation)*

entendre to hear; **s'entendre avec** to get along with

entier *(f. entière)* entire, whole

entre between, among

entrée *f.* entrance

entreprendre to undertake

entrer (dans) to enter; **défense d'entrer** keep out

envie *f.* envy; desire; **avoir envie (de)** to want (to; some of), to feel like

envoyer to send

épais *(f. épaisse)* thick

épeler to spell

éperdument madly, wildly

épinard *m.* spinach; **des épinards** spinach *(leaves used as food)*

épouvante *f.* fright; **film d'épouvante** horror film

équipe *f.* team

erreur *f.* error

escalier *m.* stairs, stairway

escargot *m.* snail

escarpin *m.* dancing shoe

espagnol Spanish; *m.* Spanish language

espérer to hope

essayer to try; to try on

essence *f.* gasoline

essuie-glace *m.* windshield wiper

et and

établir to establish, to set up

établissement *m.* establishment, place

étage *m.* floor, level; **à quel étage?** on what floor?

États-Unis *m. pl.* United States

été *m.* summer; **en été** in summer

été *(p.p. of être)*

étendard *m.* flag, banner

étendu stretched out

éternuer to sneeze

étiquette *f.* label
étonné surprised
s'étonner to be surprised
étrange strange
étranger foreign; **à l'étranger** abroad
être to be; **être de retour** to be back; **être en panne** to have a breakdown; **être en plein air** to be out in the fresh air; **être en retard** to be late; **être en train de** to be in the process of; **être en vacances** to be on vacation; **être enrhumé** to have a cold; **il était** there was
étroit narrow, tight
étude *f.* study; **faire ses études secondaires** to go to high school
étudiant *m.* student
étudier to study
eu (*p.p.* of **avoir**)
événement *m.* event
éventuellement eventually
exactement exactly
examen *m.* examination; **examen écrit** written exam
s'excuser to excuse, to be sorry
exemple *m.* example
expéditeur *m.* sender
expliquer to explain

se fâcher to get angry
facile easy
facilement easily
facteur *m.* mailman
facture *f.* bill
faim *f.* hunger; **avoir faim** to be hungry
faire to do; to make; **faire beau** to be nice weather; **se faire bronzer au soleil** to get a suntan; **faire chaud** to be warm (hot) weather; **se faire couper les cheveux** to have one's hair cut; **se faire décolorer les cheveux** to have one's hair dyed; **faire de la bicyclette** to go bicycle riding; **faire de longues promenades à pied** to go for long walks, to hike; **faire de l'auto-stop** to hitchhike; **faire des progrès** to make progress, to progress; **faire dodo** (*slang*) to go to sleep; **faire du bateau** to go boating; **faire du camping** to go camping; **faire du cheval** to go horseback riding; **faire du gâteau** to bake a cake;

faire du lèche-vitrines to window-shop; **faire du ski** to ski, go skiing; **faire du sport** to play sports; **faire le plein** to fill 'er up; **faire une croisière** to take a cruise; **faire la vaisselle** to wash the dishes; **faire enregistrer mes bagages** to have my luggage checked in; **faire la connaissance (de)** to meet, to make the acquaintance (of); **faire la cuisine** to cook; **faire le ménage** to do housework; **faire le tour du monde** to go around the world; **se faire mal** to hurt oneself; **faire partie de** to belong to; **se faire payer** to cash; **faire peur (à)** to frighten; **faire plaisir (à)** to please; **les faire réparer** to have them repaired; **faire ses études secondaires** to go to high school; **faire suivre le courrier** to have the mail forwarded; **faire un pique-nique** to picnic; **faire un tour en auto** to go for a drive; **faire un voyage** to take a trip, to travel; **faire une piqûre** to give an injection; **faire une promenade** to take a walk; **il fait beau** it is nice weather; **que feriez-vous si . . . ?** what would you do if . . . ?; **quelle température fait-il?** what's the temperature?
faire-part *m.* announcement
fait (*p.p.* of **faire**)
falloir to be necessary; to need; **il faut** it is necessary; it takes (*of time*); **il me faut** I need; **il lui faut** he needs / she needs; **il nous faut** we need; **il leur faut** they need
famille *f.* family; **en famille** with one's family, with your family
faner to wilt
fatigant tiring
fatigué tired
faute *f.* fault; **à qui la faute?** whose fault is (was) it?
fauteuil *m.* chair; armchair
faux (*f.* **fausse**) false, wrong
favori (*f.* **favorite**) favorite
féliciter to congratulate
femme *f.* woman; wife; **femme de chambre** chambermaid
fenêtre *f.* window
ferme *f.* farm
fermer to close
féroce ferocious

feu *m.* fire
feuillage *m.* leaves, foliage
fiancé engaged
se fiancer to get engaged
ficelle *f.* string
fiche *f.* form
fièvre *f.* fever
filet *m.* rack
fille *f.* girl; daughter; **fille unique** (an) only daughter; **jeune fille** girl; **nom de jeune fille** maiden name
film *m.* movie
fils *m.* son; **fils unique** (an) only son
fin *adj.* fine, thin; finely (ground)
fin *f.* end
finir (par) to end up (by), finish
flacon *m.* flask, small bottle
fleur *f.* flower
foin *m.* hay; **rhume des foins** hay fever
fois *f.* time; **la première fois** the first time
foncé dark
fonctionner to work, function
fontaine *f.* fountain
forêt *f.* forest
forme *f.* form
formule *f.* form; **formule de télégramme** telegram form
fort strong; **je t'embrasse fort** I send you a big hug (*complimentary close to a letter*); **parler fort** to speak loudly
foulard *m.* scarf
fouler to sprain
fourrure *f.* fur (coat)
français French; *m.* French language
fraise *f.* strawberry
franc (*f.* **franche**) frank
frapper to knock; **frapper à la porte** to knock on the door
frein *m.* brake
fréquemment frequently
frère *m.* brother
fripon (*f.* **friponne**) knavish, rascally
frire to fry
froid cold; **avoir froid** to feel cold
fromage *m.* cheese
fumer to smoke; **défense de fumer** no smoking
furet *m.* ferret
futur *m.* future; **au futur** in(to) the future

gagner to earn

gai happy; **avoir le cœur gai** to be happy

galerie (*f.*) **d'art** art gallery

gant *m.* glove

garage *m.* garage

garagiste *m.* garage mechanic

garçon *m.* boy; waiter

garder to watch over, tend; to keep

gare *f.* train station

gâteau *m.* cake

gauche left; **à gauche** to / on the left, to your left

gazon *m.* lawn; **couper le gazon** to cut the grass, mow the lawn

gencive *f.* gum (*of the teeth*)

généreux (*f.* **généreuse**) generous

genre *m.* type, kind

gens *m. pl.* people (*in general, an undetermined number*)

gentil (*f.* **gentille**) nice; kind; agreeable

gérant (*f.* **gérante**) hotel manager

geste *m.* gesture

glace *f.* ice; ice cream

gloire *f.* glory

gonfler to inflate

gorge *f.* throat

goûter to taste

grand big, large, tall; **à grand bruit** noisily; **de grands yeux** large eyes

grand-père *m.* grandfather

grave serious, grave

grêler to hail (*weather*)

grésiller to sleet

grippe *f.* influenza

gris grey

gros (*f.* **grosse**) big; fat; **gros mots** curse(s)

groupe *m.* group; **en groupe** with a group of people

guichet *m.* window (*in post office, bank, box office*); counter (*in bank*)

guitare *f.* guitar

habillé (de) dressed (in)

s'habiller to get dressed

habiter to live

d'habitude usually

s'habituer à to get used to

haricot *m.* bean; **haricot vert** *m.* string bean, green bean

haut high; **en haut** upstairs

herbe *f.* grass

hésiter to hesitate

heure *f.* hour; time (*of day*),

o'clock; **heures de départ** departure times; **six heures du soir** six o'clock in the evening; **à quelle heure?** when?, at what time?; **de bonne heure** early; **quelle heure est-il?** what time is it?; **vers huit heures** around eight o'clock; **à l'heure** on time

heureux (*f.* **heureuse**) happy

heureusement fortunately

hier yesterday; **hier soir** last night, yesterday evening

hirondelle *f.* swallow

histoire *f.* story

hiver *m.* winter; **en hiver** in winter; **sports d'hiver** winter sports

homme *m.* man

hôpital *m.* hospital

hors de off, outside of

hôte *m.* host

hôtesse de l'air stewardess, flight attendant

hôtel *m.* hotel

huile *f.* oil

huit eight

huitième eighth

humeur *f.* humor; **qu'est-ce qui vous met en mauvaise humeur?** what puts you into a bad mood?

ici here; **près d'ici** near here, nearby

idée *f.* idea

idiot idiotic

il he

ils they

il y a there is, there are; ago; **il y a deux jours** two days ago; **il y en a plusieurs** there are several of them; **y a-t-il** is there, are there

imaginer to imagine

immeuble *m.* building

immobilier (*f.* **immobilière**) real estate, property; **agence** (*f.*) **immobilière** rental agency, real estate agency

s'impatienter to get impatient

impensable unthinkable

imperméable *m.* raincoat

index *m.* index finger

indicatif *m.* indicative; **indicatif de zone** area code

indiquer to indicate

infinitif *m.* infinitive

infirmière *f.* nurse

s'informer to get information

inquiet (*f.* **inquiète**) worried; **avoir l'air inquiet** to look worried

inscrire to record; to register; to write

s'installer to move in

instant *m.* moment, instant

interdit forbidden; **baignade interdite** no swimming

intéressant interesting

s'intéresser à to be interested in

intérêt *m.* interest

intérieur *m.* interior

interurbain interurban, long-distance

inutile useless

invité *m.* guest

inviter to invite

italien (*f.* **italienne**) Italian; *m.* Italian language

itinéraire *m.* itinerary

jacquet *m.* backgammon

jambe *f.* leg

jambon *m.* ham

jamais never; ever

jardin *m.* garden

jardinage *m.* gardening

jaune yellow

je I

jeton *m.* token

jeune young; **jeune fille** girl

joli pretty

jouer to play; **jouer aux cartes** to play cards; **jouer aux échecs** to play chess; **jouer de la guitare** to play guitar

jouir de to enjoy

jour *m.* day; **tous les jours** every day, daily

journal *m.* newspaper; journal, diary

journée *f.* day; **toute la journée** all day (long)

joyeux (*f.* **joyeuse**) joyous; **Joyeux Noël** Merry Christmas

jupe *f.* skirt

jus *m.* juice; **jus d'orange** orange juice; **jus de pomme** apple juice

jusqu'à as far as, down to, up to; until

jusque even

juste exactly; sharp (*time*); **il est deux heures justes** it is exactly two o'clock

kilométrage *m.* mileage

la *f. (def. art).* the; *(pron.)* her, it
là there
lac *m.* lake
laid ugly
laine *f.* wool
laisser to let; to leave
lait *m.* milk
lampe *f.* lamp
lapin *m.* rabbit
laquelle which (one)
large wide; loose
latin *m.* Latin
laurier *m.* laurel
lavabo *m.* sink
laver to wash; **se laver la tête** to wash one's hair
laverie automatique *f.* laundromat
lave-vaisselle *m.* dishwasher
le *m. (def. art.)* the; *(pron.)* him, it
leçon *f.* lesson
léger *(f. légère)* light *(in weight)*
légume *m.* vegetable
lent slow
lentement slowly
lequel which (one)
les *pl. (def. art.)* the; *(pron.)* them
lessive *f.* washing *(of clothes);* wash
letter *f.* letter; **boîte aux lettres** mailbox
leur *(adj.)* their; *(pron.)* to them
se lever to get up
librairie *f.* bookstore
libre not occupied, free, unoccupied
lieu *m.* place; **au lieu de** instead of; **avoir lieu** to take place, to be held; **lieu de travail** place of work
ligne *f.* line; **ligne aérienne** airline
limité limited
linge *m.* laundry
lire to read
lisible legible
lisiblement legibly
lit *m.* bed; **lit pliant** folding bed
livre *m.* book
loger to lodge
loin far
lolo *(slang)* milk
long *(f. longue)* long
longtemps a long time; for a long time
longuement at length
lorsque when
louer to rent; to reserve
lourd heavy *(in weight)*
loyer *m.* rent

lu *(p.p.* of **lire)**
lui he, him, to her, to him, for her, for him; **lui-même** himself; **c'est à lui** it's his
luire to glow, to shine
lumière *f.* light
lundi Monday
lune *f.* moon
lunettes *f. pl.* eyeglasses; **lunettes de soleil** sunglasses
luxueux *(f. luxueuse)* luxurious

ma my
madame *f.* Mrs., Madam
mademoiselle *f.* Miss
magasin *m.* store; **grand magasin** department store; **magasin d'antiquités** antique store; **magasin de chaussures** shoe store
maigrir to get thin
maillot *m.* bathing suit; jersey; **maillot de bain** bathing suit
main *f.* hand
maintenant now
maire *m.* mayor
mais but
maison *f.* house; **maison de campagne** country house; **à la maison** at home
maître *m.* master; **maître nageur** lifeguard
majuscule capital
mal bad; poorly
mal *m.* pain; harm; trouble; *adv.* badly; **avoir du mal (à)** to have difficulty (in); **avoir mal (à)** to hurt, to have an ache; **avoir mal au cœur** to feel sick to the stomach; **avoir mal aux dents** to have a toothache; **avoir mal à la tête** to have a headache; **se faire mal** to hurt oneself; **mal de l'air** airsickness; **mal de mer** seasickness
malade sick
maladie *f.* disease
maladroit clumsy
malheureux *(f. malheureuse)* unhappy
malheureusement unfortunately
malle *f.* trunk
maman *f.* mommy, mama
manche *f.* sleeve
mandat *m.* money order
manger to eat; **salle** *(f.)* **à manger** dining room
manquer to be missing, to be lack-

ing; **il vous manque** you are missing; **tu me manques** I miss you; **vous me manquez** I miss you
manteau *m.* coat
marché *m.* market; **bon marché** inexpensive; **meilleur marché** cheaper, less expensive
marcher to walk; to march; to work *(inanimate objects)*
mardi Tuesday
mari *m.* husband
marié married
se marier to get married
marque *f.* make, brand
marron chestnut *(color)*
Marseille seaport city on Mediterranean coast
masculin masculine
matelas *m.* mattress; **matelas pneumatique** air mattress
matériel *m.* equipment
matière *f.* material; school subject; **en quelle matière vous spécialisez-vous?** what's your major?
matin *m.* morning
matines *f. pl.* morning bells, matins
mauvais bad
me me, to me, for me
mécanicien *m.* mechanic
méconnu underestimated, misunderstood
médecin *m.* doctor
médicament *m.* medicine
se méfier to distrust
meilleur better; best
même very; same; **quand même** just the same; though
ménage *m.* household; family; **faire le ménage** to do the housework
menton *m.* chin
menu *m.* menu
mer *f.* sea; **mal** *(m.)* **de mer** seasickness
mercredi Wednesday
mère *f.* mother
merveilleux *(f. merveilleuse)* marvelous, wonderful
mes my
métier *m.* occupation
métro *m.* subway
mettre to put; to display; to take *(time);* to put on *(clothes),* to wear; **mettre à** to put in; **se mettre à** to begin to; **se mettre à table** to sit down at the table
meuble *m.* *(piece of)* furniture